# How
# ISRAEL
## Became a People

# How ISRAEL Became a People

RALPH K. HAWKINS

Abingdon Press
*Nashville*

HOW ISRAEL BECAME A PEOPLE

Copyright © 2013 by Abingdon Press

All rights reserved.

No part of this work may be reproduced or transmitted in any form or by any means, electronic or mechanical, including photocopying and recording, or by any information storage or retrieval system, except as may be expressly permitted by the 1976 Copyright Act or in writing from the publisher. Requests for permission can be addressed to Permissions, The United Methodist Publishing House, P.O. Box 801, 201 Eighth Avenue South, Nashville, TN 37202-0801, or emailed to permissions@umpublishing.org.

This book is printed on acid-free paper.

**Library of Congress Cataloging-in-Publication Data**

Hawkins, Ralph K.
  How Israel became a people / Ralph K. Hawkins.
    pages cm
  Includes bibliographical references.
  ISBN 978-1-4267-5487-6 (book - pbk. / trade pbk. : alk. paper)  1. Judaism—History—To 70 A.D.  2. Jews—Origin.  3. Excavations (Archaeology)—Palestine.  4. Bible. O.T. Exodus—Antiquities.  5. Exodus, The.  6. Jews—History—To 1200 B.C.  7. Jews—History—Sources.  I. Title.
  BM165.H38 2013
  221.9'5—dc23

2012038538

All Scripture quotations unless otherwise noted are from the New Revised Standard Version of the Bible, copyright 1989, Division of Christian Education of the National Council of the Churches of Christ in the United States of America. Used by permission. All rights reserved.

Scripture quotations marked (ESV) are from The Holy Bible, English Standard Version® (ESV®), copyright © 2001 by Crossway, a publishing ministry of Good News Publishers. Used by permission. All rights reserved.

Scripture quotations marked (NASB) are taken from the New American Standard Bible®, Copyright © 1960, 1962, 1963, 1968, 1971, 1972, 1973, 1975, 1977, 1995 by The Lockman Foundation. Used by permission. (www.Lockman.org)

Chapter 3 contains material adapted from the essay originally published as "The Date of the Exodus-Conquest Is Still an Open Question: A Response to Rodger Young and Bryant Wood" and is used by permission. *JETS* 5/12 (2008): 245–66.

Figure 2 on page 30 is courtesy Shechem Archive, Semitic Museum, Harvard University.

Figure 8 on page 79 is from Michael Hasel's "Merenptah's Reference to Israel: Critical Issues for the Origin of Israel," in R. S. Hess, G. A. Klingbeil, and P. J. Ray Jr., eds., *Critical Issues in Early Israelite History* (Winona Lake, Ind.: Eisenbrauns, 2008).

Figure 14 on page 128 is from Adam Zertal's "Using Pottery Forms and Width Stratigraphy to Track Population Movements," in *BAR* 17/5 (1991): 39.

Figure 15 on page 129 is from Adam Zertal's "The Iron Age I Culture in the Hill-Country of Canaan: A Mannaaite Perspective," in S. Gitin, A. Mazar, and E. Stern, eds., *Mediterranean Peoples in Transition: 13th to Early 10th Centuiries BCE* (Jerusalem, 1998), 241.

Figure 20 on page 142 is courtesy of the Madaba Plains Project excavations at Tall al-'Umayri, Jordan. Artist: Rhonda Root © 2001.

Figure 40 on page 192 is taken from John H. Bodley's *Cultural Anthropology: Tribes, States, and the Global System*, 3rd edition (Mountain View, CA: Mayfield Publishing, 2000).

13 14 15 16 17 18 19 20 21 22—10 9 8 7 6 5 4 3 2 1
MANUFACTURED IN THE UNITED STATES OF AMERICA

*To Dr. Rodney E. Cloud,*
*to whom I am greatly indebted,*
*and for whom my reverence remains undiminished even to this day*

# CONTENTS

List of Figures . . . . . . . . . . . . . . . . . . . . . . . . . . . . . viii
Archaeological Periods. . . . . . . . . . . . . . . . . . . . . . . . . . ix
Pharaohs of Egypt's Eighteenth and Nineteenth Dynasties . . . . . . . . . . . x
Abbreviations . . . . . . . . . . . . . . . . . . . . . . . . . . . . . . xi
Acknowledgments . . . . . . . . . . . . . . . . . . . . . . . . . . . . xiii
Preface . . . . . . . . . . . . . . . . . . . . . . . . . . . . . . . . . xv
1. Why Must We Reconstruct the History of the Israelite Settlement? . . . . . . 1
2. Classical and Recent Models of the Israelite Settlement. . . . . . . . . . . 29
3. The Date of the Exodus-Conquest Part I: Biblical Evidence . . . . . . . . 49
4. The Date of the Exodus-Conquest Part II: Extrabiblical Evidence . . . . . . 67
5. Major Cities of the Conquest . . . . . . . . . . . . . . . . . . . . . . 91
6. Reconstructing the Israelite Settlement Archaeologically . . . . . . . . . 121
7. The Material Culture and Ethnicity of the Highland Settlers . . . . . . . 137
8. 'Izbet Sartah: A Prototypical Israelite Settlement Site . . . . . . . . . . . 159
9. Early Israelite Sanctuaries and the Birth of a Nation . . . . . . . . . . . 175
10. A Culture-Scale Model of the Early Israelite Settlement . . . . . . . . . 189
Afterword . . . . . . . . . . . . . . . . . . . . . . . . . . . . . . . 207
Glossary . . . . . . . . . . . . . . . . . . . . . . . . . . . . . . . . 211
Notes . . . . . . . . . . . . . . . . . . . . . . . . . . . . . . . . . 215
Index . . . . . . . . . . . . . . . . . . . . . . . . . . . . . . . . . 281

# LIST OF FIGURES

**Fig. 1.** W. F. Albright

**Fig. 2.** G. Ernest Wright

**Fig. 3.** Canaanite Sites the Bible Claims Were Taken by the Israelites

**Fig. 4.** Albrecht Alt

**Fig. 5.** George E. Mendenhall

**Fig. 6.** Norman Gottwald

**Fig. 7.** William G. Dever

**Fig. 8.** Verse Structure of the Merneptah Stele

**Fig. 9.** Kenyon's Trench 1

**Fig. 10.** Et-Tell (view NNE to tell)

**Fig. 11.** Charred Walls Inside the Canaanite Palace at Hazor

**Fig. 12.** Hazor Stele Fragment

**Fig. 13.** The Middle Bronze Age Mudbrick Gate at Tel Dan

**Fig. 14.** Types A, B, and C Cooking Pots

**Fig. 15.** The Three-Staged Process of Expansion in Manasseh

**Fig. 16.** The Madaba Map

**Fig. 17.** The Mosaic in the Church of St. Stephens, Umm er-Rasas

**Fig. 18.** The Holy City of Jerusalem as Depicted in the Church of St. Stephens Mosaic

**Fig. 19.** Map of the Settlement Pattern of the Hill-Country in Iron Age I

**Fig. 20.** Four-Room House at Tell el-'Umayri

**Fig. 21.** Collared-Rim Jar

**Fig. 22.** Thirteenth to Twelfth-Century Pottery of Cisjordan Compared to Pottery of Transjordan

**Fig. 23.** Location of 'Izbet Sartah in Relation to Iron Age I Sites in Western Samarian Hills

**Fig. 24.** Topographical Map and Schematic Plan of 'Izbet Sartah

**Fig. 25.** Schematic Plan of Stratum III

**Fig. 26.** Collared-Rim Jars

**Fig. 27.** Schematic Plan of Stratum II

**Fig. 28.** Stratum II Silos

**Fig. 29.** 'Izbet Sartah Ostracon

**Fig. 30.** Plan of Stratum I

**Fig. 31.** Aerial View of Bedhat esh-Sha'ab

**Fig. 32.** Eastern Manasseh and Sandal-Sites

**Fig. 33.** Bedhat esh- Sha'ab

**Fig. 34.** Bamah at Bedhat esh-Sha'ab

**Fig. 35.** Portion of the "Procession Road"

**Fig. 36.** Ain Dara Footprints

**Fig. 37.** Mount Ebal Enclosure

**Fig. 38.** The Iron Age I Structure on Mount Ebal

**Fig. 39.** Jebel Kebir, Located across the Valley from the Ebal Structure

**Fig. 40.** Culture-Scale and Its Features

**Fig. 41.** Ancient Israel's Progression through the Culture Scale

# ARCHAEOLOGICAL PERIODS

| | |
|---|---|
| Neolithic | 7000–4000 B.C.E. |
| Chalcolithic | 4000–3200 |
| Early Bronze Age | |
| EB I | 3200–2800 |
| EB II | 2800–2600 |
| EB III | 2600–2350 |
| EB IV | 2350–2200 |
| Middle Bronze Age | |
| MB I | 2200–2000 |
| MB II | 2000–1550 |
| Late Bronze Age | |
| LB I | 1550–1400 |
| LB II | 1400–1200 |
| Iron Age | |
| Iron I | 1200–1000 |
| Iron II | 1000–586 |
| Persian | 539–332 |
| Hellenistic | 323–337 |
| Roman | 37 B.C.E. to 324 C.E. |

# PHARAOHS OF EGYPT'S EIGHTEENTH AND NINETEENTH DYNASTIES[1]

**Dynasty 18**

'Ahmose
(1539–1514 B.C.E.)

Amenhotep I
(1514–1493 B.C.E.)

Thutmose I
(1493–? B.C.E.)

Hatshepsut
(1479–1458 B.C.E.)

Thutmose II
(?–1479 B.C.E.)

Thutmose III
(1479–1425 B.C.E.)

Amenhotep II
(1426–1400 B.C.E.)

Thutmose IV
(1400–1390 B.C.E.)

Amenhotep III
(1390–1353 B.C.E.)

Amenhotep IV/Akhenaten
(1353–1336 B.C.E.)

Smenkhare
(1335–1332 B.C.E.)

Tut'ankhamun
(1332–1322 B.C.E.)

Aya
(1322–1319 B.C.E.)

Haremhab
(1319–1290 B.C.E.)

**Dynasty 19**

Ramesses I
(1292–1292 B.C.E.)

Seti I
(1290–1279 B.C.E.)

Ramesses II
(1279–1213 B.C.E.)

Merneptah
(1213–1204 B.C.E.)

Seti II
(1204–1198 B.C.E.)

Amenmesse
(1203–1200 B.C.E.)

Siptah
(1198–1193 B.C.E.)

Twosre
(1198–1190 B.C.E.)

# ABBREVIATIONS

| | |
|---|---|
| *AASOR* | *Annual of the American Schools of Oriental Research* |
| *ABD* | *Anchor Bible Dictionary* |
| *ADAJ* | *Annual of the Department of Antiquities of Jordan* |
| *AJA* | *American Journal of Archaeology* |
| *ANET* | *Ancient Near Eastern Texts Relating to the Old Testament* |
| *AUSDDS* | *Andrews University Seminary Doctoral Dissertation Series* |
| *BA* | *Biblical Archaeologist* |
| *BAR* | *Biblical Archaeology Review* |
| *BASOR* | *Bulletin of the American Schools of Oriental Research* |
| *BDB* | *The New Brown-Driver-Briggs-Gesenius Hebrew and English Lexicon.* Ed. F. Brown. Peabody, Mass.: 1979. |
| *BR* | *Bible Review* |
| *BSac* | *Bibliotheca Sacra* |
| *BTB* | *Biblical Theology Bulletin* |
| *BWANT* | *Beiträge zur Wissenschaft vom Alten und Neuen Testament* |
| *COS* | *Context of Scripture* |
| *CR:BS* | *Currents in Research: Biblical Studies* |
| *CTM* | *Concordia Theological Monthly* |
| *EJ* | *Encyclopedia Judaica.* Ed. C. Roth and G. Wigoder. 17 vols. Jerusalem: Keter, 1996. |
| *HTR* | *Harvard Theological Review* |
| *IEJ* | *Israel Exploration Journal* |
| *JAA* | *Journal of Anthropological Archaeology* |
| *JAEI* | *Journal of Ancient Egyptian Interconnections* |

| | |
|---|---|
| JAOS | *Journal of the American Oriental Society* |
| JBL | *Journal of Biblical Literature* |
| JBQ | *Jewish Bible Quarterly* |
| JESHO | *Journal of the Economic and Social History of the Orient* |
| JETS | *Journal of the Evangelical Theological Society* |
| JPOS | *Journal of the Palestine Oriental Society* |
| LAE | *The Literature of Ancient Egypt.* Ed. W. K. Simpson. New Haven, Conn.: Yale University Press, 2003. |
| LXX | *Septuagint* |
| MT | *Masoretic Text* |
| NCE | *New Catholic Encyclopedia* |
| NEA | *Near Eastern Archaeology* |
| NEAEHL | *New Encyclopedia of Archaeological Excavations in the Holy Land* |
| NIDB | *New Interpreter's Dictionary of the Bible* |
| OEAE | *Oxford Encyclopedia of Ancient Egypt* |
| OEANE | *Oxford Encyclopedia of Archaeology in the Near East* |
| OJA | *Oxford Journal of Archaeology* |
| PEQ | *Palestine Exploration Quarterly* |
| RB | *Revue Biblique* |
| RGG | *Religion in Geschichte und Gegenwart.* Ed. K. Galling. 7 vols. 3d ed. Tübingen: J. C. B. Mohr, 1957 to 1965. |
| SJOT | *Scandinavian Journal of the Old Testament* |
| SJT | *Scottish Journal of Theology* |
| TA | *Tel Aviv* |
| TWOT | *Theological Wordbook of the Old Testament.* Ed. R. L. Harris, G. L. Archer, Jr., and B. K. Waltke. 2 vols. Chicago: Moody Press, 1980. |
| WBC | *Word Biblical Commentary* |
| WTJ | *Westminster Theological Journal* |

# ACKNOWLEDGMENTS

As with any significant project, this book could not have been completed without the assistance of many people. The faculty, staff, and students at Kentucky Christian University encouraged me throughout much of the writing process. I would like to give a special thanks to the staff of the Young Library, especially Mr. Tom Scott, who always went out of his way in his efforts to make the library a place that would be beneficial for both students and faculty, and Ms. Delores Hawk, who went above and beyond in fulfilling an endless array of interlibrary loan requests for me. Without them, I would not have been able to complete this project. The administration and faculty at Averett University, my new academic home, have provided a wonderful environment for bringing the project to completion.

Numerous colleagues helped me in various ways. Several supplied me with photos and charts, along with permission to use them. I would like to thank George Mendenhall, Norman Gottwald, and William Dever for providing me with photos of themselves; Mark Ziese for sharing photos of Jericho, et-Tell, and Dan; Adam Zertal for granting permission for the use of various charts and images; *Biblical Archaeology Review* for permission to reprint a map; the Madaba Plains Project for allowing me to reprint Rhonda Root's now famous image of the four-room house at Tell el-ʿUmayri; Christie Chadwick for use of her pottery chart; Israel Finkelstein for allowing me to reprint images from his volume on ʿIzbet Sartah; Roberto Piperno for his photo of the Ain Dara footprints; and John Bodley for the use of his culture-scale chart. Larry Herr discussed the history of the collared-rim jar with me in a series of e-mail exchanges. James K. Hoffmeier read and commented on portions of the manuscript. Paul J. Ray Jr. read several sections of the manuscript and helped me think through various aspects of the material in the course of several long telephone conversations. I am grateful to each of these colleagues for their own work and for helping me in my efforts to make my own contribution.

Several parties deserve special thanks. I am grateful to my former editor, Trent Butler, who first invited me to write this book in 2007. When I asked him when he wanted the manuscript, he said "as soon as possible." I had no idea it would take this long, and I am grateful to him for encouraging me throughout the writing process. My special thanks go to Kathy Armistead, my current editor, for taking an interest in the project and seeing it to fruition. I am honored to be publishing with Abingdon Press, and I am indebted to her for making that possible. I also want to express my sincerest appreciation to Caroline Weis, who sponsored my work at Tall Jalul in

*Acknowledgments*

2010. This work was important for my understanding of the relationship between Israel and Jordan in ancient times. The opportunities on this trip to visit and study several Moabite and Edomite sites, to make multiple excursions to Tell el-'Umayri and to the mosaic churches in Madaba and Umm er-Rasas were priceless, and I believe they have added to this work.

A special thanks to Mom and Dad, who kept our children while my wife and I traveled, and to "Aunt Carrot," who took the second shift and endured over a week with four children with fevers! Last but not least, my wife, Cathy, and our children, Hannah, Sarah, Mary, and Adam, all deserve a special thanks for not only enduring the writing of yet another book but for encouraging me in the process.

# PREFACE

The Israelite exodus from Egypt and the settlement in Canaan are two of the foundational events recorded in the Hebrew Bible. One of my goals in writing about them has been to engage as many scholars as possible in a dialogue, regardless of their ethnic identity or religious affiliation. For this reason, I have chosen to use B.C.E. and C.E. rather than the traditional B.C. and A.D. This choice is also a natural one for me, since this terminology is standard in archaeological publications. Its usage in this text is not intended to be anti-Christian in any way, and if some of my Christian readers are offended by it, I apologize and ask for your understanding.

One of the difficulties in trying to deal with a subject in which such radically opposing views are held has to do with terminology. Are those who tend to have a high view of Scripture and accept its account as being trustworthy in whole or in part to be referred to as "confessional," "maximalist," or "evangelical" scholars? And what about those who have a lower view of Scripture? Are they "nonconfessional," "secular," "minimalist," or "revisionist" scholars? I do not find any of the terminology satisfactory, since it is possible for a "confessional" scholar to be a nonevangelical, or to have a lower view of Scripture, and it is also possible for a nonconfessional scholar to have a very high view of Scripture, and so on. It is very difficult to pigeonhole a person based on his or her views of a certain segment of material within the Hebrew Bible. Nevertheless, I have had to choose one or more of these terms from time to time in trying to contrast the views of various scholars. Please note the limitations of such terminology in advance.

The exodus and conquest are also two of the most divisive subjects among scholars in the various fields of biblical studies and Near Eastern archaeology. There are those who accept the biblical accounts of these events as literally and completely true, those who believe they never happened, and a whole range of "in between" views. It seems to me that in most of the standard texts, the writer adopts a given perspective almost *a priori*, which he or she then adheres to throughout. For example, mainstream scholars do not spend a lot of time considering the early date of the exodus-conquest, and conservative or evangelical scholars do not devote a great deal of attention to the late date. Each approach tends to adhere to the standard views of their own "school" regarding these and other issues surrounding Israel's early history.

When I went to college, my advisor turned out to be the Hebrew professor Dr. Rodney E. Cloud, who talked me into taking Hebrew grammar my first semester. I fell in love with the Hebrew Bible, and spent the next six years or so studying Hebrew

Bible and biblical archaeology with him. One of the things that always impressed me the most about Dr. Cloud's teaching was that he never told us, his students, what to think. He respected us as people and wanted us to think for ourselves. Instead of teaching us one view only, he just about always presented the evidence for multiple points of view, and then he would say, tongue-in-cheek, "You paid your money, you take your pick." This is the approach I have sought to adopt in this book, which is dedicated to Dr. Cloud. My goal in writing *How Israel Became a People* has been to try to approach the subject of Israel's emergence in Canaan from a neutral perspective, to consider all the evidence, and to draw reasonable conclusions from these data. I will leave it to you, the reader, to decide to what extent I have been successful in this endeavor.

# CHAPTER 1

# WHY MUST WE RECONSTRUCT THE HISTORY OF THE ISRAELITE SETTLEMENT?

*At ten o'clock in the morning of the day following the events I have described, the trial of Dmitri Karamazov began in our district court.*

*I hasten to emphasize the fact that I am far from esteeming myself capable of reporting all that took place at the trial in full detail, or even in the actual order of events. I imagine that to mention everything with full explanation would fill a volume, even a very large one. And so I trust I may not be reproached for confining myself to what struck me. I may have selected as of most interest what was of secondary importance, and may have omitted the most prominent and essential details. But I see I shall do better not to apologise. I will do my best and the reader will see for himself that I have done all I can.*

—The narrator of *The Brothers Karamazov*, upon beginning his account of the trial of Dmitri Karamazov

When I first began teaching courses in the history of Israel or in biblical archaeology, I would devote considerable time to reconstructing the Israelite settlement in Canaan. Each time, students would ask, "Why do we need to reconstruct the history of the Israelite settlement? Doesn't the Bible give us an exact historical report as to how the Israelites came into Canaan?" Each semester, as I sought to begin teaching on the Israelite settlement, someone would inevitably raise their hand and ask these questions. It did not make sense to these students why we needed to make a full-blown historical and archaeological reconstruction of the "conquest" when we have accounts of the process in the books of Joshua and Judges. Over time, I added an entirely new component to these classes, preceding any discussion of the "conquest" itself, in which the question of *why* one must reconstruct the Israelite settlement was addressed. The answer has to do with the intent of the biblical writers. Were they trying to write a full, comprehensive history? Or were they doing something else? And if so, what was it? In this chapter, we will explore these questions first by reviewing the history of biblical archaeology and the "conquest," followed by an examination of history and historiography, and then by looking at the book of Joshua itself.

## BIBLICAL ARCHAEOLOGY AND THE "CONQUEST"

A crisis in Israelite historiography has been percolating in recent years. That the crisis may have reached a boiling point may be indicated by the recent publication of a volume of essays by European scholars who seek to address the question of whether it is even possible to write a history of Israel.[1] Many of the contributors to this volume say no. The current skepticism seems to be a swinging of the pendulum away from the Biblical Theology Movement of the 1940s through the 1960s, which was made up of North American and European Protestants who, while they acknowledged the legitimacy of historical criticism, held strongly to the concept of divine revelation in history.[2] In line with its conscious orientation to reading the Bible for the church, those associated with the Biblical Theology Movement sought to recover the Bible as a theological book, emphasize its unity, make central God's revelation of God's self in history, and stress the distinctiveness of the biblical perspective.[3] G. Ernest Wright established himself as one of the major representatives of the Biblical Theology Movement with his monograph *God Who Acts: Biblical Theology as Recital*,[4] in which he argued, "In Biblical faith everything depends upon whether the central events actually occurred," and, "To participate in Biblical faith means that we must indeed take history seriously as the primary data of the faith."[5] Wright believed "the Bible, unlike the other religious literature of the world, is not centered in a series of moral, spiritual and liturgical teachings, but in the story of a people who lived at a certain time and place."[6] If those events did not happen, then the biblical faith is erroneous. It was his understanding of the importance of the historicity of biblical events that led Wright to place such an emphasis on archaeology. He explained, "The intensive study of the biblical archaeologist is thus the fruit of the vital concern for history which the Bible has instilled in us. . . . Biblical theology and biblical archaeology must go hand in hand, if we are to comprehend the Bible's meaning."[7] Another of Albright's disciples, J. Bright, went as far as to argue that the locus of authority for the interpretation of Scripture had shifted from theological approaches to the "one admissible method for arriving at the meaning of the biblical text: the grammatico-historical method,"[8] which Z. Zevit has correctly understood to have "included control of data from excavations."[9]

This approach led to what some have perceived as a parochial and reactionary character in archaeology that became preoccupied with the idea that "archaeology confirms biblical history,"[10] and nowhere was this application of biblical archaeology seen to be more apropos than with regard to the "conquest." In the middle of the twentieth century, English language scholarship on ancient Israel was dominated by

*Why Must We Reconstruct the History of the Israelite Settlement?*

W. F. Albright, who promoted what came to be known as the "Conquest Model," which will be discussed in detail in the next chapter. Suffice it to say here that this is the theory that the Israelites gained their homeland in Canaan solely as the result of war. In 1935, Albright synthesized the archaeological evidence available at the time and made the case that enough evidence was available to reconstruct a chronological outline of the Israelite conquest.[11] By 1937, he concluded that the archaeological evidence clearly demonstrated that the Israelites had carried out a wholesale conquest of the land of Canaan at the end of the thirteenth century B.C.E.[12] This view was adopted by Albright's disciples, especially G. E. Wright.[13] Both Albright and Wright later acknowledged a somewhat more flexible interpretation of the book of Joshua and the conquest, but they continued to defend the Conquest Model with the trowel, and it reigned while they were alive.[14] The Conquest Model has often been accepted by noncritical biblical students and by many biblical scholars as the "biblical view" of how Israel emerged in Canaan,[15] and it has continued to garner some support among evangelical scholars even today.[16]

In about the mid-twentieth century, however, cracks began to show in the Conquest Model as discrepancies began to emerge between the account of the conquest in the book of Joshua (as perceived by adherents to the Conquest Model) and the archaeological evidence.[17] Wright himself acknowledged that those who had sought to "confirm the Bible" with archaeology had been guilty of "overstatement,"[18] and the use of archaeology for this purpose contributed to the demise of the Biblical Theology Movement, beginning in the late 1950s.[19] By the late 1960s, leading biblical archaeologists seemed to be seeking to distance themselves from Wright's empiricist position.[20] W. G. Dever claims that by the 1960s, the Biblical Theology Movement was dead.[21] Indeed, by the 1970s, both European and American scholars began to criticize the American school's use of archaeology in the reconstruction of Israelite history,[22] the archaeology of "conquest" had fallen out of favor, archaeology came to be seen as contradicting the book of Joshua, and the text of Joshua came to be read in ways other than as a straightforward historical report of Israel's lightning-like entrance into Canaan. In order to reach conclusions about how the book of Joshua ought to be read and understood, we must first consider how history and historiography were understood in the ancient world.

# HISTORY AND HISTORIOGRAPHY IN THE ANCIENT WORLD

Should the events recorded in the Hebrew Bible and, more specifically, in the book of Joshua, be regarded as having actually occurred? Did the author or authors intend for the reader to view the contents of the work as historical, or are modern readers naïve if they assume that? In this section, we will consider the meaning of the terms *history* and *historiography*, how historiography developed and was understood in the ancient world, and how to determine whether a text is historiographical in nature.

## Defining Terms

Historiography is among the most difficult subjects in biblical studies to define. In the study of historiography, a distinction is generally made between the terms *history* and *historiography*. B. T. Arnold notes, however, that "*history* is itself a word needing clarification, and *historiography* is inherently ambiguous."[23] Generally, we could say that "history" is the past itself, while "historiography" is the recounting of that past.[24]

Since the Enlightenment, historiography has been evaluated more and more by the criteria of modern historiographers. In the nineteenth century, Leopold von Ranke, a Prussian historian often considered to be one of the key founders of modern source-based history, staked out the parameters of history as a discipline whose primary interest was in history *wie es eigentlich gewesen ist* ("as it actually occurred"). Arnold notes that, ever since the days of von Ranke, "Modern standards of history writing have routinely been applied to ancient authors, assuming the ancients thought about history and wrote history in a way similar to modern historians."[25] In 1956, for example, R. G. Collingwood defined history as "a kind of research or inquiry" that is conducted through the analysis of evidence, and that has as its goal the acquisition of "human self-knowledge."[26] Collingwood's scientific definition obviously precludes the categorization of Mesopotamian or biblical texts from being categorized as history. M. Z. Brettler notes that his definition is "unnecessarily restrictive" and "reflects a modern bias toward scientific history, a bias which reflects the relatively recent growth of history as a university academic discipline. Few, if any, premodern works would be categorized as history if we rigidly followed Collingwood."[27]

In the 1960s, the Dutch historian Johan Huizinga defined history as "the intellectual form in which a civilization renders account to itself of the past."[28] Already in the previous decade he had defined the parameters of history. He explained that

> History adequate for our culture can only be scientific history. In the modern Western culture the form of knowledge about occurrences in this world is critical-scientific. We cannot surrender the demand for the scientifically certain without damaging the conscience of our culture. Mythic consolidations of the past can still have literary value for us as a form of play—but for us they are not history.[29]

Huizinga's remarks lower the biblical text to the level of something produced in the toddler's playroom, unworthy of even being considered when reflecting on the ancient past.

John Van Seters adopted Huizinga's basic definition of history in his major study, *In Search of History: Historiography in the Ancient World and the Origins of Biblical History*,[30] which continues to be one of the most significant studies of ancient Near Eastern history writing in modern times. In this pioneering work, Van Seters sought to illuminate the origins and nature of Israelite historiography through a comparison of it with the historiography of other ancient Near Eastern cultures. Drawing on Huizinga's definition, Van Seters argues that history must be nonpragmatic and nondidactic, and, consequently, he eliminates much that others would recognize as historical. Ultimately, Van Seters understands history to be an intellectual form of

## Why Must We Reconstruct the History of the Israelite Settlement?

corporate self-understanding, or "national history," and concludes that this kind of historiography did not develop in Israel until the sixth century B.C.E. and was the invention of the so-called Deuteronomist. While one may or may not agree with Van Seters's conclusions, "his work serves as an essential and important corrective, which has placed biblical history writers in their proper perspective as ANE (Ancient Near East) authors, and compels us to read their works on their own terms."[31] In order to appreciate the nature of the biblical history, we, too, must consider the history, development, and nature of ancient Near Eastern historiography.

## The History of the Development of Historiographical Writing in Antiquity

Owing to the wealth of ancient Near Eastern texts that have become available in modern times, we can now reconstruct at least a partial picture of the development of historiography in the ancient world. In ancient Mesopotamia, the raw materials for historiography began to appear early, in the early third millennium B.C.E. The Weidner Chronicle contains a narration of events from the Early Dynastic period of Sumerian history (the first half of the third millennium B.C.E.) down to the reign of Shulgi (2094–2047 B.C.E.). The purpose of the narrative is to show that those rulers who failed to provide fish offerings for the temple Esagil struggled while those who did flourished. A. Kirk Grayson observed that Babylon and its temple Esagil did not become important enough to warrant such special attention from Mesopotamian rulers until the first dynasty of Babylon, which led him to suggest that "certainly his or some previous writer's imagination was the source of the information about each monarch's attitude towards the provision of fish for Esagil" by the rulers in the early periods.[32] The text, therefore, is a "fanciful portrayal of the history of the cult of Esagil" and "a blatant piece of propaganda" intended to caution future rulers about the importance of Babylon and the need to adhere to its cult. The Assyrian Annals are similarly propagandistic, which prevented their authors from inquiring seriously about the past.[33] The most important Babylonian contribution to the historiographic genre is The Babylonian Chronicle Series, for which extant copies survive from the reign of Darius I (521–486 B.C.E.). These texts do not restrict their content to positive information but include negative information as well, including occasions when gods failed to be brought to religious festivals or were stolen from their temples. The texts also exhibit an interest in the politics of other nations and even report occasions when Babylon was defeated. The Babylonian Chronicle Series seems to reflect "a genuine intellectual interest in the history of Babylon itself."[34]

In Egypt, the oldest known example of historical research is the Palermo Stone, the text of which is similar to other annals, but appears like a chronicle to have been composed at one sitting through gathering information from a range of sources.[35] Another collection, the Annals of Amenophis II, is comparable to the Palermo Stone.[36] Egyptian historiography reached its peak with the Annals of Thutmose III (1479–1425 B.C.E.), which includes an extended narrative and a clear plot line and even utilizes source citations, both of which are features shared with biblical historiographic texts.³⁷ The Victory Stela of King Piye weaves together an assortment of sources, and even preserves some of their style.³⁸

The history of Egypt written by Manetho (third century B.C.E.) was basically a list with an assortment of epigrammatic stories and extended narrative occurrences woven into it. While Manetho's reasons for writing his history are not entirely clear, he does reveal a clear apologetic purpose in a statement about his desire to correct some of Herodotus's misrepresentations of Egypt.³⁹ Finally, various records that report the defeat and expulsion of the Hyksos have survived, and these can be compared with an interesting New Kingdom tale of the conflict which incorporated elements of fable and tradition into the story.⁴⁰

In Hatti, historiography developed along the same lines as in Assyria, commencing with royal inscriptions and reaching its fruition with annalistic historiography. Early texts, such as the Anitta Text,⁴¹ which dates to the Hittite Old Kingdom, are basically assemblages of royal inscriptions. An advance in the development of Hittite historiography occurred with the publication of the Annals of Hattusili I (seventeenth century B.C.E.), which contained a year-by-year narrative of the king's heroic deeds.⁴² The Ammuna Chronicle (sixteenth century B.C.E.) marks another step forward, in that its author seems to have avoided blatant propaganda in an attempt to give more temperate historical reports.⁴³ Hittite historiography burgeoned with the Annals of Mursili II (fourteenth century B.C.E.), which has survived in two different editions, the Ten-Year Annals and the Comprehensive Annals.⁴⁴ The Ten-Year Annals contain a carefully organized commemoration of the first decade of Mursili II's reign. The Comprehensive Annals, which were more thorough in every respect and represent a highly developed level of historical thought, marks the high point of Hittite historiography, despite the clear intention to honor the king. Similarly, the later Apology of Hattusili III (thirteenth century B.C.E.), which contains a long historical review of Hattusili III's ascent to the throne, was also designed to exonerate the king.⁴⁵

Historiography as a whole reached maturity in Greece. Herodotus (ca. 484–425 B.C.E.) is often credited with being the "Father of History," an eponym given to him because of his production of the *Histories*, a seven-volume history of the Greek and Persian war. Herodotus indicates that his readers should believe his accounts, and he often implies that extensive research undergirds them. Sparks notes that, "in this sense, he claimed to be doing something akin to what modern historians do: to evaluate critically various sources and lines of evidence and to arrive at a conclusion about what probably happened."⁴⁶ Despite his own claims, however, Herodotus was considered unreliable, biased, and untruthful by such exemplars as Thucydides, Aristotle, Cicero, Josephus, Plutarch, Manetho, and Libanius.⁴⁷ While modern scholars disagree about the character of the *Histories*, Sparks concludes that "a careful reading of Herodotus reveals that there is some truth in both views because at numerous points the history is accurate, but at other points Herodotus seems to have invented sources that support his opinions."⁴⁸ Thucydides (ca. 460–399 B.C.E.), a near contemporary of Herodotus, also wrote a war history, entitled the *Historeae*. While Herodotus often integrated "antiquarian" materials and mythical and legendary materials into his accounts, Thucydides undertook his own work "with a new spirit of critical inquiry that left ancient historiography behind and became the root of modern historiography's quest to write history" as it truly happened.[49] In his brief overview of the early history of Greece, before the war, however, he had to incorporate some mythical materials because of the nature of the sources available to him. Thucydides recognized this as a problem, however, and wanted his readers to be aware of it at the outset.[50] Another problem Thucydides faced was the use of oral reports. He wanted to use these reports because of his focus on political speech, but their utilization presented certain problems, which he discussed at some length.

> As to the speeches that were made by different men . . . it has been difficult to recall with strict accuracy the words actually spoken, both for me as regards that which I myself heard, and for those who from various other sources have brought me reports. Therefore the speeches are given in the language in which, as it seemed to me, the several speakers would express, on the subjects under consideration, the sentiments most befitting the occasion.[51]

Thucydides acknowledged that using oral reports meant that a certain fictive element entered his writing as he sought to reconstruct what he imagined the sources would have said and how they would have said it.[52] On the whole, however, Thucydides's goal, in his own words, was to reconstruct "a true picture of the events which have happened."[53]

Our foregoing discussion has reviewed the rise of historiography in the ancient world. Historiography developed from simpler generic types. In Babylon, the Babylonian Chronicles developed from earlier king lists. In Greece, the histories developed from earlier epics. In Egypt, works such as the Palermo Stone developed from more rudimentary annalistic records. The Greek histories are probably the closest comparable exemplars to the historical narratives in the Hebrew Bible.

Historiography did not emerge in a vacuum, however, but alongside other genres of literature. In light of this, how can we determine what texts were intended to be historiographical in nature and which were not? We have already seen that modern historians have tended to impose contemporary definitions of terms onto the ancient literature. W. W. Hallo, however, has noted that "historiography is a subjective enterprise in which each culture ultimately defines the ethnic parameters of its own past for itself."[54] We must seek to be attuned to their own definitions as we approach ancient texts.

## Determining Whether a Text Is Historical in Nature

The historiographic materials of Sumero-Akkadian literature included chronicles, royal inscriptions, and historical-literary texts. Babylonian scholars had a proclivity for "list science," and they made lists of virtually everything they found practical or worthy of note, as in the Babylonian Chronicle Series. In Egypt, this same penchant for list-making is evident in the *gnwt*,⁵⁵ the Daybooks, and the Annals of Thutmose III. It has been widely acknowledged, however, that these chronicles are not historiography; instead, their purpose was simply to make catalogues of events in their nation's past.⁵⁶ King lists *are* historical documents but, as Walton has argued, they only have "a passive, sublimated historiography."⁵⁷ J. Licht has argued that "what is usually called ancient Mesopotamian historiography does not really qualify as such," because it consists mainly of royal inscriptions, annals, and preambles to treaties. "They had the equipment to produce a historiography, but evidently felt no need for it."⁵⁸

There is a difference between the making of lists or the recording of recent events and retrospective, historical writing. Instead of simply being a list, a "historical account must be a narrative of some sort, if it is not to be simply incoherent."⁵⁹ Like the ancient Mesopotamians and other ancient Near Eastern peoples, the ancient Israelites, too, had various lists, chronicles, and other "raw-materials" for history writing. The Israelites, however, were unique in that they integrated these "raw-materials" into works of real historiography.⁶⁰ This does not solve the problem of determining whether a given text is historical in nature but, instead, only complicates it. For as soon as the "raw-materials" of history writing begin to be molded into a narrative, a number of issues come into play that may affect whether a text can be understood as historical in nature. These include proximity, literary artistry, objectivity, propaganda/didactic value, the invocation of deity/deities, and authorial intent.

## Proximity

The question of the proximity of the biblical accounts to the events they purport to record has long been a point of debate, as well as the effect that their proximity has on the reliability of the historical details contained in those accounts. In discussing the development of historiography, Kenton Sparks distinguishes between "proximate" and "nonproximate" histories.⁶¹ The royal annals of Mesopotamia, Egypt, and Hatti were written in close proximity to the events they narrated, which means that they had ready access to archival records and even to eyewitnesses. Other ancient historiographical works, however, were clearly written in distant proximity to the events they purport to recount.

The authors of nonproximate histories, writing about their subject matter from a far remove, often had to rely on inferior sources. In the Babylonian Chronicles, for example, which includes texts that deal with historical events that range from the eighth to third centuries B.C.E., the authors sometimes admit that they lacked source material for some of their accounts, in which case they must have been imaginatively reconstructed.⁶² In the Weidner Chronicle, another example of a nonproximate history, the text purports to recount the provision of fish for Marduk's temple between 2500 and 2000 B.C.E., though it appears to have been composed late in the second millennium B.C.E. The fact that Babylon did not rise to historical prominence until the latter period has led scholars to regard this text as highly anachronistic and to assume that the primary source for much of the narrative was the author's imagination. This pattern of "legend-to-history" appears to have been generally common in antiquity: "Recent periods were narrated on the basis of relatively dependable historical records (king lists, inscriptions, annalistic sources, and archives), but more remote periods were reconstructed on the basis of less dependable traditions (myths, legends, and folktales) or on the basis of less accessible traditions (such as royal inscriptions and omen texts)."[63] Implicit within Sparks's discussion is the assumption that proximate histories are more reliable, while nonproximate histories are less reliable, an idea that has become widely accepted within mainstream biblical scholarship. E. A. Knauf, for example, insists that historians ought to be concerned first and foremost with primary sources, which were produced contemporaneously with the events they purport to describe. Knauf claims that these eyewitness accounts are clearly superior to accounts produced after the events they describe, which he argues are designed "to clarify for future generations how things were *thought* to have happened."[64]

Based on his observation that the books immediately following Deuteronomy shared its theology and style, Martin Noth postulated that the same author or authors must have composed these books.[65] Based on this theory, the entire section from Deuteronomy through 2 Kings has come to be known as the "Deuteronomistic History" (DtrH), the author of which is referred to as the "Deuteronomist" (Dtr) or the "Deuteronomistic Historian" (DH). Since the account in 2 Kings ends in the sixth century B.C.E., it follows that the DtrH ultimately reflects the viewpoint of an author or authors in this period. Since the books of Joshua and Judges are part of the DtrH, Noth and others have understood the message of these books—and that of the DtrH as a whole—as one that is primarily aimed at an Israelite audience in the sixth century B.C.E. Richard Nelson, for example, while he does find predeuteronomistic materials in the book of Joshua, is convinced that "hardly any of the material it preserves is of the sort that can be directly used for historical reconstruction."

The book is primarily a product of Dtr, who produced a work that "do[es] not necessarily reflect genuine memories of Israel's origins."[66] The figure of Joshua is understood "as a forerunner for the ideological role played by later kings, and especially for the expansionistic and reforming policies of Josiah."[67] While it is not clear from his commentary whether Nelson understands Joshua to have been a historical figure or not, other scholars have concluded that the figure of Joshua is nothing more than a metaphorical portrait of Josiah invented by Dtr, a "classic literary expression of the yearnings and fantasies" of the people of Israel in later periods.[68] Regardless of whether Joshua is viewed as a historical figure, both views regard the book of Joshua as having little value as a historical source.

The history of the formation of the book of Joshua is certainly not a settled issue. One cannot deny the influence of Deuteronomy on the book of Joshua, and the book may have been put into its final form by a Deuteronomistic historian in the sixth century B.C.E. This would not preclude the use of more ancient sources.[69] The book of Joshua does contain many features that can best be explained as having their origin in the second millennium B.C.E.,[70] which could suggest that the book may have reached something like its final form centuries earlier, possibly by the time of Solomon or even earlier.[71] While the formation of the book of Joshua certainly warrants ongoing discussion, the issue of proximity is not always the decisive factor in determining the historical value of a historiographical work. If the texts author(s) had access to earlier sources, the book may very well preserve accurate memories. Drawing on examples from across the ancient Mediterranean world, E. Yamauchi makes the point that many ancient historiographical works have been relied on for the reconstruction of various histories, despite the fact that their provenance postdates the events about which they write. Yamauchi points to the following examples:

> The Homeric epics, composed five centuries after the Mycenaean era they describe, can be shown to have preserved numerous memories of the Late Bronze age, in the personal and place names and in artifacts mentioned. Roman historians use Livy to reconstruct the history of the Roman Republic several centuries before his lifetime. Classical historians use Plutarch (second century A.D.) for the history of Themistocles (fifth century B.C.), and all historians of Alexander the Great (fourth century B.C.) acknowledge as their most accurate source Arrian's *Anabasis* (second century A.D.).[72]

Ultimately, whether Joshua existed in an earlier form in the early Iron Age II or was composed of whole cloth in the sixth century B.C.E. is not the decisive factor in determining its nature as a historiographical text. In either case, as mentioned above, its author made use of a number of sources that have their origin in the second millennium B.C.E.[73] In order to further elucidate the historiographical nature of the book of Joshua, we must turn to other criteria.

## *Literary Artistry*

When a historian "puts pen to paper," the element of literary artistry immediately comes into effect. The historian has to select what materials he or she is going to include, how those materials ought to be grafted together, and what story they ought to be made to tell. As the historian carries out these tasks, he or she will make these and other decisions that will shape the narrative and thus the history that will be recounted. This raises the question of whether literary artistry compromises the stories as having a genuinely historical intent. The narrative itself does represent the interpretation of the narrator and is, therefore, to some extent artificial. In discussing the difficulties of reconstructing Mesopotamian history from the cuneiform sources, M. Van De Mieroop discusses the perception that cuneiform texts are too problematic and therefore inadequate for reconstructing history, while narratives are problem-free and therefore adequate for recreating history. A text on a cuneiform tablet, for example, may contain nothing more than a receipt for the sale of an animal, leaving every other aspect of its owner unknown. Narratives, on the other hand, are often thought of as containing sufficient information that can be taken at face value and integrated without reservation into the history-writing process. Van De Mieroop explains that it is not so simple:

> The narrative form of historical discourse also presents a fundamental paradox to the historian: its order, coherence, and completeness are appealing and intelligible, but

are imaginary. Reality does not present itself in the form of ready-made stories that come to a logical conclusion. Events occur in a sequence that often has no beginning or end that lacks coherence, and surely does not exclude extraneous facts. The realism of narrative historical representation is a dream.[74]

This truth has led some scholars, such as Robert Alter, to talk about biblical narrative as "prose fiction," or "fictionalized history,"[75] a concept that has gained popularity among biblical scholars in recent years. Philip Davies has argued that the biblical texts are, in large part, fiction.[76] For him, it follows that any attempt to make a historiographical assessment of literary texts is a "betrayal" both of literature and of the writing of history.[77]

This kind of sharp distinction between history and fiction, however, seems to be based on the kinds of modern definitions of historiography discussed earlier. Meir Sternberg counters that biblical historiography does not claim to be a "record of fact," of what "really happened," but is instead "a discourse that claims to be a record of fact."[78] In this sense, all history is "created." Events take place, but people relate and document those events, choosing which events to discuss and what aspects of those events to emphasize, thereby "creating historical texts."[79] Sternberg emphasizes that, "Whatever its faults, real or imagined, bad historiography does not yet make fiction."[80] V. Philips Long has emphasized the creative aspects of the work of ancient historiographers, but suggests that "it would be far better, at least with respect to the perceptions of the average person, to substitute a term like *artistry* to describe the historian's literary technique, and reserve the term *fiction* for the nonfactual genre of that name."[81]

## Objectivity/Bias

As noted above, king lists and other catalogues are the "raw-materials" of historiography and must be shaped into a narrative in order for history writing to occur. However, in a narrative, one still has to ask what reason the narrator has for representing the history as a narrative and whether that reason has compromised his or her objectivity. The narrator's purpose is not to recite historical occurrences in a rote fashion, which would be "list-science." Instead, the history-writing process "represents the interpretation of the narrator. The historical narrative is artificial and represents the interpretation of the narrator."[82] If the writing of history consisted solely in list making or cataloging events, objectivity would not be as elusive.

In addition to the issue of whether the original writer of the history was objective, there is also the question of whether modern historians can produce objective histories of the past. Hayden White, a postmodern historiographical critic, has argued that historians do not increase objective knowledge about the past through their writing of history; instead, they simply "generate a discourse about the past,"[83] a discourse that is just as much invented as discovered in ancient sources. Postmodern skepticism has cast extreme doubt upon von Ranke's idea that historians might recover "how it really happened." Instead, their inability to be objective leads them to produce discourses about the past that are shaped by their own biases. This skepticism has led to the crisis in historiography noted at the beginning of this chapter, which has resulted in a progressive loss of confidence in the historical value of both the biblical narratives and of most modern histories of Israel, epitomized by the rise of the minimalist school.[84] The view of historiography which has burgeoned among this school has been succinctly stated by T. L. Thompson, who sets out an empirical methodology for historiographical research:

> Sound historical research is not a highly speculative discipline, but rather is based on the very conservative methodology and simple hard work of distinguishing what we know from what we do not know, and of testing our syntheses and hypotheses to ensure that they respect the all-important separation of reality from unreality. It is only in this way that history, like any other of the social sciences, can be scientific, progressive and cumulative. To the extent that the social sciences are based on probability and analogy, they are also based on guesswork and prejudice. The heart of historical science, unlike that of the natural sciences which are predictive, is the specific and unique observation of what is known. When historiography functions "scientifically," it attempts to discover what did happen. When researchers go beyond the observable singular, they also go beyond what is known and involve themselves with the theoretical and the hypothetical.[85]

Thompson engages in circular reasoning here. In other places, he argues extensively that "social constructs" determine all knowledge, that all truth is relative, and that there is no intrinsic meaning in texts but only that which we supply.[86] And yet here he insists that historiography can function "scientifically" and thereby apprehend history "how it really happened." J. J. Collins points out that minimalists like Thompson are really "quite old-fashioned, empirical historians." He notes that N. P. Lemche even talks about "playing the von Ranke game" by differentiating so vigilantly between primary and later sources.[87] Historians must recognize that all historiography, both ancient and modern, involves selection and is ideological in nature. "The uninvolved, disinterested observer has never existed, whether as Ideal Chronicler or as Ideal Historiographer."[88] If a complete lack of bias itself disqualifies narrative writing as historiography, then no modern histories of Israel qualify as historiography.

## *Propaganda/Didactic Value*

Beyond the more mundane question of whether the biblical writers were writing their history objectively or whether they may have been biased with regard to their subject matter is the accusation that they may have been intending to produce outright propaganda, which refers to a deliberate attempt to influence the outcome of a decision-making process in a specific, desired way. Many ancient Near Eastern historiographic texts serve propagandistic functions. In Mesopotamia, for example, the Weidner Chronicle is obviously propagandistic. Its purpose is to urge its readers to provide for the Esagil cult, so they will not suffer the same fate as other predecessors who were also negligent. The Assyrian Chronicles, in addition to repeated references to the king's "military prowess," contain propagandistic details about the king's accomplishments, such as the extent of the spoils he was able to seize or how much land he was able to annex. Likewise, the Assyrian Annals are consistently propagandistic and overvalue the king and all his endeavors. The Assyrian writer of the Synchronistic History only refers to Assyrian victories over Babylon and even construes at least two defeats as victories, in what appears to be an obvious attempt to cheer on the Assyrians in their efforts to repel Babylonian invasions.[89] The Babylonian Chronicles, apparently written by scribes who were not producing an official record, lack this kind of overt propaganda and seem to have been written from an impartial perspective.

By analogy with the Assyrian and other propagandistic historiography, many scholars have argued that the biblical narratives are also driven by propagandistic purposes. G. W. Ahlström, for example, argues that the Bible contains stories that are filled with descriptions that are "ideological, rather than factual," and that the biblical authors were driven solely by an ideological pattern, with no concern for the facts.[90] K. A. D. Smelik insists that the "aim of these biblical authors was not to record history" at all.[91] Knauf clarifies the thought by explaining that "ancient Near Eastern historiography is not concerned with what actually happened. Rather, it is interested in stating what should have happened in order to construct a 'correct world.' "[92] Elsewhere, W. G. Dever similarly remarked that the Bible records history as it would have happened had (the historiographers) been in charge.[93] The biblical writers, according to this line of thought, were men whose goal in compiling the biblical documents was not simply to relay history, but to assert particular ideological agendas through narrative forms, utilizing etiology, poetry, theology, and so on. If the readers, then, approach the texts without discernment, they blindly submit themselves to being manipulated by the desires of the writers. They may unwittingly accept something as historically true that is intended to advance an idea rather than establish the historicity of an actual event.

It must be agreed that the Bible is an ideological text and that its composition was influenced in every way by the social, political, and religious bent of its writers. As K. L. Younger has pointed out, when the ancient historian(s) wrote about Israel's past, the final product was a "figurative" account, because "a narrative historian is not only a presenter of the *events* of history, but also a *presenter* of the events of history."[94] In other words, he is a "literary artist," rendering an account of the past as he perceives it.

While conceding that the narrative passages in the Hebrew Bible are ideologically driven, it must also be noted that the Hebrew Bible is, in fact, very concerned with the subject of history. This is obvious enough that Gerhard von Rad could say that "the Old Testament is a history book."[95] The problem is that history written from one's own particular sociopolitical or religious viewpoint can be generally classified as propaganda. The mass media today, the governmental press corps, and advertising in general are modern-day examples. M. Liverani points out, however, that propaganda does not necessarily always involve falsehood, or forgery, but that it is "more interested in effectiveness than correctness." The information presented through propaganda may be biased "as a result of unfair selection, cunning disinformation, and subtle connotation."[96] Liverani explains that, "It cannot be denied that the OT as a whole can be considered as a huge propagandistic work and that many texts or passages constitutive of the OT (or embedded in it) display a more or less clear propagandistic purpose, both in the political and the religious field."[97] These facts, however, do not necessarily strip away the historical value of the biblical texts. Using the narratives of 1–2 Samuel as a test case, Mark Chavalas explains that

> the intent of the author . . . was to answer the charge of wrongdoing, with an attempt to demonstrate David's innocence in the series of the events that led to his succession. The narrative of David's rise promulgates a political point of view supported by a theological interpretation of events. David's accession to the throne is portrayed as lawful because he was loyal to Saul's line and because Yahweh supported him; he also had hereditary legitimacy. . . . By virtue of the fact that he married Saul's daughter Michal, he could claim the throne through the right of Michal's inheritance. Thus it was important . . . to demand her return after their separation. David also brought Saul's relatives to his palace for political reasons.[98]

Chavalas demonstrates the propagandistic nature of those texts, in the sense that they have an apologetic function and are intended to legitimize the kingship of David in the mind of the reader. This does not, however, necessitate the alteration of facts on the part of the biblical writers. The propagandistic nature of a text does not *a priori* preclude it from having historical value, and "objective" history may very well be used by a writer for programmatic purposes.[99] "A problem occurs only when historical data is changed or embellished to enhance the propagandistic or didactic value."[100]

No history is totally objective. The process of historiography does not involve the truly objective reporting of human events, in the way that objectivity is understood above. Dillard and Longman identify four characteristics of the historiographer, none of which makes a claim to total objectivity: selectivity, emphasis, order, and application.[101] The point is, no history, even a "secular" history, can tell its readers everything about its subject. If a historiographer's goal were to be comprehensive, "it would take longer to write about an event than it does to experience it."[102] Selectivity is a necessity of space. In regard to the Hebrew Bible, in particular, Dillard and Longman point out that "the biblical historian is not interested in every aspect of the past, but focuses on the community of Israel."[103] Histories are didactic and programmatic. This does not automatically falsify the historical material they draw upon for their sources. Again, a problem only occurs when the historical data is embellished to enhance the propagandistic or didactic value. With regard to the book of Joshua, with which we are especially concerned, it is obvious that its historiographers were selective in what they presented, "but selectivity is expected when there is a didactic agenda. This is different than distortion or embellishment."[104]

## *Invocation of Deity/Deities*

Much, if not most, of Israel's historiography in the Hebrew Bible revolves around its experience of the divine in human affairs. This has led many scholars to decry the validity of the Hebrew narratives as historical in nature.[105] However, the appeal to divinity was common in ancient Near Eastern historiography. This can be illustrated with a few selections from Mesopotamian historiographic texts. The Weidner Chronicle, which reviews the reigns of thirteen rulers, attributes the success or failure of the various rulers to the intervention of Marduk. In Esarhaddon's Apology, the Assyrian king is shown to have been brought to the throne by divine election. In the Synchronistic History, which outlines the relationship between Assyria and Babylon in the ninth and eighth centuries B.C.E., the text reviews the military conflicts between the two countries over Babylonian violations of the border agreement established in the covenant between the two countries. Since the gods of each country were called upon to witness the covenant between the two countries, it only made sense that, when Babylon violated the covenant by continual breaches of the border, Assur would intervene on behalf of Assyria.[106]

It was commonplace, throughout the ancient world, for people to conceive of the will of a deity or deities as being manifested in history.[107] J. H. Walton has noted the need to recognize the cognitive environment that shapes historiography in pre-Enlightenment cultures:

> The cognitive environment in the ancient world is one in which the directive activity of deity is of primary importance. This view extends far beyond the recognition of occasional supernatural interventions. In fact, even the word "intervention" is inappropriate because it implied that there are some historical events that are not supernaturally driven. In the view of the ancient Near East, even "natural" occurrences are the result of divine activity.[108]

An important difference emerges here with regard to ancient Near Eastern conceptions of divine involvement and the way it was perceived in ancient Israel. In the ancient Near East at large, while cultures perceived divine involvement in history, polytheism precluded the conception of a singular divine plan taking in all of history. In Israelite historiography, however, monotheism allowed for the development of the conception of a single divine program being worked out by Yahweh in the history of Yahweh's chosen people, Israel. There is, therefore, a tremendous emphasis in the Hebrew Bible on recalling and remembering the past, within which Yahweh had been and continued to work out these purposes.[109] This fact betrays "a peculiar attitude to life,"[110] and "makes the Israelite attitude toward the past unique within the ancient Near East."[111] Rather than undermining the historical nature of Israel's historiographic texts, Israel's conception of divine involvement in its history seems to reinforce it.

## *Authorial Intent*

Baruch Halpern has suggested that authorial intent is another factor that may contribute toward determining whether a text is historical in nature.[112] What was it that the author meant to do, write history or fiction? This criterion has drawn fire from several scholars. John Collins has argued that it is ineffectual.[113] Susan Niditch has argued that it is "unworkable," and that it is not apparent that providing accurate record of the past was the intent of the writers of the narrative historiography in the Bible.[114] Marc Brettler has argued that this criterion is "useless" because in much of the Deuteronomistic History, "we have no ability to determine whether the author had reason to believe what he or she wrote."[115] Long ago, W. M. L. de Wette came to the conclusion that the Hebrew Bible could not be used for the reconstruction of the history of ancient Israel. He decided that the Hebrew Bible was inadequate as a historical resource, in addition to aforementioned reasons, because of authorial intent. The biblical writers, he concluded, were not intending to write history. Their purposes in writing were programmatically religious, not historical.[116] G. W. Ahlström echoes this view when he writes, "Biblical historiography is not a product built on facts. It reflects the narrator's outlook and ideology rather than *known* facts."[117] The implication here is that the ancient historiographers, because of their bias or their strong desire to propagandize, composed their work without regard for what was *known* about the past.

The idea that ancient historiographers would operate in this way defies credulity. A number of historiographers from the classical world began their work with statements of intent, in which they stressed their desire to produce reliable history. The Greek statesman and historian, Polybius (ca. 200–118 B.C.E.), begins his account of *The Rise of the Roman Empire* with such an introduction, in which he explains the dual function of his account, intended to serve both as a didactic purpose for future statesmen and also to measure the achievement of Roman ascendancy. Polybius begins by noting that "certainly mankind possesses no better guide to conduct than the knowledge of the past," and that history can serve both as a guide for those entering politics but also for those who desire to learn "how to bear with dignity the vicissitudes of Fortune."[118] In articulating his intentions, Polybius suggests:

> There can surely be nobody so petty or so apathetic in his outlook that he has no desire to discover by what means and under what system of government the Romans succeeded in less than fifty-three years in bringing under their rule almost the whole of the inhabited world, an achievement which is without parallel in human history.[119]

In isolation, this excerpt may appear to have come from an author whose devotion lay with Rome, and yet Polybius was a Greek who had served in the Achaean League, an organization that strove to maintain a friendly but independent policy toward the Romans, but who had also been taken as a political prisoner by the Romans and held for eighteen years in Rome. He was clearly not writing the foregoing quote as a partisan on behalf of Rome, but as a historian relatively free of national biases and committed to the search for truth with regard to the phenomenon of Roman ascendancy. In the latter part of his work, after having made a statement that he was concerned may surprise readers of his account, Polybius made the following qualification:

> If this appears incredible to any of my readers, let him remember that the present writer is especially mindful of the fact that it is the Romans above all who are likely

to read this book, since the greatest number and the most brilliant of the achievements which it describes belong to them, and that it is impossible that they should either be ignorant of the facts or prepared to pardon an author who utters false statements. It is obvious then that nobody would willingly expose himself to their inevitable disbelief or contempt. This fact should be borne in mind throughout the whole of my history, whenever I may appear to make any surprising statement about the Romans.[120]

Livy (59 B.C.E.–17 C.E.), while writing about a century later and as a Roman citizen, expressed "some misgiving" about writing a history of Rome from its earliest days. He writes:

> I am aware that for historians to make extravagant claims is, and always has been, all too common: every writer on history tends to look down his nose at his less cultivated predecessors, happily persuaded that he will better them in point of style, or bring new facts to light. But however that may be, I shall find satisfaction in contributing—not, I hope, ignobly—to the labour of putting on record the story of the greatest nation in the world.[121]

Livy goes on to note, however, that his task is "immensely laborious," such that "adequate treatment is hardly possible." Interestingly, he explains that, while few readers will be interested in his account of Rome's beginnings and "will wish to hurry on to more modern times and to read of the period, already a long one, in which the might of an imperial people is beginning to work its own ruin," he believes that the study of Roman antiquity has special rewards for both himself and his readers.[122] Livy goes on to explain that the sources available to him for earliest Rome consisted of "old tales with more of the charm of poetry than of a sound historical record," but he does not propose to either affirm or refute the reliability of these materials. Even "when antiquity draws no hard line between the human and the supernatural," Livy simply concludes that "it adds dignity to the past," and he does not seek to disparage it. The writer goes on to explain that these issues are "trivial matters" compared to the "much more serious" issue of tracing out the moral decline of the nation in order to discover the remedy to cure it. He explains that

> the study of history is the best medicine for a sick mind; for in history you have a record of the infinite variety of human experience plainly set out for all to see; and in that record you can find for yourself and your country both examples and warnings; fine things to take as models, base things, rotten through and through, to avoid.[123]

Livy closes his introduction by expressing his hope that his zeal for Rome's past has not prejudiced his judgment and reiterating the fact that his goal is to write a fair and balanced account of Rome's early history.

Polybius and Livy both include detailed statements of their intents. Unfortunately, the biblical writers do not. The statements of Polybius and Livy do, however, make an important point, and it is that "in a void, any and all of the historian's reports could be arbitrary and unbiased—and his convictions conjure up suspicions that the evidence for them is concocted. In his social setting, however, the historian is answerable to the expectations of his contemporaries."[124] While Ahlström suggests that the biblical historians' own bias and desire to propagandize led them to put their own ideology above *known* facts, analogy suggests that ancient historiographers—including the biblical historiographers—would have been restrained from falsification by the fund of shared knowledge. The authors of these texts were trying to accomplish something with their writings, and their readers were able to compare those purposes with what they knew to be true.

Having reviewed the rise of historiography, it seems clear that ancient Israel was unique in its early emphasis on historical writing. Even though the writers of this historiography utilized literary artistry, were never completely objective, had didactic purposes, and invoked their god Yahweh, these factors, as we have seen, are not sufficient criteria for withholding a general historiographical ascription to the Hebrew narratives. However, the nature of each text as historiography and the historical value of each text must still be assessed in light of its own apparent purposes. The question that now faces us is, what were the specific historiographical purposes of the writer(s) of the book of Joshua?

## THE BOOK OF JOSHUA

Biblical scholars and archaeologists alike have often assumed that the main historiographical purpose of the book of Joshua is to report Israel's conquest of Canaan. T. Butler, for example, suggested that the book of Joshua was assembled by a compiler who emphasized "the conquest of the land in which Israel conquered and maintained control until the days of the compiler."[125] Likewise, G. Mitchell concludes that the book of Joshua is primarily about conquest and mass destruction.[126] Archaeologist W. G. Dever understood the biblical traditions as being focused primarily on the theme of "conquest."[127] Several scholars who might be described as minimalists have rejected the historical veracity of the book of Joshua because of their understanding of conquest as its main theme and their own conclusions that the working out of this theme in the book does not correspond with the archaeological record.[128] Some scholars have taken the study of the book of Joshua in a different direction by focusing not on Joshua alone, but as a part of the Deuteronomistic History (DtrH). M. Noth, who pioneered this approach, interpreted the book of Joshua primarily through the lens of the Deuteronomistic Historian (Dtr), and encouraged other scholars to do so as well. He explained that, to understand the book of Joshua, "we had better ignore, to begin with, the usual division of this historical complex into 'books,' for this was undoubtedly a secondary process in the history of the tradition and closer investigation is required before we can decide whether it took place before or after Dtr."[129]

Noth's work has been very influential, and many scholars have followed his lead with regard to the interpretation of the book of Joshua. R. Polzin, for example, interprets the book of Joshua in terms of the overall concerns of the Deuteronomist. Since he understands the interpretation of the Law to be the main theme of the Deuteronomist, he also identifies this as the main theme of the book of Joshua.[130]

While identifying conquest as the primary theme of Joshua is commonplace, it may be based on a superficial reading of the book. Likewise, reading the book of Joshua solely through the lens of Dtr may obscure the historiographic purposes of the book. In order to identify the historiographic purposes of the book of Joshua, we must read it closely and on its own terms. There are two things in particular that we should take note of. First, we must observe what the book does *not* say. Second, having realized what the book does not say, we must then seek to discover what it *does* say.

## What the Book of Joshua Does Not Say

Sometimes what a writer leaves out is just as important as what he or she includes. As discussed above, authors cannot include everything, and they carefully select what they will include based on whether those materials will help them accomplish their historiographical goals. One of the ways authors practice selectivity is through a literary device called "gapping." Meir Sternberg explains that all literary works establish a system of gaps that must be filled in by the reader in the process of reading.[131] Every literary work raises a number of questions in the minds of the readers, but only gives explicit answers to a few of these. The remaining questions—or "gaps"—must be answered or filled in by the reader on the basis of clues found in the text itself. Sternberg includes the following Hebrew nursery rhyme as an example:

> Every day, that's the way
> Jonathan goes out to play.
> Climbed a tree, what did he see?
> Birdies: one, two, three!
> Naughty boy! What have we seen?
> There's a hole in your new jeans!

How did a hole come to be in Jonathan's new jeans? Even a child can draw conclusions about how this must have come about—*based on the information given in the rhyme*—though the point is never explicitly made. Sternberg explains that "gap-filling ranges from simple linkages of elements, which the reader performs automatically, to intricate networks that are figured out consciously, laboriously, hesitantly, and with constant modifications in the light of additional information disclosed in later stages of reading."[132] I will use two examples, one from the Hebrew Bible and another from the New Testament, in order to elucidate how biblical historiographers utilize gapping.

### *The Coronation of David*

The Bible contains two reports about the coronation of David, each different in emphasis. According to 1 Sam 31, David was anointed king only over the tribe of

Judah after the death of Saul. At the same time, Abner installed Ish-bosheth, Saul's son, as king over the northern tribes (2 Sam 2:1-4, 8-10). It was not until two years later—when Abner and Ish-bosheth were assassinated (2 Sam 3:12-39 and ch. 4)—that the elders of northern Israel approached David in Hebron, made a covenant with him, and anointed him "king over Israel" (2 Sam 5:1-3). Although these details reveal that David's reign began, in a sense, haltingly, the writer of 1 Samuel includes them out of an apparent desire to stress that David did not usurp the throne.

The Chronicler leaves out any material describing the period from the death of Saul to the installation of David in Hebron by the elders of the northern Israelite tribes (2 Sam 1–4). In other words, he omits the description of events that transpire during that two-year period of David's reign over Judah, which coincides with the reign of Ish-bosheth in the North. Instead, the Chronicler places the story of David's coronation in Hebron over all Israel (1 Chr 11:1–3//2 Sam 5:1-3) immediately after the story of the death of Saul (1 Chr 10//1 Sam 31), thus creating the impression that the two events occurred one after the other without any time having elapsed between them. This impression is strengthened in the mind of the reader by the verse "therefore he (God) slew him (Saul) and turned the kingdom over to David, the son of Jesse" (1 Chr 10:14b). This phrase "bridges the gap" between the story of the death of Saul (1 Chr 10:1-14a) and the story of the installing of David (1 Chr 11:1-3). The Chronicler uses this literary-chronological proximity to "erase" the two-year interval between the two events. He apparently wants to portray David as the king who ruled over all the tribes of Israel, both Northern and Southern, throughout his reign.[133]

## *The Spread of the Church*

The writer of the book of Acts has the spread of the gospel to the Gentiles begin with Peter's call to visit with and evangelize Cornelius (Acts 10). Cornelius is often regarded as "the first Gentile convert."[134] Peter preaches to the Gentiles (Acts 10:34-43), and they receive the Holy Spirit (Acts 10:44-48). The writer of Acts "officially" launches the Gentile ministry with Peter, because Peter, along with Jesus' brother James and the sons of Zebedee, was one of the main leaders of the Jerusalem church. However, when we read a bit farther in Acts, we find that conversions had already been taking place as far away as Phoenicia, Cyprus, and Antioch (Acts 11:19). Based on this fact, one wonders if congregations may have already formed in some of these locations. In any case, news of this eventually was heard by the church in Jerusalem, and they sent Barnabas to Antioch to verify that there were believers there (v. 22). How had the gospel arrived at these remote areas? Did not Acts 10 say that the Gentile mission only just began with Peter's trip to see Cornelius?

The spread and growth of the early church really began as early as Acts 2, when "devout Jews from every nation under heaven" (v. 5) had come to Jerusalem for Pentecost, a festal celebration of the wheat harvest fifty days after Passover. The text reports that "Parthians, Medes, Elamites, and residents of Mesopotamia, Judea and Cappadocia, Pontus and Asia, Phrygia and Pamphylia, Egypt and the parts of Libya belonging to Cyrene, and visitors from Rome, both Jews and proselytes, Cretans and Arabs" (vv. 9-11) were all present when the gospel was first proclaimed. The text goes on to report that on "that day about three thousand persons were added" to the church (v. 41). These people took the gospel with them back to their home countries.

Following this initial spread and growth of the early church, a further development ensued. After the stoning of Stephen (Acts 7:54-60), "a severe persecution began against the church in Jerusalem, and all except the apostles were scattered throughout the countryside of Judea and Samaria" (Acts 8:1). The text reports that "those who were scattered went from place to place, proclaiming the word" (8:4). What we see here is that the gospel was initially spread when new believers returned to their homes after Pentecost (Acts 2) and, later, when the Christians were scattered by persecution (Acts 8). When the author of Acts portrays Peter as pioneering the evangelization of the Gentiles (Acts 9:32–11:18), he is not denying those earlier forays of the gospel into Gentile territory, nor is he contradicting himself; rather, he is showing the legitimacy of the Gentile mission by emphasizing Peter's role in it.[135]

## *Joshua and the Israelite Settlement*

Like the foregoing examples from the books of Chronicles and Acts, the writer of Joshua is "preaching," and to make his point, he carefully selects what material to include and what material to leave out. The author of the book of Joshua is not trying to write a comprehensive, secular history of the process by which Israel entered into the land. He does not discuss what kinds of villages they established when they entered the land, how they ordered their domestic lives, what kinds of pottery they used, what sort of house structure they used, or any of these other kinds of details. These are the kinds of facts, however, for which historians and archaeologists are searching in the gaps, and their absence from the book of Joshua suggests the historiographer's interests were other than producing a scientific-historical reconstruction of the appearance of Israel in Canaan. This is not to say that the book of Joshua has no historical value. On the contrary, even though the writer(s) of this book employed literary artistry, was not dispassionate, had didactic purposes, and appealed to the Hebrew god, Yahweh, none of these issues provide an adequate reason for refusing to acknowledge that the book of Joshua is generally historiographical in nature. The question is where, exactly, did the historiographer's interests lie? In order to answer this question, we must look at what the book of Joshua *does* say.

## What the Book of Joshua Does Say

As mentioned above, Bible readers often think of the book of Joshua as being primarily an account of conquest. Instead of being primarily concerned with giving an account of a conquest, the writer of the book of Joshua was dealing with religious concerns. The book of Joshua is "preaching" about how the covenant promises made to Abraham in Gen 12:1-3 will continue to be realized based on Israel's adherence to the covenant. When one reviews the major events of the book of Joshua, it becomes evident that the concerns of the author are primarily religious in nature rather than historical.

- After introductory materials, the book opens with God leading Israel into the promised land (religious procession) (Josh 3).
- There, a new generation is circumcised and the Passover is celebrated.
- Joshua has a vision (Josh 5).
- Jericho is taken (Josh 6), but only one verse describes the battle (v. 21). The entire chapter is focused on religious processions around the city; even the verse that describes the battle (v. 21) is really about religious adherence: "they devoted [the city] to destruction" (חרם, *herem*), a religious idea.
- Two chapters contain a lengthy description of the taking of Ai, but its primary interest is in a case of covenant violation and how that threatens to bring Israel's progress to a halt (Josh 7–8).
- An altar is built and a covenant renewal ceremony is carried out on Mount Ebal (Josh 8:30-35).
- The longest section of the book concerns the *allotment* of the land— *done on paper at Gilgal* (Josh 13–21). This section envisions the territories that Yahweh will give to the Israelite tribes if they will carry through with the conquest.
- At the end of the book, the historiographer records another covenant renewal ceremony (Josh 24).

All of the aforementioned activities are religious in nature, not military. Battles are recounted in the book of Joshua, but compared to the overall mass of religious events recorded, they are few in number. David Merling has recently made the case that the few accounts of military victories in the book of Joshua have a special function, which is to serve as "confirmation events."[136] These events testify to what God could and would do if Israel were faithful to the covenant and if they carried through with the conquest of Canaan. The book of Joshua reports, however, that while Israel did have initial victories, they did not carry through from conquest to settlement.

The book of Joshua makes it clear that the conquest was incomplete. The early battles were sorties from a base established at Gilgal, not settlement. Merling has written at length about Gilgal, the site where the Israelites camped and from which they launched these sorties.[137] The Israelites camped at Gilgal after having crossed the Jordan River (Josh 4:19), and it was there they circumcised the new generation (Josh 5:1-9), and celebrated the Passover (Josh 5:10-12). The Israelites returned to Gilgal after each circumambulation of Jericho (Josh 5:14), and it was there the Gibeonites sought Joshua out in order to establish a covenant with him (Josh 9:6), an act that evoked the attack of a coalition of the kings of five important southern city-states

(Josh 10:1-5). After defeating this coalition, "Joshua returned, and all Israel with him, to the camp at Gilgal" (Josh 10:15). Two campaigns are then carried out, one in the south (chaps. 9–10) and the other in the north (chap. 11), after which it is reported that "the land had rest from war" (Josh 11:23) and that Israel possessed the land (chap. 12). The text acknowledges, however, that "much of the land still remains to be possessed" (Josh 13:1-7) and that Joshua and the Israelites are still residing in Gilgal (Josh 14:6), and that some tribes failed to drive out the indigenous inhabitants of the land (e.g., 15:63).

Joshua was "old and advanced in years" when the allotment began (Josh 13:1), and it was when he was about to "go the way of all the earth" (Josh 23:14) that he summoned the leadership of Israel and reminded them that the promise still remained, that "the LORD your God will push them [the indigenous inhabitants of the land] back before you, and drive them out of your sight" (23:5). Judges 1:1–2:5 confirms that, following Joshua's death, the Israelites failed to follow through and complete the conquest.[138]

Joshua is historical in nature; however, it utilizes its historical material *primarily for the purpose of preaching*, not for writing an exhaustive, secular history that explains Israel's appearance in the land of Canaan, with all its sociological, domestic, economic, and agricultural details.

# THE NECESSITY OF A METHODOLOGY FOR RECONSTRUCTING ISRAEL'S SETTLEMENT IN CANAAN

We have, therefore, two pictures of Israel's history, one constructed by the faith of Israel and the other by modern critical scholarship. Commenting on this reality, Gerhard von Rad wrote:

> It would be stupid to dispute the right of the one or the other to exist. It would be superfluous to emphasize that each is the product of very different intellectual activities. The one is rational and "objective"; that is, with the aid of historical method and presupposing the similarity of all historical occurrence, it constructs a critical picture of the history as it really was in Israel.[139]

Von Rad suggested that "the fact that these two views of Israel's history are so divergent is one of the most serious burdens imposed today upon Biblical scholarship." He goes on to say, however, that one should not explain one of the portrayals as historical and the other as unhistorical, because even the kerygmatic picture is based in the actual history and was not invented from whole cloth. He concludes that "the particular way in which Israel's faith presented history is still far from being adequately elucidated."[140] Our concern in this book will not be with the kerygmatic history per se, but with the "objective" history, i.e., what actually happened in the process of Israel's appearance in the land of Canaan. How did Israel come to be in the land? When they failed to drive out the Canaanites, how did they "live with the people" (as in Josh 15:63)? How did the Israelites define themselves ethnically and religiously, in contrast to the indigenous inhabitants of the land of Canaan? A historical and archaeological reconstruction that would answer these questions would be motivated by a completely different set of concerns than those that motivated the author of the book of Joshua, whose concerns were primarily religious.

If it is necessary to reconstruct early Israel's settlement in Canaan, then how are we to go about the process of doing so? In 1946, the French historian Fernand Braudel outlined three "speeds" or dynamics of history with which the historian could be concerned,[141] as follows:

1. History of events, with which traditional history writing has been concerned. This is the fastest moving, according to Braudel, but also the most superficial current in the historical stream of events. This is the history of rulers and wealthy merchants, of wars and treaties, of foreign exchanges and monopolies, and any other element of the social hierarchies that has the power to "manipulate exchange to their advantage and disturb the established order."[142] This stream of events hovers above the market economy and is comprised of its upper limit.

2. Social history, which includes the history of family, government, evolution of institutions, and so forth.

3. *La longue durée*, referring to "history over the long term," which includes the history of people's relationship to their natural environment.

The second and third streams are much slower and constitute the everyday material life, which includes the labor and exchange carried out by countless numbers of forgotten villagers. The lives of ordinary people throughout the ages have been preoccupied with the quest for food, clothing, and shelter and have, consequently, been made up of "repeated actions, empirical processes, old methods and solutions handed down from time immemorial."[143] These everyday events of material life constitute the deepest undercurrents of history. The third stream of history, the *longue durée*, is history over the long duration, which, again, seeks to understand how human history has both shaped and been shaped by the environment.

As we seek to reconstruct early Israel's appearance in Canaan, we will seek to take into account all three of these dynamics of history; we will take into account the natural conditions, but we will also focus on events. Most of all, we will seek to reconstruct the social history of early Israel's appearance in Canaan.

In carrying out this study, we will use two main texts.[144] First, we will use the Hebrew Bible, but with an eye for the two traditions between which Rainer Kessler distinguishes in the text, the "intentional" and the "unintentional" traditions. Kessler observes that "almost everything that interests us in our attempt at social-historical reconstruction appears only incidentally in the texts we use as our sources."[145] As an example, Kessler points to Jeremiah 32, in which Jeremiah buys a field during Nebuchadrezzar's siege of Judah. Jeremiah bought the field with seventeen shekels of silver,

## Why Must We Reconstruct the History of the Israelite Settlement?

which he weighed out for his cousin (Jer 32:9). The text goes into some detail about the exchange:

> I signed the deed, sealed it, got witnesses, and weighed the money on scales. Then I took the sealed deed of purchase, containing the terms and conditions, and the open copy; and I gave the deed of purchase to Baruch son of Neriah son of Mahseiah, in the presence of my cousin Hanamel, in the presence of the witnesses who signed the deed of purchase, and in the presence of all the Judeans who were sitting in the court of the guard. In their presence I charged Baruch, saying, Thus says the LORD of hosts, the God of Israel: Take these deeds, both this sealed deed of purchase and this open deed, and put them in an earthenware jar, in order that they may last for a long time. For thus says the LORD of hosts, the God of Israel: Houses and fields and vineyards shall again be bought in this land. (Jer 32:10-15)

While this text includes details about Jeremiah's business transaction, its goal is not to educate readers about mercantile activity in the sixth century B.C.E. Instead, its goal is to inform readers about something theological: Yahweh's promise that, despite the impending exile, Israel still had a future in the land into which Yahweh had brought them. The writer of Jeremiah was not concerned with whether silver was weighed or paid in coins, but with the foregoing theological thesis. Kessler concludes that, "In general, we can say that the narrative texts of the Old Testament are interested in events, and simply *assume* the circumstances within which the events occur as background."[146] Throughout our study, we will pay careful attention to "unintentional" details about the text that may have a bearing on Israel's early social history and especially its early appearance in the land of Canaan.

Our other major source "text" will be that of archaeology. By this I do not mean, however, archaeology as a "proof-text," the kind that brought the pendulum swinging back against the Biblical Theology Movement, discussed at the beginning of this chapter. Beginning at the point of decline of the Biblical Theology Movement, Syro-Palestinian archaeology began to burgeon as a separate discipline, distinct from biblical studies,[147] and it is the methodology of this discipline that we will be using. The New Archaeology is heavily influenced by New World archaeology and anthropology and is, in fact, often referred to as "anthropological archaeology."[148] W. G. Dever suggests that a consensus recognizes the following six major emphases within the New Archaeology. These are: (1) the use of cultural-evolutionary paradigms; (2) a multidisciplinary orientation; (3) the necessity for a holistic approach; (4) the adoption of scientific methods for the formulation and testing of laws of cultural change; (5) the value of ethnography and modern material culture studies; and (6) the potential of archaeology for elucidating patterns of human thought and action.[149] Dever goes on to suggest that ultimately the goals of archaeology are to investigate and explain culture, which is defined as a specific people group's adaptation to the environment, their patterned individual and social responses, and the recognition that these features of culture are ever-changing.[150] Herein lies the approach I will be taking in this volume: this will not be a retelling of the narrative of the book of Joshua, nor will it be an effort to illuminate the details of the book of Joshua by use of

25

archaeological remains. Instead, my goal in this volume is to reconstruct the emergence of early Israel as a socio-ethnic entity with its own distinctive culture in the central hill-country of Canaan.

The New Archaeology is closely intertwined with anthropology, which is very relevant to the student of biblical history in and of itself. Anthropology is especially interested in the phenomena of culture, particularly in how a given culture originates, how it persists, and how it changes or resists change. John Rogerson notes that anthropology "is interested in the comparative studies of societies and cultures, seeking to formulate general theories about how culture changes in response to such things as alterations in the environment, population increase and control, and the introduction of new technologies."[151] Beyond dealing with the illumination of specific practices within Israelite society, there are some benefits that could result in a closer partnership between sociocultural anthropologists and biblical archaeologists. These were explored in a 1988 article by Ø. S. LaBianca, in which he suggested that sociocultural anthropology offers two things, in particular, to Syro-Palestinian archaeology. These are: (1) master concepts that can help integrate the results of multidisciplinary investigations, and (2) models that may prove helpful in conceptualizing the dynamic cultural processes to which changes in the observed archaeological record may be attributed.[152] We will draw on some of anthropology's master concepts throughout this study as we seek to understand Israel's emergence as a cultural entity in the highlands. In the final chapter, we will seek to articulate an anthropological model for the emergence of early Israel in Canaan.

Some have argued that archaeology should be exercised as an independent discipline and that it alone is sufficient for the reconstruction of Israelite history. S. A. Rosen, for example, argues that "the role of archaeology as an independent discipline within the historical sciences still apparently requires legitimization."[153] In order to demonstrate that archaeology can function as a discipline "independent of standard text-based historical reconstruction," Rosen offers an archaeological reconstruction, without reference to ancient written sources, of the pastoral nomads who existed on the periphery of the Roman/Byzantine frontier.[154] Rosen concludes that archaeology "addresses issues not even conceived of in the texts" and that "the history of this people is as important and legitimate a scholarly concern as that of any other people."[155] While these are valid points, Rosen's argument seems to overstate the case. Archaeologists can certainly write their own narratives and, as Rosen notes, "prehistorians do this all the time." However, the absence of texts to provide interpretive constraints has resulted in the production of some narratives that stretch credulity.[156] Thompson, Ahlström, and Coote and Whitelam have all sought to produce histories of Israel that utilize this approach of relying primarily on archaeology, but because they reject the biblical textual tradition as post-Exilic, Dever rejects their works as "monologues" rather than dialogues between text and data.[157] The fact is that excavated data has the same limitations as texts. While artifacts are "facts," their meaning "is no more self-evident than that of texts, and they become data only when one can read them properly and can place them in the context of significant questions."[158]

Dever suggests that, like texts, artifactual data are also "selective," not by an editorial process but by the natural processes that select at random what will be preserved and therefore represented in the archaeological record. Rather than considering either texts or archaeological data as more "primary" than the other, the limitations of both texts and physical data should be recognized, and a "holistic approach to [all] the source materials bearing on . . . the ancient Near East" should be adopted.[159]

# CONCLUSION

In this chapter we have sought to answer the question of why we must reconstruct the history of the Israelite settlement in the first place. Through a review of the definition and development of historiography, we have argued that the biblical account of the "conquest" is indeed historiography. At the same time, the biblical account is kerygmatic in nature. This does not rule out its historiographical character, but it does mean that its writer(s) did not share the same concerns as the modern historian who is seeking to produce a scientific-historical reconstruction of the appearance of Israel in Canaan, which is the task of this book. Throughout the remainder of this study, therefore, we will not rule out the books of Joshua and Judges as valuable sources of historiographical data, and we will indeed give due attention to the various kinds of data contained therein, including "intentional" and "unintentional" traditions. In undertaking our study, however, we also recognize that our objective is fundamentally different than that of Dtr. For this reason, we must avail ourselves of as much extrabiblical data, both textual and artifactual, as we have at our disposal. We must then seek to utilize and interpret these data with a holistic approach.

CHAPTER 2

# CLASSICAL AND RECENT MODELS OF THE ISRAELITE SETTLEMENT

While embarking on a historical and archaeological study of the early Israelite settlement in Canaan, it makes sense to stop and survey the scholarly landscape. The study of Israelite origins in the land of Canaan has been a subject of study and controversy for well over a hundred years, and it shows no signs of abating. Interest in the study of early Israel has continued to grow in recent years, despite the insistence of N. P. Lemche that "debate in this area is almost at an end."[1] In this chapter, we will review the classical and recent models of Israelite origins in Canaan. We should note at the outset that few scholars today accept any of these models outright. Contemporary theories of the Israelite settlement are, however, either built on one of the classic models or have been constructed in response to one of them. It is important, therefore, to review these models before looking at current propositions. After reviewing the three classical models, we will look at some recent reconstructions of the Israelite settlement. We should also note that these models are efforts to provide an explanation for the identity of the *majority* of the first Israelites. None of these models are trying to account for every last person who became a part of the Israelite people—each recognizes the outsiders who joined the Israelites and assimilated among them, a fact recognized in the Hebrew Bible itself.[2] Instead, the classical models are efforts to understand what the major process was that led to the change from the system of Egyptian-ruled city-states in Canaan to a decentralized system of small villages in the highlands. The goal in this chapter is not to provide an exhaustive examination of the classical and recent models of Israelite origins in Canaan, since there have been a number of excellent surveys and detailed analyses in recent years.[3] Instead, we will review the models and briefly discuss each one's strengths and weaknesses. Afterwards, we will consider how the models all share certain weaknesses, as well as how they all interrelate.

# THE CLASSICAL MODELS

## The Conquest Model

The Conquest Model is built on the idea that the settlement of the Israelite tribes in the land of Canaan was a process that was undertaken primarily through violent warfare. It has conventionally been thought of as following the biblical account most closely, and has been assumed to be the most "biblical" model. William Foxwell Albright (1891–1971) (**Fig. 1**) often referred to as the "dean" of American archaeology in the twentieth century, articulated this theory, and his disciples in America and Israel helped disseminate it. It would be difficult to overestimate Albright's impact on the fields of Near Eastern archaeology and biblical studies.[4] He held the position of W. W. Spence Professor of Semitic Languages and the chair of the Oriental Seminary at Johns Hopkins University from 1929 to 1958, and directed the American School of Oriental Research from 1921 to 1929. He excavated a number of sites, one of the most important of which was that of Tell Beit-Mirsim, where Albright honed the pottery chronology that Petrie had first pioneered in 1891. Many of the great archaeologists of the twentieth century were trained by Albright at Tell Beit Mirsim, including Cyrus Gordon, John Bright, James Kelso, and Nelson Glueck.

*Fig. 1*

Albright's theory essentially followed the biblical story of the Pentateuch and Joshua, which he believed was based on underlying history. After having left Egypt in an exodus event, the Israelites migrated through the desert and ultimately invaded Canaan from the east. Albright believed that the invading Israelites were ethnically and religiously distinct from the indigenous population of Canaan, whom he described as "crude and depraved,"[5] and the Israelites were united in their effort to overtake the Canaanites' land. As the unified Israelites carried out this conquest, Albright interpreted the biblical narrative as if the invading Israelites attacked *numerous* cities—not just Jericho, Ai, and Hazor—and he sought to tie destructions of Canaanite cities with invading Israelites. He looked for burn levels at Jericho, Ai, and Hazor that coincided with the time of the Eighteenth Egyptian Dynasty (**Fig. 2**), which had been accepted by a number of scholars in the early twentieth century as the correct context for the exodus.[6] Hazor appeared to have a destruction layer that dated to about 1400, but no such burn layers could be found in the same

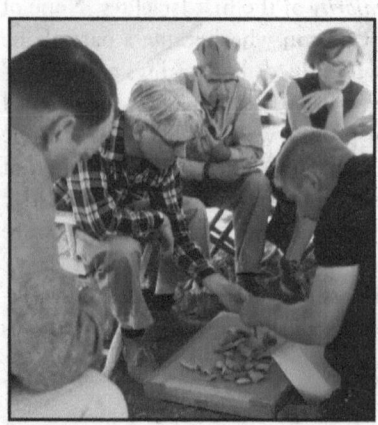

*Fig. 2*

time frame at Jericho or Ai. A number of Canaanite sites did, however, seem to have been destroyed in the thirteenth century B.C.E., such as Bethel, Debir, Eglon, Hazor, and Lachish. He considered these as evidence of the conquest, which he concluded must have occurred in the thirteenth century rather than in the fifteenth century.[7] He explained that "the progress of excavation and of philological interpretation of inscriptions has made it absolutely certain, in the writer's judgment, that the principal phase of the Conquest must be dated in the second half of the thirteenth century."[8]

G. E. Wright (1909–1974), who earned his doctoral degree under Albright in 1937, became another extremely influential leader in American archaeology during the twentieth century. Wright agreed with his professor that the archaeological data supported the idea that "a planned campaign such as that depicted in Josh 10–11 was carried out."[9] Although he recognized that these conclusions stood in some tension with a "face-value" reading of the biblical data—which may seem to suggest a fifteenth-century exodus-conquest, he also agreed with Albright's thirteenth-century date, which he rationalized on the basis of a symbolic reading of some of the numbers involved.[10]

The Conquest Theory reigned supreme during the lifetimes of Albright and Wright, although, as early as the 1960s, archaeological data had begun to emerge that presented problems for it. It began to appear that a number of sites mentioned in the biblical account may not have been occupied in the thirteenth century B.C.E. When thirteenth-century destructions did appear, they could not be as neatly correlated with Israelite invaders as was once thought, and some of them seemed too widely separated in time to have been the result of a single campaign, even if it was drawn out.[11] Albright, Wright, and others recognized the need to temper the Conquest Theory in later years. A few years before his death, Albright admitted that "at present we cannot propose any safe reconstruction of the actual course of events during the period of the Israelite settlement in Palestine."[12] Wright observed that a closer reading of Joshua made it clear that the biblical author was "quite aware of much left to be done" in terms of taking the land.[13] Bright also recognized that the Israelites' conquest of Canaan must have been "vastly more complex than a simplistic presentation . . . would suggest."[14] Tempering the theory did not, however, mean redefining what conquest meant, and the Conquest Theory remained just that, a theory of Israel having acquired its territory by war. Even after the deaths of Albright and Wright, as new archaeological data emerged that sometimes did not seem to cohere with the biblical data, disciples such as John Bright continued to argue that there was "impressive" evidence for a violent conquest at the end of the thirteenth century B.C.E. and that none of the newer data "can be held flatly to refute the theory."[15] Likewise, Yigal Yadin reflected that "in its broad outline the archaeological record supports the narrative in Joshua and Judges as Albright said."[16] Others, even those who believed that the Joshua narratives were schematized, also held that Israel's arrival in Canaan must have been accompanied by some degree of violent incursion.[17] The Conquest Model continued to enjoy support among evangelicals into the 1980s and mid-1990s,[18] though alternative models began to be proposed as early as the late 1950s, and by the

1970s, the Conquest Model had come to be seen as deeply flawed and inadequate for understanding Israelite origins in Canaan.[19]

The criticisms had to do both with the way the proponents of the Conquest Theory used archaeology and the way they interpreted the Bible. As discussed in chapter 1, their usage of archaeology was mainly in the service of theology. G. Ernest Wright was seen as a major leader of the Biblical Theology Movement, and in his book *God Who Acts: Biblical Theology as Recital*,[20] he insisted that "in Biblical faith everything depends upon whether the central events actually occurred."[21] If those events did not happen, Wright argued, the biblical faith is untrue. His emphasis on archaeology, in other words, was at least partially based on his understanding that the historicity of biblical events was essential for faith. Bright has even insisted that the locus of authority for the interpretation of Scripture had shifted from theological approaches to the "one admissible method for arriving at the meaning of the biblical text: the grammatico-historical method,"[22] which implied the use of biblical archaeology.

The reactionary character that developed in archaeology resulted in the idea that "archaeology confirms biblical history,"[23] and this idea was implemented nowhere more clearly than in the development of the Conquest Theory and the efforts to demonstrate its truth through the archaeological record. As for their interpretation of the Bible, proponents of the Conquest Theory understood the book of Joshua to require a wholesale destruction of the land of Canaan at the time of the Israelite settlement, and critics responded that a demand for this magnitude of destruction was clearly an overreaching beyond what the biblical text required.[24]

Archaeologists argued that this magnitude of destruction was not reflected in the archaeological record. J. Maxwell Miller, for example, noted what he perceived to be a disparity between the biblical account of the conquest and the archaeological record. He observed that "the cities which do present archaeological evidence of having been destroyed at the end of the Late Bronze Age are, for the most part, not the ones which figure prominently in the biblical conquest traditions" and when there are Late Bronze Age destructions, they may have been due to localized causes.[25] W. G. Dever, a longtime critic of the Conquest Model,[26] summarized the archaeological data that was available in 1992 in a chart,[27] which I have slightly revised here:

| Site Name | Biblical Reference | Biblical Claim | Archaeological Data |
| --- | --- | --- | --- |
| Zephath/ Hormah | Num 21:1-3; Judg 1:17 | "Destroyed" | No LB occupation (if correctly identified as Tel Masos) |
| Jericho | Judg 6:1-21 | "Destroyed" | No LB II occupation |

| | | | |
|---|---|---|---|
| ʿAi | Josh 8:24 | "Destroyed" | No LB II occupation |
| Bethel | Josh 8:17; Judg 1:22-28 | "Destroyed" | Destruction layer at end of LB II |
| Jerusalem | Josh 10:1-27; Judg 1:8, 21 | Variant accounts | LB II occupation, but without destruction |
| Libnah | Josh 10:29, 31 | "Destroyed" | Site unidentified |
| Lachish | Josh 10:31, 32 | "Destroyed" | Level VI destroyed ca. 1150 B.C.E. |
| Hebron | Josh 14:13–15; 15:13, 14; Judg 1:10 | Capture implied, but no destruction described | No evidence |
| Debir | Josh 10:38, 39; 15:15–17; Judg 1:11-13 | "Destroyed" | No LB II destruction (if Kh. Rabûd) |
| Makkedah | Josh 10:28 | "Destroyed" | If Kh. el-Qôm or Tel Erani, no LB II destruction |
| Eglon | Josh 10:34–35 | "Destroyed" | Site unidentified |
| Hazor | Josh 11:10–13 | "Destroyed," but described later as still in existence | Lower City violently destroyed ca. 1230 |
| Dan | Judg 18:11-28 | "Destroyed" | Destruction layer ca. 1200 |
| Gaza | Judg 1:18 | "Taken" | No evidence |
| Ashkelon | Judg 1:18 | "Taken" | No evidence |
| Ekron | Judg 1:18 | "Taken" | No evidence |
| Heshbon | Num 21:25–30 | "Destroyed" | No LB II occupation |
| Dibon | Num 21:30 | Implied destruction | No LB II occupation |
| Medeba | Num 21:30 | Implied destruction | No evidence |

*Fig. 3 Canaanite Sites the Bible Claims Were Taken by the Israelites*

Dever notes that of the nearly twenty identifiable sites dating from the Late Bronze Age to the Iron Age I, only Bethel and Hazor have destruction layers that could even be considered to have been wrought by the Israelites. He regards the destruction layer at Lachish as dating too late to be connected with the Israelites, and at the time of his writing, the destruction layer at Dan was as yet unclear.[28] Dever further stressed that even in the cases of Bethel and Hazor, there was "no conclusive data to support the notion that Israelites were the agents of destruction." He concludes:

> Thus the "conquest" model derived principally from the book of Joshua, so promising in the beginning, is now seen to have fared rather badly in more recent research. We must conclude that as an overall model for understanding the origins of Israel, the whole notion of a literal "Exodus-wilderness wanderings-Conquest" episode is now unproductive and indeed detrimental, since it is challenged by current archaeological and historical research.[29]

K. L. Younger observes that "the conquest model was doomed from the beginning because of its literal, simplistic reading of Joshua."[30] As we saw in chapter 1, it may be more accurate to call it a *mis*reading of Joshua, since the Conquest Model "assumes massive destruction of property as well as population, whereas the book of Joshua suggests no such thing."[31] Indeed, Joshua does claim that cities were taken and kings killed, but only three cities—Jericho, Ai, and Hazor—are specifically claimed to have been burned. Charts listing "destruction layers" suffer from the same kind of simplistic reading of the data that undermined the Conquest Theory.[32] Nonetheless, the Conquest Theory as a whole has fared so poorly both theologically[33] and archaeologically that it has been almost entirely abandoned by both biblical scholars and archaeologists.

Despite rejection of the Conquest Theory as a whole, D. Merling has observed several corollaries of the theory unique to it that should be taken into account.[34] First, Albright's relationship to the Bible and his apparent dogmatism as to its confirmation by archaeology was one of the reasons for the rejection of the Conquest Theory. As discussed above, the model came to be seen as parochial and apologetic. However, when one looks at Albright's life and his own statements about both the Bible and archaeology, he does not appear to have been the dogmatic fundamentalist some have perceived him to have been. Albright claimed to have originally been a biblical skeptic who had been inclined to approach biblical literature "mythologically."[35] Burke Long argued that there had never been such a conversion, and that Albright had always been a conservative Christian and that he remained so throughout his life.[36] Albright was well-known, however, for changing his mind on issues of both major and minor importance, including matters of chronology, early Israelite history, and other matters,[37] and J. E. Wright suggests there is no reason not to take Albright at his word with regard to having gone through a skeptical or "liberal" phase.[38]

While he did regard the Bible as generally accurate, Albright was ready to emend this viewpoint if he believed there was external evidence demanding it. With regard to the conquest, he noted "the Israelite tradition is not uniform and our biblical sources vary considerably."³⁹ Neither did Albright believe excavation results were necessarily conclusive. He observed that "the results of excavations are ambiguous and sometimes in apparent contradiction with the [biblical] tradition."⁴⁰ In fact, he said, "archaeological discoveries have compelled us to modify the standard tradition of the Conquest, as reflected in Joshua."⁴¹ An example of this modification is his suggestion that the history of Bethel was adopted and used as if it belonged to the city of Ai.⁴² Albright was not a fundamentalist, but described himself as an adherent of neo-orthodoxy, a movement in which Scripture was viewed not as the Word of God itself, but as the *vehicle* for the Word of God.⁴³ This view allowed for a general acceptance of biblical criticism, in which respect neo-orthodoxy retained at least some aspects of nineteenth-century liberal theology. Because of these views, neo-orthodoxy was largely unacceptable to Protestant evangelicalism or to fundamentalism.⁴⁴ The point is, Albright's Conquest Theory was not slavishly bound to a wooden reading of the biblical text, and one should not necessarily reject every aspect of it on the assumption that it was.⁴⁵

A second aspect of the Conquest Theory that grows naturally from the foregoing point is Albright's theorem that "the ultimate historicity of a given datum is never conclusively established nor disproved by the literary framework in which it is imbedded: there must always be external evidence."⁴⁶ Albright asserted that the literary record of an event must be corroborated by additional, concrete evidence—specifically, archaeological evidence—in order for it to be proven historically. The impact of Albright's theorem on generations of biblical scholars and archaeologists alike cannot be overstated. It is commonly stated that archaeology is no longer the "hand-maiden of the Bible," and the idea that "archaeology confirms biblical history" is considered obsolete.⁴⁷

The new sociopolitical-interpretive situation in biblical scholarship, according to Walter Brueggemann, is that of *postmodernism*. Brueggemann explains that "I have no special brief for that term, but take it as a shorthand reference to the end of a cultural period that was dominated by objective positivism that made a certain kind of historical scholarship possible, and that granted interpretive privilege to certain advantaged perspectives."⁴⁸

The term *positivism* recalls a school of philosophy developed by Auguste Comte in the nineteenth century. Comte had asserted that each branch of knowledge passes successively through three different theoretical conditions: "the theological, or fictitious; the metaphysical, or abstract; and the scientific, or positive."⁴⁹ Comte believed that the first of these is "the necessary point of departure of the human understanding" and the second is a transitional state, but the third is the "definitive state" of human understanding.⁵⁰ When the definitive state of human understanding has been attained, then "reality can be apprehended objectively and that data (facts) should be separated from the theories that explain them (interpretations)."⁵¹ This approach sought to set aside simple hypothesizing about the motivations that gave rise to social phenomena "in favour of careful observation and experiment regarding how social phenomena manifested themselves and related to each other in the real world."⁵² This positivism seems to underlie G. Ernest Wright's certainty that "archaeology confirms biblical history."[53] Positivism "has become somewhat passé in contemporary philosophical theory,"[54] and Hebrew Bible studies have moved beyond historical-critical studies[55] to such approaches as foundationalism, canon criticism, *a seriatim* reading,[56] and others that focus on theological issues within the text rather than historical issues that underlie the text. Scholars who continue to argue for historicity of events recounted in the texts that deal with early Israel are labeled "traditionalists," "maximalists," "positivists," or "neo-conservatives."[57]

The implication is that, clearly, archaeology cannot prove the Bible, and anyone who seeks to do so is engaging in parochialism. While this has become widely accepted,[58] biblical commentary often belies this conclusion as commentators make recourse to archaeological data in order to either validate or invalidate particular readings of a given text. A case in point is the book of Joshua, commentaries for which have often been assigned by series editors to archaeologists or ancient Near Eastern textual scholars because of the abundance of references to historical geography, sites, and other subjects that are naturally within the purview of these scholars. Whether the authors of commentaries on Joshua are archaeologists or biblical scholars, however, they have almost always made recourse to arguments based on archaeology, which suggests that the belief that "archaeology confirms biblical history" is still held by confessional and nonconfessional scholars alike. I am not arguing that archaeological data does not have a relationship to discussions about the historicity of events; I believe it does. I am simply pointing out that Albright's legacy of positivism lives on, even among those who disparage it.[59]

A final corollary of the Conquest Theory to be taken note of is Albright's acceptance of the biblical portrayal of the Israelites as already having had a clear ethnic identity upon their entrance into Canaan.[60] Those who held to the Conquest Theory never doubted this, and it was unique to the Conquest Theory in its day. Few contemporary models of Israelite emergence would accept this, and most scholars believe that Israel's ethnic identity developed during the settlement in the highlands or sometime later. Albright's view of Israel's ethnic unity is interesting in light of the renewed attention being given to Israelite ethnicity, a subject that will occupy a great deal of focus throughout this work.

## The Peaceful Infiltration Model

Between the world wars, European scholars looked for alternatives to the Conquest Model. Albrecht Alt (1883–1956) (**Fig. 4**), a leading German Protestant theologian, proposed an alternative understanding of Israel's entry into Canaan, known as "the Peaceful Infiltration Model."[61] Alt had come to believe that literary-critical research had done all it could do to reconstruct the early history of Israel and that a new approach was needed that could approach the subject from outside the biblical texts in order to bypass the barriers erected by the redactors. Alt sought to use extra-biblical sources contemporary with the time of Israel's settlement in order to build a history of the territorial divisions of the land of Canaan. His argument was that this history would then provide the context for evaluating the traditions embedded in the Deuteronomistic History (hereafter DtrH). Alt utilized mainly Egyptian sources and concluded that Shechem was the only significant city-state left in the hill-country between Jerusalem and the valley of Jezreel in the fourteenth century B.C.E. After the decline of Egypt's Nineteenth Dynasty about a century later, the hill-country between Jerusalem and Jezreel still appeared to be essentially unoccupied. The biblical traditions place the initial settlements of the Israelites in this sparsely inhabited region. Since he was working out his theory long before the period when archaeological surveys began in the West Bank, he did not have specific evidence for the infiltration or the settlements he imagined the Israelites founded. Instead, he based his reconstruction on analogy and hypothesized that the Israelites were not a unified people who entered Canaan in a blitzkrieg, but they were a mixture of unrelated and disparate nomadic or seminomadic peoples from the surrounding regions, all of whom worshiped different gods,[62] who peacefully immigrated into and out of the land of Canaan on a seasonal basis, following their herds, for many years, perhaps even centuries, before they began to settle in permanent villages in the highlands, away from Canaanite cities. Whereas Alt believed that the Philistines came to Canaan in one event,

*Fig. 4*

> The outward details of the immigration of the Israelites into Palestine were completely different; this was no single movement completed in a relatively short time, as it appears, I admit, in the later literary works of the Israelite tradition, particularly in the Book of Joshua. It was in fact a series of movements by single tribes and bands which may well have lasted for several centuries; and in the majority of cases they did not proceed by force of arms, so that although the accounts of individual military victories over older towns may well be correct, they insinuated themselves into thinly populated or even totally unpopulated districts where there was no chance of serious opposition.[63]

Alt hypothesized that a second stage of settlement occurred late in the Iron Age I in which the Israelites undertook military action in order to expand their territory. In this stage, which corresponded with the descriptions in the book of Judges, individual tribes waged battles over land. As the settlements increased in number, occasional battles broke out between the new Israelites and the Canaanites. As the cities declined and the Egyptian empire lost its grip on Canaan, the Israelite settlers gradually became the dominant force in the land.

Martin Noth (1902–1968), who had been a student of Alt's, developed the Peaceful Infiltration Theory further in his history of Israel. Like Alt, Noth understood the Israelite entrance into Canaan as a process in which they followed their herds, summering in the hill-country and wintering in the deserts until, when they had finally found permanent homes in the highlands, they ceased to return to their winter pastures. It only made sense to Noth that the seminomadic Israelites would settle down in the highlands since he thought that "semi-nomads always hanker after a more settled life in the coveted agricultural countryside."[64] According to Noth, the process of Israel's immigration and eventual settlement in the highlands took about two hundred years. It began around the end of the Amarna Age, during the second half of the fourteenth century, and burgeoned around 1200 B.C.E.[65] Noth also stressed that the Old Testament tradition "is unquestionably right in regarding the tribes not as indigenous to Palestine but as having entered and gained a footing there from the wilderness and steppe at a definite point in time."[66] He argued that even if the traditions had not explicitly stated the outside origin of the Israelites, one could infer it from their lifestyle in the highlands, as well as the tribal traditions preserved in the Hebrew Bible.

One of the most ardent adherents of the Alt-Noth hypothesis was Yohanan Aharoni (1919–1976). Aharoni had immigrated to Palestine in 1933, when the issue of how the ancient Israelites had originated in the ancient land of Canaan was a subject of intense debate. Aharoni began his archaeological career as antiquities inspector for Galilee under the newly founded State of Israel and from 1950 to 1955 conducted a survey that culminated in his doctoral dissertation for the Hebrew University of Jerusalem, entitled *The Settlement of the Israelite Tribes in Upper Galilee*.[67] A devoted follower of Alt, Aharoni believed that in his survey of upper Galilee he had found evidence of a centuries-long settlement process.[68] The fact that so few of the Iron Age I sites were fortified seemed to him to demonstrate the peaceful nature of this settlement. He observed that the biblical accounts of the conquest repeatedly note that the tribes of Israel were unable to pit themselves against the strong cities of the plain (e.g., Josh 17:18), and that is why they initially settled in the highlands.[69]

J. A. Callaway (1920–1988) played an important role in promoting a modified form of the Alt-Noth hypothesis in the United States. Callaway grew up as a conservative Southern Baptist on a farm in rural Arkansas and went to seminary as a ministerial student in 1951. During his graduate work, after having read Albright's seminal volume, *From the Stone Age to Christianity*,[70] Callaway began to pursue an interest in archaeology.[71] He began his archaeological field work as a staff member at Shechem under G. E. Wright, where he spent a number of seasons. During the 1961–1962 academic year, he had opportunity to study under Kathleen Kenyon, an experience that also had a strong impact on his thinking. But it was during these years spent working to uncover the city of Ai (1964–1972) that a number of things happened that would lead Callaway to abandon the Albright model forever. First, not only did he not find evidence of a Late Bronze Age II destruction at et-Tell, he concluded it had not been occupied at all during that period, which meant if the Israelites were invading, there had been no one there for them to conquer.[72] Second, as Callaway investigated the communal life of the village of et-Tell, he utilized the New Archaeology and sought to reconstruct the cultural life of the village. He concluded that its inhabitants had largely been farmers.[73] As he began to assess the archaeological data related to the early Israelite emergence in Canaan, Callaway concluded that Jericho and Ai did not fit into the Conquest Theory, and that the Albright school was unconvincing because of the way it "too easily" made connections between destruction layers and the biblical texts.[74]

Once Callaway synthesized his findings, he concluded that the theories of Alt provided the best starting point for understanding the early Israelites, though he had decided that the early Israelites had originated from within the land of Canaan rather than outside of it. Callaway postulated that the highland settlers as a whole had been, first and foremost, farmers, and only secondarily had they been herders. In a survey of the location and remains of archaeological sites in the central hill-country, Callaway argued that several discoveries of artifacts in the villages between Jerusalem and Jezreel (including a cuneiform tablet found at Taanach, "pots full of pebbles" found at Taanach, Megiddo and et-Tell that may have been a type of foundation deposit related to agricultural rites, a cuneiform tablet from Beth-shemesh that contains a birth incantation written in Ugaritic, an inscribed jar handle from Raddana in early Canaanite script, and numerous other bronze and pottery artifacts) all "have their cultural parallels in the coastal and lowland regions."[75] He argued that "these are not the kinds of objects that warlike Yahwists from Transjordan would be expected to have in their homes, nor are the other evidences cited above what one would expect to see in the lifestyle of nomads recently settled in villages."[76] Callaway concluded that "these settlers came to the highlands with fixed cultural patterns of village life" they had brought with them from the lowlands and coastal region *west* of the hill-country.[77] They had probably migrated to the highlands to escape the pressure imposed by the incoming Sea Peoples. "Thus the hill country settlers migrated *to escape wars and violence*, and sought out in their remote and isolated mountain-top villages a place of refuge from the strife and disruptions in the more fertile plains."[78] Callaway realized his conclusions may trouble believers who wanted to take the Bible literally, but he believed that his conclusions had important and positive spiritual implications. He wrote:

> The research at Ai compels us, in my opinion, to review and evaluate the Deuteronomistic History's presentation of Israel's origins and ascertain more realistically its relevance for today's world. Foremost among the items that should be reviewed is the "preaching" of holy war in Joshua 1–12 which, taken literally for centuries by conservative and fundamentalist Christians, has made Bible-belt church members in particular the most militant segment of our population in every war we have fought. Who can conceive of the waste of resources and life, as well as the damage to the social and religious fabric of our society, that wrong interpretation of the conquest of Ai, and of Canaan, have wrought! If we take seriously the redirection of our thinking occasioned by the findings at Ai, then it may be that Satan made another mistake when he gave the site of Ai to the archaeologists.[79]

Callaway believed that his Altian reformulation of Israelite origins more accurately reflected Christian values of peace than did the Conquest Theory.

The Peaceful Infiltration Model held great appeal for a variety of reasons. Chief among these would probably be that it still saw the brunt of the Israelites as having entered the land of Canaan from outside the land, and yet it was also compatible with the idea that the Israelites came from mixed backgrounds. The theory also made sense to those who thought the settlement had likely occurred as a gradual process. The theory did not rely on either the Bible or on archaeology, but this was also seen as an advantage by many. Manfred Weippert, a student of Noth's, insisted the Peaceful Infiltration Theory was more objective than the Conquest Theory because it was not influenced by either the Bible or by archaeology.[80]

The theory also had shortcomings, of which I will only mention a few. First, some have argued that the Peaceful Infiltration Theory fails to deal with the apparent similarities between the material culture and religion of the incoming Israelites with that of the indigenous population. If the Israelites originated from outside the land of Canaan, these critics ask, then why does their material culture so closely resemble that of the indigenous population? Second, the Peaceful Infiltration Model was based on nineteenth-century concepts of nomadism that are now known to be wrong. Alt had regarded nomadism as an intermediary evolutionary step between hunter-gatherers and settled agriculturalists, and he suggested that the Israelites were in this process of moving from one stage to the other.

Ethnographic studies have revealed that nomadism was not some kind of intermediate stage in evolutionary development at all. Instead, we now know that pastoralists existed—and still exist—alongside settled populations throughout ancient Near Eastern history.[81] Rural populations have fluctuated between nomadism and sedentarization in the ancient Near East throughout its history. Pastoral nomads exist symbiotically with settled populations, and "the process of nomadization of rural households is best understood as a form of resistance, a sort of natural response by the rural population to the exploitative undertakings of urban elites."[82] The evolutionary influence that undergirded the Peaceful Infiltration Model is no longer viable. Third, the Peaceful Infiltration Theory fails to explain why the Hebrews composed the stories of the exodus-conquest if their origins were the result of a peaceful, evolutionary process. If the Israelites entered the land in a gradual process that occurred peacefully over several centuries, why does the Hebrew Bible tell such a different story of the origins of Israel?

## The Social Revolution Model

In 1962, G. E. Mendenhall (1916– ) (**Fig. 5**) took the discussion about Israelite origins in a whole new direction with his article, "The Hebrew Conquest of Palestine,"[83] in which he proposed what came to be called the Peasant's Revolt Theory. Mendenhall forthrightly admitted that the purpose of his article was an attempt to offer an alternative "idea model" to Albright's Conquest Model and Alt's Peaceful Infiltration Model.[84] He rejected the basic assumption of both Albright and Noth—that Israel came from outside the land—and instead interpreted Israel's formation within the turbulent context of the Late Bronze-Iron I transition. The gist of this theory was that the indigenous Canaanite peasantry rebelled, albeit nonviolently, against Canaanite overlords and retreated to the central hill-country. There, they met a small band of slaves who had escaped from Egypt and who had experienced a theophany of Yahweh in the Sinai wilderness and had also settled in the central hill-country. The larger Canaanite group rejected the society they had abandoned and joined the emerging religious community of Hebrews. The early Israelites, therefore, were essentially indigenous, formed through revolution and conversion. Mendenhall suggested there is one observable feature in human life, that "fashion is constantly changing."[85] Mendenhall postulated that every tenth generation—or roughly every 250 to 300 years—societal pressures build to the point of eruption. It is the "rhythmic pattern of history" that produces the macro changes in society, while micro changes are the "natural product of life."[86] For Mendenhall, the peasant revolt of the Canaanites came about during one of those cycles. Mendenhall, however, did not intend to minimize or do away with the religious factor, which he thought was very significant and had played a major role in the origins of early Israel. It was the Yahwistic faith revealed at Sinai, rather than ethnicity, that bound the new social organization together.

Fig. 5

Norman K. Gottwald (1926–) (**Fig. 6**), one of Mendenhall's students, supported the basic ideas of Mendenhall's Peasant's Revolt Theory, but interpreted and modified it through the lens of Marxism. In his magisterial *Tribes of Yahweh: A Sociology of the Religion of Liberated Israel, 1250–1050 B.C.E.*,[87] Gottwald made the case of ancient Israel not being spawned by religious experience, but by political unrest steeped in class struggle. He modeled his approach after his own sociological experiences in the civil rights struggles, antiwar (Vietnam) movement, "anti-imperialist" activities, criticisms of North American capitalism, and church and school politics.[88] Taking his model from Europe's medieval period, or even seventeenth-century France, Gottwald writes about "serfs," "lower class," "aristocrats," "free citizenry," and "Canaanite feudalism." Like their later protégés, Israel's predecessors lived outside the dominant society of Canaanite feudalism and eventually broke away from this oppressive culture. Violent conflicts erupted, caused by "tension between urban-based statism and rural-oriented tribalism."[89] Gottwald proposed that the repressed classes threw off the bondage of the city-state structure, and through a series of peasant rebellions, a social revolution was brought about that was "free agrarian, and lacked a state form of government and class system."[90] Mendenhall had emphasized the possibility that there was some history behind the stories about the exodus and the wandering in the wilderness, and that it was the religious views of the people involved that created the new Yahwistic community in the highlands. Gottwald focused more on the internal process, the role of the lower-class Canaanites themselves, and less on the exodus group that may have inspired them to revolt. While he did view the worship of Yahweh as having been instrumental in uniting peoples of diverse backgrounds into a unified people in the highlands, his particular argument, based on Marxist philosophy, was that they had already emerged as a growing coalition of people opposed to the city-states.

Fig. 6

The theories of Mendenhall and Gottwald have often been combined and referred to collectively as the "Mendenhall-Gottwald Hypothesis," although Mendenhall saw his theory as distinctly different from that of Gottwald, whose *Tribes of Yahweh* he excoriated as "an endless series of hyphenated pseudo-social science" and summed up as "truly a tragic comedy of errors."[91] Mendenhall stressed that he had only used the term "peasant's revolt" once in his 1962 article and that in publications since then he had emphasized that the Israelite movement was "much more a cultural and ideological revolution than a political one."[92] Likewise, in subsequent publications, Gottwald dropped the use of the term "peasant revolt"[93] "because it invites a too simplistic association with European peasant uprisings."[94] While the distinctions between the theories of Mendenhall and Gottwald are recognized, their theories continue to be referred to collectively, albeit now as the Social Revolution Model.

The Social Revolution Model has been influential in leading biblical scholars to make use of the social sciences and to focus attention on the Canaanites as the possible source from which the Israelites emerged. Those who embrace it argue that it helps explain why the material culture of the Iron Age I Israelites is so similar to that of the Canaanites. Mary Louse Musell, for example, has argued that the break between the Late Bronze and Iron Age I cultures predicted by both the Conquest and Peaceful Infiltration models has not been proven. While there is evidence of some cities having been destroyed and new, small agricultural communities having been founded, "there is no evidence of the arrival of a new, invading or settling people from the desert who establish themselves in central Canaan." The continuity between the cultures of the Late Bronze and Iron Ages, she argues, demonstrates that the highland villages must have been populated by people who had left the cities during the degeneration of Canaanite culture.[95]

The Social Revolution Model has been criticized for a number of reasons. First, it has been argued that the Social Revolution Model goes too far beyond the evidence, particularly in the application of Marxist ideology to the emergence of early Israel. A. F. Rainey criticized both Mendenhall and Gottwald, but especially *The Tribes of Yahweh*. He concluded that "Gottwald's efforts to make the early Israelites into some kind of idealized peasants, bearing the torch for the 'New Left' under the banner of Yahweh, is merely an amateur's attempt at pseudo-Marxism."[96] Second, it has been argued that there is no archaeological evidence that a "peasant revolt" occurred. Coastal Canaanite cities such as Acco, Tel Keisan, Tel Yoqne'am, and Tell Qiri, as well as Megiddo, were all continuously occupied from the thirteenth to the eleventh centuries B.C.E.[97] In and of itself, however, this criticism cannot disprove the Social Revolution Model, since a revolution may be directed more at the ruling classes and not necessarily the buildings and walls of the cities. A revolt may not leave behind much evidence of destruction.[98] Third, if the highland settlers successfully defeated the Canaanite kings, as Gottwald claims, then why did they not take over the best land? If the excellent agricultural land of the lowlands had become available as a result of a social revolution, it does not make sense that the Canaanites who had rebelled against their oppressors would then retreat to the mountains. Fourth, and probably most important, the Social Revolution Model fails to offer a sufficient explanation for why the Hebrew Bible gives an account at such variance with the reconstruction of the theory.

I agree with Mendenhall that the emphasis in the biblical accounts is on "the major symbolic expressions of divine aid, the Exodus and Sinai covenant," with which all the highlanders identified.[99] But Mendenhall suggests that because the whole community embraced this salvation story, "the mainstream of tradition emphasized what all had in common instead of particular acts or experiences of a single group."[100] According to the theory, this *was* the experience of one element of the new society. If an element of the Canaanite society had either peacefully withdrawn from the cities or violently revolted against their Canaanite overlords, would not this group have also felt that their experience was one of salvation brought about by Yahweh? Why would it not have been included in the biblical account? Mendenhall suggests it may have been that the official version of Israelite history composed during the monarchy "was understandably loathe to describe the process by which villagers rejected the sovereignty of the kings who ruled them."[101] I find this unconvincing, and while the model makes important contributions, the lack of biblical attestation for this model seems to me to be a substantial obstacle for acceptance of the theory in its complete form.

# RECENT MODELS

Several newer models have been proposed in recent years, most of which are amalgamations of the Peaceful Infiltration Model and the sociological model. There are still numerous proposals that view the first Israelites as having come from outside Canaan. Two of the most notable of these have been those of Baruch Halpern and Donald Redford. In 1983, Halpern published *The Emergence of Israel in Canaan*, which was for many years the standard handbook on the Israelite settlement.[102] Along with considering the available archaeological evidence, Halpern takes the biblical traditions into serious consideration as literary evidence. Halpern rejects the Social Revolution Model because he does not see any evidence for retreat from the cities to the hill-country and he sees the archaeological evidence as too ambiguous to draw such conclusions.[103] Speaking broadly, he argues that the collared-rim jar and the four-room house do not characterize Late Bronze Age Canaanite centers, while they are typical of Israelite settlements in the Iron Age in both Cisjordanian and Transjordanian sites.[104] Neither does he think it necessary to posit a social revolution in order to explain the ideology of decentralization in the early Israelite traditions, but argues these would have either already been present or developed naturally among peoples living in the highlands.[105] When the textual and archaeological evidence are taken together, Halpern argues, they point to an origin for the early Israelites from outside the land of Canaan. The movement may have consisted of groups of people who originated from the direction of Haran, as well as other peoples east of the Jordan. The Bible identifies this population as *Hebrews*, a term used in the Bible by foreigners to refer to the Israelites. Some of these Hebrews "may have been propelled into Transjordan by the stick of Assyrian expansion at the end of the thirteenth century."[106] Some of these migrants developed into the nations of Ammon, Moab, and Edom. Halpern postulates that a small group of pastoralists who had been tending sheep in the Wadi Tumilat migrated out of Egypt in order to avoid corvée. As they migrated through the desert, they transversed the "land of the Shasu of YHWH," a location mentioned on an Egyptian list of Shasu groups, which must have been where they acquired their Yahwism.[107] Somehow, these Yahwists came into contact with elements that were homesteading down the King's Highway in Transjordan, and together they coalesced into "Israel." Although Halpern suggests that we cannot know the exact relationship of the exodus to the Israelite settlement in Canaan, he argues:

> What we *do* know is that the Exodus was certainly central to the ideology of the Israelites in Canaan already in Iron I. The victory at the sea in Exodus 15, the tradition that *YHWH* marched forth from Edom to conquer Canaan, the Egyptian reference to the land of the Shasu of *YHWH* all point to the same conclusion. Sometime, relatively early in Iron I, Israel began to subscribe to a national myth of escape from Egypt, mediated by a god residing in the south (and outside Canaan), with the purpose of establishing a nation in Canaan. That national myth—justifying the Israelite land claims in Canaan—became a call to arms, a doctrine of Manifest Destiny, for a people newly arrived from the north and east.[108]

Donald Redford articulated his position in his 1992 book, *Egypt, Canaan, and Israel in Ancient Times*,[109] in which he approached the origins of early Israel from the perspective of Egyptian history. Redford does not put any stock in the biblical traditions of the patriarchs or the exodus, and he believes scholars should abandon their attempts to find historicity in them. Instead, Redford points to the Shasu, who had lived south and east of Canaan and who had been a longtime threat to the people of Canaan and an irritation to Egypt, as a likely source for the Israelites. He suggests that the Israel mentioned on the Merneptah Stele (ca. 1210 B.C.E.) may have been a Shasu enclave that after 1200 B.C.E. began to found small villages in the highlands, where the Egyptians could not reach them.[110]

Since the nomadic Shasu did not have architectural traditions of their own, they adopted the four-room house type, which Redford believes belonged to the material cultural tradition of the lowlands, as well as other aspects of their material culture.[111] Redford also argues that the highland settlers were also distinct in their religion. Rather than worshiping the Canaanite gods, they worshiped a god called Yahweh, who Redford argues, like Halpern, had already been worshiped by some Shasu. He bases this on the appearance of "Yhw in the land of the Shasu" on an Egyptian list of Shasu groups, mentioned above. Redford argues that this was a location named after the god Yahweh, which must have been located in Edom, and from which Yahwism originated when a tribe of Edomites migrated northwest and assimilated among proto-Israelite tribes in the mountains of Canaan.[112]

The models of Halpern and Redford both make an important contribution in bringing attention to the Shasu. Halpern especially makes an important contribution by pointing to the connection between the beginning of Israel and the neighboring states of Ammon, Moab, and Edom, which are all viewed in the Hebrew Bible as close relatives of the Israelites.[113] More recent theories have built on these points of contact with Transjordan and with the Shasu. R. W. Younker has traced these connections out in a series of important studies.[114] He observes that during the transition from the Late Bronze to the Iron Age, there was a rise in the kin-based countryside. Rural, kin-based groups evolved into a more complex tribal organization that opposed the state, in this case Egypt.[115] Local tribal peoples such as the Ammonites implemented an avoidance strategy by retreating to marginal frontier zones in the highlands or deserts and, in many cases, underwent nomadization. One such group fleeing the settled regions was the Shasu, who had migrated to Transjordan, outside the direct sphere of Egyptian influence. Despite their use of nomadization as an avoidance strategy, these were essentially sedentary peoples, so when Egypt experienced a hiatus in its domination in the latter part of the thirteenth century, the Shasu took the first opportunity to resettle both in the highlands of Cisjordan and Transjordan. Because of the social fluidity provided by the system of tribal genealogies, the Shasu, along with other sedentarizing peoples, were able to coalesce into "Israel." Younker concludes that "the Iron Age represents a new social evolutionary trajectory in which Canaan's old urban order is permanently disrupted and the kin-based elements evolve into a new level of social organizational complexity that leave them on top."[116]

T. E. Levy and A. F. C. Holl accept the desert origins of the early Israelites and, like Younker, point to the Shasu as a possible source of origin for the early Israelites.[117] Levy and Holl stress that the Shasu people were not an ethnic group tied to any specific region but that they "seem to represent a social class of nomads who reflect an ancient equivalent of the term 'Bedouin,' which crosscuts different ethnic groups and relates more to a generic socioeconomic subsistence organization devoted to pastoral nomadism."[118] They suggest that Israel was probably one group among many Shasu moving out of the steppe lands in search of areas in which to settle.[119] Drawing on ethnographic parallels of sedentarizing Shuwa-Arab pastoralists in the Chad Basin of north central Africa, Levy and Holl show how the highland settlers underwent a process of ethnogenesis by which they became Israelites and separated themselves from the larger groups of Shasu nomads. This process involved the development of distinctive manners, customs, and worship, and "probably peaked and crystallized during the Late Bronze-Iron I period within the context of Philistine expansion and renewed imperial Egyptian expansion."[120]

While the foregoing recent models have, like the Conquest Theory and the Peaceful Infiltration Model, held that the Israelites entered Canaan from outside the land, many other newer models either hold a middle ground or argue along the lines of the Social Revolution Model that the Israelites were indigenous to the land of Canaan. Volkmar Fritz represents a middle ground with his Symbiosis Hypothesis, in which he observes that there are both similarities and differences between early Israelite and Canaanite material culture.[121] Fritz suggests that the new highland settlements have a lack of uniformity, and that their pottery is very close to that of the Canaanites. He notes specifically that the inscription on the 'Izbet Sartah ostracon is written in the proto-Canaanite alphabet, which indicates similarities in the languages of the highlanders and the Canaanites.[122] On the other hand, he argues that the four-room house is too dissimilar from the houses in Canaanite cities to have evolved from them. On the basis of the dissimilarities between the two cultures, Fritz concludes that the new settlers could not have been former inhabitants of the Canaanite cities and that they were unrelated to the Canaanites.[123] Based on the similarities, however, he postulates the new settlers must have had close contact with the Canaanites over a long period of time. This must have happened when the nomadic Israelites entered the land and gradually developed close economic relationships with the Canaanites. While the Israelites became self-sufficient in the highlands, they retained aspects of the Canaanite material culture that had developed in their own culture over their years of contact with the Canaanites.

The view that the Israelites originated from among the indigenous population of Canaan appears to have become the most popular view today, and it is taught in many graduate schools and seminaries as fact. The argument that the first Israelites were Canaanites has also become the favored model of scholars who sometimes refer to themselves as "deconstructionist" biblical scholars,[124] but who are known to many as "minimalists." These scholars generally view Israel as derived entirely from the Canaanite population and its history as state propaganda produced at a later period, some as late as the Persian period.[125] An analysis of the minimalist approach goes well beyond the scope of this volume, and cannot be undertaken here.[126]

William G. Dever (**Fig. 7**), one of the most prolific writers on early Israel, has long argued along the lines of the Social Revolution Model that Israel emerged from the indigenous population of Canaan, and has synthesized his arguments in *Who Were the Early Israelites and Where Did They Come From?* In this work, Dever argues that the continuity between the Late Bronze and Iron Age I material decisively supports the conclusion that ancient Israel emerged from the indigenous Canaanite population, which occurred when disaffected Canaanites withdrew to the hill-country during and after the transition from the Late Bronze Age to the Iron Age I, and ultimately came to see themselves as "Israelites."[127] The withdrawal of the hill-country settlers from Canaan was not, however, a "flight from intolerable conditions or necessarily a revolutionary Yahwistic fervor . . . but rather simply a quest for a new society and a new lifestyle. They wanted to start over. And in the end, that was revolutionary."[128] Dever suggests that "Land reform must have been the driving force behind, and the ultimate goal of, the early Israelite movement."[129] He argues that agrarianism is about more than land; it is utopian. Dever points to other rural revolutionary developments as analogies for understanding his early Israelite utopian community.

*Fig. 7*

For example, the Oneida Community of the 1800s in New York was founded as a perfectionistic society on principles of absolute equality. Another experiment in rural communal living was carried out in the early 1800s at New Harmony in southwestern Indiana. In New York, the eighteenth-century Shaker movement was characterized by a commitment to absolute equality, temperance, and simplicity in all things. The Amish have probably been the most successful example of withdrawal.

Dever claims that "all these and many other reformist movements in history are essentially agrarian—that is, based on principles of land reform and shared agricultural production."[130] He sees all of these movements as focused essentially on social causes. "All older models are now obsolete," he states, and the only remaining contribution will be to illuminate the context in which this occurred.[131]

While we will consider the issue of continuity in later chapters, I would note here that none of the groups that Dever uses for analogies were motivated by social issues or the ideal of agrarian reform. Instead, they were all founded expressly as religious groups, basing their formation on specific biblical concepts. The Harmony Society, for example, which was founded in 1785 by George Rapp (1757–1847) in Württemberg, Germany, was one expression of the Separatists. Rapp both believed and taught that his Harmony Society was the physical embodiment of the woman clothed with the sun in Revelation 12:1. This "sunwoman" became incarnate when Rapp's "church of the brethren" presented its articles of faith, which dealt with its views on the church, baptism, Holy Communion, and other matters, and was consequently formed outside of the established church.

When the government of Württemburg issued a serious warning to Rapp, he moved to America in order to seek out a haven for his followers. He made his first payment on a parcel of land in Pennsylvania in 1804. When articles of agreement were drawn up for the Society in 1805, they included that members would give up all property and submit to the laws and regulations of the congregation. In his documentary history of the movement's years in Indiana, K. J. R. Arndt stresses that "the real binding force of the Society was, of course, not this agreement but the special message implicit in the faith of the Society that it was the embodiment of the Sunwoman in Saint John's vision and the doctrine taught by George Rapp that harmony would follow the Second Coming of Christ when all things would be restored to their original harmony that existed before Adam and the fall of man."[132] The letters and documents that have survived from the Harmony Society, compiled and edited by Karl J. R. Arndt, seldom reveal the religious motivation behind the Society, since it was very private and religiously self-contained. One letter, however, written by Frederick Rapp on December 19, 1822, in reply to Samuel Worcestor of Boston, who expressed an interest in starting a similar society in Boston and had written to inquire about the details of the nature of the Society, does. Rapp's long reply may be one of the most important letters related to the Society, since it explains the religious foundation of the Society and the details of its organization.

> Of all those evils and calamities [of the modern world] Harmonie knows nothing; Eighteen years ago she laid the foundation and plan for a new period, after the original Pattern of the primitive church described in the 2 & 4 chapter of the acts and since that time we lived, although unnoticed, covered with ignominy and contempt, yet happy in peace, for all our temporal as well as Spiritual Union became every year more perfect, and now our Community stands proof, firm and unmoveable upon its Rock of truth. . . . Taking a worldly view, our diligence and Labour are amply rewarded, we suffer no want whatever.[133]

Rapp apologized for there being no books or brochures about the Society he could send, and explained they did not have a written or printed constitution or law to regulate the Society. Instead, an agreement was made with newcomers that they would lead a Christian life and that, if they could not, they could withdraw from the community. He went on to explain:

> No community established upon the principles of ours can exist without the prohibition of exclusive property, which always creates motives for individual self interest and operates as an inherent & irresistible principle to bring on confusion and decay; Therefore all schemes to form Societies similar to Harmony without practicing the Religion of Jesus Christ in prohibiting individual property have gone to wreck.[134]

Clearly, the motivation for the founding of the Harmony Society was a very specific conception of what it meant to be a real Christian community. The same could be said for each of the other social reform movements cited by Dever. Religion is important, and while there have been communal groups that were founded on the basis of a secular vision,[135] communal groups appear to typically be motivated by a religious vision.[136] Seeking to explain early Israelite origins by strictly social or economic motivations fails to explain the persistent biblical claim that the earliest Israelites were motivated by a religious vision.

# CONCLUSION

The classical and contemporary models of the Israelite settlement all have strengths and weaknesses, some of which have been considered in this chapter. The Conquest Theory is generally seen as having been discredited, and some scholars suggest that a consensus is emerging that most of the early Israelites evolved from among the Canaanites.[137] Indigenous models are "in vogue,"[138] and they have made some positive contributions to the debate about early Israelite origins, including the thesis that groups other than the Israelites were represented among those who moved to the highlands during the Late Bronze-Iron Age transition, possibly including Habiru, resedentarized pastoralists, and potentially even immigrants from Anatolia. While indigenous models are "in vogue," it would be an overstatement to say that infiltration or immigration models are passé. In fact, there is an increasing awareness of the need to consider the role of the Shasu, mentioned in Late Bronze Age Egyptian texts, as well as other immigrants from Syria and Transjordan, in reconstructing the early Israelite settlement.

Norman Gottwald's observation that most of the contemporary models seem to be constructs on a continuum that simultaneously interpret some of the evidence in the same way while disagreeing on others is probably correct.[139] Most of the newer models are oriented toward the social sciences, and they tend to have similar approaches and interpretations of the data, even when they disagree on substantial issues. All of these models are, therefore, interrelated to some degree or another, and while some of their aspects may need to be either refined or even rejected, it may be that they can each contribute something toward reconstructing the Israelite settlement.

CHAPTER 3

# THE DATE OF THE EXODUS-CONQUEST

## PART I: BIBLICAL EVIDENCE

The date of the exodus-conquest has been a subject of academic inquiry for over a century.[1] Since the first quarter of the twentieth century, the early date for the exodus-conquest has become more or less standard among evangelical scholars.[2] Before the decipherment of Egyptian hieroglyphs, many readers naturally gravitated toward the long-lived Ramesses II as the pharaoh of the oppression. Ramesses is mentioned in Exodus 1:11 as the name of one of the store cities that the Hebrews built for the pharaoh. Ramesses II had, indeed, produced many monuments and left behind ruins of monumental buildings in Egypt. It seemed natural, therefore, to imagine the ancient Hebrews participating in the construction of those projects. With the identification of Ramesses II as the pharaoh of the oppression, his son Merneptah, who succeeded him on the throne, naturally became the pharaoh of the exodus. Based on this reasoning, the biblical exodus was securely located by scholars within the Nineteenth Dynasty of Egypt (1293–1185 B.C.E.) throughout the nineteenth century.[3]

In 1896, this understanding came under challenge. That year, Sir William Flinders Petrie discovered a monument in the ruins of Merneptah's mortuary temple at Thebes. This Merneptah Stele makes reference to Israel as a people living in Canaan by Merneptah's fifth year, which is the date of the inscription: 1210 B.C.E. This new data appeared to require that Israel had already been settled there by the end of the thirteenth century B.C.E. Placing Israel in Canaan this early in the reign of Merneptah raised obstacles for his having been the pharaoh of the exodus. Israel obviously could not have left Egypt in the first year of Merneptah's reign, wandered in the wilderness for forty years, and then appeared in Canaan as a settled ethnic group in his fifth year. The radical reduction of the duration of the wilderness wandering that this would require presented an insurmountable obstacle for evangelicals. There were two primary responses to these difficulties.

First, some scholars continued to work toward locating the exodus during the Nineteenth Dynasty. In order to do this, the identification of the pharaohs involved had to be adjusted. By moving these identifications back, Seti I could then be identified as the pharaoh of the oppression, and Ramesses II as the pharaoh of the exodus. Up until about 1925, this position was widely held by scholars—both evangelical and otherwise.

A second approach was to begin looking for a date in other periods. This approach seems to have been pioneered initially by James Jack, who challenged the thirteenth century B.C.E. date in his 1925 book, *The Date of the Exodus in the Light of External Evidence*. Jack argued that both biblical and extrabiblical evidence pointed to a mid-fifteenth-century B.C.E. date. The Masoretic text (MT) of 1 Kgs 6:1 dates the departure from Egypt at 480 years before Solomon's fourth year as king. Solomon's accession date can be securely fixed at 970 B.C.E., thanks to synchronisms between biblical and Assyrian texts.[4] This would set Solomon's fourth year of reign at 966 B.C.E. Working backward 480 years from 966 produces a date of 1446 for the exodus.

This date seems to be supported by the statement in the historical reflections of the Hebrew judge, Jephthah. Toward the end of the Judges period, probably early in the eleventh century B.C.E., the Ammonites were making hostile advances on Israelite territory in Gilead. Jephthah argued against the Ammonites' aggressive moves on the basis that Israel had a right to the land because they had already occupied it for three hundred years (Judg 11:26-27). If 1100 B.C.E. is taken as an approximate date for Jephthah's activities, this would place the taking of the Transjordan under Moses (Num 21) around 1400, about forty years after the departure from Egypt.[5]

Since Jack's work in the 1920s, many scholars, particularly evangelicals, have continued to argue for a fifteenth-century B.C.E. exodus. For many evangelicals, it has come to be perceived as the "biblical date" of the exodus.[6] This early date, as such, is often held very strongly by evangelical scholars, who sometimes criticize other evangelicals who opt for the later date. For example, in the late 1990s, Daniel Browning, a professor of religion at a Baptist college, published an article in which he summarized the data on the emergence of Israel as it relates to the biblical traditions and concluded that the late date was the only plausible time period for the events in question.[7] In a paper he presented at the annual meeting of the American Schools of Oriental Research the following year, Browning related that following the publication of the article, he "was quietly chastised" by other evangelical scholars for being "too hard on the early date for the Exodus."[8] In another example, Eugene Merrill, an evangelical scholar, wrote a glowing review of K. A. Kitchen's book, *On the Reliability of the Old Testament*, but suggested that Kitchen's treatment of the date of the exodus could "threaten his credibility as a historian."[9]

When I published a short article suggesting that there may be good reason for evangelicals to consider the late date,[10] I was accused of seeking to "discredit" the Bible, to negate its credibility, of "seeking ways to show that the Bible is not to be trusted in historical matters," and of either supporting or directly advancing "radical revisionism."[11] My point in mentioning these examples is to say that there is tremendous pressure on conservative scholars to assume the early date as the "biblical date" of the exodus-conquest. We cannot, however, adopt an *a priori* conclusion, but must seek to let the data speak for itself. In this chapter, two passages will be considered that generally serve as starting points for the discussion of the date of the exodus-conquest, namely 1 Kgs 6:1 and Exod 1:11. We will also consider that a number of passages that Rodger Young has recently proposed contain either clear references or allusions to Jubilee Years or Sabbatical Cycles, which reinforce an early-date exodus-conquest.

# THE 480 YEARS OF 1 KINGS 6:1 AND THE CHRONOLOGY OF JUDGES

## A Literal Interpretation of the Number 480

The premier datum for those who adhere to the early date for the exodus-conquest is 1 Kgs 6:1, discussed above. Rodger Young argued that the 480 years of 1 Kgs 6:1 are "entirely consistent with the chronology of the book of Judges . . . whereas a thirteenth-century exodus cannot be reconciled with its time spans and sequences."[12] Young notes that the length of the period of the judges cannot be reconstructed by simply adding up the numbers in Judges,[13] but that pericopes must be distinguished based on whether they are sequenced or unprovenanced. Once unprovenanced pericopes have been identified, the interpreter must then "seek the most reasonable time to assign to the unprovenanced passages," after which the sequenced and unprovenanced pericopes can be harmonized. Young concludes that, "with the proper literal approach to the text, the pericopes in Judges are compatible with the 480th-year datum of 1 Kgs 6:1."

I do not deny the possibility of a literal interpretation of the number 480 based on a literal harmonization of the numbers in Judges. Indeed, Robert Boling suggested that the "most plausible" solution "is one which simply adds together the first 4 years of Solomon's rule, the 42 regnal years of Saul and David, the 136 years from Tola to Eli, the 200 years of peace under the saviors, the 53 years of oppression, and the 45 years implied in Josh 14:1. The total is 480."[14] This tabulation, however, is still a harmonization. On a straightforward reading, the lengths of time recorded as having transpired between the exodus and the beginning of construction on the temple seem to have exceeded 480 years.[15] While Wood insists there is a "biblical" chronology laid out with regard to the exodus-conquest,[16] Hoffmeier argues that "biblical chronology does not provide us with an absolute date for the exodus."[17] I have shown that a literal reading of the numbers could produce a duration of 515 years from the exodus to the beginning of construction on the temple;[18] D. I. Block reaches an aggregate total of 593 years;[19] and Hoffmeier tabulates 633 years.[20] There was apparently confusion about the duration from the exodus to the beginning of construction on Solomon's temple in the ancient world as well. The LXX records 440 years instead of 480 (1 Kgs 6:1). Josephus gives two different numbers for the period. In his *Antiquities* he reports the duration as covering 592 years,[21] and in *Against Apion* he recounts it as 612 years.[22] Surely the authors of the LXX were concerned to give the "scriptural" length of the period from the exodus to the founding of the temple! And surely Josephus did not want to be regarded as unreliable in his reporting. The point, however, is simply that the actual length of time spanned by this period is not as unambiguous as Young and Wood want to insist.

Young notes recent articles by Paul Ray[23] and Andrew Steinmann,[24] both of whom have sought to harmonize the 480 years of 1 Kgs 6:1 with the chronology of Judges. While these authors recognize some degree of overlap among some of the judgeships, they seem to generally view the appearance of the judgeships in the book of Judges as occurring more or less in chronological order. On the basis of his determinations of which judgeships overlap and which do not, Steinmann even reconstructs an "absolute" chronology.[25] Younger, on the other hand, notes several problems with working out a chronology for the period, including the unknown amount of overlap, the author's use of numbers, and the inadequate historical presentation of all of the judges, especially the "minor" judges.[26] Younger also notes that although many scholars believe Eli and Samuel functioned as judges in Israel, they are not included in the book of Judges.[27]

These difficulties were observed long ago by the Jewish statesman, philosopher, and Bible commentator Don Isaac Abravanel (1437–1508), who noted that Samuel may not, in fact, belong at the *end* of the period of the judges.[28] Abravanel also observed that the two stories at the end of the book of Judges could have taken place at any time at all during the period of the judges. Rabbi Felix observes the fact that the book of Judges begins with the Hebrew ו (*vav*), and suggests on that basis the placement of 1 Samuel after Judges in the canon may not necessarily be to indicate that the events it records follow chronologically after those in the preceding book. He proposes instead that the placement of the book there may be to provide a contrast between Judges and Samuel. Younger concludes, "It is important to remember that the book is very much a selective presentation designed to reinforce the author's didactic message" and "the precise chronology of the period of the judges is unknown."[29]

## The 480 Years as 12 Generations

Conservative scholars who have gravitated toward the late-date exodus-conquest have always recognized it contradicted a literal reading of the number 480 in 1 Kgs 6:1. One of the ways of coping with this has been to explain the number 480 symbolically. G. E. Wright, for example, took this approach, and suggested that the number 480 symbolized 12 generations of 40 years each.[30] This approach has been followed by many biblical scholars who accept the late date. Young argues that "the reduction of the 480 years into twelve generations of forty years fails because of [the] wrong practice of equating the 'generation' with a period of forty years." Throughout the Old Testament, however, 40 years is considered both a generation (e.g., Psalm 95:10) and an era (e.g., Judg 3:1, 5:31; 1 Sam 4:18; et al.). As Hoffmeier observes, the connection with a generation probably began with such statements as: "For the people of Israel walked forty years in the wilderness, until all the nation, the men of war who came out of Egypt, perished" (Josh 5:6 ESV), and "For forty years I loathed that generation" (Ps 95:10 ESV).³¹ Through regular usage as such, the number 40 appears to have come to mean something to the effect of "a long time," which is how Hess recently rendered it in line 5 of his translation of the Moabite Stone.³²

Young also argues that the word דּוֹר ("generation") does not refer in any of the passages under discussion to a period of time. He explains that, "this could not be the meaning in the case of Israel in the wilderness because every parent who had children twenty years old or older died together with those children; this would have been two generations dying in the wilderness if the meaning were a lapse between the birth of the parent and the birth of the child." While the term דּוֹר is usually translated as "generation," the study of the Hebrew word and its Semitic cognates suggests that it may be more accurately translated as "a lifetime" or even "a cycle of time."³³ D. N. Freedman and J. Lundbom note, "with this meaning *dor* becomes a measure of time or a period of time."³⁴ They explain:

> Like other ancient peoples, the early Hebrews dated long periods by lifetimes. They divided long periods of time into segments corresponding to the life-span of a generation. This is the meaning of *dor* in Gen. 15:16. The difficulty came in attaching numerical values to a generation, and the *'arba 'me 'oth* in Gen. 15:13 were reckoned as 400 years (4 generations of 100 years each). The idea that four generations equals 400 years, which lies behind Gen. 15:13, is undoubtedly based on an artificial scheme which assigns 100 years to a generation.³⁵

The years included within a דּוֹר are not consistent, but vary from one passage to another. For example, in Job 42:16, four generations cover 140 years. The dynasty of Jehu is said to have included four generations, which reigned for only 70 years (815–745 B.C.E. (2 Kgs 10:30; cf. 15:12). It appears that in these and other cases דּוֹר can and does describe a period of time.³⁶

## The 480 Years as a Symbolic Number

According to writer(s) of Kings, exactly 480 years elapsed from the time of the Exodus to the beginning of the building of the temple. Solomon reigned 40 years and, after his reign, if one adds the number of years reigned of all the kings of Judah, from the division of the monarchy to the destruction of the temple, one reaches a total of 394. Another 50 years passed from the destruction of the temple to the foundation of the second temple in Cyrus's second year (Ezra 3:8-9). According to biblical chronology, therefore, another 480 years passed from the first temple's foundation to that of the second temple. When this data is taken together, it yields a schematic pattern of 2 x 480 years centered on the foundation of the first temple (1 Kgs 6:1). It may be that the author(s) of 1–2 Kgs emphasized the number 480 in 1 Kgs 6:1 in order to place the building of the temple right at the center of biblical history.³⁷ Conservative scholars have objected to this 2 x 480 schema, in part because it is assumed to be the product of critical methodology.³⁸ Julius Wellhausen, for example, recognized the 2 x 480 schema, and postulated that the author of the text designed it artificially by adding up the numbers from the time of the first temple to the founding of the second temple and then projecting this figure back into the time between the exodus and the beginning of construction on the first temple. In Wellhausen's reconstruction, the 480 of 1 Kgs 6:1 is derived from the subsequent regnal data of 1–2 Kgs and is artificially applied to the period prior to the first temple.[39] Critical scholars since Wellhausen have generally agreed with his derivation of the number 480 in 1 Kgs 6:1.[40]

Critical scholars have supposed the correspondence of the 480 of 1 Kgs 6:1 with the 480 of the period from the first temple to the return from exile is artificial, and it was imposed by an editor who wanted to draw a connection between the two eras. This is not, however, a necessary conclusion, since it can be shown that the number of years from the destruction of the first temple to the founding of the second temple either equal to or approximately 480.[41] I noted above the plausible solution proposed by Robert Boling, and others have offered similar reconstructions.[42] Based on the aforementioned difficulties with working out a chronology of the period of the judges, I am inclined to take the number 480 as a figurative number, an approximation of the duration from the exodus to the beginning of construction on the first temple. Regardless of exactly how the author of 1 Kings derived the number 480 in 1 Kgs 6:1, it corresponds, at least generally, with the length of the time that transpired in the subsequent period to the return from exile. This correspondence does not imply that any of the numbers are "falsifications." As Clyde Miller so cogently observed, "God, who was providentially guiding the affairs of Israel, could have so utilized [specific periods of time] as to give them symbolic significance as a result of Israel's actual history. This certainly seems to be what God was doing with those many regulations in the law which gave the number seven symbolic significance."[43]

Young argues, however, "[The] problem with these schemes is that they are just too clever." He wonders "what purpose this might serve, since the pattern had to wait until modern times to be discovered." Young assumes that the notion that the 480 of 1 Kgs 6:1 corresponded with another period of 480 spanning the era between the first temple and the return from exile originated with Wellhausen,[44] and he argues that "there is no indication that ancient readers would have understood it in any other sense." However, Abravanel observed this correspondence over 300 years before Wellhausen and noted that there must have been some unknown divine plan behind these time frames.[45] The contemporary rabbinic commentaries on the *haftarot* generally follow this view.[46] As noted above, Nahum Sarna suggested that the plan behind this arrangement may have been to portray the building of the first temple as "the central point in the biblical history of Israel."[47] Interestingly, rabbinic commentators have viewed the number 480 as recurrent throughout their history. Based on the midrashic principle that "the actions of the forefathers are a sign for the children,"[48] rabbinic commentators have believed that, through the story of the forefathers, the Torah also teaches the outline of what to expect in later periods of Jewish history.[49] According to this timeline, there were approximately 480 years from Abraham's recognition of God until the emergence of the Hebrews as a free nation.[50] The same number of years then passed from the exodus until the building of the first temple in Jerusalem. After the building of the first temple, 480 years elapsed until the second one was built. Another 480 years transpired until the rebellion of Bar Kochba. After an equal amount of time, the Talmudic period ended and that of the Geonim began. After another 480 years, the Rif and Rabbeinu Gershom lived, ushering in the period of the Rishonim in Spain and Germany. This period also lasted about 480 years, until the time of Rav Yosef Karo and Rav Moshe Isserles, the authors of the *Shulchan Aruch*. The production of this work inaugurated the period of the Acharonim, during which Jewish scholarship and life was centered in and around Europe. This period came to an end some 480 years later with the Holocaust.[51] The point is, Orthodox Jews have regarded their history as having occurred in these cycles or eras. The tendency to break history into eras has been a feature of numerous cultures from antiquity on,[52] and so the possibility of its presence in the Bible should not be surprising.

In the writings of the patristic[53] commentators, few deal in detail with chronological matters. The reason for this is that the patristic writers did not share the focus on historical-critical matters with which modern readers are concerned. Their approach to interpreting Scripture is primarily allegorical or typological,[54] and when they do discuss numbers, they tend to interpret them in this manner. The interpretation of the number 480 in 1 Kgs 6:1 does appear in the Anglo-Latin church fathers. The Venerable Bede (ca. 672–735), whose exegetical method follows that of Ambrose, Jerome, Augustine, and Gregory the Great, wrote a commentary on the Solomonic temple in which he makes ample use of allegorical and typological interpretation.[55] In treating 1 Kgs 6:1, Bede encourages his readers to "learn the spiritual mystery attaching to this period," and explains it as a multiple of 4 x 120. He notes that the number 4 is "very appropriate to evangelical perfection" because it corresponds with the number of the Evangelists. In addition, it makes sense to Bede that the duration of the period between the exodus and the building of the temple would be comprised of multiples of 120, since that was the life span of Moses, the great legislator.[56] The number 120 is also the count of the men who received the Holy Spirit in the earliest church.[57] The fact that the number 120 corresponded with both the life of Moses and the number of those who received the Spirit in the early church proved, for Bede, "that those who use the law legitimately, that is, those who recognize and embrace the grace of Christ in it, are deservedly filled with the grace of his Spirit so that they may become more ardent in his love."[58] There is certainly precedent in both Jewish and Christian traditions for interpreting the number 480 in 1 Kgs 6:1 symbolically.

# THE IDENTIFICATION OF JUBILEE AND SABBATICAL CYCLES

In a series of articles, Young recently proposed that a number of Jubilee years and Sabbatical cycles can be identified in the Hebrew Bible and these, in turn, comprise an important argument in favor of the early date for the exodus.[59] Discussed here will be the two Jubilee years that Young points to in the Talmud, as well as some of the years he claims were Sabbatical years.[60]

# Jubilee Years

## Ezekiel 40:1

The first passage Young argues points to a Jubilee year is Ezek 40:1, in which Ezekiel notes he received a vision in the twenty-fifth year of the captivity, and it was בְּרֹאשׁ הַשָּׁנָה, "at the beginning of the year." The *Seder 'Olam* and the Talmud claim that a Jubilee year occurred at this time.[61] While Young[62] asserts that Ezekiel's notation that it was "the beginning of the year" is a reference to the seventh month of the year, Tishri, this is not agreed upon among commentators. While some commentators have understood this to be a reference to Tishri,[63] most have interpreted it as a reference to Abib (Nisan).[64] The following reasons suggest that it should be understood as a reference to Abib (Nisan):

1. The Torah stipulated that the New Year was to be inaugurated with Abib (Nisan).[65] In the course of the instructions about the departure from Egypt and the Passover, Exod 12:2 states that "this month shall mark for you the beginning of the months; it shall be the first month of the year for you." While the year of Jubilee was to begin on 7/10, the Day of Atonement, no autumnal month is ever called the first month.[66] The custom of beginning the year with Tishri was eventually adopted, but not until long after the captivity.

2. It seems doubtful that Ezekiel, a priest (1:3), would have contradicted the Torah with regard to such an important issue as the liturgical calendar.[67] Hummel notes that the liturgical rituals prescribed in Ezek 45:18-25, which also presuppose a spring New Year, confirm that he did not.[68] Hummel concludes that, "even if a calendar whose year began in the autumn had already been accepted in everyday life in the OT era, there is no indication that the liturgy had ever abandoned its ancient method of beginning the year in the spring (Nisan)." Keil suggests that בְּרֹאשׁ הַשָּׁנָה "is a contracted repetition of the definition contained in Exod 12:2, רֹאשׁ חֳדָשִׁים רִאשׁוֹן לְחָדְשֵׁי הַשָּׁנָה, and signifies the opening month of the year, i.e., the month Abib (Nisan)."[69]

3. The usage of the civil calendar throughout the book of Ezekiel corresponds with an interpretation of Ezek 40:1 as a reference to Abib (Nisan) as the beginning of the year.[70]

Young argues that the fact that the date is given as "on the tenth day of the month" is indicative that Ezekiel saw his vision at the beginning of a Jubilee year. Ezekiel's calendrical reference, however, is not indicative, as the tenth day of the month carries importance in the first as well as in the seventh month.[71] Eichrodt suggests that the tenth day may have held special significance in the priestly terminology.[72] May observes that it was on the tenth day of the first month that the Hebrews entered into the promised land (Josh 4:19; cf. also Exod 12:3). In addition, following its construction and dedication, the glory of Yahweh filled the Tent of Meeting on the first day of the first month (Exod 40:1-38), an occasion with which Ezekiel may intend to draw a parallel since it will be on this same day that Yahweh will enter the new temple (43:1-5).[73] Keil concludes that "the tenth day of this month was the day on which the preparations for the Passover, the feast of the elevation of Israel into the people of God, were to commence, and therefore was well adapted for the revelation of the new constitution of the kingdom of God."[74]

The rabbinic traditions that Young relies on (*b. Arak* 12a) are attempts to resolve the chronographic indicators in Ezek 40:1, which explains the lengthy discussion among the sages attested to therein. These discussions witness to the academic speculation that took place in the Jewish academies, in which the various phrases in Ezek 40:1 were discussed and interpreted. Michael Fishbane explains that the assignment of a seventeenth Jubilee to the passage is a back-assessment, and the conclusions drawn about Ezek 40:1 are midrashic speculation, as Rabbi Eleazar of Beaugency (twelfth century) pointedly acknowledged in his commentary on Ezek 40:1.[75]

## *Josiah's Eighteenth Year*

The second Jubilee Young points to is one that *Seder 'Olam* and the Talmud claim was observed in the eighteenth year of Josiah.[76] The claim that a Jubilee was celebrated at this time is very weak.[77] The account in 2 Kings only records two phases of Josiah's reform: first, the purification of Judean religion (23:1-20, 24-27) and second, an effort to centralize worship in Jerusalem along with the celebration of the Passover in Jerusalem. The celebration of the Passover festival during the Josianic reform is very significant, as the text reports that this marked the first time that this holy day had been observed since the days of Joshua (2 Kgs 23:21-23). If the priests had allowed the Passover to go unobserved since the days of Joshua, it seems extremely unlikely that they would have kept meticulous track of the sabbatical and Jubilee cycles.

## Sabbatical Years

Young identifies a number of Sabbatical years in Scripture, though none of them is identified as such in Scripture.

## *Jeremiah 34:8-10*

The first case he cites is that of Jer 34:8-10, which reports a release of slaves during the Babylonian siege of the sixth century B.C.E. After the Babylonian siege had begun (ca. 588 B.C.E.), the people made a solemn covenant to release their slaves, apparently hoping thereby to gain the favor of Yahweh. However, after some time, the Egyptians extended aid to Israel, and the Babylonians consequently lifted the siege (Jer 37:6-11). Following the cessation of the Babylonian siege, the Israelite slave owners took back their slaves. Young argues that, based on the release of the slaves, this must have been a Sabbatical year. However, the term used here is דְּרוֹר, "release," from the legislation in Lev 25 regarding the Jubilee year, instead of שְׁמִטָּה (*shemittah*) or "remission," which is the term used for the year of remission in the legislation for the Sabbatical year (Deut 15:9). This is indeed a perplexing passage, as vv. 8b-11 seem to refer to a general liberation of slaves, as in a Jubilee year (Lev 25:39-55), while vv. 14-15 refer to the release of slaves who have served six years, in accordance with the legislation for the Sabbatical year (Deut 15:12-18). The release proclaimed by Zedekiah does not, therefore, conform to either passage, but seems to combine them both in a kind of mass manumission. Hyatt suggested that the action described here must have been a release by special proclamation of the king under an emergency situation,[78] much like the ancient Near Eastern practice of *mesharum* acts. Keown, Scalise, and Smothers describe the *mesharum* as follows:

> The king, usually on the occasion of his accession to the throne, would declare a temporary measure of debt relief. F. Kraus's study of Old Babylonian *mesharum* texts reveals that they were not enacted at fixed intervals of years but rather in response to specific needs. They provided a way to exalt the new king as protector of the weak by alleviating excessively oppressive debt loads resulting from wartime disturbances of the economy or poor harvests. Law codes published later in the reign usually included provisions for gaining release from debt slavery. If such regulations had been followed during the previous king's reign, the *mesharum* act would have been unnecessary.[79]

Keown, Scalise, and Smothers suggest that Zedekiah's proclamation of release is like the Babylonian *mesharum* acts. "Neglect of the customary means of limiting the servitude of debtors (Deut 15) had created a situation ripe for the king's proclamation (v. 14b)."[80] That the customary means had been neglected is made clear by Jer 12–14, which reviews the law of release and then notes that it had not been followed in Israel's history:

> The word of the LORD came to Jeremiah from the LORD: Thus says the LORD, the God of Israel: I myself made a covenant with your ancestors when I brought them out of the land of Egypt, out of the house of slavery, saying, "Every seventh year each of you must set free any Hebrews who have been sold to you and have served you six years; you must set them free from your service." But your ancestors did not listen to me or incline their ears to me. (Jer 34:12-14)

Verse 15 states the people had only recently repented for this and did what was right in the eyes of Yahweh "by proclaiming liberty to one another." Apparently the law had been disregarded for years. The people's repentance was short-lived, however, and it was not long after the release had been put into effect before the Hebrews recaptured their slaves and "brought them again into subjection to be your slaves" (v. 16). This was a case of "foxhole religion" or "death-bed repentance."[81] During a time of siege, Zedekiah sought to compel the people to act in a way that reflected the values of the Law, but when the siege was lifted they took their slaves back. If the entire passage reveals anything, it surely highlights the perpetual neglect by Israel of its Sabbatical Year laws and their concomitant provisions of justice, and since these years culminated in the year of Jubilee, it also suggests the observance of the year of general manumission was also not regularly practiced in the life of Israel.

## Isaiah 37:30

Another of Young's supposed Sabbatical years is connected with a sign offered by Isaiah in the midst of the Assyrian siege: "This year eat what grows of itself, and in the second year what springs from that; then in the third year sow, reap, plant vineyards, and eat their fruit." According to Young, "This has no explanation unless that year was a Sabbatical year." The natural reading of this passage, however, followed by most commentators, is that the context for this passage has to do with the fact that the land had been ravaged by the Assyrian siege, not that it was a Sabbatical year. The sign given by Isaiah is a promise of restitution offered to a remnant of Judah and Jerusalem, with the understanding that the change in fortune would only unfold gradually, over a three-year period. Hans Wildberger writes:

> It is assumed in the present case that the inaction caused by the war has hindered people from planting the fields. Since working the fields fully would not be possible in the second year either, only "wild growth" would be available for food. This would indicate that the need would be even more severe the second year, since one could expect only a very minimal harvest that would grow from the few seeds that would have fallen as the first harvest was gathered. But the third year would bring normalcy back to what had been a threatening situation. One would sow again and would get to harvest—a miracle that would be seen as a sign from Yahweh for his people, assuring them that he had turned back toward them again.[82]

The second year of Isaiah's prophecy, in which the people would be dependent on volunteer growth, is probably simply an indication that the land was in a sad condition due to the occupation of the Assyrians, and there are no indications in the text that this was a Sabbatical year.[83]

In the case of the Sabbatical Year Young finds that in the eighteenth year of Josiah the reading of the Law (2 Kgs 23:2) was not on the occasion of a Sabbatical year since, as we saw above, Israel's ancestors had failed to implement the Sabbatical Year system (Jer 34:14).[84] Instead, the text states explicitly this was a covenant renewal (2 Kgs 23:3),[85] which also included the reading of the covenant document.[86] Far from showing the continuity of Israel's piety, the text suggests that the contents and commands of this newly discovered document had long since been forgotten and had therefore gone unobserved. Walter Brueggemann cogently explains that

> the negative counterpoint of this act, implied and not stated, is that over long years of carelessness and indifference, covenantal dimensions of life have been forgotten and neglected, so that through ethical carelessness, religious indifference, and theological heterodoxy, Israel's peculiar identity and vocation in the world have been abandoned. Thus, the narrative presents Josiah's act as an act of such profound

importance that it parallels the founding act of Moses at Sinai and the renewing act of Ezra. This act is nothing less than the recovery of a lost destiny.[87]

As in the case of Zedekiah's *mesharum* act, rather than showing the people's piety, this occasion reinforces the fact of Israel's neglect of the Law and the revolutionary nature of Josiah's reinauguration of its observance. Young's other postulated Sabbatical years are either inferred or depend entirely on rabbinic tradition. Just as is the case with the Jubilee years, "there is no direct reference to a sabbatical year being observed in the OT period . . ."[88]

## The Use of the Supposed Sabbatical Year and Jubilee Cycle Data

On the basis of the two Jubilees he has identified in the Talmud, Young points to Lev 25:1-10, which states the Israelites were to begin counting tithes, Sabbatical years, and Jubilees upon their entrance into the land of Canaan.[89] On this basis, Young counts backward from the seventeenth Jubilee (Ezek 40:1) in increments of 49 years[90] to 1406 B.C.E. as this inaugural date. There are at least three problems with Young's methodology and conclusions.

First, the conclusions Young draws from the dating are not in accordance with the rabbinic chronology that serves as the basis of his work. Based on the postulated seventeenth Jubilee of Ezek 40:1, which Young dates to the Day of Atonement, Tishri 10 of 574 B.C.E., Young counts backward to 1406 B.C.E., where he places the Israelite entrance into Canaan. Since Israel was to start counting the cycles when they entered the land of Canaan (Lev 25:1-10), Young dates this as the first Jubilee and counts forward accordingly. This is not in accordance, however, with the rabbinic materials that Young claims substantiate his early-date exodus-conquest. According to the *Seder 'Olam Rabbah*, the Israelites did not begin counting Sabbatical and Jubilee cycles until fifteen years after their entrance into the land of Canaan:

> One has to say that 14 years Israel spent at Gilgal, seven when they were conquering and seven when they were distributing. After that (Josh 18:1) "All the congregation of the Children of Israel assembled at Shiloh and there they put up the Tabernacle." At that moment, they started to count years for tithes, sabbatical years, and Jubilee years (Josh 22:1-2). "Then Joshua called the Reubenites, the Gadites, and the semi-tribe of Manasse and said to them: you kept everything that Moses, the Servant of God, had commanded you; you listened to my voice for all orders that I gave you." Joshua sent them to their tents and blessed them. On their return they built a big altar for view. Joshua celebrated with them the first sabbatical year; he died before he finished the second one.[91]

An interesting problem emerges here. The author(s) of the *Seder 'Olam Rabbah* notes that fourteen years passed after the Israelites first entered Canaan, and then states that Israel "started to count years for tithes, sabbatical years, and Jubilee years." *Seder 'Olam* seems to say that what occurred upon the Israelites' entrance into Canaan was that they began counting, not that they celebrated a Jubilee year. The injunction in

Lev 25:1-7 has also been variously interpreted. Verse 2b states that, "When you enter the land that I am giving you, the land shall observe a sabbath for the LORD," and the following verses then go on to explain how the regulations for the Sabbath year are to be observed:

> Six years you shall sow your field, and six years you shall prune your vineyard, and gather in their yield; but in the seventh year there shall be a sabbath of complete rest for the land, a sabbath for the LORD: you shall not sow your field or prune your vineyard. You shall not reap the aftergrowth of your harvest or gather the grapes of your unpruned vine: it shall be a year of complete rest for the land. You may eat what the land yields during its sabbath—you, your male and female slaves, your hired and your bound laborers who live with you; for your livestock also, and for the wild animals in your land all its yield shall be for food.
> 
> You shall count off seven weeks of years, seven times seven years, so that the period of seven weeks of years gives forty-nine years. Then you shall have the trumpet sounded loud; on the tenth day of the seventh month—on the day of atonement—you shall have the trumpet sounded throughout all your land. And you shall hallow the fiftieth year and you shall proclaim liberty throughout the land to all its inhabitants. It shall be a jubilee for you: you shall return, every one of you, to your property and every one of you to your family. (Lev 25:3-10)

Some interpreters have understood Lev 25:2 as saying that, upon entering the land of Canaan, Israel immediately celebrated a Sabbatical year.[92] In this case, "it resembles the practice of the *mīšarum* issued by the Babylonian kings during the year of their accession to the throne."[93] It seems more natural, however, to understand Lev 25:3-8 as an explanation of how the Sabbath mentioned in verse 2 was to be carried out. If this is correct, then "the principle of Sabbath rest is now applied to a seven-year period in which the final year is to be observed as a Sabbath to the Lord."[94] If *Seder 'Olam Rabbah* is correct that the Israelites only "started to count years for tithes, sabbatical years, and Jubilee years" after they had been in the land for fourteen years, and if they began counting the first year of the first Sabbath year cycle in the following year, then they would not have celebrated a Jubilee until they had been in the land some sixty-five years.

In any case, Young counts backward from a hypothetical Jubilee year in 574 B.C.E., based on Ezek 40:1, to 1406 B.C.E., the year in which he argues that Israel entered Canaan. The date of the exodus according to *Seder 'Olam Rabbah*, however, has been calculated to about 1313 B.C.E.[95] or 1312/1311 B.C.E.[96] Subtracting 40 from 1312/1311, the rabbis reached a date of about 1272/1271 B.C.E. for the entry into Canaan.[97] The rabbinic chronology is not, in fact, in accordance with the early date.

The second problem has to do with Young's methodology for utilizing the rabbinic materials. Young admits rabbinic calculations were inaccurate, noting, for example, "rabbinical calculation methods were not capable of correctly calculating that there were forty-nine years between Josiah's eighteenth year and Ezekiel's vision," and yet he argues that their traditions regarding the Jubilee are correct. Young accepts as historical the rabbinic traditions that support his argument, while ignoring the many egregious errors in rabbinic chronology. The scheme of *Seder 'Olam Rabbah* begins at Creation and ends with the destruction of the temple in 70 C.E. The chronology is very condensed, with the length of the Egyptian sojourn abbreviated by taking the figure in Exod 12:40 to include the patriarchs' years in Canaan. Its dates for the exile are inaccurate by over a century and a half, dating the exile to 423 B.C.E. The discussion of the post-biblical period in *Seder 'Olam Rabbah* is controlled by Daniel's 70 weeks, or 490 years,[98] in which the Persian period is allotted only 34 years, abbreviating it by some 165 years.[99] The idea that *Seder 'Olam* contains "genuine historical memory" is very weak. The fact that it depends on biblical numerology (especially Daniel's prophecy of the 490 years) to calculate reign lengths and other figures both demonstrates its author's lack of extrabiblical historical information and leads to egregious errors. I have already mentioned the problems with the Talmudic materials. Young argues that these rabbinic materials "can be taken as a historical reference independent of the scriptural record, the same as if some ancient document from the Near East mentioned a date that could be tied independently to a biblical date."[100] There are very serious problems with using a source from the fifth century C.E. (or later), namely the Babylonian Talmud, to determine the date of events that took place in the late second millennium B.C.E.[101] The bottom line, however, is that "rabbinic and/or Talmudic information is almost never considered reliable for chronology,"[102] and not only that but their traditions about the Jubilee cannot be considered as reliable. The fact is, "there is simply no evidence of a national jubilee in the extant historical documents of Israel."[103] The silence of the historical documents does not prove that it never happened, but it does prevent us from reconstructing a biblical chronology on that basis.

A third area I would identify as problematic in Young's argument is the idea that symbolic numbers cannot be used in a narrative. Young began his discussion of the Jubilee and Sabbatical cycles by suggesting that only scholars influenced by redaction criticism would "seek to impose a non-literal 480 years in the midst of an otherwise historical account." The inclusion of a symbolic number in the midst of a historical account would not, however, be evidence that a document had been redacted. Indeed, biblical materials regularly incorporate genre changes.[104] In the midst of the narratives of the conquest, we have nine chapters comprising a series of border descriptions (Josh 13–19);[105] in the midst of the narrative of Abimelech's attempt to establish a monarchy, we have a fable about trees (Judg 9:7-15). Prophetic books often contain passages belonging to different genres, even within the same chapter. For example, Isaiah 5 begins with a poem (vv. 1-7), shifts to a series of oracles of woe (vv. 8-23), turns next to a series of proclamations of divine judgment (vv. 24-25), and concludes with a poetic description of the Assyrian army (vv. 26-30). The New Testament is no different. In the midst of narratives about the life of Jesus, we have sermons (e.g., Matt 5:1–7:28), prayers (e.g., Matt 6:9-13), and even fictional parables (e.g., Matt 22:1-14). Bruce Chilton notes, "throughout the Bible, differing genres often appear within individual works, which indicates that genres do not represent fixed types of communication to which biblical books can be made to conform."[106] Arguing that a symbol cannot occur in the midst of a historical account is unreasonable.

At present, two possible options seem to present themselves as the best contenders for understanding the 480 years of 1 Kgs 6:1. The first is that the 480 years constitute an Israelite *Distanzangabe*, or given distance,[107] a term denoting a large block of time linking the founding of a temple or the restoration of a cult to earlier events. Hoffmeier points to the case of Tukulti-Ninurta's declaration that 720 years had elapsed between the time of the initial construction of the Ishtar Temple in Ashur and his own reconstruction of it at the beginning of his reign. Julian Reade suggests that the 720 years is probably not literal, but that it may derive either from "12 times 60" or from taking the number of kings listed in the king list between the two monarchs, which is 45, and multiplying that number by 16, thought to be the average reign length, thus producing the number 720.[108] Hoffmeier concludes his discussion of the number 480 with these questions:

> Could it be that the 480 years of 1 Kgs 6:1 is an Israelite *Distanzangabe*? If so, its purpose was not to provide a historical datum per se, but rather to create a link between the building of Israel's temple and the event that led to YHWH becoming the God of Israel. The same is true of Assyrian and Egyptian *Distanzangaben*. The connection of all these texts to the construction of a temple must be taken seriously. Is the 480-year figure in 1 Kgs 6:1 an example of the use of a large symbolic number rather than a literal number and does it represent a "convention of the penman's milieu"?[109]

The second option is the previously discussed idea of the number 480 as a product of 12 x 40. In a recent discussion of this, Dale Manor has noted that a careful reading of Chronicles, in combination with Exodus, reveals that there were twelve generations from the exodus to the high priest who presided over the construction of Solomon's Temple.[110] Based on the possibility that 12 generations were involved, Manor notes the prospect that the number 40, instead of always functioning as an arithmetic number, may have sometimes functioned as a metaphor for a generation. Noting that some Egyptian sources indicate that his twenties would often be the time when a man would father a child,[111] Manor suggests that if one rounds the number to 25 and multiplies it by 12 generations, the result is 300 years. Adding 300 years to the fourth year of Solomon's reign produces a date of about 1266 B.C.E., "well embedded in the reign of Ramesses."[112] These two approaches are closely related, both viewing the number 480 as designed to constitute an "era" between the time of the exodus and the beginning of the construction of the first temple.

# THE BOOK OF EXODUS

## Reference to the Supply City of "Rameses"

### *Exodus 1:11*

This passage, which states that the Hebrews were put to forced labor and compelled to build a supply city for the pharaoh was one of the main reasons that Egyptologists held to a late-date exodus-conquest throughout the twentieth century.

The biblical text refers to this supply city as "Rameses," and it was well known that Ramesses II (1279–1213 B.C.E.) had built a city named Pi-Ramesses, which means "House of Ramesses," in the northeastern delta.[113] Based on this information, scholars naturally concluded that the exodus occurred either late during the long reign of Ramesses II, or during the reign of Merneptah, his thirteenth son. Labib Habachi, a Coptic Christan Egyptologist, began investigating the site of Qantir in the 1950s, which he had concluded was to be identified as Pi-Ramesses, and although it took a few decades, a consensus began to emerge that Qantir was indeed Pi-Ramesses.[114] A German team began excavating the site in 1980, and the picture that has emerged is of a city that flourished from about 1270–1120 B.C.E., and that there was no city known as Ramesses there during the Eighteenth Dynasty.[115] These data have seemed to support the earlier supposition about an exodus during the Nineteenth Dynasty.

As discussed earlier, James Jack appears to have been the first to question the late-date. Jack recognized that the identification of the thirteenth-century Pi-Ramesses with the supply city of Ramesses in Exod 1:11 presented a problem for a fifteenth-century date. He sought to deal with this by arguing that the later editor of the text modernized the name in order to make it more easily identifiable for readers in his own day.[116] This position has continued to be held by many evangelicals, including C. Aling, G. L. Archer, E. H. Merrill, M. F. Unger, B. G. Wood, and L. J. Wood.[117] Editorial glossing did occur in the Hebrew Bible but, as Hoffmeier has observed, typically both the former name and the contemporary name occur together.[118] For example, Gen 14:2 refers to "Bela (that is, Zoar)."[119] In cases such as this, the formula used includes the old name + הוא + the new name. This formula, a "verbless clause of identification,"[120] is an obvious sign of editorial updating of an outdated toponymy. Longer descriptions of name changes also occur, such as when Jacob slept at a certain place and dreamed of the stairway to heaven when he was traveling to Haran. On this occasion, the text says "he called that place Bethel; but the name of the city was Luz at the first" (Gen 28:19). While the toponym Ramesses (רעמסס) occurs five times in the Hebrew Bible, the formula "old name + הוא + new name" is never used, nor is a longer explanation ever given. Hoffmeier concludes, therefore, that "there is no evidence within these five passages to suspect that 'Ramesses' is an editorial gloss."[121] This comports well with Hoffmeier's previous findings that the geographical terms found in Exodus and Numbers correspond with the Nineteenth Dynasty but not with earlier periods.[122]

Some conservative scholars have also argued that even if the name Rameses in Exod 1:11 is not a modernization, it may still reflect an Eighteenth rather than a Nineteenth Dynasty context.[123] Rodger Dalman, for example, said the reference to the region as the "land of Rameses" in Gen 47:11 may indicate that it was associated with this name during the Middle Kingdom. He notes that the name "Ramose" was used twice in Eighteenth Dynasty texts and argues that Ramose and Ramesses were the same name.[124] If Ramose was the name behind the toponym in Exodus 1:11, however, the Hebrew should read רעמס instead of the MT's רַעְמְסֵס. The fact is that, while the name Ramose does occur before the Nineteenth Dynasty, the name formula for Rameses, which means "Ra bore him," does not appear until the Nineteenth Dynasty or the thirteenth century B.C.E.[125] The MT reproduces the name Ramesses, which was first documented in the Nineteenth Dynasty, and this corresponds with the rule of the pharaoh with the most copious construction record, Ramesses II, whom we know built a city that he named after himself. There is no archaeological or textual evidence to support the theory that the region was known as Ramesses or that there was a city known as Ramesses there during the Eighteenth Dynasty. Pi-Ramesses only flourished from about 1270 to 1120 B.C.E., after which it was replaced by Zoan, which became the dominant city of the northeast Delta for the next thousand years.[126] If one believes that the Torah or some early form of it was composed or compiled sometime between the thirteenth and twelfth centuries B.C.E., then it makes sense that the texts would use the contemporary name of the city. According to this view, "the reference to Ramesses in Genesis . . . is a cogent argument that the same author who wrote Genesis also wrote Exodus and Numbers."[127]

In sum, it appears that the mention of the store city of Ramesses in Exod 1:11 continues to suggest a thirteenth-century B.C.E. date for the exodus.

# CONCLUSION

In this chapter, biblical data was examined with a view to identifying the date of the exodus-conquest. We considered two passages that frequently serve as starting points for approaching this chronological problem, namely 1 Kgs 6:1 and Exod 1:11. The previous passage states that the exodus occurred 480 years before Solomon's fourth year as king. Since Solomon's accession date can be securely fixed at 970 B.C.E., his fourth year would be 966. Working backward 480 years from 966 B.C.E. produces a date of 1446 for the exodus, a date that seems to be supported by the statement in the historical reflections of the judge Jephthah (Judg 11:26-27). Many evangelicals have held to 1446 as the "biblical" date of the exodus since at least 1925, when James Jack made the case for it in his 1925 volume, *The Date of the Exodus in the Light of External Evidence*.

We also examined a number of passages that Roger Young has recently argued contain clear references or allusions to Jubilee Years or Sabbatical Cycles, which would reinforce an early-date exodus-conquest. In the case of the number 480, it cannot be harmonized with the period of the judges, for which the precise chronology remains unknown. It seems more likely that the number 480 is intended to be a symbolic number, which is how it appears to have been understood by the church fathers, rabbinic commentators, and Jewish philosophers. With regard to Jubilee Years and Sabbatical Cycles, there do not appear to be any clear examples of either in the Hebrew Bible, and thus they cannot serve as a chronological anchor for calculating the date of the exodus-conquest. The only piece of data from the Hebrew Bible that seems to provide a clue to the date of these events is Exod 1:11, which states that the Hebrews were put to forced labor and compelled to build a supply city called "Rameses" for the pharaoh. The city of Qantir, discovered in the 1950s, has been identified with

Pi-Ramesses, and the archaeological data suggest that it only flourished from about 1270–1120 B.C.E. In sum, the biblical data provides little clear information regarding the date of the exodus-conquest. The naming of the city of Rameses is the only reference that may provide chronological clarity, and it seems to situate the events of the exodus-conquest in the thirteenth rather than the fifteenth century B.C.E.

CHAPTER 4

# THE DATE OF THE EXODUS-CONQUEST

## PART II: EXTRABIBLICAL EVIDENCE

In the previous chapter, we looked at biblical evidence related to the discussion about the date of the exodus-conquest. In this chapter, we will consider extrabiblical data, beginning with texts and then supplementing them with an examination of material conditions in the eastern Mediterranean world during the transition from the Late Bronze to the Iron Age.

## CANAANITE TEXTS

### The Amarna Correspondence

Amarna Correspondence is the name given to a collection of cuneiform tablets found in 1887 at a location about two hundred miles south of Cairo by a Bedouin woman digging ancient mud-brick to use as fertilizer. Scholars came to call the site el-Amarna after the name of the Bedouin tribe that lived there. The site turned out to have been the capital of Pharaoh Akhenaten (Amenophis IV, 1353–1337 B.C.E.), famed for having acknowledged only one deity, Aten, the Egyptian sun god. A total of 382 tablets were discovered, each of which now has its own identity number and the prefix *EA*. The majority of the el-Amarna tablets, which date to the time of Akhenaten and are written in Akkadian, the *lingua franca* of the day, are housed in Berlin, the British Museum, and the Egyptian Museum (Cairo).[1] The tablets can basically be divided into two groups, the first of which consists of forty-three tablets containing diplomatic correspondence between Egypt and the great powers of western Asia (Babylon, Assyria, Mitanni, Hatti, and Alashiya). They deal with political matters, trade agreements, arrangement of diplomatic marriages, exchange of presents, gift inventories.[2]

The second group has an important bearing on reconstructing the Israelite settlement. It consists of 307 tablets containing the communications between the

Canaanite city-states of Syria-Palestine and the pharaoh, to whom they were vassals. This group of tablets consists mostly of routine expressions of loyalty from tributary rulers, who address pharaoh as "my lord," and provide a fairly detailed picture of Egyptian power in Canaan, recording the conflicts of the local rulers who ask for help against each other.[3] I will discuss this situation and its importance for the Israelite settlement later, but want to focus here on a people group called the Habiru that are mentioned in sixteen of the el-Amarna tablets, and also on the question of whether or not there may be a relationship between them and the Hebrews in the period of the Late Bronze/Iron I transition. I will introduce the Habiru, review the factors that led scholars to associate them with the Hebrews, and then consider three factors that seem to mitigate against this association, including linguistic factors, usage of the terminology, and the temporal and geographic range of the Habiru.

## *Habiru*

The Habiru were a population group on the social and political margins of the ancient Near East from about 1850–1150 B.C.E. The earliest known references to this group occur in Sumerian texts from the middle of the third millennium B.C.E., and the latest are in Mesopotamian texts that date near the end of the second millennium.[4] They first came to the attention of biblical scholars, however, when the Amarna letters were discovered in 1888–1889, and it was observed that some sixteen of the letters to Amenophis IV (ca. 1352–1336 B.C.E.) from city-states within Canaan mention the Habiru as a threat and ask for help from the pharaoh in order to defend themselves against these marauders. A cursory reading of the texts suggests that the Habiru were taking over the highlands of Canaan. In writing to the pharaoh, the king of Gezer claimed that Egypt's Canaanite holdings were at risk of being lost to the Habiru (EA271), and the king of Jerusalem likewise claimed that these raiders had "plundered all the lands of the king," and that, if the pharaoh did not provide archers soon, then "lost are the lands of the king" (EA286). This same king went on to report that the sons of Labayu, the ruler of Shechem,[5] had "given the land of the king to the [Habiru]" (EA287), and that "the land of the king is lost . . . the [Habiru] have taken the very cities of the king" (EA288) and that "the land of the king deserted to the [Habiru]" (EA290).

Due to the apparent similarity between the names Habiru and Hebrew and the proximity of their location and time, scholars quickly reached the conclusion that the Amarna Habiru and the Israelites were one and the same, and that the Amarna texts provided extrabiblical evidence of the Hebrew conquest of Palestine.[6] B. G. Wood, for example, writes that "One could not ask for a more accurate description of the Israelites shortly after entering the land of Canaan."[7] He suggests that "by examining the historical records to see who was in control of the highlands after the mid-fourteenth century B.C.E., we can confirm the identity of these [Habiru] forces. Although the data are meager, nevertheless sufficient information is available to ascertain that it was the Israelites."[8] Similar conclusions are reached by a number of scholars, including

F. M. Cross, N. K. Gottwald, M. D. Hiebert, and S. D. Waterhouse, all of whom correlate the biblical Hebrews with the Habiru.[9]

There are at least three main problems with associating the Habiru with the Hebrews. First, it is linguistically impossible to correlate the Hebrews with the Habiru. On the surface, "Hebrew" and "Habiru" look similar. And so the biblical term *'ivrim* (עִבְרִים) has often been thought to have either been derived from the term *Habiru*[10] or even to be linguistically equivalent to it.[11] However, based on usage of the term *Habiru* in Egyptian and Ugaritic documents, it has become clear that the second consonant should most properly be read as a *p* rather than a *b*, which means that the term is more correctly written as *'apiru*.[12] The words *Hebrew* and *'apiru* are thus substantives of a different type and do not appear to have ever been related.[13] Instead of being derived from *'apiru*, P. K. McCarter has suggested that *'ivri* is a gentilic of *'ever* (עֵבֶר), which means "region across" or "region beyond."[14] In this case, the term *Hebrew* would be intended "to distinguish the family of Abraham (thus the reference in Gen 14:13 to 'Abram the Hebrew') from the indigenous population of Canaan and from foreigners."[15] More recently, D. Fleming has suggested that the biblical term *Hebrew* derives from *'ibrum*, a term in Mari for back-country herders that was notably prevalent among the Binu Yamina tribespeople of southwest Syria.[16] The *'ibrum* were "mobile pastoralist communities that ranged across southwestern Syria during the Mari period," but who retained ties to their settled communities through the ideology of tribal identity. The term *'apiru* carries a different meaning altogether. A. F. Rainey, following the work of R. Borger, suggests that the term *'apiru*, on the basis of the Syriac cognate *'apir*, means something like "dusty." He explains that "the social outcasts or refugees, runaways, who bore this pejorative appellative, had to 'hit the road,' thus they were covered with dust."[17]

A second point is related to the first, and it is that it appears that the *'apiru* do not represent an ethnic group but a social phenomenon, the background of which is very different from that of the Hebrews. The *'apiru* often appear to have urban backgrounds, and while they appear in a variety of work-related positions, for the most part they functioned as mercenaries, brigands, agricultural personnel, and construction workers. The Hebrews, on the other hand, are reported to have had their origins in pastoralism.[18] The term "Hebrew" itself is a gentilic, like "Canaanite" or "Moabite." If it is derived from *'ever*, then it would mean something like "the man from beyond," which is how the LXX renders it. If Fleming is correct that it derives from *'ibrum*, then it would mean something like "the one from the back country," which would seem to be a better social fit for the biblical Hebrews. Many of the occurrences of the word *Hebrew* are in the book of Genesis, where the term is used in contrast with "Egyptian,"[19] and in 1 Samuel, where it is used in opposition with "Philistines."[20] The term *Hebrew* is clearly used in these contexts as an ethnicon.

A third factor which seems to mitigate against an association of the Hebrews with the *'apiru* is that the latter were practically omnipresent in the Fertile Crescent throughout much of the second millennium.[21] As mentioned before, their appearance ranges in date from the middle of the third millennium to near the end of the second millennium, and they range in location all across the Fertile Crescent. Cuneiform texts from all across the ancient Near East refer to the *'apiru*, including cuneiform texts from numerous Levantine, Anatolian, northern Mesopotamian, and southern Mesopotamian cities. The Egyptians used the term in their hieroglyphic inscriptions too. The temporal and geographical range is simply too broad for there to be a direct connection between the *'apiru* and the Hebrews. A straightforward identification of the Hebrews with the *'apiru* is untenable, but it also fails to recognize the complexity of the sociopolitical landscape during the Late Bronze Age.

# EGYPTIAN TEXTS

In addition to the Akkadian texts from the rulers of the Canaanite city-states,[22] there are several Egyptian texts that have a bearing on reconstructing the emergence of Israel in Canaan. These include a number of texts that mention another nomadic group known as the Shasu, an inscribed column base fragment stored in the Egyptian Museum in Berlin, and the famous Merneptah Stele. We will examine each of these in turn, beginning with texts that discuss the Shasu.

## Shasu

Egyptian texts throughout the New Kingdom period mention the Shasu, another nomadic people in Syria-Palestine besides the *'apiru* who caused the Egyptians trouble. Though they were active in the Negev, Palestine, and Syria, they appear to have been more concentrated in the hills of Transjordan. The term *šzśw* (*shasu*), which first occurs in the early Eighteenth Dynasty, was a generically used Egyptian term for desert dwellers. It appears to have been derived from the verb *šzś*, which means to "go," "pass through," or "wander," and described a social class rather than an ethnic unity.[23] In this respect, the term *Shasu* is analogous to the modern term *Bedouin*. In the Egyptian sources, however, the Shasu are not described as pastoralists but as raiders who are viewed with disdain by the Egyptians. The parade example of this disdain is found in Papyrus Anastasi I, in which the scribe describes the dangers an Egyptian would face when traveling through Shasu country. While the traveler might encounter lions, leopards, or bears, he would, in fact, be "hemmed in on all sides by Shasu," whom he describes in these frightening terms:

> The face of the pass is dangerous with Shasu, hidden under the bushes. Some of them are 4 or 5 cubits, nose to foot, with wild faces. Their thoughts are not pretty, they do not listen to cajoling.[24]

The Shasu are here described as being 2.5 to 3.5 meters (8.2 to 11.4 feet) tall, a description that is clearly a stereotype. The point of the text is to convey the idea that the Shasu are ferocious savages. As such, they were sometimes the object of military action in northern Sinai and the Negev, as in the celebrated battle reliefs of Seti I at Karnak,[25] where the warriors appear with pointed beards and some sort of article of clothing wrapped around their upper bodies, and fight with small duckbill axes and spears. There is an interesting variation in the headgear of the Shasu depicted on these reliefs: some wear droopy caps, while others wear caps with short fringes on the back. It may be that the variations reflect different clans or tribes of Shasu, though this cannot be known for certain without some kind of textual confirmation.

In some texts, the term *Shasu* is combined with a second name that may either be a tribal name or a geographical region. Several of these have been of special interest to biblical scholars. The Nineteenth Dynasty Papyrus Anastasi VI, which dates to around 1192 B.C.E., refers to the Shasu of Edom, who were allowed to pass by the Fortress of Merneptah in order "to keep them alive and to keep their cattle alive."[26] The Edomites were a tribal people named after their eponymous ancestor, Esau, also known as "Edom," the brother of Jacob.[27] In this case, Edom is both a tribal name and a geographical area. A topographic list in Ramesses II's thirteenth-century Hypostyle Hall at 'Amrah West, which was copied from Amenhotep III's earlier temple at Soleb, which dates to around 1400 B.C.E., contains a group of six names, all of which are preceded by the words "Shasu land of." The first author to discuss these six "Shasu lands," B. Grdseloff, thought that all of them were located in Edom and northern Transjordan.[28] This was based on several identifications within the list. To begin with, the first "Shasu land" on the list is associated with the name *śe-'-r-er*, which he identified as "Seir," equated with Edom in the Hebrew Bible. The second "Shasu land" is associated with the name Laban, which is in fact identified as a Transjordanian toponym in Deut 1:1. The fifth "Shasu land" is associated with the name *yhwz*, which Grdseloff did not hesitate to identify with Yahweh. The proximity of "Shasu land of Seir" to the "Shasu land of Yahwa" led Grdseloff to conclude that these Shasu lands were both in the region of Edom, that one of them bore the name of Yahweh, and that this reinforced the theory that the cult of Yahweh originated from among the Kenites.[29]

Since Grdseloff first published his article, many scholars have adopted his reconstruction with practically no revision. Minimalist scholars have latched onto it as evidence that Yahwism evolved or originated from sources external to the Israelites. Donald Redford, for example, writes:

> For half a century it has been generally admitted that we have here the tetragrammaton, the name of the Israelite god "Yahweh"; and if this be the case, as it undoubtedly is, the passage constitutes the most precious indication of the whereabouts during the late 15th century BC of an enclave revering this god.[30]

Redford agrees that the land of the Shasu of Yahweh was located in Edom, and he argues that Yahwism originated when a tribe of Edomites migrated northwest and assimilated among proto-Israelite tribes in the mountains of Canaan. Gösta Ahlström had made a similar argument in 1986 by pointing to Judg 5:4, which commemorates the time when Yahweh "went out from Seir, when you marched from the region of Edom." Ahlström not only concluded that Yahweh originally came to Israel from the Edomites, but also that Mount Sinai must be in Edom.[31] Maximalist scholars, while they reject the idea that Yahwism originated from among the Edomites, have seen the topographical list at 'Amrah as locating early Israelites, identified as Shasu by the Egyptians, in the region of Edom as they travelled en route to Canaan from Egypt. Charles Aling and Clyde Billington have insisted that this "fits perfectly with the Early Date of the Exodus, but . . . presents major problems for those scholars who believe that the Exodus took place during the reign of Pharaoh Ramses II in the 13th century BC."[32]

Michael Astour's landmark study of the 'Amrah list, however, raises serious problems for the foregoing conclusions. First, Astour observes that, in the Egyptian name *śe-ʿ-r-er*, the letter *r* occurs twice, whereas it occurs only once in Seir. Astour notes that, while this phenomenon is usually explained as a simple case of duplication, the two *r*'s are not geminated but are, instead, separated by a vowel.[33] The Egyptian name *śe-ʿ-r-er* cannot be equated with the biblical Seir. Second, while "Laban" is named as a Transjordanian toponym in Deut 1:1, the name is not unknown elsewhere. It is also associated with Paddan-aram, for example, which may have been another name for Haran. Both names appear to refer to the same general area of northwest Mesopotamia.[34] Another town called Laban was located on the southern coast of Canaan near the Wadi al-'Aris.[35] Third, Astour's study shows that the geographical context in which the name *śe-ʿ-r-er* occurs suggests that it was located in Middle Syria rather than Edom.[36] Hoffmeier observes that, "if Astour is correct, the toponym containing the supposed divine name is placed hundreds of miles north, and thus either is not YHWH or is too far removed to have had any influence on Israel."[37] It also shows that the Shasu were not confined to the Sinai, Negev, and Transjordan, but were also located in northern and southern Palestine, Syria, and even Egypt, a fact already attested to in the textual sources.[38]

In addition to these arguments, the Hebrew Bible claims that three generations of Hebrews lived in Canaan before they immigrated to Egypt, and yet they were called Hebrews. Once in Egypt, they remained there for two to four centuries, during which time the Egyptians knew them as "Hebrews."[39] According to the biblical account, once they had left Egypt, they wandered in the wilderness for two generations. After they had settled in Canaan, they encountered the pharaoh Merneptah, who, while he recorded the encounter on a stele,[40] referred to them not as "Shasu" but as "Israel." As enticing as the identification of the Israelites with the Shasu may be, there still seem to be obstacles to a *carte blanche* identification of the Israelites with the Shasu.

Whether the ancient Israelites can be equated with the Shasu or not, it is clear from Papyrus Anastasi VI that, in addition to their other locations, there were Shasu in the region of Edom. Recently, as part of the Wadi Fidan Regional Archaeological Project, T. E. Levy and R. B. Adams discovered and excavated the largest Iron Age site in the survey, the Wadi Fidan 40 cemetery, one of the best-preserved tombs dating to the Iron Age.[41] The cemetery clearly reflects a population with a pastoral nomadic economy that can provisionally be identified with the Shasu. Based on surface distribution of grave structures, it appears that about 3,500 graves are located at this mortuary site, of which sixty-two circular graves were excavated. Ceramic grave goods were absent, while wooden bowl offerings were used instead. These attributes, along with others, indicate that the cemetery belonged to a pastoral group.[42]

This is a very significant excavation because it provides some of the first evidence for Iron Age pastoralists in Edom. The most ubiquitous grave offerings found in the Wadi Fidan District 40 Cemetery are beads, and a group of about 2,004 beads have been found in the excavated graves. These were strung in necklaces, bracelets, and anklets. Interestingly, there is an almost complete lack of copper among the mineral assemblage used for the beads. Levy, Adams, and Muniz postulate that the avoidance of copper by the Iron Age populations of the Wadi Fidan 40 Cemetery raises "the possibility that this population was not interested in the wealth of copper ores available nearby."[43] Levy has argued that the Israelite prohibition of making molten gods or images of God may have been an element of early Israelite ethnogenesis, as the early Israelites sought an avoidance strategy to distinguish themselves from the Edomites, for whom metallurgy was a key element of their own ethnogenesis.[44] This Shasu burial ground may represent a nascent Yahwist group that sought to distinguish itself from the early Edomites. Incidentally, a number of glass beads were also found in the burials that are similar to Egyptian beads of the early first millennium, "and an Egyptian origin [for the beads] cannot be ruled out."[45] The Wadi Fidan District 40 Cemetery is certainly suggestive of an early Israelite identification with the Shasu and, while it cannot be definitively established at this time, "the archaeological and textual/historical linkages . . . suggest that in this case the archaeological record supports the biblical and historical/textual evidence."[46]

As enticing as it may be to identify the Hebrews with the 'apiru of the Amarna tablets or the Shasu of the Egyptian texts, we must proceed with caution. During the transition from the Late Bronze to the Iron Age, the Eastern Mediterranean was surrounded by a periphery peopled by inhabitants who had a complex relationship with those who lived in the heart of the states. The peripheries could not support a sedentary lifestyle, and the pastoral economy in these zones relied on transhumance, the annual transfer of flocks between winter and summer pastures, a process that followed established routes. There were many such people groups who lived this way, and sorting them out is extremely complex, if not impossible. Understanding the very nature of nomadism has also proved to be a challenge. In his recent synthetic study of *The Eastern Mediterranean in the Age of Ramesses II*, Marc Van De Mieroop includes an insightful study of nomadic population groups in the region during the Late Bronze Age, and he makes two important observations that bear on our discussion of the 'apiru, the Shasu, and the Hebrews. The first observation has to do with the difficulty in identifying and distinguishing between the numerous nomadic populations. Van De Mieroop notes that one of the reasons for this difficulty is the lack of accuracy in the ancient sources with regard to the use of their names. A large number of names are preserved for these people, including the Lullumu, Qutu, Sutu, Habiru, Shosu, Medjay, and many others, and while one might think that these refer to well-defined groups of people, tribes, or tribal associations, the names are loosely applied in the ancient sources and appear to have been intended to allude to a way of life rather than necessarily to specific groups.[47] To further complicate matters, he demonstrates that terms used to refer to nomadic people in specific areas changed over time. In northern Syria during the second millennium, for example, there is a succession of names from Suteans, to Ahlamu, to Arameans. While it may be that these terms originally referred to different people groups that could be distinguished from one another, the terms were used interchangeably at one time or another in Syria-Palestine and in Mesopotamia.

The Suteans may have been a clearly defined group in northern Syria in the early second millennium, but it appears that their name evolved into a common designation for pastoral nomad, which could then pass from one language to another with reference to entirely different groups of people. It was picked up by the Hittites and applied to the Gasga, a nomadic people from the north of Anatolia who were not at all related to the people of northern Syria. Similarly, the name of the Gutians, a people who dwelled in the Zagros Mountains in the third millennium, was adopted by the first millennium Babylonians as an appellation for the Persians.[48] Van De Mieroop suggests nomadic groups may have been distinguished early on in their existence, but their names simply became terms of disparagement later on, and "the confusion of names partly reflects the ideology that nomadic people were outside history, and thus could be designated with outdated terms."[49] It is clear from the sources that their authors often had little knowledge about nomadic peoples other than their names, which they apparently did not use with precision.

A second observation Van De Mieroop makes about nomadic populations that is important for our discussion is that their main attribute in ancient Near Eastern texts, both from antiquity and more recently, is fierceness.[50] This is important because, in the discussion about the terms *'ivrim* and *'apiru*, it is sometimes assumed that military actions on the part of the *'ivrim* imply that they should be identified with the *'apiru*. In reading Gen 14:14, for example, Gottwald views Abraham's command of 318 warriors as counter to the peaceful role of the pastoralist, and this suggests to him that the patriarch is actually an *'apiru*.[51] The implication seems to be that if the term *'ivrim* has to do with pastoral nomadism, then that implies a peaceful role and precludes military activity, while *'apiru* suggests banditry. If ancient Hebrews engaged in military activity at all, therefore, then they must also have been *'apiru* and, in fact, the terms *'ivrim* and *'apiru* must have corresponded. This idea of pastoral nomads as peaceful wanderers is based on nineteenth-century perceptions of nomadism as an intermediary evolutionary step between hunter-gatherers and settled agriculturalists.

Ethnographic studies have revealed, however, that nomadism was not an intermediate stage in evolutionary development at all. Instead, we now know that pastoralists existed—and still exist—alongside settled populations, throughout ancient Near Eastern history. Rural populations have fluctuated between nomadism and sedentarization in the ancient Near East throughout its history. Ø. S. LaBianca explains that "the process of nomadization of rural households is best understood as a form of resistance, a sort of natural response by the rural population to the exploitative undertakings of urban elites."[52] And the reality in the ancient world, at least according to the literary sources, was that almost all interactions between states and nomadic groups were said to be military in nature.

In almost all the sources, pastoral nomads are depicted as stereotypically uncivilized, violent, and dangerous. Modern anthropological studies have confirmed that nomads—both ancient and modern—are not merely pastoralists, but they are also warriors. A. M. Khazanov, for example, affirms that "nomadic associations . . . in all circumstances . . . emerge for military-political reasons."[53] This seems to contradict the contemporary scholarly reconstruction of an idyllic coexistence between transhumant herdsmen and settled people. Anthropological studies have concluded that clashes between transhumant pastoralists and settled populations were more likely the exception rather than the rule and pastoralists and farmers complemented one another economically.[54] Van De Mieroop suggests the focus on hostilities and military clashes in the sources may simply reflect the concerns of those tasked to write governmental accounts—military clashes are a natural preoccupation of such works. These arguments, however, seem to belie numerous ethnographic studies that have shown that, in pastoral societies, all men are warriors, and they mobilize to act militarily when facing a dispute, injury, or threat. Philip Carl Salzman argues that, in pastoralist societies, "raiding and warfare is endemic, and violence is a way of life."[55] Salzman points to raiding for camels among the Bedouin, raiding villages to steal cattle, burn huts, and gain access to new territory by the Nuer, and raiding Persian villages for slaves, livestock, and carpets by the Sarhadi Baluch. Pastoralist groups have even been known to sometimes succeed in conquering and ruling settled societies.[56]

Besides knowing how to herd or farm, men in pastoralist societies must know how to fight, and they often devote a great deal of time to training to fight. The Maasai of Kenya and Tanzania, for example, are famous for their skill as warriors, which they focus on developing whenever they are not preoccupied with their pastoral work.[57] Wellhausen had observed that, in the early Arab empire, "the citizen list was the army register, the tribes and families forming the regiments and companies."[58] This "citizen army" brought region after region into military submission to the Muslim Empire for an entire century (632–732). Salzman argues that "what is absent in segmentary, tribal societies is civil peace, in which disputes and conflicts are resolved according to specified rules, without recourse to violence."[59] Regardless of the extent to which tribal societies include a militaristic bent, the point is that the ideas of pastoral nomadism and military activity are not mutually exclusive. Abraham could have engaged in military activity as a Hebrew without also being an *'apiru*[60] or a Shasu.

## An Inscribed Column Base Fragment in the Egyptian Museum in Berlin

Thus far, there have been no references to Israel discovered in Egyptian texts dating from the fifteenth to the fourteenth centuries B.C.E. In 2001, Manfred Görg claimed that he may have found one included in a partially preserved list of names inscribed on a column base fragment, now stored in the Egyptian Museum in Berlin.

The surviving names are Ashkelon, Canaan, and a third name that is incompletely preserved, but which Görg interprets as "Israel."[61] Bryant Wood has pointed to this translation as possible evidence that Israel was in Canaan already in the fifteenth-century B.C.E.[62] Hoffmeier, however, has argued that Görg's reading "is plagued by serious linguistic and orthographic problems that preclude it from being Israel."[63] If Hoffmeier's criticisms hold, then the Merneptah Stele remains as the sole reference to Israel from ancient Egypt.

## The Merneptah Stele

In 1897, W. M. F. Petrie published a stele that he had found in the ruins of Merneptah's mortuary temple at Thebes,[64] which contains a hymn that includes an account of a triumph over Asiatic peoples, including Israel, in its last poem. Merneptah, whose name means "beloved of Amun," was the twelfth son of Ramesses II. (Merneptah lived into his early 90s, outliving many of his sons.) He became the heir apparent and commander-in-chief of the army in Ramesses' fifty-fifth year and essentially took over the reign of Egypt during his father's final twelve years. When his father died in 1212 B.C.E., Merneptah became the fourth pharaoh of the Nineteenth Dynasty. He continued to live in Ramesses, the capital his father had built in the eastern Delta. By the end of Merneptah's third year, he made a campaign to Canaan, probably to quell unrest, since Egypt hadn't campaigned there since Ramesses II's twenty-first year—about fifty years earlier. During this campaign, Merneptah encountered Israel and bragged of defeating the fledgling nation. Merneptah's Canaanite campaign can be dated to the first few years of his reign, ca. 1210 B.C.E.[65] It consists of twenty-eight lines, all of which are complete. It's been described as a hymn to Merneptah, since it was written in a poetic style and is laudatory in nature. It begins with the exact day the text was composed in his fifth year of rule, and then is followed by twenty-six lines describing Merneptah's victory over the Libyans and the Sea Peoples, also in the fifth year of his reign. The last two lines seem to be an "addendum," giving a retrospective account of an earlier campaign to Canaan. This section reads as follows:

> The (foreign) chieftans lie prostrate, saying "Peace." Not one lifts his head among the Nine Bows. Libya is captured, while Hatti is pacified. Canaan is plundered, Ashkelon is carried off, and Gezer is captured. Yenoam is made into non-existence; Israel is wasted, its seed is not; and Hurru is become a widow because of Egypt. All lands united themselves in peace. Those who went about are subdued by the king of Upper and Lower Egypt . . . Merneptah.[66]

These lines were originally considered revolutionary, because they were understood to attest that by the end of the thirteenth century B.C.E., the Israelite tribes had achieved sufficient status to be deemed worthy of being defeated by the king of one of the most powerful nations on earth. This is the most important extrabiblical document relating to Israel's origins, in that it is the only direct reference to Israel found in Egyptian records and the only reference to Israel outside the Bible before the divided kingdom. In recent years, however, the appearance of "Israel" in the Merneptah stele has been challenged on several grounds, including the interpretation of the name, the location, and the nature of the group in question. There have been a number of detailed studies of these and other issues related to the stele in recent years, which we will summarize and reference here as we seek to determine the Merneptah Stele's contribution to reconstructing early Israelite origins.

## The Name of Merneptah's Israel

Since the discovery and initial publication of the Merneptah Stele, its use of the term *Ysr'el* has been understood as the earliest record of the name "Israel" yet discovered.[67] Beginning in the twentieth century, however, the identification of Merneptah's *Ysr'el* with the Israel of the Bible began to be challenged. Martin Noth argued that the group mentioned in the Merneptah Stele referred to an older group that bore the name "Israel," but who "for some now obscure historical reason passed it on to the 'Israel' that we know."[68] Noth did not offer any evidence for his conclusion, however, and no evidence has ever suggested that another "Israel" existed besides the one known from the Hebrew Bible. Otto Eissfeldt suggested that the term *Ysr'el* in the Merneptah Stele should really be read as "Jezreel."[69] Kenneth Kitchen effectively rebutted Eissfeldt's theory in 1966,[70] but contemporary scholars have continued to subscribe to it, either in whole or in part, including Philip Davies, Diana Edelman, Othniel Margalith, and Thomas L. Thompson.[71] The argument has been taken up most recently in an article by Ingrid Hjelm and Thomas Thompson, who argue that there are at least five different possible ways of translating the term *Ysr'el*, including "Sharon," "Yeshurun," "Asher," "Asher'el," and "Jezreel."[72] In a series of publications, Michael Hasel and Kenneth Kitchen have each provided definitive refutations of the argument that Merneptah's "Israel" should really be translated "Jezreel."[73] Their arguments can be summarized in three points. First, *Ysr'el*, as it appears in the Merneptah Stele, cannot be translated as "Jezreel." The Merneptah Stele is a New Kingdom period text and during this period the Hebrew sign for *zayin* was rendered as a *d* or a *t* and not as an *s*, which is what appears in the term *Ysr'el* in the Merneptah Stele. Second, the Egyptian term *Ysr'el* does not contain the Egyptian equivalent of an *ayin*, which would be necessary for it to equate with Jezreel. Third, the term *Ysr'el* contains a determinative for "people" rather than that for a geographical location. These three reasons cumulatively provide evidence against translating the Egyptian term *Ysr'el* with "Jezreel."

## The Location of Merneptah's Israel

In addition to the translation of the term *Ysr'el* on the Merneptah stele, its location has also been a subject of dispute. Eissfeldt's 1966 reading of *Ysr'el* as "Jezreel" was not only an argument for reading the term as a territorial designation rather than as the name of a people group, but it also situated Merneptah's *Ysr'el* between the hills around Samaria and the hills of Galilee. Although Eissfeldt's reading has long been considered discredited by Egyptologists,[74] some scholars continue to subscribe to it, as we saw above. Davies, for example, concedes that the alternative reading "Jezreel" is rendered "less likely" by criticisms such as the ones reviewed above, but he goes on to imply that the fact that Merneptah would have found it easier to fight in the plain of Jezreel than in the highlands may yet suggest that the translation of *Ysr'el* as Jezreel is correct.[75] Ahlström also argued that *Ysr'el* was a territorial term, but he sought to make a case that it applied to the central hill-country. He insisted that it was only with the development of the monarchy that the territorial term was taken up and applied to the highland settlers as a political entity. According to this view, the later political entity of Israel was distinct from the geographical territory of Israel first mentioned in the Merneptah stele.[76]

One of the major weaknesses of the argument that Merneptah's *Ysr'el* is a territorial appellation is the determinative with which it is connected. When Egyptian materials make reference to enemies that are countries or states, they are always preceded by the determinative sign for "foreign country" (the throw-stick plus the three-hills sign). This is the case with the specific Canaanite cities mentioned in the Merneptah stele. The term *Ysr'el*, however, is preceded by the determinative sign for a "people" rather than that of a "land" or "territory." Ahlström argues that this "does not necessarily contradict this proposal" that Merneptah's *Ysr'el* is a territorial appellation, because "determinatives were generally used rather loosely by scribes, especially when a people was called by the name of the territory they inhabited."[77] This argument has also been taken up by Lemche, who writes that "the inscription's use of determinatives is inconsistent."[78] The claim, however, is patently untrue. Kitchen has examined the stele in great detail in search of grammatical errors and has concluded that, out of 3,300 hieroglyphic signs, only about half a dozen "can possibly be regarded as serious scribal slips affecting the understanding of the text in any significant way."[79] In addition, Hasel has conducted numerous studies of determinative usage in New Kingdom texts and has found that they are used with extraordinary consistency.[80] The use of the determinative for "people" in conjunction with *Ysr'el* in the Merneptah stele is exactly what it appears to be, the naming of a people group rather than a territory, and it seems almost indisputable that this people group can be equated with biblical Israel.[81]

If one can accept that the Merneptah stele refers to Israel, then the question becomes one of whether or not the stele locates them and, if so, where. Nearly all investigators agree that the Canaan section of the Merneptah stele has a chiastic structure, a poetic format which has matching, or mirror image, elements before and after a focal, or climactic, point. Exactly how this format should be laid out has been a matter of heated discussion. The best arrangement so far may be that of Michael Hasel (**Fig. 8**), in which he explains the relationships between the various elements of the poem as follows: A and A' summarize the content of the poem as having to do with the binding of pharaoh's enemies; B and B' are what might be called global terms that describe Egypt's domination over entire lands and/or nations in the eastern Mediterranean; C and C' focus in on regions within these larger territories; while section D consists of the names of individual city-states and/or people groups

|  |  |  |
|---|---|---|
| **Verse Structure of the Merneptah Stele** | | |
| Binding of enemies | A | The princes are prostrate, saying "Peace!" Not one raises his head among the Nine Bows |
| Lands/Nations | B | Desolation for Tehenu; Hatti is pacified |
| Region | C | Plundered in Pa-Canaan with every evil |
| Cities/People | D | Carried off is Ashkelon<br>Captured is Gezer<br>Yenoam is made nonexistent<br>Israel is laid waste, his seed is not |
| Region | C' | Hurru is become a widow because of Egypt |
| Lands/Nations | B' | All lands together, they are pacified |
| Binding of enemies | A' | Everyone who was restless has been bound |

*Fig. 8*

he claimed to have conquered during his Canaanite campaign.[82] Roland de Vaux observed that the names Ashkelon, Gezer, Yenoʿam, and Israel are all mentioned between Canaan and Hurru, which are synonymous. Since Ashkelon and Gezer are in the south and Yenoam is in the north, he concluded Israel must either be in the north or in the center.[83] This conclusion, that Merneptah's Israel appears to have been located primarily in the central hill-country and Upper Galilee, has been confirmed by contemporary scholars and represents a near-consensus.[84]

## *The Nature of Merneptah's Israel*

If the name and location of this "Israel" have been agreed upon, its nature is still under dispute. Martin Noth argued that the Merneptah stele was of no help in understanding the nature of early Israel since, as mentioned above, it is "impossible to say with any certainty what the 'Israel' referred to here actually was in the Palestine of circa 1225 B.C., whether it was already the 'Israel' of the twelve tribes in the form known to Old Testament tradition or some still older entity"[85] Finkelstein states that the Merneptah stele does not provide "any clue" for the size or sociopolitical organization of the Israel mentioned therein. Thompson has repeatedly insisted that since this Israel is paired with Canaan, drawing boundaries between the two groups is uncalled-for.[86] Hjelm and Thompson together have argued that Merneptah's term *Israel* refers to the whole population of Canaan and not to the predecessors of biblical Israel.[87]

The two foregoing arguments are dispelled by the evidence from the stele. First, Hasel's explanation of the relationships between the various elements of the poem dispels the arguments of Hjelm and Thompson that Merneptah's "Israel" is simply another name for Canaan. Israel is not paired with Canaan, contra Hjelm and Thompson, but with Ashkelon, Gezer, and Yenoam, which are all names for cities and/or people groups defeated by the pharaoh. These four entities are paired together between the two C elements of the poem, where Canaan and Hurru are synonymously named as the region in which the pharaoh carried out his subjugations. Second, the assertion that nothing can be known about the nature of the Israel mentioned in the Merneptah stele is contradicted by the use of the determinative in the inscription. As mentioned above, the term *Ysr'el* is preceded by the determinative sign for a "people," which consists of a throw-stick for foreigners plus the man+woman over plural strokes, rather than that of a "land" or "territory." It is clear that the Israel referred to in the Merneptah stele is not a state but a socio-ethnic group. Kitchen insists that the use of the determinative leaves no doubt about the nature of Merneptah's Israel, that it is "the mark in numberless instances of a people-group, and not a settled state with an urban center. So far as Merenptah's soldiers, record-keepers, and this stele's scribe were concerned, this 'Israel' was a people-group in western Palestine, and neither a land nor a mini-state."[88]

As the only ancient Egyptian text containing a reference to Israel, the Merneptah stele is incredibly significant and has a direct bearing on the discussion about the date of the exodus and conquest. According to the early-date exodus-conquest, the period of the conquest and the judges began to transpire around 1406 and continued into the fourteenth century B.C.E. Since Egypt continued to exercise hegemony over Canaan and Syria from 1400 to 1250 B.C.E., the idea that Israel could attack vital Egyptian interests in Canaan without evoking a response stretches credulity. Scores of geographical texts and toponym lists are extant, and these preserve hundreds of toponyms from Canaan relating to the fifteenth and fourteenth centuries B.C.E., but none of them include a single reference to Israel or any of its tribes.[89] Neither do the biblical records, which include Mesopotamians, Moabites, Philistines, Canaanites, Midianites and Ishmaelites, Amorites, and Ammonites as having been among Israel's enemies.[90] If the exodus occurred in the thirteenth century B.C.E., then Merneptah's campaign may be understood as a response to Israelite expansion during the period of the judges.

## GREEK AND PHOENICIAN TEXTS

In a recent article, Anthony J. Frendo has called attention to Greek texts that explicitly attest to the tradition that early Israel emerged on the basis of military operations led by Joshua son of Nun.[91] These texts have not, as far as I am aware, ever been cited in any of the commentaries on Joshua or in any study on the emergence of Israel in Canaan. Their contents, however, are extremely important because they provide early extrabiblical attestation to the tradition that there was a military dimension to the early Israelite settlement. In the sixth century C.E., the Greek historian Procopius (ca. 500 C.E.), who served under Belisarius, general of the eastern emperor

Justinian, wrote an eight-volume work entitled *History of the Wars of Justinian*. In the course of his account, Procopius reports that Canaanites had built a fortress at a place called Tigisis, in Numidia. He notes they had left two columns with a Phoenician inscription in which they claimed they had fled from Joshua the son of Nun. Procopius writes as follows:

> They [the Canaanites] also built a fortress in Numidia, where now is the city called Tigisis. In that place are two columns made of white stone near by the great spring, having Phoenician letters cut in them which say in the Phoenician tongue: "We are they who fled from before the face of Joshua, the robber, the son of Nun."

This fascinating account automatically raises a number of questions, including the reliability of Procopius as a historian, the location of the city of Tigisis, where he claims these columns stood, and the date at which they were erected. With regard to the reliability of Procopius, he is generally regarded as very dependable. He received formal training in rhetoric and law, after which he received his post as a counselor on the staff of Belisarius. He was later made an assessor. After accompanying Belisarius on his Persian (527–531), African (533–536), and Italian (536–540) campaigns, Procopius remained in Constantinople, where he was appointed prefect of the city in 562. It should not be surprising that someone with his educational training and administrative roles would have been able to read Phoenician. He utilized written sources in Greek, Latin, and probably also Syriac, and there seems to be no reason to assume that he would not have been familiar with Phoenician as well. With the rise of Tyre and Sidon within Phoenicia and the growth in trade and overseas expansion in the first millennium B.C.E., Phoenician spread to Cyprus, Greece, North Africa, southwest Spain and the Balearic Islands, western Sicily, Sardinia, and Malta. Krahmalkov reports that "western Phoenician (Punic), the language of the Carthaginian state and its vast empire, rivaled in importance Greek and Latin in classical antiquity."[92] In North Africa, its usage continued well into the common era, with native speakers ranging from patristic writers to Roman emperors. In any case, even if Procopius could not read Phoenician, Browning notes that, "as Belisarius' confidant, [he] had direct and comprehensive acquaintance with military affairs and was favorably placed to interrogate eyewitnesses of what he had not himself seen."[93] If he could not have read the stelae himself, however, he could certainly have had someone translate them for him.

Also related to the question of whether Procopius can be considered reliable as a historian is the issue of ideology. P. C. Schmitz has argued that Moses of Khoren postdates Procopius, and that the (fictional?) Procopius stelae are probably simply an example of later Christian etiological writing, in this case intended to explain the Canaanite diaspora.[94] Schmitz has not, however, successfully demonstrated that Procopius was an ideologue who was writing Christian etiology. While some scholars had initially thought that Procopius was either a Jew or a Christian, it is not clear that he had any religion at all, and instead of having been an ideologue, he appears to have been skeptical about Old Testament revelation.[95] R. Browning compares Procopius to

Thucydides and concludes that "Procopius was a careful and intelligent man, of balanced judgment and sincere in his desire to establish the truth."[96]

As for the location of Tigisis, it cannot be determined conclusively, since several places bore the name in antiquity. Procopius narrows it down by specifying that the Tigisis to which he was referring was in Numidia, which is modern North Africa. In light of several factors that Frendo considers, he suggests that the city "is very likely to have been found somewhere in one of the modern North African countries of Tunisia or Algeria."[97]

As for the date of the inscribed columns Procopius claims to have seen, one might assume that they were carved in the sixth century C.E., shortly before Procopius saw them. There is, however, an even earlier reference to the two inscribed columns in Moses of Khoren (b. ca. 370–d. ca. 486 C.E.), an Armenian historian who lived and died before Procopius was even born.[98] P. C. Schmitz, however, has argued that Moses of Khoren postdates Procopius.[99] This cannot be said definitively, however, since the dates for Moses of Khoren are still under dispute.[100] The information contained in the Phoenician inscription is attested in even earlier materials, such as a Latin translation of the *Chronicon Paschale*, an anonymous work that claimed to be a universal history that began with the creation of the world and concluded with the events of about 630 C.E.[101] The original Greek text of this quotation dates to 234 B.C.E.[102] During this period, there were Jewish settlements throughout the Roman provinces of North Africa, including Tunisia and Algeria. If descendants of the Canaanites had fled to this area, they may have resented the growing Jewish population in the location where they had made their homes, and inscribed the columns about Joshua "the robber" to taunt them.

Procopius's two inscribed columns and the traditions to which they attest provide astounding extrabiblical attestation of the tradition that there was a military dimension to the early Israelite settlement. Paul Schröder, the nineteenth-century Phoenician scholar, upheld their authenticity,[103] and there does not seem to be any reason for modern scholars to doubt the existence of the inscribed columns. Frendo concludes that "it seems that in the central and western Mediterranean areas inhabited by the Phoenicians there had been a constant tradition in antiquity according to which these seafarers had once fled from Joshua who had invaded their land in the Levant. The two inscribed columns mentioned by Procopius show that the Canaanites/Phoenicians had this same self-awareness."[104] Modern scholars must incorporate the data from these "long-lost" Phoenician inscriptions into their study of early Israelite history.

# CONDITIONS IN PALESTINE

If we are to understand the ancient Near Eastern stage onto which ancient Israel emerged in the Late Bronze-Iron Age I, we cannot restrict ourselves to the southern Levant but must familiarize ourselves with the entire Eastern Mediterranean world. The age of Ramesses II was a time when powerful states throughout the Eastern Mediterranean shaped the society and economy of the region together through both peaceful and military processes. During the years 1500 to about 1350 B.C.E., the superpowers of Mittanni, the re-unified Egyptian state of the New Kingdom, Assyria, Babylonia, and Hatti all emerged. Thutmose III also mentions the kings of two states, Asy and Tanaya, neither of whose identity is certain. Asya may be associated with Cyprus, and Tanaya with the Greek mainland. Akhenaten clearly regarded the king of Cyprus as one of the great rulers of the Eastern Mediterranean, and the Aegean world seems to have housed a powerful state as well. The Elamite state emerged on the eastern fringe of the Eastern Mediterranean in around 1400.

From 1500 to 1350 all these states sought to expand, and their main area of conflict was Syria, which formed an interstitial zone. The most famous battle that occurred in this era was the battle of Qadesh, in middle Syria, fought between the Hittite King Muwatalli and Ramesses II, after which the northern part of what Egypt had considered its zone of influence came under Hittite control. In 1260, Ramesses concluded a peace treaty with the new Hittite king, Hattusili III, although Qadesh remained under Hittite control. All the states in the Eastern Mediterranean, however, either disappeared or were drastically reduced in size within 100 to 150 years, though the reasons for this are not entirely clear.

In 1250, the Eastern Mediterranean was still peaceful and stable. But these conditions began to deteriorate. Hattusa was abandoned at some point either during or after the reign of its last known king, Suppiluliuma II, and there is evidence of fires in the royal citadel and other official buildings. Egyptian sources report that foreign "Sea Peoples" suddenly overran Hatti. The accuracy of the account is questionable, however, since the destructions were localized and selective, and since a royal dynasty that continued Hittite traditions for centuries afterward survived in Carchemish. Similarly, several destructions occurred in the Mycenaean world, but they were not due to a single event and occurred over the course of several years. It appears that people of the Mycenaean world migrated east, including to Cyprus, where some sites were destroyed. Rather than having been devastated, however, it appears that power in Cyprus was subsequently centralized in coastal centers and that the island appears to have flourished for another century.

Ugarit was violently destroyed around 1200, but other cities in the area, such as Byblos, survived. In addition, Egyptian influence over Palestinian territories weakened, and Merneptah (ruled 1213–1204) and Ramesses III (ruled 1187–1156) both described having had to fight invading forces consisting of Libyans and "Peoples of the Sea," who wreaked havoc in Anatolia, northern Syria, and Cyprus before they attacked Egypt by land and sea. These descriptions are not completely accurate, however, as we know that some of the states they report as having been destroyed continued to survive (Carchemish and Alashiya), and the names of some of the attackers are known from prior sources.[105] It is clear, however, that Egyptian power had begun to wane. Further east, the city of Emar, on the Euphrates, was sacked soon after 1187; in Assyria, the assassination of King Tukulti-Ninurta I that had occurred in that country in 1207 had already brought that country's militarism to an end; and Babylonian power was shaken by an Elamite invasion in the mid-twelfth century. The changes brought about by the aforementioned turmoil were radical. The great states lost much of their power, and some disappeared completely. The level of economic activity sharply declined. As a result, culture declined, and there is little in the way of building remains, art, or even texts to illuminate this period. There was minimal urbanization during this period, and many people either lived in villages or migrated with their herds. New arrivals gained political power, including the Libyans in Egypt, Arameans in Syria and Mesopotamia, Persians in western Iran, Philistines and Israelites in Palestine, and others. By the time that historical data begins to become available again, in about the tenth century B.C.E., the Eastern Mediterranean world had undergone a great deal of change.

In *The Eastern Mediterranean in the Age of Ramesses II*, introduced above, Marc Van De Mieroop seeks to understand what caused these major historical changes in the history of the Eastern Mediterranean. The author approaches this question by focusing on the region of Palestine, which was at the center of the Eastern Mediterranean world. In the Late Bronze Age the area was the home of thriving city-states under Egyptian suzerainty, while several territorial states, including Israel and Judah, controlled the region during the early first millennium. Many of the old cities had been destroyed and new villages had been established in previously unoccupied highland zones. New population groups had arrived, including the Philistines, Israelites, and Moabites, and they wrote in their own languages rather than Babylonian in cuneiform. The inhabitants of the region differed from those who had inhabited it two hundred to three hundred years earlier, and the two periods are separated by a Dark Age, making it difficult to determine how the transition occurred. The Israelite conquest has been understood to have been the catalyst for change in the area: a new people entered Canaan, caused the urban traditions to come to an end, and colonized previously unsettled areas. Van De Mieroop notes the difficulties with the conquest theory that led to new theories focusing on social tension and, later, to other theories that emphasized migration. In recent years, scholars have begun to stress continuity over change, and some have suggested that there never was a Dark Age but instead that a new age simply evolved out of the previously existing Canaanite culture.[106]

As an example for the difficulties in interpreting the situation in Palestine, Van De Mieroop notes the difficulties of archaeological interpretation in the wider Eastern Mediterranean world, which can sometimes be construed to point to abrupt change while at other times to continuity. As an example, he cites the case of Hattusa, where the royal citadel, parts of the defensive walls, and temples throughout the city were burned down during the reign of Suppiluliuma II, the last Hittite king. Obviously, the destruction could have been caused by outside invaders. However, the fact that only public architecture was destroyed may suggest that the attack was not against the general population, but against the elite, which could suggest that the destruction was the result of a popular uprising. The excavator, Jürgen Seeher, has recently argued that the buildings were emptied and abandoned before they were destroyed, and that King Suppiluliuma II and his entourage left the city with the

## The Date of the Exodus-Conquest: Part II

contents of the buildings before they were attacked. Van De Mieroop concludes that "the burnt layers as evidence of violent citywide destruction fit well with the idea that the Hittite Empire ended in sudden disaster; today's reinterpretation suits better the now widespread view of gradual change and continuity."[107]

Van De Mieroop reviews some of the major causes that have been suggested for the end of the Bronze Age and notes some of their problems. First, he discusses invasions/migrations and destructions as a potential cause of the end of the Late Bronze Age. Many ancient texts present this image. For example, Ramesses III reports a sudden attack of "Sea Peoples" in 1180 B.C.E.:

> The foreign countries made a conspiracy in their islands. All at once the lands were removed and scattered in the fray. No land could stand before their arms, from Hatti, Kode, Carchemish, Arzawa, and Alashiya on, being cut off at [one time]. A camp [was set up] in one place in Amurru. They desolated its people, and its land was like that which had never come into being. They were coming forward toward Egypt, while the flame was prepared for them. Their confederation was the Peleset, Tjeker, Shekelesh, Denyen, and Weshes, lands united. They laid their hands upon the lands as far as the circuit of the earth, their hearts were confident and trusting: "Our plans will succeed!"[108]

The impression one gets from this account is that these island attackers were previously unknown immigrants. It is clear, however, from the accounts of the battle of Qadesh, that some of these Sea Peoples (Dardana, Lukka, and Shardana) were already serving in both the Hittite and Egyptian armies as early as ca. 1274 B.C.E., in the time of Ramesses II. Van De Mieroop concludes that "Ramesses III's portrayal of sudden invasions was thus certainly false."[109] Other data that have previously been understood as strengthening the general picture that invasion caused a collapse of the system have also recently begun to be reexamined, and a closer examination of the evidence for violent invasions reveals weaknesses and contradictions. Van De Mieroop writes:

> The Egyptian picture of a coordinated and sudden attack is refuted by the fact that two kings living several decades apart told essentially the same story and that long-known people were involved. The much later Greek accounts of migrations are too confused and contradictory to be useful. Ugarit's letters could bring to light something about the city's last days, but that is not certain. Moreover, they talk about small groups of ships—seven and twenty—not about a massive attack that would explain the destruction of the city that archaeology shows. The archaeological evidence of devastation throughout the Eastern Mediterranean spans several decades, so it does not validate the idea of a sudden wave of attacks.[110]

The idea of invasions as a source of historical change was very popular in the late nineteenth and early twentieth century, when colonization was seen in a positive light. In today's climate of anticolonization, however, few regard invasion in a positive light and, consequently, the Sea Peoples and others have come to be seen as having played less of a role as agents of historical change. While invasions may have been a contributing factor, Van De Mieroop suggests that they can no longer be regarded as the sole and crucial factor that led to the end of the Late Bronze Age.

A second potential explanation for the end of the Late Bronze Age discussed by the author has to do with natural causes, including earthquakes or climate change, which have become popular subjects in contemporary historical writing. While some cities may have come to an end as a result of earthquake activity, however, this would not have led to the end of the entire Bronze Age. Likewise, climate change may have meant a drier environment or even famines around 1200 B.C.E., but people had confronted years of drought before and found ways of coping with them.[111]

The third potential explanation for the end of the Bronze Age Van De Mieroop discusses is social tension, an idea which became especially common in the 1960s. Throughout the book, the author stresses the inequalities of Late Bronze Age societies. Van De Mieroop summarizes:

> Palace elites maintained a very high standard of living at the expense of the general populations. They separated themselves physically from the people by residing in restricted areas, they enjoyed a cosmopolitan lifestyle that made them more familiar with elites abroad than with their own countrymen, they buried themselves with staggering amounts of wealth, and so on. Admittedly, the economic conditions of the mass of the populations are hard to reconstruct. But in certain societies, especially in the Syro-Palestinian area, it seems that the numbers of farmers were very small in relation to the numbers of couriers they had to support. We estimate that a rural population of some 31,000 to 33,000 supported an urban one of some 6,000 to 8,000 at Ugarit. The figures are not firm, but reliable enough to suggest that too few people produced the income that enabled the urban elite to live in lavish circumstances.[112]

Van De Mieroop goes on to discuss similar difficulties throughout the Eastern Mediterranean and concludes that while social discontent was certainly not the only cause of the end of the Late Bronze Age, it must have been a significant contributing factor.

In addition, Van De Mieroop addresses the question of whether there was, in fact, a crisis in the twelfth century at all. He notes that, in reading the essays collected in *The Crisis Years: The 12th Century B.C. from Beyond the Danube to the Tigris*,[113] one gets the impression that no crisis occurred. A number of the essays emphasize that many Late Bronze Age practices continued into the Iron Age, numerous centers were *not* ruined, and specific regions were largely unaffected by the disturbances that did occur in specific areas of the Eastern Mediterranean. In the twelfth century, Cyprus flourished, Ugarit was soon resettled, and many Levantine harbors survived intact. For many of the contributors to this work, the changes in Palestine were gradual, and the various archaeological sites show a great deal of dissimilarity. In inland Syria, Babylonia, and Egypt, continuity is clearly evident. In this book, the early Iron Age was not a dark age. Instead, it is regarded as a time that signaled a new age that was being built on the remains of Canaanite civilization. Similarly, a section of a 2000 conference that focused on "The Dark Age That Never Was" consisted of speakers who insisted that the early Iron Age in the Eastern Mediterranean was not a period of decline, but a period in which social, economic, and political conditions were simply reconfigured.[114]

The current trend in scholarship, Van De Mieroop observes, "is to downplay the crisis aspect of the end of the Bronze Age and to stress the continuity with later periods."[115] Van De Mieroop concedes that many elements of the Bronze Age that were once thought to have disappeared did, in fact, continue after that period. The Hittite kingdom, for example, once thought to have ended with the sack of Hattusa, is now known to have survived in cities in the south of Anatolia and northern Syria. In addition, he notes that other examples from politics, economics, religion, culture, and social structure could be cited. It is certainly clear that Braudel's statement that "The twelfth century B.C. brought such catastrophes that the preceding centuries seem benign by comparison" is an overstatement that few would agree with today.[116] Van De Mieroop argues, however, that "the present focus on continuity is not without its modern intellectual bias, however," and he observes that

> Throughout the historical discipline many prefer to consider indigenous developments as motors of change over external influences and the arrival of foreigners. Invasion theories are out of fashion. Local histories are in style, and scholars like to stress the peculiarities of each case they investigate. Moreover, many do not like the idea of revolutionary change. In this view, revolutions do not really occur but there are only adjustments to existing systems that can be somewhat abrupt. Therefore they stress continuity.[117]

Van De Mieroop, however, sees the end of the Late Bronze Age as more than "a mere ripple" in the historical development of the region. He insists there was an interruption, and the most important change that happened was the disappearance of the Eastern Mediterranean system he describes in this volume.

In the final pages of the book, Van De Mieroop summarizes several clear characteristics of the Late Bronze Age system he has described in detail throughout the book. First, it was based on palaces located in urban centers, which linked together the political, social, economic, and cultural aspects of life in the Eastern Mediterranean. The economic system fostered by these palaces favored a small elite at the expense of the masses. Second, this system was international in character, fostering extensive intercultural interaction and exchange, both materially and intellectually. These fundamental characteristics disappeared around 1200 B.C.E. and, in this sense, the system collapsed. Van De Mieroop summarizes:

> Many of the palaces ceased to exist and the others were seriously weakened. The disappearances mostly happened in the western part of the Eastern Mediterranean, the Aegean, Anatolia, and the Levant. In other regions once mighty states—Egypt, Assyria, Babylon, and Elam—were reduced in size, losing access to resources from territories they had previously controlled. The loss of resources made it impossible to sustain their responsibilities as centers of redistribution, which affected all levels of society.[118]

The international framework crumbled, and new influential groups and individuals did arise, some of whom were likely immigrants from outside the Eastern Mediterranean, while others may have been formerly powerless elements of local populations. For example, Libyans settled in the Nile Delta, Arameans penetrated into many areas of Mesopotamia and, in Syria-Palestine, both nomadic and disenfranchised people settled in villages and cultivated fields in zones that, until that time, had gone unexploited. "Everywhere people had to create new lifestyles with a mixture of old and new that depended on local circumstances. They did build new societies on the ruins of the past; in some areas those ruins were still very prominent, whereas in others little survived."[119]

The question of what triggered these transformations cannot be answered with the citation of a single cause or event. Van De Mieroop suggests that the Late Bronze Age system contained the seeds of its own demise. International competition, foreign immigration, indigenous rebellion, drying of the climate, and other factors that were a part of the Late Bronze Age system held it together for three hundred years, but also caused it to begin to unravel. And once that began to happen, the resulting instability created the opportunity for others to begin to develop new living conditions.

S. Bunimovitz has raised questions about the relationship of the new highland settlements in Canaan and to the societal collapse at the end of the Late Bronze Age.[120] How long did Egyptian hegemony continue into this period, how far did it reach into Canaan, and how does this impact our reconstruction of the early Israelite settlement? Egyptian involvement in Canaan probably began after Thutmose III's military campaign to Canaan (ca. 1475 B.C.E.), but it was only after Amenhotep II's third campaign, three decades later, that the Egyptians imposed direct control over the region. Egypt was the dominant power in Syria-Palestine until around 1350, when Hittite expansion under Shuppiluliuma I (ruled 1350–1322) began to present a serious challenge to that dominance.

Egypt's influence in the region waned for a time, but it appears that Sety I (ruled 1290–1279) and Ramesses II (ruled 1279–1213) reestablished Egypt's military credibility, though their influence in northern Syria remained limited. The Hittite presence led to a change in Egypt's approach to ruling southern Syria and Palestine. Instead of depending on local administrative systems, Egypt now established direct control under its own officials. These officials lived in residences and garrisons built expressly for this purpose and they brought goods from their homeland with them so that they could continue to live a lifestyle similar to the one they experienced in Egypt. At the same time, locals increasingly adopted Egyptian behavior. Southern Syria-Palestine thus became annexed territory, although this process was less thorough than it was in Nubia.

A similar scenario is articulated by M. R. Adamthwaite, who argues that Egyptian occupation is clearly attested at sites all over Palestine until around 1150 B.C.E.[121] He points to sherds inscribed in hieratic discovered at Lachish that may indicate the operation of an Egyptian taxation system there during the Ramesside period, and he argues that a bronze plaque bearing the prenomen of Ramesses III gives a *terminus post quem* for the gatehouse where it was found. He points to similar data at Megiddo and Beth-shan, and concludes that "the Late Bronze era was one of Egyptian presence and occupation. Furthermore, this picture is so pervasive that on present historical-chronological schemes an Israelite presence much before 1150 B.C.E. is hard to reconcile with it."

B. M. Bryan has recently challenged this prevailing view of direct Egyptian governance of Canaan.[122] She argues that Canaan was administered by local, not Egyptian, rulers, who adapted some elements of pharaonic iconography to represent themselves. There is an increase of Egyptian style objects in the early twelfth century, but she suggests that this reflects a desire on the part of Canaan's ruling elite to emulate the superior Egyptian culture. Bryan's elite-emulation theory has been severely criticized, however,[123] and the current consensus appears to be that in the thirteenth century, "Egypt's agenda changed from a more 'hands-off' approach to a stronger imposition of military and administrative rule that impacted the country as a whole."[124] Carolyn Higginbotham, however, has made a strong case that both the textual and the archaeological evidence fail to provide a complete correlation with what we expect from either direct Egyptian rule or an elite-emulation model. She argues that the data suggests that each model applies to some degree in Ramesside Canaan.[125] In any case, the situation changed after the death of Merneptah, who was followed by a succession of four very weak rulers who basically abandoned Canaan for the next quarter century (ca. 1213–1185 B.C.E.).

Some have suggested that the political vacuum in the central hill-country of Canaan created by this hiatus of Egyptian domination appears to have been the most likely window of opportunity for the establishment of the new highland settlements, and that it corresponds with the ceramic chronology of these sites.[126] This seems too late, however, to place the emergence of the Israelites in the central hill-country of Canaan. One of the most outstanding Iron Age I sites, Mount Ebal, which we will discuss in chapter 9, was founded in the mid-to-late thirteenth century B.C.E.[127] In addition, the destruction of Hazor appears to have occurred in about 1230 B.C.E.[128] The book of Joshua specifically states that Hazor was the only town situated on a mound that Israel burned (11:13). If the Israelites are indeed to be associated with the destruction of that Canaanite city, they would have to have been in the land by that time.

If Egyptian military and administrative rule did continue until the death of Merneptah at locations such as Megiddo and Beth-shan, these centers lay in the plains, and the absence of defensive walls among the highland settlements may suggest that those who settled there, at least during this period, may have thought of the Egyptians as either incapable or at least not interested in penetrating the hill-country where these villages were located.[129] Y. Aharoni observed that Thutmose III's topographical lists did not even include the lower parts of the Galilee, the Shephelah, the Negev, the highlands of Judah and Ephraim, the southern end of the Jordan Valley, Gilead, or the southern part of Transjordan.[130]

Kitchen argues, on the basis of a text at Ramesses II's temple in Luxor, that during his conquest of Moab, the pharaoh circled the southern highlands of Canaan without entering them.[131] It does appear that the Egyptians had a low view of the highlands during the Nineteenth Dynasty, which can be illustrated with an Egyptian letter by a royal official named Hori that was used for training apprentice scribes. In a summary catalogue of places in the Egyptian empire in Asia, Hori describes the Syro-Palestinian highlands as a dangerous place inaccessible with chariots, which must be disassembled and carried if one is to ascend there. The highlands are populated by wild animals and bandits, who hide under the bushes. Some of these bandits, Hori claims, are seven to nine feet tall. Those who venture into these areas will be seized with trembling and will constantly be breaking into a run out of fear that an enemy is behind them. For those who venture into the highlands, Hori concludes, "Thou seest the taste of pain!"[132]

# CONCLUSION

Based on our foregoing analysis of the extrabiblical textual data, an identification of the ancient Hebrews with the Habiru does not seem tenable. Linguistic factors, usage of the terms, and the temporal and geographic range of the Habiru seem to mitigate against such an association. There are many affinities between the ancient Hebrews and the Shasu, yet we cannot make a carte blanche association of these two groups either. The difficulty in identifying and distinguishing between the numerous nomadic populations of the Late Bronze Age Mediterranean world should caution us against easy associations, and studying the nature of nomadism during this period may indicate that the representation of the Hebrews in the Bible comports well with the portrayal of nomadic peoples in the extrabiblical sources, especially that of the Shasu. If the ancient Hebrews were not Shasu, however, they must have closely resembled them.

With regard to the extrabiblical textual data that reveal conditions in Canaan, it appears that, by the middle of the Eighteenth Dynasty, the Egyptians viewed the highlands with disdain and had little interest in the area. The political vacuum created by Egypt's disinterest in the area would have allowed for Israelite settlement there in either the fifteenth or the thirteenth century B.C.E., though the biblical and extrabiblical evidence we have examined in this chapter suggest the latter date. Regardless of one's preferences, the Merneptah stele clearly sets a *terminus ante quem* of about 1210 B.C.E. for the arrival of the Israelites in Canaan.

CHAPTER 5

# MAJOR CITIES OF THE CONQUEST

In this chapter, we will review the historical and archaeological data relevant to the Hebrew Bible's reports that the early Israelites took these cities militarily. Our focus will be on undertaking a balanced reading that neither reads more into the text than it claims nor diminishes what it does claim.

## JERICHO

Joshua 6 reports the attack and conquering of the city of Jericho. The text reports that Jericho "was shut up inside and out because of the Israelites" (6:1). YHWH told Joshua that YHWH was handing Jericho over to him, "along with its king and soldiers" (v. 2). Joshua and the warriors were to walk around the city once a day for six days (v. 3), with "seven priests bearing seven trumpets of rams' horns before the ark" (4a). On the seventh day, seven circumambulations were to be completed, with the priests blowing on the trumpets all the while (v. 4b). At the end of this process, the priests would issue a long blast with their trumpets, and with that sound "the wall of the city will fall down flat, and all the people shall charge straight ahead" (v. 5). Joshua relayed these commands (vv. 6-7), and the process began (vv. 8-14). At the end of the series of marches on the seventh day (vv. 15-16), the priests blew the trumpets, Joshua instructed the people to shout, and then repeated the instructions about how "the city and all that is in it [were to be] devoted to the LORD for destruction," except for Rahab and her house, who were to be spared (vv. 17-19). As soon as the people shouted, "the wall fell down flat; so the people charged straight ahead into the city and captured it. Then they devoted to destruction by the edge of the sword all in the city, both men and women, young and old, oxen, sheep, and donkeys" (vv. 20-21).

This portion of text seems to describe Israel's first victory in Canaan as a major conquest, and as such, its *realia* generated an interest going back into antiquity. Eusebius, probably writing before the Edict of Milan in 312 C.E., noted that remains of Jericho's earlier cities were still visible at the site.[1] Jerome acknowledged the same some sixty years later[2] and in 333, the "pilgrim of Bordeaux" reportedly explored it.[3] But early Christian interpreters seldom, if ever, showed any concern for historical issues in their exegesis of Joshua 6, concentrating instead on spiritual exegesis.[4] Later

Jewish commentators carried out a similar form of exegesis, which focused on spiritual rather than historical issues.[5] It was only in the nineteenth century that a focus on identifying the site and its remains began to emerge. In 1838, E. Robinson and E. Smith explored a village situated in the midst of the vast plain of the Jordan Valley, called Erîha, which they explained as "a degenerate shoot, both in name and character, of the ancient Jericho."[6] In the end, however, they remained unsatisfied with the location of "the former Jericho."[7] Today, most accept an identification of the oldest city of Jericho with the main mound of the oasis, Tell es-Sultan (M.R. 192.142).

## History of Excavations at Tell es-Sultan

The first preliminary excavations were carried out at Jericho in 1868 by Charles Warren, who cut east-west trenches across the mound and sank some eight-foot square shafts down to bedrock. In doing so, he cut through the Early Bronze Age town wall and missed the famous Neolithic tower by just about three feet; therefore he concluded that there was nothing to be found on the mound of Jericho.[8] But it appears that either few biblical interpreters were aware of Warren's work at Jericho or they did not see it as relevant for the exegesis of Josh 6. The Reverend F. B. Meyer, for example, interpreted Josh 6 in a way very much reminiscent of the spiritual exegesis of the Patristic period.[9] Even Keil and Delitsch, who so often concerned themselves with historical-critical issues, failed to mention it and, likewise, carried out a spiritual exegesis.[10]

The first scientific excavations at Tell es-Sultan were carried out from 1907–1909 and again in 1911 under the direction of Ernst Sellin and Carl Watzinger. They excavated a considerable portion of the tell, discovered a section of the Middle Bronze Age glacis on the northern, western, and eastern sides of the tell, and found segments of walls dating to the Early Bronze Age. Sellin and Watzinger dated the walls to the first half of the second millennium, which appeared to confirm the biblical story of the city's capture by Joshua.[11] Watzinger, however, later revised his views and concluded the outer revetment had been destroyed in about 1600 B.C.E. and the walls dated to the third millennium B.C.E.[12]

Within just a few years, John Garstang, who disagreed with Watzinger's findings, undertook a new excavation. During the years 1930–1936, Garstang carried out excavations that exposed material from the Neolithic, Early, Middle and Late Bronze Ages, and the Iron Age. Garstang found five tombs on the west side of town that dated to the Middle Bronze Age. On the tell, Garstang excavated two major constructions, the "Palace," which he concluded had been founded in the Middle Bronze Age, and the "Middle Building," the associated pottery of which he dated to the Late Bronze Age I.[13] With respect to fortifications, Garstang excavated a series of walls in his City IV, which he dated to the end of the Late Bronze Age I.[14] The main defenses followed the upper brink of the city mound and consisted of two parallel walls. The outer wall was about six feet thick and the inner wall twelve feet thick. Investigations along the west side showed continuous signs of destruction and burning. This wall was only preserved where it abutted the citadel, or tower, where it was preserved to a height of eighteen feet. Everywhere else it had fallen into the space between the two walls, which was filled with ruins and debris. The remains of the outer wall had fallen down the slope. The excavator dated the destruction of the Late Bronze Age City of Jericho, along with its walls, after 1400 but before 1385 B.C.E., and concluded that "the destruction of the Fourth City corresponds in all material particulars with the Biblical narrative of the Fall of Jericho before the Israelites under Joshua."[15]

In his commentary on the books of Joshua and Judges, Garstang works backward from the number 480, given in 1 Kgs 6:1, to the date of 1400 B.C.E. for Joshua's invasion of Canaan,[16] and it is to this date that he narrows down the destruction of the Fourth City at Jericho.[17] Garstang's conclusions were criticized by Albright, who argued that his dates were too early.[18] Consequently Garstang modified his date to a time period between 1400 and the accession of Akhenaton (ca. 1370–1353 B.C.E.).[19] Albright himself placed the destruction of Jericho sometime before 1220 B.C.E.[20] Vincent, too, argued that Garstang's dates were "extremely too high," and insisted that they needed to be brought down at least a century.[21] He proposed a date for the fall of Jericho between 1250 and 1200 B.C.E., a view with which Schaeffer and de Vaux both agreed.[22] Garstang did not, however, bring his conclusions about the end of City IV any lower than the mid-fourteenth century B.C.E.

Almost two decades after Garstang dug at Jericho, excavation techniques improved dramatically with the innovations of Sir Mortimer Wheeler and Dame Kathleen Kenyon with regard to stratigraphical methods. Dame Kenyon excavated at Jericho from 1952 to 1958, in an effort to clarify the results of her predecessor, John Garstang. She excavated several tombs ranging in date from the Early Bronze Age I to the Roman period. Over the course of her excavations, she dug three main trenches on the western, northeastern, and southern ends of the mound (**Fig. 9**).

Fig. 9

In addition, she excavated a number of squares on the tell, which were either partially or fully excavated to bedrock. Of particular relevance for this study are the Late Bronze Age walls in Garstang's City D, which he associated with the destruction of Jericho by Joshua. Kenyon argued that these were misdated, and she identified them as two successive phases of a Bronze Age town wall.[23]

In her initial review of Garstang's work at Jericho, Kenyon concluded that there was a gap in occupation at Jericho on both the tell and in the tombs from the end of the Middle Bronze Age II (ca. 1550 B.C.E.) until the early Iron Age.[24] In 1954, however, after several seasons of excavation, Kenyon discovered Late Bronze Age remains and revised her position.[25]

Kenyon found portions of three walls on the northern edge of the tell, although only the stone foundations survived, and some of the stones of these foundations were missing. To the south of one of these walls, a very small area of intact floor survives. A *tabun* was situated on the floor and, next to it, a dipper juglet was found.[26] The juglet was crushed but complete, and Kenyon dated it to the fourteenth century.[27] She concluded that there clearly *had* been occupation at Jericho during the Late Bronze Age II, and she imagined that "the small fragment of a building which we have found is part of the kitchen of a Canaanite woman, who may have dropped the juglet beside the oven and fled at the sound of the trumpets of Joshua's men."[28]

While Kenyon ascertained that there had been a Late Bronze Age town at Jericho, she concluded that the latest occupation at the site should be dated to the third quarter of the fourteenth century B.C.E., a date "which suits neither the school of scholars which would date the entry of the Israelites into Palestine to c. 1400 B.C. nor the school which prefers a date of c. 1260 B.C."[29] She admitted the possibility, however, that "a yet later Late Bronze Age town may have been even more completely washed away than that which so meagerly survives." Kenyon stressed repeatedly in numerous publications the extensive damage that erosion had done at Tell es-Sultan. However, some scholars dismissed the idea that erosion could have eliminated a Late Bronze Age occupation at Tell es-Sultan as special pleading.[30] Kenyon stressed, however, that most of the summit of the tell, even the houses of the Middle Bronze Age town, which had housed a considerable number of people, had all vanished. In addition, most buildings had also washed away on the east slope. Despite construction of the town of 1400 B.C.E. on top of the wash that interrupted this process, once it was abandoned, the erosion continued and removed most of it. So if there were walls in the Late Bronze Age, there is no trace left of them.

No one can conclusively say there were no Late Bronze Age walls, because much of the city's defenses from other periods were destroyed, and even the summit of the Middle Bronze Age rampart only survives in one place. Kenyon suggested that the Late Bronze Age inhabitants must have reused materials, or they may have built a new wall above it, of which nothing remains.[31] Some argue that this is also "special pleading." Aaron Burke, for example, in his recent study of the evolution of Middle Bronze Age fortification strategies in the Levant, argues that this possibility "finds no support," and that "no walls of any Early or Middle Bronze Age site lasted for three hundred years without needing to be rebuilt."[32] Many sites, however, show evidence of continuity from the Middle Bronze Age II to the Late Bronze Age with respect to fortifications, and their inhabitants made no effort to renovate or repair the ramparts.[33] This leaves open the question of whether these fortifications may have continued to be used by Late Bronze Age occupants at the site of Jericho.[34] Alternatively, the possibility that either a stone or mud-brick wall may have been built atop the Early Bronze Age wall also finds clear precedent. At Bethsaida, for example, Iron Age walls were constructed on top of the Early Bronze Age walls. Why should the inhabitants of the city not have taken advantage of earlier work and existing elevation?

Even after Kenyon's excavations at Tell es-Sultan, the Late Bronze Age at Jericho is still best represented in Garstang's published and unpublished materials, which Piotr Bienkowski suggests should be reexamined. In examining the tombs on the west side of town that Garstang dated to the Middle Bronze Age, Bienkowski found that they were reused in the Late Bronze Age II. But not much can be said about the "Palace," owing to the scarcity of published data about it. Almost twenty years later, when Kenyon undertook work at Jericho, she thought that no dating evidence related to this building had been published at all and so was unclear about its date. She suggested that it may even be Iron Age.[35] The only part of this building that had survived *in situ* was the foundation, and Garstang had only excavated a small area of the building.[36] He dated the founding of this building to the Middle Bronze Age II, but Bienkowski observed that four sherds from the palace appear to date to the Late Bronze Age.[37] If the Jericho palace was built in the Middle Bronze Age, it obviously still stood in the Late Bronze Age and appears to have been in use during that period. The evidence is insufficient to go beyond these approximations.

The second major construction that may date to the Late Bronze Age is what Garstang called the "Middle Building," because it is situated between the Middle Bronze Age and Iron Age levels.[38] The Middle Building measured about 47 x 39 feet and had seven rooms, one of which may have been a courtyard. A terracotta figurine of a naked female, measuring about 3.5 inches high, found in one of these rooms, has clear Late Bronze Age parallels.[39] The pottery found in association with the Middle Building clearly dates from the Late Bronze Age IIA or early IIB.[40] The Middle Building may have been built and used from about 1425/1400 to about 1275 B.C.E. As with the "Palace," however, a lack of stratification makes it impossible for a definitive dating of the building to be established.

Bienkowski concludes that it seems "extremely unlikely" there were city walls at Jericho in the Late Bronze Age, and the actual area of occupation was probably limited to the area around the Middle Building.[41] He suggests that a small, unfortified Jericho would not have been unusual in Late Bronze Age Canaan, since about 37 percent of known settlements were less than 2.5 acres in size, and the vast majority of these were unfortified.[42] Gonen suggests that, while Jericho may have been similar, there may have been either a fortified palace or a ceremonial gate.[43] In any case, the relationship between the work of Garstang and Kenyon and the issue of the extent of Late Bronze Age Jericho warrants further consideration. In the meantime, the assumption shared by virtually all biblical scholars today, and many archaeologists, of there being no Late Bronze Age remains found at Tell es-Sultan is simply incorrect.

As we have seen, the archaeological data make it clear that there was occupation in the second half of the Late Bronze Age, though it cannot indicate anything beyond this general conclusion.[44] Kenyon herself believed that the data was insufficient cause to reject the general historicity of the account of the conquest of Jericho. She observed that "all the canons of historical criticism demand that we accept the main facts of the story of the conquest of Jericho as authentic, for it was obviously an event of great importance in the ultimate dominance of the Israelites in Palestine, and the wealth of detail makes it clear that it was a faithful verbal record handed down for generations until it was incorporated in a written record."[45] At the same time, Kenyon did not believe that one had to accept the exact chronological succession of subsequent events or the nearly immediate conquest of the rest of the land. Instead, she followed Aharoni in concluding that the Israelite penetration into the land occurred very gradually and, to a great degree, peacefully.[46] The scholarly world in general, however, perceived Kenyon's findings as having been negative with regard to Jericho's habitation in the Late Bronze Age, and this perception would play an important role in ongoing biblical studies.

Subsequently there have been renewed excavations at Jericho. In 1997, an Italian-Palestinian team resumed excavations at the tell, under the direction of N. Marchetti, L. Nigro, and I. Sarrie. They have exposed portions of the Early Bronze III rampart in Areas B and D, and have made correlations with the earlier excavations of Sellin and Kenyon. As a result of the discovery of a mud-brick wall on top of the Middle Bronze II glacis, as well as a tower that may have been part of a city-gate, they were able to check the chronology of the fortification system.[47] Unfortunately, the work of the Italian-Palestinian team has not discovered any new data related to the Late Bronze or Iron Age I and has no contribution to make to the interpretation of Josh 6.

## The Impact of the Archaeological Findings at Jericho on Biblical Studies

M. Noth published his *Überlieferungsgeschichtliche Studien*[48] in 1943, almost ten years before Kenyon began excavating at Jericho, and his articulation of the idea of the Deuteronomistic History[49] (DtrH) had important implications for the understanding of the book of Joshua as historiography. Noth argued that the history found in the books of Deuteronomy through 2 Kings was the work of a single author (the Deuteronomistic Historian [Dtr]) writing shortly after 562 B.C.E., the date of the last recorded event (2 Kgs 25:27-30). Noth explained that Dtr "did not write his history to provide entertainment in hours of leisure or to satisfy a curiosity about national history, but intended it to teach the true *meaning* of the history of Israel from the occupation to the destruction of the old order."[50] The purpose of Israelite historiography, therefore, was understood to be theological and etiological.[51] This is not to say that Noth believed the history recounted in the Hebrew Bible is fictitious; indeed, he accepted the essential historicity of Israel's national epic.[52] However, Noth saw the Israelite emergence as "a long process which certainly did not begin with the conquest of cities."[53] Noth explained:

> On the contrary, the attacks on isolated Canaanite cities probably did not take place until the Israelite tribes had established themselves in their vicinity, in uninhabited or only sparsely inhabited areas and had thus gained a footing for themselves in Palestine. The occupation of Canaanite cities which were situated for the most part on the borders of Israelite territory, may be thought of at most as the very last stage in the process of occupation, if it is not in fact even better to think of it as a development and rounding off of the process of occupation, and a coming to terms with the earlier inhabitants after the real occupation was over.[54]

## Major Cities of the Conquest

The stories of the conquests of Canaanite cities are, according to Noth, etiological legends based on the fact that these cities were already in ruins. Their destruction had already taken place before the Israelites' occupation, so the Israelites were able to simply take possession of them. Noth had already explained this with regard to Josh 6 long before Kenyon's excavations.[55] When Kenyon published her aforementioned findings on the wall, however, Noth saw this as a confirmation of his etiological reading of Josh. 6. He believed that such an impressive wall as the one that should have stood at Late Bronze Age Jericho could not have disappeared without leaving any trace. The fact that extensive excavations had been carried out at the tell suggested to him the improbability that the wall still remained to be found elsewhere on the site. For Noth, therefore, the absence of any evidence of the wall presented unequivocal proof that the wall did not exist.[56]

There seemed to be a confluence of the two streams of Noth's hypothesis of the Deuteronomistic History and the archaeological findings that had begun to emerge from Tell es-Sultan, and many biblical commentators writing on the book of Joshua have followed its flow. The recognition of etiological elements in the book of Joshua has led to extremely low estimates of their historicity, and the archaeological data has been understood as substantiating those conclusions.[57]

Writing in the wake of Noth, J. A. Soggin understands Josh 6 primarily as a liturgical text that includes a symbolic action representing "conquest," in which only a minimal part of the original narrative has been retained. The text is a complicated conglomeration of different strata that may include: the Benjamite saga of Rahab; an Ephraimite recension introducing Joshua; a national recension by the compiler of which virtually nothing remains; a first recension introducing the ark; and a second recension concerning the ark. Verse 6, along with elements in verses 8, 10, and 16b-20, are all Deuteronomic re-elaboration and glosses (vv. 4, 13, 15b).[58] As a result of this understanding, Soggin concludes that "the historicity of the fall of Jericho in the ritual circumstances described in this chapter seems extremely unlikely."[59] Soggin notes that, as a liturgical text, the passage poses no problem, but "for the historian the true problems only begin with the artificial rehistoricization carried out either by the 'compiler' or later by Dtr."[60] Soggin then reviews the archaeological findings at Jericho, and concludes by citing the aforementioned conclusions of Noth, and explains that "this situation . . . is what we would expect to find after our analysis of the literary condition and tradition history of ch. 6."[61] While Soggin's reading of Josh 6 appears to be based on his literary-critical understandings of the text, he sees the excavation results from tell es-Sultan as verification for his interpretation.

J. Gray also posits an etiological explanation for the story of a march around the city by silent warriors who then raise a shout at a given signal, after which the walls collapse and the city is taken and put under the ban. He explains that this "is possibly the tradition of the Rachel group, later Ephraim and Benjamin. It may reflect their surprise at finding such a site as Jericho by its strong spring and with ample evidence of its former strength virtually an open settlement, if not actually derelict."[62] To substantiate this idea, Gray cites Kenyon's tentative dating of the fall of Late Bronze

Age Jericho to ca. 1350–1325 B.C.E.[63] The same approach is followed by R. Nelson. At the beginning of his commentary on Joshua, in a section entitled "Joshua and History," Nelson discusses the difficulty with ascertaining how earliest Israel came into being. He concludes that "one thing has become increasingly clear, however. The archaeological record does not support Joshua's story of a conquest by a people arriving from outside Palestine."[64] Nelson notes that Jericho does not appear to have been "occupied in a significant way" in the Late Bronze Age II, and there could not therefore have been a conquest of Jericho. Nelson goes on to explain that Joshua's real value lies in what it can reveal about the later generations who compiled it. "The needs of an increasingly centralized monarchy would have favored the growth of a unified narrative of origins," and "any such narrative was bound to tell of a unified invasion and successful conquest from the outside, for that would be the best way to coordinate Israel's presence and claim on the land with its deeply-rooted tradition of an exodus from Egypt and its poems and tales of Yahweh as Divine Warrior."[65] In this scheme, the etiological stories in the book of Joshua of "victories over vanished peoples provided a natural explanation for the ruined cities that dotted the landscape."[66] The stories in Joshua functioned as a "myth of origins" to bolster Judah's national identity and pride.

In his commentary in the *New Interpreter's Bible*, R. B. Coote engages in an extensive discussion of the compositional history of the book of Joshua. He explains that, following the death of Moses, Joshua leads the Hebrew people in "an orgy of terror, violence, and mayhem," in order to reach "the savage goal toward which God's creation of Israel and delivery of Israel from slavery in Egypt appears to point from the start."[67] Coote argues that, among other things, "the notion of a unified conquest involving mass murder," along with the disagreement of the story with the archaeological evidence of the period before the Israelite monarchy, indicate that the book of Joshua "was not composed all at once as an accurate account of an episode in the history of pre-monarchic Israel," but an account of a gradual composition that took place "from two hundred to six hundred years after the supposed events occurred."[68] In his reconstruction of the compositional history of Joshua, Coote explains that the book of Joshua was not the original ending of the pre-priestly Tetrateuch, which preceded DtrH. The pre-priestly Tetrateuch consisted of two strands of narrative, the early house of David's history of Israel (J), and a slightly later northern Israelite supplement (E). Coote writes that "the J and E strands give little indication of how God's promise of land is to be fulfilled. They seem to take it for granted that David (in the case of J) and the kings of Israel (in the case of E) possess sovereignty over the land of Israel, as sanctioned by God, and devote most of their attention to other concerns."[69]

These strands, Coote argues, cannot be traced into Deuteronomy and Joshua. These strands do not end with a conquest, but with their own respective themes, E with Exodus and J with Numbers. Coote insists that these strands not only "fail to refer to a conquest," "but they also give no indication that the promise of the land is to be fulfilled in a *blitzkrieg* and attempted ethnic cleansing. Nor is there a hint of God's command to exterminate the Canaanites, to say nothing of the particular contours and emphases of the book of Joshua."⁷⁰ Ultimately, the story of Joshua's conquest is patterned on Josiah's "reconquest," and is designed to function as a tool to pressure and compel all his subjects into full submission to his reign. Coote explains:

> The historian wants to terrorize the populace, particularly its recalcitrant political leaders, into submission to Josiah by showing what happens to a class of people ("Canaanites") whose interests are opposed to the interests of Josiah's monarchy and of the peasantry under him. The writer shows that obedience to Josiah can take precedence over supposed ethnic affiliation: Canaanites can submit and be saved (Rahab, the Gibeonites), and if a Judahite belonging to the Israelite in-group disobeys the commander-in-chief, he can be repudiated and killed (Achan).⁷¹

Josiah's court historiographer, therefore, "uses the rhetoric of warfare and nationalism as an encouragement and a threat to its own population to submit voluntarily to the central authority of a government struggling to organize itself and to [re]create its own ideological framework of inclusion. In order to justify violent action [to that end], the dynamics of the literature of warfare usually consist of a division [often outrageously overstated] between self and other."⁷² Coote finds "much about the book of Joshua . . . repulsive, starting with ethnic cleansing, the savage dispossession and genocide of native peoples, and the massacre of women and children—all not simply condoned but ordered by God. These features are worse than abhorrent; they are far beyond the pale."⁷³

Coote's reconstruction of the compositional history of the book only partially ameliorates Joshua from its imperialistic themes, as the final product is still understood as a propagandistic tool for nationalistic purposes, which are potentially oppressive and discriminatory. In any case, Coote turns to the archaeological evidence to substantiate his reading of the text as ahistorical, and explains that "archaeological evidence . . . fails to agree with a Late Bronze Age destruction of Jericho and with few, if any, of the other episodes of destruction described in Joshua."⁷⁴ He suggests that Jericho "had no significant occupation during the Late Bronze Age, when the incidents in Joshua would have occurred."⁷⁵ To a degree, this may exculpate the ancient Israelites from the genocide with which it is associated in the book of Joshua.

C. Pressler stresses that Joshua is not historical or military reporting, but theological or even doxological literature. She stresses that "the truth of this liturgically shaped story has less to do with facts about something that happened long ago and more to do with the ongoing reality of divine sovereignty and divine generosity."⁷⁶ Pressler turns immediately, however, to a review of the archaeological evidence, and notes that, "given the purpose of the narrative, [the fact that] archaeological evidence casts doubt on the historicity of the Jericho account should not come as a surprise."⁷⁷ After summarizing the history of excavation, Pressler concludes that "at best, Jericho was a poor, small, unwalled village when Joshua was supposed to have conquered it. More likely, it was an uninhabited ruin."⁷⁸ The book of Joshua began to receive its final shape in the late seventh century B.C.E., during the reign of King Josiah, who led the nation of Judah in a program of nationalistic expansion and religious reform during a period of Assyrian weakness. "The stories in Joshua, re-presenting Israel's past as one nation—with one central leader, under the rule of one God—supported Josiah's nationalistic program."[79]

Likewise, J. F. D. Creach also understands that the book of Joshua "must be classified as the kind of history that was written in the ancient world to trace national origins and to support nationalistic goals"[80] and appeals to the archaeological evidence for support. He concludes that the city of Jericho, along with that of Ai, "seem to have been small, unwalled settlements at that time and throughout the Late Bronze II period (1400–1200 B.C.)."[81]

Most scholars have taken similar approaches to those discussed above, both in terms of the way they have drawn conclusions based on the work of Dame Kenyon and in the way they have incorporated those conclusions into their commentaries on Joshua.[82] Some, however, have sought other explanations. M. H. Woudstra, for example, responded to Kenyon's findings by asserting that "the question of [site] identification must be left open," as "there are still various unexplored tells in the vicinity."[83] Another scholar, B. Wood, has argued for a return to Garstang's dating of the fall of City IV on the basis of his own examination of the pottery and other materials from Jericho that only became available in Kenyon's final reports, published posthumously only in the 1980s.[84] Wood suggests that Kenyon's methodology in dating some of the pottery remains at Jericho was flawed, since it relied on imported pottery types from tombs for its typology rather than the more common local, domestic wares that were found much more widely throughout the mound. He argues that some of the pottery she identified as Middle Bronze Age should actually be dated to the Late Bronze Age I. Bienkowski has vigorously challenged Wood's conclusions[85] and has insisted that Kenyon's original dating of these pieces was correct. Wood responded with a cogent rebuttal,[86] but because he had only made his case in the popular publication *Biblical Archaeology Review* rather than in scholarly journals, his arguments have gained little traction. Since Wood's case supports an early-date exodus-conquest, evangelical commentators often point to his work. D. M. Howard Jr., for example, suggests that "if he is correct—and his evidence is very persuasive—then the archaeological evidence from Jericho fits the biblical picture very well."[87] When viewed by itself, however, the pottery Wood uses for redating purposes appears to be Middle Bronze IIC (1650–1550 B.C.E.).[88]

## The Relationship between Archaeological Data and the Hebrew Bible

The current consensus of archaeologists[89] and biblical scholars[90] is that the results of the excavations at Tell es-Sultan contradict the account of the conquest of Jericho as presented in the book of Joshua. Chronicling the ways in which archaeological excavations have influenced scholarly interpretation of Josh 6 suggests at least two things. First, I would suggest that the logic of these commentators, as exhibited in their discussions of Josh 6, reveal the ongoing influence of positivism. The commentators on Josh 6 each demonstrate a subtle acknowledgment of the belief that archaeology can prove the Bible. Since archaeologists did not find evidence of the biblical events of Jericho at Tell es-Sultan, then the biblical account has been disproved. D. Merling observes that "the logic and corollary to this logic would be: the truthfulness of the biblical text has been disproved by archaeology; therefore, it is also possible that archaeology could have proved the truthfulness of the Bible."[91] Merling concludes: "In short, whether [biblical commentators, historians, and/or archaeologists] are willing to admit it or not, their acceptance that the Bible has been disproved is evidence that they believe that archaeology can prove the Bible."[92]

What this means is that positivism is still a philosophical premise that underlies much of modern scholarship. This assertion leads to the second, which has to do with the implications of positivism. Despite the criticisms we noted in chapter 1, I do not believe the influence of positivism, as well as other social science assumptions,[93] is wholly negative. As G. A. Herion suggests, it "often work[s] to restrict historical reconstructions by imposing limits on the range of understandable options available to historians even prior to an examination of the evidence."[94] This can be seen in the survey of scholarly interpretations of Josh 6, which all seem to perceive the archaeological evidence as presenting an "either-or" choice. Either the evidence supports the biblical account of Joshua's conquest of Jericho, or it does not. However, if historians are to escape these limitations on the range of understandable options, a more nuanced understanding of the relationship between text, archaeology, and history is necessary.

The relationship between archaeological and textual data, in this case, the Bible, is a controversial subject about which there is wide disagreement. B. Halpern has suggested that archaeologists and textual scholars usually engage in a "monologue." He explains that "we have the madness of textual analysis, with its vast range of explications and over-publication, in which standards of evidence vary disastrously, and in which there is a frequent and lamentable tendency for readers to respond to publications without understanding the questions they pose."[95] Some scholars, who have become fed up with what they view as an over-reliance on "subjective" texts, argue that archaeology should write independent histories, free of any reliance on texts at all. S. A. Rosen, for example, as noted in chapter 1, argues that archaeology should be used "independent of standard text-based historical reconstruction."[96] J. M. Miller, however, has called into question the very possibility of constructing frameworks for the interpretation of artifacts from Iron Age Palestine without using concepts from the Bible. He argues, "Simply to use the name 'Israel' in association with the Iron Age means to draw on written sources."[97] Similarly, B. Halpern has accused those who attempt to dispense with the biblical text in the process of writing histories of Israel of "abdicating" the historian's responsibility to consider the text carefully for what information it might provide.[98] Instead of trying to reconstruct the history of Israel or an episode within that history based solely on either texts or archaeology, scholars must recognize the limitations of both texts and physical data, and a "holistic approach to the source materials bearing on . . . the ancient Near East" should be adopted."[99]

While the current consensus among archaeologists may be that the results of the excavations at Tell es-Sultan completely contradict the account of the conquest of Jericho in the book of Joshua, these were not the conclusions of Dame Kathleen Kenyon herself. She discovered Late Bronze Age walls and buildings at Jericho, which suggested to her that the site was inhabited during the Late Bronze Age, even if only sparsely. And, this small Late Bronze Age settlement at Jericho also came to an end by destruction.[100] She had insisted, however, that archaeology *does not* provide an answer as to how Jericho factored into the experience of early Israel in Canaan. Many of the commentators' discussions reviewed above acknowledged this Late Bronze Age occupation at Jericho, but still argue that the archaeological data *does* provide the answer as to what role Jericho plays in the early history of Israel. And their argument is that it contradicts the biblical account of Joshua's conquest of Jericho. While there are remains for Late Bronze Age habitation at Jericho, these are dismissed because they do not correspond with what readers of Joshua believe they *should* find at Late Bronze Age Jericho based on their reading of Joshua. A holistic reading of Joshua 6 should acknowledge the limitations of both the text and the physical data.

## A Careful Reading of Joshua 6 and Its Implications

In a series of articles, D. Merling and R. S. Hess pointed out some limitations of the text that seem to have been overlooked by modern interpreters. Chief among them is the fact that the meaning of the text is limited to its own milieu, and when modern, twenty-first-century readers forget that and impose their own presuppositions on the text, it will precondition what kinds of results they expect to find archaeologically.[101] A careful reading of the text of Joshua must be carried out to determine what the text actually says about the city of Jericho and what scholars might expect to find in the way of its archaeological remains. R. S. Hess has recently insisted that what is meant by "city," what kinds of walls and gate are pictured, the role of the "king," the probable size of his army, and other issues in the text all need to be reexamined.[102] I will comment on the definition of the term *city*, the walls of Jericho, and the role of the king. For further discussion, I will refer readers to the aforementioned article by Hess.

Modern readers can hardly help but interpret the word עִיר (*city*) through the lens of modern Western civilization. J. A. Dearman, for example, defines a city as a "sedentary communal existence, with basic social institutions and shared building projects," and notes that the term by itself "does not preserve much specificity," and "can be used for almost any settlement."[103] He adds, however, that "related architectural vocabulary . . . such as gates, walls, and temples, helps in defining a city."[104] Dearman goes on to discuss examples of cities with these characteristics, which may reinforce the assumption that עִיר refers primarily to a substantial, urban kind of settlement. T. M. Willis defines a city as "a settlement with walls and one or more gates."[105] These impressions of what a city is have had a great impact on the way scholars have conceived of biblical Jericho in Josh 6:1.

## Major Cities of the Conquest

In the nineteenth century, Keil and Delitzsch, for example, assumed that the "city" of "Jericho was not only the first, but the strongest town of Canaan, and such was the key to the conquest of the whole land,"[106] though the biblical text itself nowhere states this. Modern commentators have continued to make these kinds of assumptions about Jericho. S. L. McKenzie, for example, notes that "Jericho was the oldest city in Canaan and a legendary symbol of Canaanite might. As such, it symbolized Canaan."[107] While Jericho was an important ancient city, the site itself was relatively small; the seventy-eight-foot high tell spanned only about 10 acres. The abundant water supply provided by the perennial spring, Ain es-Sultan, located east of the tell, and the fact that the situation of the site at one thousand feet below sea level created a tropical climate conducive to agriculture, were both factors that made Jericho desirable. The location of Jericho near the Dead Sea created economic opportunities, and it was located near a major ford in the Jordan River. L. F. DeVries explains that this meant that the city

> was a gateway from the Transjordan and the plains of Moab to western Palestine . . . situated on the major east-west trade route that controlled the flow of traffic from the Transjordan area westward into the central hill country, including the city of Jerusalem located approximately fourteen miles southwest of Jericho, as well as traffic that moved eastward from western Palestine into the Transjordan. Jericho was also located on an important north-south highway that connected the city with Bethshan to the north. Consequently, the possession of Jericho carried with it numerous benefits, including control of the major entrance to western Palestine from the Transjordan, control of the water rights and the oasis-like garden land east of the city, and the control of mineral traffic in the Dead Sea area.[108]

While DeVries makes important points here, one should not overstate the importance of Jericho. R. G. Boling stresses that "it is not quite accurate to say that Jericho commands the approaches to the central highlands," and he notes that "there are a number of routes" that those entering the land could take "without being blocked by forces based at Jericho."[109] Nothing in the text of Joshua indicates that Jericho played such an important, legendary role in the Israelite imagination as McKenzie thinks. While the adjective גָּדוֹל, "great," is attached to the city of Gibeon (Josh 10:2), and Hazor is described as "the head of all those kingdoms" (Josh 11:10), Jericho is never designated by anything except the term עִיר. Hess notes that this term does not always signify a metropolis, but can be used for small villages (e.g., 1 Sam 20:6) and even tent encampments (Judg 10:4; 1 Chr 2:22-23).[110] He notes with special interest the use of עִיר for fortresses, as at Rabbah of Ammon, where the term designates the citadel (2 Sam 12:26), or at Jerusalem, where the term was used for the fortress of Zion (2 Sam 5:7, 9; 1 Chr 11:5, 7).[111] The site of Tell es-Sultan is not large (only about 10 acres), but it does hold a strategic position at the entrance to several of the main roads that lead from the Jordan Valley into the central hill country. Hess suggests that it may have been a fort maintained by one or more of the hill-country sites to guard the passes to the city or cities.[112] G. E. Wright had already suggested this long ago, even though he, too, went on to write about the "great city."[113]

Jericho's walls and gates have also been the subject of reader embellishment. As early as the fourth century B.C.E., it seems that the urban surroundings of the translators of the LXX influenced the way they read the Hebrew text of Josh 6:1. While the MT reads סֹגֶרֶת וּמְסֻגֶּרֶת, which simply means that the city "was tightly shut up," the LXX reads Συγκεκλεισμένη καὶ ὠχυρωμένη, "shut up and fortified." The MT of Josh 6:1 does not, however, mention fortifications, though the assumption that the text implies that they were there continues to be reflected in modern commentaries. In R. D. Nelson's commentary, for example, the author reads Josh 6:1 as implying that the inhabitants of Jericho locked themselves up behind "impregnable walls."[114] The fact that Kenyon's excavations did not find a Late Bronze Age fortification system with walls and gates has led many to conclude that the archaeological data contradicts the biblical story.

However, the typical Hebrew word for "wall," חוֹמָה, only appears twice in Josh 6, and nowhere does the text indicate what kinds of walls were envisioned. Kenyon suggested that the inhabitants of Late Bronze Age II Jericho may have reused the walls of the Middle Bronze Age II city.[115] Merling notes that "while her suggestion is possible, it is equally possible that the Jericho that the Israelites attacked had walls that were a single line of unbaked mud-bricks or were composed of a small circle of mud-brick houses built side by side."[116] A circle of buildings could certainly have included an inn, as well as government or military quarters. As for the Hebrew term for "gate," שַׁעַר, it does not occur in Josh 6, but is inferred in verse 1 from its two occurrences in 2:5 and 7. The biblical story relates that Jericho had a gate, but one cannot, simply by reading the story, draw any conclusions about the gate, whether it was huge and impressive or small and fragile.

Hess notes that "the strongest textual objection to the image of Jericho as a fort occurs with the appearance of the king of Jericho."[117] Aside from its occurrences in Josh 2:2-3, the Hebrew word for "king," מֶלֶךְ, (*mlk*) occurs only once in Josh 6:2. If a traditional king is intended, then Jericho was the center of his realm and his subjects would have lived around the site and in the surrounding vicinity. Since the text seems to describe a largely uninhabited region, from Adam in the north to the Dead Sea in the south, and since this is reflected archaeologically, this is also seen as evidence that Josh 6 was composed in a later period by writers whose familiarity with monarchy is projected back into this text. Through a careful study of semantic equivalents in Akkadian and Ugaritic texts, Hess suggests that the *mlk* root "may have appeared as a verb in West Semitic during the fourteenth and thirteenth centuries, with the sense of a ruler or administrator, though not necessarily the sole king who answers to no one."[118] Through specific evidence in the El Amarna tablets, Hess makes the case that, during this time, "a noun from the root *mlk* carries the sense of a commissioner responsible to his overlord for the military security of a region."[119]

Based on this data, as well as others not discussed here, both Merling and Hess conclude that Jericho in the Late Bronze Age II was not a metropolitan center, but was more likely an outpost or fort, maintained perhaps by one or more hill-country sites such as Bethel or Jerusalem.[120] Hess suggests that "it could have guarded the passes to these

## Major Cities of the Conquest

cities and also provided a means of monitoring and perhaps collecting taxes from those traveling in the Jordan Valley."[121] During the period of the judges, Jericho appears to have functioned in a similar capacity, but this time under the auspices of Transjordanian peoples. During this period, at least some of the Israelites were "defeated" by an alliance of Moabites, Ammonites, and Amalekites, who stationed "King Eglon" at Jericho in order to monitor and maintain Israel's subservience (Judg 3:12-14).

Almost thirty years ago, drawing on 1 Cor 15:14, in which the apostle Paul argues that "if Christ has not been raised, then our proclamation has been in vain and your faith has been in vain," G. W. Ramsey asked whether "if Jericho was not razed, is our faith in vain?"[122] He was concerned with the question of whether the theological premises of the Bible could still be tenable if the historical episodes on which they claimed to be based had not actually happened or had not actually happened in the way that the Bible claims they did. In addition to Ramsey, many others have sought to resolve this question theologically.[123]

While biblical studies have seen many trends emerge that do not concern themselves with historical-critical issues, we have seen in this chapter that the theses of many interpreters are often predicated on archaeology. Josh 6 is a prime example of this. Most commentators today understand the book of Joshua as part of the DtrH, and find varying degrees of historicity behind its narratives. While some commentators continue to find a high degree of historical reliability in the book of Joshua, it seems that a majority have concluded that the book is primarily theological and etiological. Both of these groups, however, appear to believe that "if Jericho is not razed, then our faith is in vain," and therefore make recourse to archaeology in order to verify their respective approaches. I am not arguing that one should *not* appeal to archaeology. Instead, my purpose has been to show that the choices made by the interpreters about how the archaeological data from Tell es-Sultan relate to Josh 6, whether for the sake of building a "minimalist" or a "maximalist" reconstruction of the events,[124] have been based on the reader's conception of what is being envisioned therein.

Interpreters of Josh 6 have often understood it to be describing a massive military assault on a huge, heavily fortified, metropolitan city that served as the center of the realm of a traditional king. Based on the sparse remains at Tell es-Sultan datable to the Late Bronze Age II, the archaeological data has been conventionally understood as contradicting the Bible. "Some blame the Bible for its weakness, while others blame archaeology for its limitations. [The] real blame lies in false expectations."[125] Following the work of Merling, Hess, and others, when one undertakes a close study of the Hebrew text of Josh 6 to see what the text actually says, the idea that it describes a massive military assault on a huge, heavily fortified, metropolitan city that served as the center of the realm of a traditional king turns out to be a chimera.

## AI

The second city that features in the Conquest account is called הָעַי, which is a combination of city name, עַי, plus the definite article, הָ, or "the," which would make the name of the city "the Ai," instead of just "Ai." In any case, the city is first mentioned as a landmark in the account of Abram's early migration into the land of Canaan, where it is said to be located east of Bethel (Gen 12:8; 13:3).

Joshua's conquest of Ai is recounted in Josh 7:2-5 and 8:1-29. The text claims that "Joshua burned Ai, and made it forever a heap of ruins, as it is to this day" (Josh 8:28). Subsequent texts note that Gibeon was "larger than Ai" (10:2) and that Ai is located "next to Bethel" (12:9). In the *Onomasticon* of Eusebius, the Bishop of Caesarea explains that Ai was located as a minor ruin east of Bethel, which he locates twelve Roman miles north of Jerusalem, on the right side of the road that leads to Neapolis (modern Nablus).[126] This identification in the *Onomasticon* does not help locate the site of Ai definitively, since there are other small ruins in the area.

In 1838, Edward Robinson (1794–1863) suggested two sites, et-Tell and Khirbet Haiyan, as possibilities for the location of Ai.[127] Since he did not see any evidence of ancient settlement at et-Tell, he favored Khirbet Haiyan. In 1866, on the basis of biblical references and the topography of the area, Captain Charles Wilson identified Ai with et-Tell.[128] Before the end of the first quarter of the twentieth century, there were several efforts to identify biblical Ai.[129] In 1924, however, W. F. Albright conducted a surface survey of the region east of Bethel, and he concluded that et-Tell was the only Canaanite ruin east of Beitin, which he identified as Bethel, that was a viable candidate for biblical Ai.[130] Albright's article, along with his subsequent writings,[131] more or less established et-Tell (**Fig. 10**), a 27.5-acre site east of modern Beitin (which is conventionally identified as Bethel), as the accepted location of biblical Ai, which few have questioned since.

*Fig. 10*

## History of Excavations at et-Tell

John Garstang (1876–1956) made soundings at et-Tell in 1928 and opened eight trenches, but never published his findings. He claimed that he had excavated Late Bronze Age pottery on the site that dated to ca. 1400 B.C.E.,[132] but this pottery has never been found, making a second opinion impossible. The supposed discovery of a 1400-B.C.E. city supported Garstang's date for Jericho, confirming an early-date reconstruction of the exodus-conquest.

Judith Marquet-Krause (1906–1936), an Israeli, who studied French, Akkadian, Syrian, and Armenian at the École des Hautes Études and Near East at the Louvre du École, began working with John Garstang at Jericho in 1932 or 1933, where she dealt with artifacts discovered in graves. When she was twenty-seven, Baron de Rothschild asked her to lead an archaeological team to excavate the city of Ai. Marquet-Krause accepted and eagerly went to et-Tell to confirm the description in Joshua of Ai as a royal Canaanite city that was conquered by the Israelites. In 1928 Garstang had sketched what he thought was the complete site, and Marquet-Krause confined her excavations to this area.

In the first campaign, she uncovered a so-called palace, a part of an Iron Age I village, and tombs in a necropolis northeast of the tell. In 1934, she continued work on the Iron Age village, excavated fortifications in the lower city, and discovered the "sanctuary" on the acropolis. In a final campaign in 1935, she sought to complete the excavation of the Iron Age village and discovered it had been built on top of remains from the Early Bronze Age and there was no evidence of any occupation between those two periods. All of the remains in the lower-city dated to the Early Bronze Age, and the Iron Age village appeared to be confined to the acropolis. Marquet-Krause concluded that Ai had been an important city during the Early Bronze Age, but that it had been completely destroyed and abandoned at the end of that period.

The unfortified village from the early Israelite period appeared to have been founded peacefully on an abandoned site in about 1220 B.C.E., and existed until about 1050 B.C.E., when it was abandoned.[133] Following the interpretation of her mentor, M. R. Dussaud, Marquet-Krause reached the conclusion that there had been no conquest at Ai, and that the account in Josh 7–8 must be legend rather than history.[134] Martin Noth followed this interpretation, stressing the etiological role of the conquest account.[135] Needless to say, this conclusion was controversial, and several scholars attempted to cope with it with various proposals, including Albright's hypothesis that the destruction he had found at Bethel had been applied to the city of Ai.[136]

J. A. Callaway went to et-Tell in May of 1964 and, as a devout Southern Baptist, entertained hopes of "bridging the widening gulf between the biblical accounts in Joshua 7–8 and the actual evidence of the ruin itself."[137] He extended the areas excavated by Marquet-Krause but was only able to confirm her conclusions that the site had been abandoned at the end of the Early Bronze Age and had remained so until around 1200 B.C.E., when it appeared to have been peacefully settled. Callaway thought that et-Tell may not be the correct location for Ai, and he pursued alternatives.[138] In 1964, he conducted a sounding at Khirbet Haiyan, but found no pottery earlier than the Roman period. In 1966, he excavated a large area at Khirbet Khudriya and discovered fifteen tombs in the adjacent Wadi Asas. One tomb, located far down the valley east of Khudriya, dated to the Middle Bronze Age IIB, but all the others contained no evidence earlier than Late Hellenistic. There was no evidence in any of the tombs of the Late Bronze or Iron Age II. A third site, Khirbet Hai, was explored on a one-day expedition, but all the surface pottery and architecture appeared to be Mamluk (1291–1516 C.E.), although some pre-Byzantine sherds were found on the small, unfortified site. Callaway concluded that "there is no Late Bronze evidence in the region east of Bethel that I can find," and this led him to construe with Albright's earlier statement that there is no other viable candidate for Ai than et-Tell.[139]

Callaway was still convinced, however, "that there is too much historical evidence to call the conquest of Ai legend or etiology."[140] Callaway suggested that there were two closely limited Iron I phases at Ai, the first being a three-acre Canaanite village and the second simply a repair of the same buildings. He proposed that the Israelites infiltrated from Transjordan, took the Phase 1 village, and established the Phase 2 village. He had already concluded that the destructions of Bethel, Lachish, Tell Beit Mirsim, and Hazor in the Late Bronze Age could not be attributed to an invasion of the Israelites and proposed that the conquest be redated to the Iron Age I. He wrote that "the emerging picture of the conquest that I see in the archaeological evidence is one of minor scale raids on small villages like the Phase I settlement at Ai, but mainly it is a picture of political integration with the Iron Age I inhabitants of the land, such as those at Gibeon."[141] Callaway felt that Albright's Conquest Theory was no longer tenable, but he was not ready to accept Noth's etiological views, which he believed were unacceptable. He thought his proposal retained "the essential historicity of the conquest," even though it scaled it down significantly.[142]

Callaway went on to direct nine seasons of excavation from 1964 to 1976, but his work only reinforced the conclusions of Marquet-Krause. The city was inhabited as early as 3200 B.C.E., and a 27.5-acre walled city was developed beginning at the beginning of the Early Bronze Age I, about 3100 B.C.E. The buildings and fortifications were remodeled in the Early Bronze Age II (2950–2775 B.C.E.) and reconstructed in the Early Bronze Age III (2775–2400 B.C.E.). The site was destroyed in 2400 B.C.E. and abandoned for the next 1,200 years. A small, unfortified village with agricultural terraces was founded on the site at the beginning of the Iron Age I, around 1200 B.C.E. Callaway estimated the population of this early Iron Age I village at about 150 to 300 people.

## The Impact of Archaeological Findings at et-Tell on Biblical Studies

By 1985, Callaway reached the conclusion that the evidence at Ai could not be forced to support an Israelite Conquest, and in an article with the evocative title, "Was My Excavation of Ai Worthwhile?" he admitted that "the Joint Expedition to Ai worked nine seasons between 1964 and 1976 and spent nearly $200,000, only to eliminate the historical underpinning of the Ai account in the Bible."[143] He insisted, however, that his work had not been in vain, and the challenge to generations of "positivistic" historical reconstructions was forcing scholarly thinking in new directions. In his struggle to make sense out of the data, Callaway embraced Alt's theory of a two-staged process of settlement, in which the Israelites peacefully immigrated into Canaan and only later engaged in military activities as they sought to expand their territory. As Callaway examined the village culture in the highlands, he concluded that the inhabitants were first and foremost farmers who had fixed patterns of village life prior to their settlement. As he examined the material culture more closely, he came to believe that it most closely resembled that of the Canaanite cities in the lowlands. While he embraced Alt's thesis that the highland settlers were peaceful immigrants, he rejected the idea that they came from Transjordan and concluded instead that they had come from the Canaanite cities in the lowlands and coastal regions north and west of the central hill-country.[144] Since Callaway was a Southern Baptist, these conclusions were very controversial among evangelical scholars,[145] but they were embraced by mainstream scholars and reflect the consensus that exists among many scholars today about the Israelite settlement.[146]

The absence of Late Bronze Age remains at et-Tell have led scholars to reach a variety of conclusions. Like Callaway, many scholars have concluded that the biblical story of Ai must be legendary or etiological. Other scholars have concluded that et-Tell may be incorrectly identified as the location of biblical Ai. There have, in fact, been other candidates for biblical Ai since the beginning of the study of the Hebrew Bible's historical geography.[147] A most intriguing example of an alternate location for Ai is that of Khirbet el-Maqatir, which is located about a mile southeast of et-Tell. Edward Robinson visited this site the same day that he visited Beitin and was told by the locals that it was biblical Ai. There was a Byzantine church on the site, but he concluded that there was no evidence of any other ancient site.[148]

When Ernst Sellin visited the site, he was also told that it was ancient Ai. In fact, he reported that the locals called it "Khirbet Ai."[149] The site was explored during the survey of the hill-country of Benjamin in 1981, and pottery of the Middle Bronze Age, the Iron Age I, Hellenistic, and Roman periods was found.[150] Bryant Wood explored the site of Khirbet el-Maqatir in the early 1990s and found ancient walls on the surface of the ground about two hundred meters down the southeast slope of the site. Wood began excavations at the site in 1995 and discovered, in addition to some late Hellenistic/early Roman and Byzantine remains, a small fortress on the southeastern slope that he has dated to the Late Bronze Age I, along with a poorly made Iron Age I domestic structure built into the ruins of the Late Bronze Age I wall. The walls of the Late Bronze Age I fortress appear to have been about four meters wide, and the discovery of calcined building stones, bedrock, and a possible ash layer in several places suggest that it was destroyed by fire.[151]

While the possibility that Khirbet el-Maqatir may be an alternate location for biblical Ai is intriguing, especially in light of local traditions, there are several obstacles to its identification as such. First, its identification as biblical Ai depends on the identification of Bethel, formerly named Luz,[152] since the Hebrew Bible states that Ai is east of Bethel (Josh 7:2; 8:9, 12) and in the vicinity of Bethel (Josh 12:9). Wood proposes that the traditional identification of Bethel with Beitin, a connection first made by Robinson, is mistaken, and that Bethel should be correctly identified with el-Bireh, which is about two miles southwest of Khirbet el-Maqatir.[153] It seems, however, that the archaeological evidence and the historical references continue to support the traditional identification of Bethel with Beitin.[154] Second, Khirbet el-Maqatir is not on a tell, but is a ruin situated two hundred meters beneath the summit of the hill off of which it is found. Third, the plans that have been published reflect very little excavation, but consist mostly of reconstruction.[155] There does not seem to be enough there to reconstruct a Late Bronze Age I fortress. Fourth, the site of Khirbet el-Maqatir is thus far completely lacking in Late Bronze Age II remains. While the Late Bronze Age I pottery remains might cohere well with an early-date exodus-conquest, it is problematic for a late-date exodus-conquest. The evidence that is available at present is not convincing for identifying Khirbet el-Maqatir as biblical Ai. Even though locals may have called the site "Khirbet Ai," this only means that they recognized it as a ruin, which is the literal meaning of the Hebrew word עַי. Despite these reservations, the possibility of an alternative location for biblical Ai should not be ruled out *a priori* and certainly warrants further consideration.

## Rereading the Account of the Conquest of Ai

Rather than viewing the biblical story of the conquest of Ai as completely legendary or etiological or concluding that Ai must be incorrectly identified, David Merling has proposed a third alternative, discussed in part with regard to Jericho. This way suggests rethinking the purpose of the text and the limits of archaeology to "prove" the Bible. As in the case of Jericho, the tendency among maximalists and minimalists has been to believe that archaeology can prove the Bible. While minimalists have pointed to the absence of evidence at et-Tell from 2400 to 1200 B.C.E., maximalists have looked for corollaries between the archaeological data and the biblical account, either at et-Tell or elsewhere.

In one recent study, for example, Peter Briggs designed a criteria screen for the identification of the city of Ai consisting of fourteen features that represent "the empirical correspondence between that narrative and the material time-space context that the narrative purports to represent."[156] The first three parameters of the criteria screen form a predicate criteria screen, in that they provide what Briggs sees to be the minimum set that is capable of distinguishing between viable and nonviable candidates for the biblical Ai. These are: (1) a site located in the Benjamin hill-country and destroyed in the first half of the Late Bronze Age IIA (1400–1300 B.C.E.); (2) a small site with an area less than seven acres; and (3) a fortified site with a wall and a gate. These three criteria, however, appear to be flawed from the outset. Briggs's first criterion automatically rules out et-Tell because of its *a priori* adoption of a date in the Late Bronze IIA. His second criterion sets a limit on the acreage for Ai based on a wooden reading of Joshua 10:2, which notes that Gibeon was larger than Ai. Since Gibeon was at least seven acres, then this must be the maximum acreage for the area of Ai. The Hebrew, however, states that Gibeon was גְּדוֹלָה מִן־הָעַי, which could be translated literally as "greater than Ai." This does not necessarily imply that Gibeon was larger than Ai in terms of its acreage, but it implies that it was superior to Ai in some way. Hess suggests that the expression may mean that the security at Gibeon was better than that at Ai, whose walls Israel did not breach.[157] Briggs's third criterion, that Ai was a fortified city with a wall and a gate, are also an inference.

Like Jericho, Ai is described as an עִיר, which, although it can be translated as "city," can mean a variety of other things, including fortress, small village, and even tent encampment.

In the roster of Manasseh's eastern lands, as the writer lists the cities of this territory, he substitutes עִיר with חַוָּה, which means "campsite" or "tent-village."[158] Later, the author uses עִיר in apposition to חַוָּה. This kind of usage of the term עִיר is clearly indicative of the lifestyle of nomadic peoples and makes it clear that contemporary understandings of "city" in passages that reflect Late Bronze-Iron Age I settings may not always be what modern readers expect.[159]

The biblical account of the taking of Ai is brief and succinct, with virtually no details. Merling observes:

> The entire episode of the actual destruction of Ai is presented in three Hebrew words ... ("and Joshua burned Ai," Josh. 8:28). This story does not tell us that the gate was destroyed. It does not tell us how much of the site was burned. It does not tell us that any specific building on the site was destroyed. It does not even inform us that there was a building on the site. For all we know, those living at הָעַי were living among the ruins of the previous Middle Bronze Age city, and the fire set burned the grass that covered its surface. After all, its name "the ruin" (Heb. עַי) might have been a literal description.[160]

Could it be that et-Tell is the correct location of biblical Ai, that its current occupants lived among the ruins of the Middle Bronze Age city, and that they experienced a sort of scaled-down conquest? These possibilities certainly warrant further consideration. The possibilities are intriguing. If Ai is to be correctly identified with Khirbet el-Maqatir, this could be correlated with a fifteenth-century B.C.E. Israelite entrance into Canaan. If Ai is correctly identified with et-Tell, which I believe is the case, then it could cohere with a thirteenth-century B.C.E. Israelite emergence with a scaled-down level of military engagement.

# HAZOR

The book of Joshua claims that Hazor was "the head of all those kingdoms" (Josh 11:10), and that Jabin, its king, led the forces of five Canaanite city-states in an attempt to prevent further Israelite incursion into the land of Canaan. The Canaanite forces are described as "an enormous host, as numerous as the sands on the seashore—and a vast multitude of horses and chariots" (Josh 11:4). With Yahweh's help, however, Joshua defeats this multitude and then turns back to capture Hazor. The Bible reports that of all the cities subdued in the Israelite conquest, Hazor alone was torched (Josh 11:11). Because of the importance ascribed to Hazor in the biblical account of the conquest, this city has been under constant examination by archaeologists and biblical scholars for almost a century. In this section, we will introduce the site, its appearance in ancient texts, and give an overview of its excavation and the archaeological data produced by those excavations. We will then focus in on two critical issues that are still under dispute, the date of Hazor's destruction and the identity of its destroyers.

## The Site and Its Historical Importance in Canaan

The site of Tell el-Qedah was first identified as biblical Hazor as early as 1875, on the basis of geographic references in 1 Maccabees and Josephus.[161] The location of the site at the junction of the main roads from Sidon to Beth-Shean and from Damascus to Megiddo gave it a position of strategic importance, making it possible for whoever controlled Hazor to dominate northern Palestine.[162] The site is made up of both an upper and a lower city. The tell itself is only about fifteen acres, but the Canaanite city spilled over the northern edge of the tell and across the fields below, and encompassed more than two hundred acres total. Under the Canaanites, the city flourished from the eighteenth to the thirteenth century B.C.E. and, at its peak, may have had a population as high as thirty thousand.

The prominence of the city of Hazor is also attested in ancient texts as early as the nineteenth or eighteenth centuries B.C.E. The seventeenth-century Mari archives include fourteen references to Hazor, which make it clear the city played a key role in the political and economic relationships of its northern and eastern neighbors. Hazor is mentioned in only four of the fourteenth-century Amarna letters, but these references show the city was still a significant political force in the region during the Late Bronze Age II. Hazor appears again in Papyrus Anastasi I, a thirteenth-century text ascribed to Ramesses II, where it is used as a landmark to identify a ford across the Jordan River.[163] Hazor must have still been inhabited at this time, since using an abandoned tell would not have been very helpful in a land dotted with tells.

Archaeological excavations at Hazor began with John Garstang, who conducted preliminary excavations at the site in 1928. Yigal Yadin conducted major excavations at the site from 1955 to 1958 and also from 1968 to 1970. Excavations were renewed under Amnon Ben-Tor in 1987, and have continued from 1990 until the present time.[164] Twenty-one strata have been exposed, though we are concerned primarily with those dating to the Late Bronze Age and the Iron Age. The Late Bronze I city shows a great deal of continuity with the preceding Middle Bronze IIB city, which had been destroyed about 1550 B.C.E. Based on the similarity between the two cities, one might conclude that the Late Bronze I city was built by the population of the previous city, who had abandoned it for a time following its destruction. The Late Bronze IIA city of the Amarna period was substantially different from its predecessor. The defensive architecture of this level only experienced minor changes, while the Area H temple was rebuilt on a plan similar to known Alalakh temples. This Late Bronze IIA city was violently destroyed by fire at the end of the fourteenth century B.C.E.

The final Late Bronze IIB city, dating to the thirteenth century, displays a noticeable deterioration when compared to its predecessor.[165] Imported vessels are fewer in number, and it may be the fortifications fell out of use. In Area A, a well-preserved Canaanite palace was discovered. Thick walls and lower sections lined with skillfully finished basalt orthostats suggest that this structure had been at least a two-story building. This Canaanite city was destroyed in a fiery conflagration. Across the site, a thick layer of ash—in some places three feet deep—attests to the intensity of the blaze (**Fig. 11**). Timber used in construction of the palace along with oil stored in *pithoi* contributed to the ferocity of blaze. Though it is clear that the destruction occurred sometime after 1300, the exact date has been disputed. Based on the pottery, Yadin dated the destruction of the Canaanite city to the last quarter of the thirteenth century B.C.E., with an approximate date of 1230 B.C.E. He confidently suggested that the city was destroyed by Joshua as described in the Bible, although in recent years others have suggested other culprits, which will be discussed below.

*Fig. 11*

## Reconstructing the History of Hazor in the Late Bronze Age

In recent years, several evangelical scholars have sought to correlate the history of Late Bronze Age Hazor with an early-date exodus-conquest.[166] Most prolific among those who take this approach is Bryant Wood, who has identified the destruction of Stratum 2 of the lower tell and Stratum XV in the upper tell, both of which were destroyed in the fifteenth century, with Joshua. He has identified the destruction of the Late Bronze IIB city, which is found in Stratum 1a and XIII, with Deborah and Barak and their victory over Jabin and Sisera.[167] Both the biblical and the extrabiblical data seem to militate against this view.

First, the biblical text never claims that Deborah and Barak attacked Hazor. In Judges 4, Israel is said to have been "sold" into the hand of "Jabin of Canaan, who reigned in Hazor," whose general, Sisera, lived at Harosheth ha-goiim, the location of which is unclear.[168] The Israelites took up a position at Mount Tabor (v. 6), and Sisera was drawn out to meet the Israelites by the Wadi Kishon (v. 7). A battle between the two groups commenced here, by Mount Tabor and near the Wadi Kishon (vv. 12-16), in a location some twenty-five miles south of Hazor. The biblical text reports that Yahweh "subdued" King Jabin of Canaan. J. K. Hoffmeier points out that the word translated "subdued" is the Hebrew וַיַּכְנַע, which must have been a play on the word כְּנַעַן, with which it sounds similar.[169]

At the conclusion of the prose account, the text notes that, with the aid of Yahweh, the Israelites "destroyed" King Jabin (v. 24). The text specifically says that the Israelites הִכְרִיתוּ אֶת יָבִן, which literally means that they "cut off" or "killed" Jabin. The text reports a victory over Jabin and his army in the vicinity of Mount Tabor, near the Wadi Kishon, twenty-five miles south of Hazor. The text says nothing about a battle at Hazor.

Second, extrabiblical texts seem to militate against the idea of an Israelite military victory over Hazor at the beginning of the Late Bronze IIA, around 1400 B.C.E. In two of the Amarna letters, the princes of Tyre and of Ashtaroth complain to the pharaoh that Abdi-Tirshi, the king of Hazor, had joined forces with the Habiru and captured several of their cities.[170] Abdi-Tirshi, however, insists that he is innocent of this accusation.[171] Abdi-Tirshi claims that, during this time, Hazor was still loyal to Egypt. There is also an Egyptian text, Papyrus Anastasi I, dating to the time of Ramesses II that may contain some overlooked evidence about the status of Hazor as late as Late Bronze IIB. In this text, the Egyptian scribe reports that Hazor is said to be a destination to which the Egyptian *mahir* would travel.[172] The Egyptian term *mj-h'-jr*, which J. P. Allen understands to be a "logistics officer," comes into Hebrew as מָהִיר, which, while it is usually translated as "prompt" or "quick,"[173] can also carry the derivative meaning of "skilled." In Psalm 45:2 and Ezra 7:6 it is joined with סֹפֵר and clearly carries the derived meaning of "skilled."[174] While the Hebrew scribe was typically someone involved with the Temple apparatus,[175] the Egyptian *mahir* was a skilled officer who went into the field. The fact that a *mahir* would travel to Hazor implies that it was still intertwined with Egyptian affairs at this point.

The data do not cohere with a destruction of Hazor by the Israelites in an early-date exodus-conquest. While the Late Bronze IIA city was violently destroyed by fire around the end of the fourteenth century, the city was rebuilt and continued to exert a strong influence in the region while acknowledging Egyptian hegemony, apparently into the thirteenth century. Yadin was probably correct in attributing the destruction of Late Bronze IIA Hazor to Seti I.[176] Hazor suffered some decline in the Late Bronze IIB, but, despite that, it remained an important political force in the region until the destruction of its final Late Bronze IIB city, the date of which has remained unclear until recently.

During the 1999 excavation season, a stone fragment inscribed with hieroglyphs was discovered (**Fig. 12**). The small fragment, measuring only about four inches wide, three inches high, and two inches thick, was found in the cult complex on the northern slope of Hazor's acropolis, in the debris of a mud-brick wall that collapsed when the final Late Bronze Age city was destroyed. James Allen published a preliminary description and translation of the fragment, in which he concluded that the fragment may have originally been part of the upper surface of an offering table, and could date "to as late as the third decade of Ramesses II's reign."[177] K. A. Kitchen has recently made a detailed study

*Fig. 12*

of the fragment and has translated the surviving text as follows: "[. . . Noble? And Coun]t, Sem-priest, Director of all clothing ('kilts'), chief [ . . . ]."[178] Kitchen makes a detailed study of these four titles and their usage in ancient Egyptian, and concludes that it dates to the New Kingdom and is consistent with standard Ramesside production of the Nineteenth Dynasty, which equates to the thirteenth century B.C.E. Based on the specific combination of titles and those who bore them during this period, Kitchen identifies four possible candidates who could have been responsible for leaving this monument at Hazor. In the end, however, he narrows it down to the vizier Prahotep, who boasted of engaging in foreign affairs and who had the specific title "Royal Envoy to the land of Hatti," as well as the title "Mouthpiece of the King in Every Foreign Land." No other similar role has been recorded for other viziers of Sethos I or Ramesses II. Kitchen notes that after Year 42, Ramesses II married his second Hittite princess, and it may have been that Prahotep was sent to meet her at Hazor, the biggest center in northeastern Canaan between Egypt and Hatti. If so, he may have taken the offering table to Hazor to commemorate the occasion.[179] Regardless of why he took the monument to Hazor, it provides us with datable Egyptian data for how long the city of Hazor survived into the Late Bronze Age. It lasted long enough for the vizier Prahotep to set up a monument there sometime around 1240–1230 B.C.E.

## The Identity of the Destroyers

The question of the identity of the destroyers of Late Bronze IIB Hazor continues to be a subject of debate. Yadin attributed the destruction to the Israelites, but other scholars have proposed alternative identifications. Aharoni associated it with Deborah and Barak.[180] V. Fritz attributed the destruction of the final Late Bronze city of Hazor to the Sea Peoples.[181] Finkelstein argues that either a Sea Peoples' group or a rival Canaanite city are as viable candidates as anyone.[182] Most recently, Sharon Zuckerman has argued that Hazor was not destroyed by outside marauders at all, but by an internal rebellion.[183] In chapter 4, we discussed the fact that colonization was seen in a positive light in the late nineteenth and early twentieth centuries, and consequently the idea of invasions as a source of historical change was very popular during those years. In today's climate of anticolonization, however, few regard invasion in a positive light; consequently, outside agents have come to be seen as having played less of a role as agents of historical change. Archaeologists and historians of the Eastern Mediterranean basin have for the last twenty years or so focused on internal factors as they have sought to explain change within the various cultures of this region. These trends, of course, contributed to the development of the peasant's revolt theory in the 1960s, and Zuckerman builds on them here.

Zuckerman points to the lack of archaeological evidence for warfare at the site, including human victims or weapons, as proof that Hazor was not destroyed by outside invaders.[184] She focuses on the decline that thirteenth-century Hazor experienced and observes that "traces of deterioration and partial abandonment are visible in most public buildings and communal areas."[185] She argues that these deteriorating architectural and material features "reflect signs of crisis and disintegration of the royal strategy which was carefully planned and executed during the 14th century," a strategy of control over the city and its inhabitants.[186] This dominant ideology elicited the resistance and, ultimately, rebellion of the inhabitants of Hazor. As part of their rebellion against the powers-that-be, the people of Hazor carried out "termination rituals," in which they blocked passages and sealed installations in the temple, the Podium Complex, and various other locations on the site associated with the Hazor elite and its religious establishment.

While Zuckerman's argument may lead the way to further study of the culture of Hazor in its last days, there are several weaknesses with it in terms of explaining the end of Late Bronze Age Hazor. First, her argument is based entirely on silence.[187] While there is clear decline in Late Bronze IIA Hazor, this does not automatically indicate the inability of an elite class to maintain control over an oppressed populace. Zuckerman's hypothesis is just that, a hypothesis. Second, her claim that Hazor was not attacked by outsiders is based on an absence of evidence. Despite ongoing excavation, only a small portion of the tell has been excavated and, although the lack of remains of human victims or weapons is compelling, concluding that they will not be found anywhere on the tell may be premature. Third, if the temple, Podium Complex, and other administrative buildings represented part of the "establishment" at Hazor, it does not make sense that the inhabitants who rebelled against the system would have taken such care to ritually dispose of its vestiges.

Zuckerman argues that "it is obvious that these stones were laid by people who knew the original function of the building, recognized the importance of its plan and associated features and intended to obliterate its ritual symbolic function." If Zuckerman is right that the blockages are signs of "termination rituals," this does not seem to cohere with the desire to "obliterate" the function of the building. It may, however, be possible that these sites were sealed in an effort to protect them from outside invaders. Eleven objects, on the other hand, including Egyptian royal statues and Canaanite statues of deities and kings, were intentionally mutilated. This is made clear by the fact that their heads and hands were primarily targeted. Ben-Tor's interpretation of these disfigurements as cases of "political iconoclasm" motivated by political reasons makes a lot more sense.[188]

In an earlier article, Ben-Tor enumerated the possible candidates who may have carried out such a destruction of Hazor and its statues.[189] These candidates include (1) the Sea Peoples, such as the Philistines; (2) a rival Canaanite city; (3) the Egyptians; or (4) the early Israelites.

Hazor is located too far inland to have been of interest to the Sea Peoples, who were maritime traders who tended to settle along the coastline. In addition, hundreds of thousands of potsherds have been discovered at Hazor, none of which have been among the well-known repertoire of the Sea Peoples. The possibility that another Canaanite city destroyed Hazor also seems unlikely, in light of the Bible's report that Hazor was "the head of all those kingdoms," a position attested by other ancient sources. This seems to rule out the possibility that a petty Canaanite city-state could have carried out the destruction of Hazor. Since the mutilated statues were Egyptian and Canaanite, it would seem unlikely that Egyptian or Canaanite marauders would have destroyed statuary depicting their own kings and gods. This leaves the Israelites, who were specifically commanded to destroy the altars of the Canaanites (Deut. 12:1-7), as the only apparently viable candidates.

## (LAISH) DAN

The tribe of Dan was originally supposed to occupy a territory in the northern hill-country (Josh 19:40-48). When they were unable to gain a foothold in their allotted territory, the Hebrew Bible claims the tribe moved north, conquered a Canaanite city named Laish, and changed its name to Dan (Judg 18). It is not clear whether the whole of the tribe migrated north and took part in the conquest of Laish or what strategy the conquerors used in order to take the city. The text states only that six hundred armed men of the family of the Danites set forth (Judg 18:16), that they came upon Laish, "a people quiet and unsuspecting," killed them, and "burned down the city" (18:27). Dan first appears in the Hebrew Bible when it is used as a landmark, under the name Dan, in Gen 14:14, and it is known from several extrabiblical texts, including the eighteenth-century B.C.E. Egyptian Execration Texts,[190] a Mari text,[191] and a list of Thutmose III.[192] Edward Robinson identified Laish with Tell el-Qadi, located in the far north of Israel at the base of Mount Hermon.[193] Excavations began at the site in 1966 under the direction of Avraham Biran, but the identification of the site with biblical Dan was not certain until after the Six-Day War, when a bilingual inscription in Greek and Aramaic was found that included a vow to the "god who is in Dan" or "to the god of the Danites."[194] The tablet confirms the identity of Laish as biblical Dan, and the site has come to be known today as Tel Dan.

*Fig. 13*

The large pre-Israelite city of Laish covered about fifty acres during the Middle Bronze Age and may have had a population from 7,500 to 10,000. It was heavily fortified, with sloping ramparts that measured over 25 feet thick, and a triple-arched gateway (**Fig. 13**).[195] This city was violently destroyed, probably by the Egyptians, in the late sixteenth or early fifteenth century B.C.E. The subsequent Late Bronze Age architectural remains were heavily damaged by later Iron Age I activity, but there were numerous important discoveries from this period.[196] It seems clear that there was a smelting industry at Laish during the Late Bronze Age, as indicated by the discovery of furnaces, slag, and the muzzles of blow pipes. A Mycenean tomb contained the remains of over three dozen people, along with hundreds of grave goods, including a magnificent "Charioteer" vase painted in red and black, the only whole vessel of its kind yet found in Israel. The beginning of the Iron Age at the site (Stratum VI) is characterized primarily by two features. First, there is a relatively large number of pits, some stone-lined, in all the areas excavated, and second, the characteristic vessels associated with the pits are large pithoi, including collared-rim jars and cooking pots. Any remaining structures of the Middle or Late Bronze Ages ceased to be used, and the early Iron Age inhabitants built pits in their places. The Mycenean and Cypriot vessels so characteristic of the Late Bronze Age at Laish disappear, and are replaced by the aforementioned rustic vessels. Many have associated the change in material culture from the Late Bronze Age to the early Iron Age I at Laish with the Danite conquest of the city, recounted in Judges 18.[197] Others have argued that this conclusion "is based more on the biblical story than on archaeology."[198] Does the transition from the Late Bronze to Iron Age I signify a change in the population? If so, can the inhabitants be identified? If the inhabitants were Israelites, is there any evidence that they "conquered" and burned the Canaanite city of Laish?

While Judg 18 does give an account of an Israelite tribe in search of a territory for settlement, and it does claim that this tribe settled at Laish, the archaeological evidence independently suggests that Stratum VI represents an Israelite settlement. First, the numerous pits or silos found in this phase are similar to the ones built by those who settled the highlands during the transition from the Late Bronze Age to the Iron Age I.[199] This type of pit or silo, which is so characteristic of the new highland settlements of Iron Age I, has come to be known as a "settlement pit" and is associated with early Israelite culture.[200] Second, the collared-rim jars found in Stratum VI are not derived from any previous Canaanite tradition, but resemble those found in the central hill-country at Shiloh, Ai, Bethel, Tell el-Ful, Giloh, and ʽIzbet Sartah, among other places.[201] While some scholars maintain that the collared-rim jar has its precedent in a Canaanite prototype, it does not appear in any Late Bronze Age strata of Canaanite Laish.[202]

Biran notes that it only appears after the destruction of Stratum VII, at the end of the thirteenth century B.C.E. The new elements of material culture and the change in lifestyle evident at Laish suggest to Biran that a new population settled at the site. He writes that "it seems inconceivable to me that the same people who enjoyed the highly developed material culture of the Late Bronze urban civilization would suddenly revert to a life-style that can only be characterized as semi-nomadic, with people dwelling in tents and storing food in large jars deposited in pits or silos."[203] The material culture and lifestyle evident at Laish in the Iron Age I mirrors that of the central hill-country settlers in the same period. For Biran, the "inescapable conclusion" is that the collared-rim jar was introduced at Laish by the tribe of Dan. Third, despite Manor's declaration that "no evidence for widespread destruction by fire on this transitional horizon has been found" at Laish,[204] the excavator reports that a thin layer of destruction by fire marks the end of Canaanite Laish at about 1200 B.C.E.[205]

Biran suggests that Dan "may well serve as a case study for the examination of the synthetic approach to biblical, historical, and archaeological research."[206] When looked at archaeologically, three pieces of physical data—the destruction of the Late Bronze Age stratum by fire, the change in lifestyle represented by the appearance of the pits or silos, and the appearance of the collared-rim jar—independently suggest that Laish was occupied by Israelites during the transition from the Late Bronze Age to the Iron Age I. The account of the Danites' migration and settlement in Judges 18 is the longest such account in the Hebrew Bible. Malamat suggests that, as an account of a campaign on a solely tribal level, rather than one set against the national background, it appears realistic.[207] Based on the confluence of archaeological and biblical data, Biran concludes that "there is no reason to doubt the historicity of the event or the narrative, although the date of this migration is by no means certain."[208] Lawrence Stager agrees and suggests that "the biblical traditions and the archaeological evidence converge so well that there can be no doubt that the Danites belonged to the Israelite . . . federation."[209]

# CONCLUSION

The four cities that the Hebrew Bible specifically claims were burned during the infiltration of the Hebrews into the land of Canaan were Jericho, Ai, Hazor, and Dan. The site of Jericho is problematic, since much of the remains dating between the Middle Bronze Age and the Iron Age II eroded away. However, the fragmentary domestic architecture, along with the limited Late Bronze Age remains recovered by Garstang, makes it clear that Tell es-Sultan was occupied during the Late Bronze Age. Jericho may have been smaller, with a fortified palace and a ceremonial gate, or the massive wall and defensive constructions from the Middle Bronze Age could have been used by Late Bronze Age inhabitants.

The archaeological data does not decisively prove there is not a historical nucleus to the Hebrew Bible's claim that early Israelites sacked the city of Jericho. At et-Tell, the site appears to have been abandoned from 2400 until about 1200 B.C.E., when a small Israelite village of about 150 to 300 people appears to have been peacefully established. However, the biblical Ai may still be incorrectly identified or, if et-Tell is the correct location, it may have had inhabitants who lived among the ruins of the Middle Bronze Age city, where the Israelites may have defeated them and set fire to their tents. Hazor provides clear evidence of destruction, and the data seems to point toward an identification of the early Israelites as the culprit. Likewise, the Late Bronze Age city of Laish, located at Tell el-Qadi, ended in destruction in about 1200 B.C.E., and a confluence of archaeological data with a tribal tradition of immigration seems to clearly reinforce the identity of the new settlers as the Danites.

While the evidence from these four sites is mixed, it seems to cohere with the claim of the Hebrew Bible that the emergence of Israel in Canaan involved some efforts on the part of the Hebrews to overtake at least segments of the indigenous population militarily. However, these are the only sites that the Hebrew Bible reports were burned by the Hebrews. It makes no sense, therefore, to look for conflagration layers at every site dating to the Late Bronze-Iron Age I transition in the land of Canaan. However, as we saw in chapter 2, this is exactly what generations of researchers have done, and the negative results yielded by this approach have led many to the conclusion that the account of the Hebrew Bible is completely inaccurate. Instead of focusing on tell archaeology and the search for more conflagration layers, we should consider looking to the rural countryside, where the vast majority of the newcomers to Canaan lived in the Iron Age I.

## CHAPTER 6

# RECONSTRUCTING THE ISRAELITE SETTLEMENT ARCHAEOLOGICALLY

When we turn our attention away from the tells of urban Canaan to the rural countryside and the central hill-country, we find evidence of dramatic settlement activity early in the twelfth century B.C.E.[1] Beginning in the 1960s, Israeli archaeologists began conducting surface surveys in the West Bank—Judea and Samaria—the heartland of early Israel. By the 1980s, a wealth of new archaeological data had begun to accumulate, which allowed scholars to reevaluate the traditional models. These data, first synthesized in English by Israel Finkelstein in 1988, revealed a network of hundreds of late-thirteenth- to eleventh-century B.C.E. small, unwalled villages, most of which were in the hill-country extending from the lower Galilee to the northern Negev.[2] In this chapter, we will review the results of these surveys and seek to understand their relationship to the emergence of Israel.

## THE GALILEE

The Galilee includes the area contiguous with the west side of the Sea of Galilee, and can be subdivided into the Upper Galilee, which is rugged and mountainous, and the Lower Galilee, where the hills are transected by four broad valleys.[3] Y. Aharoni, who conducted a pioneering archaeological survey of the region in the early 1950s, began to reveal the settlement pattern of the Upper Galilee as the first effort to study the Late Bronze-Iron Age I transition in a regional perspective.[4] Since the 1950s, others have further surveyed and excavated in the region. The comprehensive survey of Western Galilee conducted by R. Frankel has yielded new information on the Late Bronze Age settlements in the northern part of Upper Galilee.[5] The number and size of settlements decreased, which suggests a cultural decline in the Late Bronze Age. The main centers of population were in the valleys, but at least six Late Bronze Age sites have been recorded, and extrabiblical sources name a few others.[6] The picture of the Upper Galilee that emerges from the written and archaeological data shows city-states situated in the valleys. In the early Iron Age I, small settlements that had not been occupied in the Late Bronze Age began to appear, and the large settlements that had existed at Hazor and Dan in the Late Bronze Age were replaced by small settlements.[7] The Bronze Age city of Kinneret was reestablished in the Iron Age I, but only after a gap, and very little of the first city of this period (Stratum VI) remains. The Stratum V city was fortified with a wall and was well-planned, and reflects the Canaanite traditions of the Late Bronze Age.[8] Frankel's intensive survey, covering about 77 square miles, revealed forty sites dating from the early Iron Age, the sizes of which tended to range from 2691 square feet to five acres. Most of these sites were situated on hills, and few of them had building remains.[9] Many of them were not founded until the latter half of the period, suggesting a delay in the establishment of villages in this region during the Iron Age I.

In the northernmost area of Lower Galilee, not a single Late Bronze Age site has been discovered. The southern area of Lower Galilee, however, was the fringe of the Canaanite settlement system of the Jezreel Valley and the Plain of Acco, and two major mounds have been discovered in this region. The first site, Tel Hannathon, which may be associated with biblical Hannathon (Josh 19:14), extends over twelve acres. The second, Tel Gath-Hepher, situated on the northern slopes of the Nazareth Range, spans fifteen acres. A few small, rural settlements are located in the vicinity of these tells. Another major Late Bronze Age site, Tel Rekhesh, which covers an area of ten acres, is located in the eastern Lower Galilee. While the southern area of Lower Galilee did have a few major sites, the overall picture is one of sparse settlement in the Late Bronze Age. The Late Bronze Age is "one of the poorest periods in the history of Lower Galilee."[10] Z. Gal points to Amarna tablet 148, which portrays the region as an area inhabited only by groups of 'Apiru, and contested by both the kings of Tyre and Hazor.[11] The Iron Age I marked the beginning of a major change in the settlement of Lower Galilee. In this period, around twenty-five sites were discovered, concentrated primarily in the southern part of the region. Gal observes that "these are in fact very small settlements but they create a pattern of settlement completely different from that of the Late Bronze Age."[12] These sites were typically established near small springs, characteristic of southern Lower Galilee, ranged from two-tenths to one acre, and were short-lived.[13]

## THE JEZREEL AND BETH-SHEAN VALLEYS

The Jezreel Valley is a fertile basin found between the hills around Samaria and the hills of Galilee. It served as the main road between the coast and the Jordan Valley. The Beth-Shean Valley then continues toward Transjordan. Together, these valley roads functioned as part of an international system that connected Transjordan with the Mediterranean Sea, and the Jezreel and Beth-Shean Valleys were located at a strategic crossroads upon this route. Because of the strategic location of this crossroad, these valleys have seen clashes between numerous ancient powers. And because of the unusual fertility of the Jezreel Valley, which was famous for its grain production, it was the home of several important Bronze Age sites, including Megiddo and Jokneam, which both stood near the mouth of the main access road from Egypt.[14] Likewise, the Beth-Shean Valley housed several Bronze Age sites, including Beth-Shean, located on Tell el-Husn, a ten-acre mound on the bank of the Harod River, and Rehov, one of the largest mounds in the land of Israel (25.7 acres), located between the Gilboa Ridge and the Jordan River.[15] Because of the location of these sites on the major east-west highway across northern Israel, Egypt sought and appears to have successfully maintained control of them throughout the Late Bronze Age. Both cities attest occupational gaps following the loss of Egyptian hegemony, and there was a decline in the material culture of the valley cities in general.[16] In the late Iron Age I and early Iron Age II, some of these sites began to recover their former standard of living, and smaller sites, such as Taanach and Afula began to prosper.[17]

# THE CENTRAL HILL-COUNTRY

The central hill-country of ancient Israel includes the geographical region located between the Shephelah and the Judean wilderness, and is an almost unbroken feature that stretches south from the mountains of Lebanon to the Red Sea, broken up only by the Plain of Esdraelon. The higher elevation, more temperate climate, and greater precipitation facilitated the production of more abundant grain crops. M. D. Green notes that "because of their favorable environment and agricultural fertility the hill countries of Israel and the Transjordan were heavily settled throughout antiquity."[18] In his seminal volume, *The Archaeology of the Israelite Settlement*, I. Finkelstein observed that the vast majority of all Iron Age I settlements west of the Jordan River were located in the central hill-country, with 90 percent of them situated within the territories of Ephraim and Manasseh.[19] We will first review the surveys of Ephraim and its vicinity, as well as the territories of Benjamin and Judah, but will reserve the territory of Manasseh for extended treatment in the following section.

The 1968 survey of Judaea, Samaria, and the Golan had already shown that Ephraim had been fairly densely settled in the Early and Middle Bronze Ages, but was sparsely settled in the Late Bronze Age.[20] A new archaeological survey of southern Samaria was conducted from 1980 to 1987, as one component in a comprehensive regional project, which also included excavations at Shiloh.[21] Data from the survey have appeared in various published works, the first two volumes of the final report most recently.[22]

The survey of southern Samaria reveals a settlement pattern similar to that of the foregoing surveys. Only nine Late Bronze Age sites have been discovered in Ephraim, including Beit Ur et-Tahta, Beitin, Tell Abu Zarad, Khirbet Seilun (Tel Shiloh), Khirbet el-Marjama, Khirbet er-Rahaya, Khirbet Urma, and two unnamed sites, with Beitin boasting a relatively large settlement.[23] Most of the Late Bronze Age sites fell out of usage at the end of this period, and those sites where occupation did continue shrank in size. "During Iron I," "an influx of settlers overran the region."[24] The number of newly founded sites in the Iron Age I, reported in the current publication of the southern Samaria survey, stands at 134.[25]

Thorough archaeological surveys have been carried out in many of the areas bordering southern Samaria. The territory to the immediate south was surveyed by teams working under the auspices of the Archaeological Staff Office for Judaea and Samaria; the foothills to the west were surveyed in the 1970s by two teams, one from the Institute of Archaeology of Tel Aviv University and another by Shavit; the area to the east was surveyed by Y. Spanier, working under the auspices of the Archaeological Staff Office of Judaea and Samaria.[26]

Further south, the territory of Benjamin included the city of Jerusalem, where massive structures, including fortifications, dating to the Middle Bronze Age II clearly indicate social organization. It is unclear, however, whether the Middle Bronze fortifications remained in use in the Late Bronze Age; there appears to be no evidence that they were repaired in this period.[27] The status of the Iron Age I Jebusite city is also unclear, since neither Kenyon nor Shiloh uncovered any substantial Iron Age I remains during their respective excavations on the slope of the City of David. The absence of data, however, is not conclusive, since about half of the supposed tenth-century city lies beneath the present-day Temple Mount and remains unknown archaeologically, and much of the area south of the Temple Mount has been razed down to bedrock.[28] One surviving feature that may be indicative of Late Bronze-Iron Age I Jerusalem is the "stepped stone structure" in Area G of the City of David, sometimes associated with the biblical מִלּוֹא (*millo*).[29] This exceptionally large structure is unique in the archaeology of Iron Age Israel and appears to have functioned as the retaining wall of a large building that has not survived. The pottery found beneath its foundation fit a date during the transition from the Late Bronze Age to the Iron Age I, and domestic structures built above it date from the ninth to eighth centuries B.C.E. These factors suggest that the "stepped stone structure," along with whatever it supported, was likely built sometime between the thirteenth and tenth centuries B.C.E.[30] Thus, while tenth- through ninth-century Jerusalem appears not to have been a large urban center, "it cannot be claimed that the city did not exist or did not contain monumental structures."[31]

In the area around Jerusalem, few Iron Age I sites have been discovered. Z. Kallai identified seven in the 1968 survey, but these are clustered in a limited geographical strip on the desert fringe.[32] U. Dinur, N. Feig, and F. Geldstein carried out surveys in the hill-country of Benjamin under the auspices of the Archaeological Staff Office for Judea and Samaria and discovered additional Iron Age sites.[33] Only two distinctly Iron Age I sites in the vicinity of Jerusalem have been excavated: Tell el-Ful,[34] about three miles north of the city, and Giloh,[35] about three miles to the southwest. In an area of about ninety-seven square miles around Jerusalem, however, only about thirty Iron Age I sites have been discovered. The area south of Jerusalem, in the northern part of the territory of Judah, yielded only tiny settlements in the Late Bronze Age and virtually no Iron Age I sites.[36]

# THE NEGEV DESERT

Late Bronze Age remains are absent in the Beer-Sheba Valley and the Negev Highlands.[37] A small enclosed settlement was built at Tel Masos in the Middle Bronze

Age II, which may have existed to administer economic and political contacts with pastoralists to the south. There is a gap following this period, and the site appears to have been newly settled in the early Iron Age I,[38] a settlement that was originally identified by the excavators as Israelite.[39] A number of features, however, make it difficult to accept the site as a typical Israelite settlement,[40] and a consensus has emerged that its inhabitants were made up of a mixture of backgrounds, including seminomads, *fellahin* from the southern coastal plain or the Nile delta, and other nomadic groups such as Amalekites.[41] At the smaller site of Beer-Sheba, no Late Bronze Age remains have been found, and a rudimentary settlement consisting of pits and huts was founded in the mid-twelfth century B.C.E.[42] It appears that groups of different origins gradually settled in the area during this time frame, some of whom came from the central hill-country.[43]

# MANASSEH

It has long been recognized that Manasseh played a central role in the Israelite settlement.[44] The Hebrew Bible claims that Manasseh was given the largest allotment of territory of all the tribes in the central hill-country (Josh 17:1-13). Seventy percent of all Iron Age I sites in the country of Israel are located in the territory of the tribes of Ephraim, with the oldest having been discovered in Manasseh.[45] The natural passageways to Transjordan and to the King's Highway are in the territory of Manasseh—through the Wadi Far'ah and along the Wadi Zerqa.

The biblical data suggest a picture of Manasseh as "the cradle of the Israelite clans and tribes that originated from there."[46] Because of the abundance of biblical material on Manasseh, scholars have been drawn to the study of Manasseh since the earliest years of the twentieth century.[47] The survey of Manasseh was begun in 1978, under the direction of Israeli archaeologist Adam Zertal, and has continued now for over a quarter of a century.[48] The Manasseh survey team has covered more than 966 square miles by foot, which is about 80 percent of the central hill-country area. The survey territory extends from the Jordan Valley to the Mediterranean coastal plain, which provides a cross section of western Palestine. This makes a comparison among different geographical units possible. Hundreds of Iron Age I sites have been processed,[49] producing a wealth of data regarding the central hill-country settlement from ca. 1250 to 1000 B.C.E. Because of the large quantity of new data produced, the survey of Manasseh has been called "one of the most important ever undertaken in the land of Israel."[50]

The survey team examined the pattern of settlement in the Manasseh territory from the beginning of the Calcolithic (ca. 4500–3150 B.C.E.) to the end of the Ottoman (ca. 1300–1922 C.E.) periods. For the purposes of this study, the periods ranging from the Middle Bronze Age II to Iron Age II are of particular interest. The Middle Bronze Age IIB was a prosperous time in Canaan. The population was high, lived in fortified towns, and had a rich material culture. Seventy-two settlements were established in the Manassite territory during this period, as a result of "a considerable 'wave' of settlement" which began in this period,[51] a number double that of the Early Bronze Age I. In the Late Bronze Age, the number of settlements sharply declined, with only a quarter of the Middle Bronze Age IIB sites remaining.

Zertal suggests that this decline may be attributed to the destruction of settlements by the pharaohs of the New Kingdom who sought to eliminate the Hyksos, which would accord well with the general historical picture, since the New Kingdom pharaohs incorporated Canaan into the Egyptian Empire during this period, draining the region through taxation and occasionally stamping out rebellions. The fact that culture suffered and the number of settlements declined during this period is now well known.[52] No new sites were established during the Manassite territory during this period, but there was a large increase in settlements in the Iron Age I. Fifty-six settlements with pottery of this period were found in the Shechem syncline, three times the number of Late Bronze sites. Thirty-eight of these sites were established on virgin soil or rebuilt after having been abandoned for some time.

In the Manassite territory overall, over 450 Iron Age I sites have now been discovered, a considerable increase that Zertal interprets as the incursion of an outside population. The Iron Age II witnesses a peak of settlement expansion in the Shechem syncline, with most of the Iron Age I sites continuing directly into this period. In most of these sites, life continued without interruption from the time of their establishment in the Late Bronze-Iron Age I into Iron Age II.[53] When the continuity between the Iron I and Iron II sites is viewed in contrast to the discontinuity between the Late Bronze Age and Iron I sites, it "may be interpreted as an indicator of the ethnic homogeneity of the two societies."[54]

The survey of Manasseh has discovered a number of new sites in this period located in the Wadi She'ir region, particularly in the Sebastiyeh section, where Samaria would become the new capital of the northern kingdom of Israel. There were thirty-five new sites in these areas, twenty-six of which were founded *de novo*. Zertal concludes that the new settlements, and the density of the sites in their respective areas, can be attributed primarily to the increase in the importance of Samaria. Viewing this settlement pattern over the millennium from the start of Middle Bronze IIB to the end of Iron II has led Zertal to conclude that the Iron Age I settlements were sites of Israelite settlement in the Manasseh hill-country.

One aspect of the survey of Manasseh that has been revolutionary has been its exploration of the eastern valleys and desert fringes of east Manasseh, an extensive area encompassing about 193 square miles. The survey of this region was carried out over a fourteen-year period, from 1980 to 1994, with over five hundred days of step-by-step fieldwork invested in the process.[55] The publication of the survey of east Manasseh is paramount because this area was largely unknown to research, and about 80 percent of its sites have never been published elsewhere. East Manasseh has been one of the lesser-known and lesser-researched areas of the central hill-country in particular and of the Holy Land in general, because of its location, lack of famous historical sites, and difficult conditions for exploration. This component of the survey, therefore, presents much previously unknown data and brings to light an entire previously unknown region. The landscape units surveyed include the Zebabdeh Valley, Ras es-Salmeh, Tubas Valley, Wadi Malih, Ras Jadir, the Buqei'ah, Jebel Tammun, Wadi el-Far'ah, Ras Humsah, and the Desert Fringes.[56] The survey shows that, in the Late Bronze Age I–II, there was a sharp decline in settlement, with few sites continuing from the Middle Bronze Age II and no sites founded on virgin soil, followed by a dramatic increase in settlement in the Iron Age I.[57] The landscape units of Wadi Malih and Wadi el-Far'ah are particularly interesting, since these served as natural "highways" through the desert fringes and mountains of Manasseh. In the Wadi Malih, thirty-four sites were found, though they were mainly tiny sites. Wadi Far'ah, on the other hand, is the richest of all the landscape units in East Manasseh in terms of settlements. There are a few sites from the Chalcolithic Period and nineteen from the Early Bronze Age I. Sites are rare in the Middle Bronze Age I, with 50 percent of these continuing into the Late Bronze Age. The number of Iron Age I sites rises. The number and size of sites increases in Iron Age II, but begins to decrease in Iron Age III, and continues to do so in the Persian and Hellenistic Periods.

Building on the foregoing data related to East Manasseh, Dror Ben-Yosef has recently conducted an in-depth study of the historical and archaeological evidence for the settlement of the Jordan Valley during the Iron Age I.[58] He demonstrates the radical nature of the changes in the Jordan Valley from the Late Bronze to the Iron Age I. While there were only eleven settlements at the end of the Late Bronze Age, their number increased to 116 during the Iron Age I. These changes are unprecedented, and represent an increase of 1,045 percent, the most radical change in pattern of any region in Israel during this time frame.

The valley just west of the Jordan River stands out as the location of the most sweeping changes, while changes are less evident further west at this early stage. In the desert frontier and in the eastern valleys, the number of settlements increased by 460 percent, while they increased by 330 percent in the Shechem syncline and, in the area between Nahal 'Iron and Nahal Shechem, by 300 percent. Ben-Yosef concludes that this kind of radical change can only be explained by the migration of a massive new population. The impact is earliest and strongest in the east and, since the area maintained a stable settlement pattern from the Late Bronze Age into the Iron Age II, these new inhabitants must have come from outside Canaan, most likely from across the Jordan River. The archaeological data demonstrates these migrants were mostly nomads and seminomads.

The settlements consisted mainly of elliptical enclosures and cave sites, compound enclosures, and "sandal-shaped" enclosures and, very rarely, tell sites. None of the enclosure-type settlements, all of which were founded on virgin soil in early Iron Age I, can be linked to a road, a water source, or nearby agricultural land, but were instead established in remote areas. These sites contained a severely limited ceramic repertoire, with virtually no imported vessels, and with the cooking pot as the most abundant vessel type. Sickle blades, which are characteristic of agricultural settlements, are absent at these sites. These enclosure-sites appear to have been designed for settlements with an economy based on pastoralism, and they appear to have been seasonally occupied in the winter and deserted in the summer, when their populations would leave for cooler areas in the Samarian hills or the mountains of Gilead. The "sandal-shaped" enclosures, which are unique to this area, were built at the bases of natural slopes, which formed something like a natural stadium. These "sandal-shaped" enclosures, discussed more extensively in chapter 9, may have served as places of assembly. The data all points to a homogenous settlement pattern of an enclosed nomadic group with no central political authority.[59] Ben-Yosef concludes that during the earliest part of the Iron Age I, the region appears to have been under the control of ethnically homogeneous tribes or large, extended families of nomadic or seminomadic pastoralists who had immigrated into the Jordan Valley, probably from the area east of the Jordan River.

Zertal has argued that an examination of the pottery assemblage and its distribution across the Manassite territory demonstrates this east-to-west movement of the early settlers. The pottery of the more than two hundred Iron I sites was analyzed according to the percentages of different kinds of cooking pots, with special attention to the development of their rims. Three types of cooking pots were identified in the Manasseh territory, including types A, B, and C (**Fig. 14**). The Type A cooking pot is a direct continuation of the Late Bronze cooking pot and has been solidly dated to the thirteenth century B.C.E., when it was used throughout Canaan.[60] This cooking pot has an averted, triangular, or "folded rim," and is "a very thick vessel, made of dark brown clay with pieces of quartz in it."[61] This Type A cooking pot predominates in the eastern areas of the

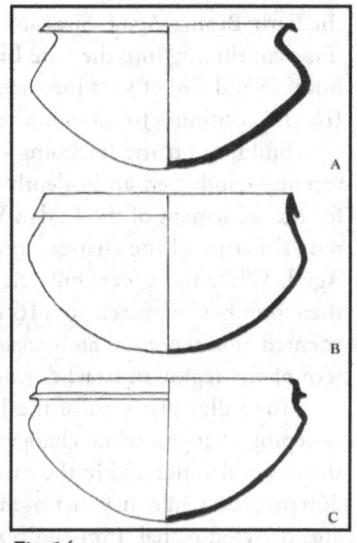

*Fig. 14*

Manassite territory, near the Jordan Valley. More than four dozen sites in the Jordan Valley and in the desert fringes had high percentages of these vessels. In addition, sites along the Wadis Far'ah and Malih, which were the ecological pipelines leading westwards from Transjordan and the Jordan Valley, were replete with this early type of cooking pot.[62] The Type B cooking pot has a sharp, adze-shaped rim, and is assigned primarily to the twelfth century B.C.E.[63] The use of Type B cooking pots rose in the syncline's interior—in the eastern valleys and in central Manasseh—while the use of Type A declined.[64] The Type C cooking pot has a low ridge, and is the latest in the series, dating to the eleventh and tenth centuries B.C.E.[65] These pots tended to be found in sites farther into the interior of the Manassite territory, while Types A and B were virtually absent. This data seems to suggest a gradual infiltration of population elements into the central hill-country from the east to the west. In light of these and other data,[66] Zertal postulates a three-staged process of geographic expansion (**Fig. 15**).[67]

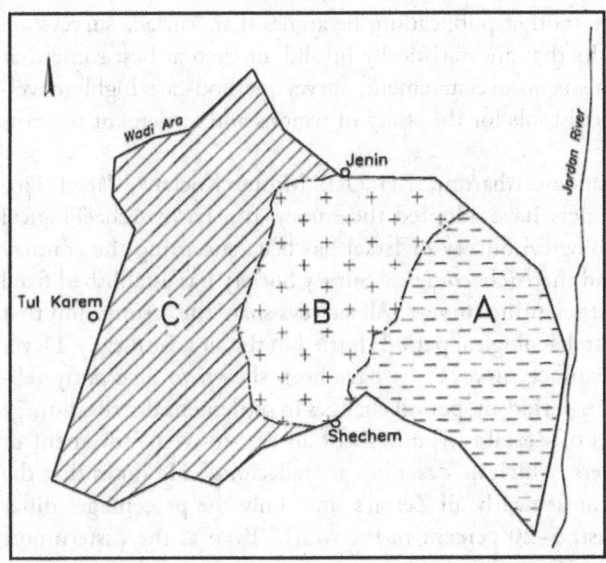

Fig. 15

The settlement process began in the Jordan Valley and eastern Manasseh (stage A), where sites were discovered mainly along the Wadis Far'ah and Malih. During this stage, dating to approximately the middle of the thirteenth to the middle of the twelfth centuries B.C.E., the settlers were seminomads, with an economy based on sheep husbandry, in the process of sedentarization. The second phase of settlement occurred in the desert fringes and eastern valleys of Manasseh (stage B), and seems to have been a later phase than the first. Many of the sites—enclosures and villages—discovered in this phase of settlement were founded adjacent to Late Bronze Age sites, which may suggest, to some degree, a complementary existence with the indigenous population. During this phase, the settlers moved to an economy based on a mixture of sheep-raising, wheat and barley farming, and possibly some limited cultivation of olive groves and vineyards. This phase involved the beginnings of sedentarization, as these migrants both grazed their flocks in the forest park of the evergreen oak, which apparently covered these valleys, and also began to practice sedentary agriculture as they settled along the fringes of the central valleys.

The final stage of the settlement process, and the latest in the series, involved penetration into the western and northern hill-country (stage C). In this final stage, the settlers utilized terrace agriculture and cultivated crops, such as olive trees and vineyards, that were well-suited for the terra-rossa soil. The implications of Zertal's reconstruction are profound, since no one has ever identified an entrance into Canaan from the east archaeologically.

Zertal's interpretation of the data has evoked a mixed response. L. E. Stager has dismissed it as "unconvincing."[68] Dever has been Zertal's most vocal opponent, criticizing the reconstruction on the basis of the survey approach, the hypothesized east-to-west movement based on the ceramic inventory, and the idea of a Transjordanian origin for the settlers. Dever's first criticism is that the conclusions were drawn from surveys. He writes that "statistics of this sort, based as they are solely on scant materials from surface surveys, are meaningless. They certainly cannot bear the weight of Zertal's sweeping generalizations about a Transjordanian, pastoral-nomadic origin for early Israel."⁶⁹ In another publication, he argues that "surface surveys are notorious for yielding results that are statistically invalid, or even at best somewhat misleading."⁷⁰ However, this is an overstatement; survey methods are highly developed and are widely accepted tools for the study of regions and settlement patterns within those regions.⁷¹

Nelson Glueck, Yohannan Aharoni, Zvi Gal, Moshe Kochavi, Israel Finkelstein, and other researchers have adopted the survey as a basic archaeological research tool. The Archaeological Survey of Israel has been surveying the country consistently since 1965, and the Archaeological Survey Society has established fixed procedures for carrying out scientific surveys. All surveys share the assumption that surface pottery represents archaeological periods buried in the site. Ironically, Dever himself has written that "surface surveys . . . have been shown to give fairly reliable statistics—especially on period-by-period changes in settlement distribution."⁷² Dever's second criticizm is of Zertal's hypothesis of an east-to-west movement of the early hill-country settlers, which he describes as "fallacious." He notes that the Type A cooking pots "occur at nearly all Zertal's sites: only the percentages differ (over 20 percent to the east, 5–20 percent to the west)." Even at the easternmost sites there was some of the Type B pottery present, albeit a smaller percentage. Dever argues that "if there are any early cooking pots there at all, then the site was established in the early twelfth century. It may have been small, it may have grown later, but it has to have been established in the earliest phase of settlement. In short, there *was* no general movement of peoples from east to west."⁷³ He concludes that Zertal's postulation of an east-to-west settlement pattern is "bogus," and that he has "been seduced by the later biblical notion of outside immigration, against all current archaeological evidence."⁷⁴

Postulating the movement or spread of populations through the use of pottery finds, however, is not "fallacious" or "bogus," but is, in fact, a methodology called "width stratigraphy" that has been used by many scholars, including K. Kenyon, P. Gerstenblith, Dothan, A. Caubet, L. Stager, and others in following population movements.⁷⁵ The theory of an east-to-west settlement pattern on the basis of pottery distribution is in full accordance with the conventions of archaeological method. Dever's final criticism is that the presence of any Type A pottery in a site in zone B or C means that it must have been founded in the early twelfth century. On this basis, he insists that all the sites were founded contemporaneously. This argument, however, ignores the fact that pottery sequences always overlap. Typically, one form gradually declines as another increases.⁷⁶ It seems plausible that the most natural interpretation of the distribution of Types A, B, and C cooking pots across zones A, B, and C of the Manassite territory is as a settlement pattern. As Ziony Zevit argues, "this distribution cannot be accounted for if all these settlements were established at the same time, if the pattern of settlement was random, or if it moved . . . from west to east."⁷⁷ When stages A, B, and C are examined together, they suggest a general east-to-west pattern of settlement.

# TRANSJORDAN

There has been a tendency to ignore or at least minimize Transjordan in studying the early history of Israel. Transjordan is often understood to lie outside of the promised land, since some textual traditions treat the Jordan River as its eastern boundary (e.g., Num 34:1-12).[78] The biblical tradition does contain an account of Gad and Reuben requesting and receiving land in Transjordan (Num 32), but the scholarly consensus seems to be that these traditions reflect a later period and that these tribes were first located west of the Jordan.[79] In addition, half of the tribe of Manasseh, who had also received a land grant in Transjordan, is conventionally thought to have migrated to Transjordan from the west during the period of the judges.[80] The accounts of Israelites receiving territorial allotments in Transjordan are simply part of the later creation of a territorial self-definition and a history that provided a foundation narrative for an Israelite state.[81] Discussions of archaeological data from the Late Bronze-Iron Age transition in Transjordan generally reflect this scholarly consensus and treat the region and its corresponding material data as external to Israelite territory.[82] In responding to claims that the ancient Israelites may have been pastoralists who migrated into Canaan from Transjordan, Dever argues that there is little Late Bronze Age context for either urban sites or pastoral nomads, and that efforts "to provide archaeological justification for the nomadic ideal in ancient Israel are simply nostalgia for a biblical past that never was."[83] He argues that "all the evidence" shows that "there is simply no archaeological evidence that 'Earliest Israel' *was ever in* Transjordan."[84]

The fact that Israelites were in Transjordan is clearly attested, however, both in biblical and extrabilical sources. Although the date of the composition of the Pentateuch and its sources are a subject of ongoing debate, a number of passages there claim that Israelites received territorial allotments in Transjordan and settled there.[85] Both Dtr and the Chronicler contain traditions about Israelite settlement east of the Jordan as well.[86] The Moabite Stone reports the Gadites "had lived in the land of 'Atarot forever, and the Moabite King Mesha only took it by force."[87] It also states the Israelites had inhabited Nebo, and it was only when the Moabite god Chemosh ordered Mesha to take it that he did so. Interestingly, the Moabite Stone claims that Omri had taken possession of "a[ll the lan]d of Madaba," as if it was a fairly recent occurence, while the Hebrew Bible claims that it had been settled much earlier in Israel's history.[88] The Moabite Stone, of course, dates to the ninth century B.C.E., but it clearly suggests that an Israelite presence in Transjordan had been a reality as far back as the Moabites could remember. While the extent of the Israelite presence in Transjordan is unknown at present, the Moabite Stone does attest that the Moabite plateau had always been known to the Moabites as an area with a mixed population.[89]

Long ago, Albrecht Alt recognized there must be a connection between the settlement patterns in Israel and in Ammon, Moab, and Edom.[90] Indeed, recent studies of the settlement patterns and accompanying archaeological data demonstrate there was an increase in settlement in central and northern Transjordan in the Late Bronze

II.[91] The process of sedentarization is evidenced by the establishment of a series of both walled and unwalled settlements.[92] The number of sites increased in the early Iron Age I.[93] Collared-rim jars and four-room houses appeared at a number of these sites.[94] While this does not prove the ethnic identity of the inhabitants of these sites, it is characteristic of the Israelite settlement in Canaan. Herr has noted the strong similarities of the material culture at Tell al-'Umayri with that of the highlands of Cisjordan.[95] It is one of the earliest Iron I sites in Palestine, contemporary with Mount Ebal and Giloh, contains the same limited repertoire of pottery and finds as highland sites in Cisjordan, and shares a material culture most similar to the hill-country north of Jerusalem, particularly from the region of Shechem.

The most frequent bowl type at 'Umayri is the "Manasseh bowl"; two collared-rim storage jars bear the same potter's mark as some jar rims from Ebal; some of the seals from 'Umayri are similar to trapezoidal seals from Ebal; and over thirty seals are similar to a kind of Cisjordanian seal. The same material culture is reflected in the Iron I levels at Hesban, Tell Jawa, and Tall Jalul, and Herr has suggested that "one may entertain the possibility that these four sites represent a contemporaneous regional cultural entity."[96] Building on F. M. Cross's "Reubenite Hypothesis," which postulates that the tribe of Reuben played a dominant role in early Israelite society,[97] Herr proposes that the Iron I settlements at these sites may have been Reubenite.[98] P. J. Ray Jr. has recently agreed, suggesting that the earliest Iron Age settlement at Hesban was a small, unfortified Reubenite village.[99] Similarly, R. W. Younker has suggested that the material culture at Tall Jalul may reflect a Reubenite presence at the site in the Iron Age I.[100] The Iron Age I settlement at Tell Jawa (Stratum IX) is limited, but the similarities between its material culture and that of Tell el-'Umayri, Hesban, and Tall Jalul during the same period are evident.[101]

Rainey has suggested that the fact that the Jordan River was a political and military barrier from 1967 to 1993 may be at least partly responsible for the tendency to overlook evidence from Transjordan in reconstructing the early history of Israel.[102] As we saw in chapter 2, Callaway decided that parallels for the material culture of the early Israelites was to be found in the coastal and lowland regions to their west.[103] He did not have access to the archaeological evidence from Jordan. As we have seen above, however, neither the biblical nor extrabiblical sources appear to have regarded the Jordan River as a barrier that prevented interaction between the cultures on either side of it.[104]

## Later Perceptions of the "Holy Land" as Comprising Both Cisjordan and Transjordan

In a tour of churches in and around Madaba, I found that many of the mosaics contain maps of the Christian Near East. All of these maps seem to depict the ancient Near East as a homogenous unit, with no division between Cisjordan and Transjordan. The sixth-century C.E. Madaba map, located in St. George's church, for example, is a depiction of the "Holy Land," with Jerusalem at its center (**Fig. 16**).[105]

It views the Near East from the vantage point of the Mediterranean Sea and includes both Cisjordan and Transjordan. While some have argued that it was based

Fig. 16

primarily on Eusebius's geographical lexicon to the Bible, the famous *Onomasticon*, less than 20 percent of its sites can be found on the Madaba Map. Clearly, it was intended to be a record of the contemporary Near East in the sixth century, and it depicted it as a region whose cities saw themselves as part of a shared culture.

At the Church of St. Stephen at Umm er-Rasas, a huge mosaic facing the apse depicts a parade of cities on both sides of the Jordan River (**Fig. 17**).[106]

Fig. 17

On its left side are those cities on the west side of the Jordan River, beginning with Jerusalem, which is called the "Holy City" (**Fig. 18**).

Jerusalem is followed by Neapolis, Samaria Sebaste, Caesarea, Diospolis (Lod), Eleutheropolis (Betogabri, Beit Guvrin), Ascalon, and Gaza. On the other side, cities to the east of the Jordan River are depicted, beginning with Philadelphia (Amman) in the north, and then, working south, Madaba, Heshbon, Belemount (biblical Ba'al Ma'on), and Characmoba (Kerak). G. W. Bowersock notes that "this limited scope for the cities of Transjordan contrasts strikingly with the broad sweep of cities on the other side of the Jordan, extending as far as Caesarea on the coast to the north and Gaza on the coast to the south."[107] While the artist was located in Jordan, his gaze "looked westward more than to the interior." The designers of these mosaics clearly saw themselves as part of a region with a shared culture. While one might object that this is because these mosaics originate in the Christian Roman Empire, this cannot be sustained, since mosaics in other regions do not attest to the same kind of shared culture. North Africa, for example, is not characterized by a shared culture during the same period, but by internecine struggles among Christians.[108] The region is characterized by a proliferation of private villas and fortress-villas with mosaics that reflect ethnic and religious disparity rather than homogeneity.[109] The Near East, on the other hand, following the suppression of the Revolt of Bar Kokhba in the second century C.E., reflects a common culture that was generally peaceful.[110] While these conditions date to a far later period than the one under study here, they may serve to reinforce the idea that the perception of the Jordan River as a political and military barrier is a modern rather than an ancient one. In antiquity, Transjordan clearly had a role to play in the early history of Israel. The archaeological data do not rule out the biblical tradition that the Hebrews migrated north from the outskirts of Moab to the Mishor plains, through southern and northern Gilead, and into Bashan. Indeed, it seems to support it.[111]

*Fig. 18*

# CONCLUSION

By the 1980s, a wealth of new archaeological data had begun to accumulate, which allowed scholars to reevaluate the traditional models. Much of the new data came from surface surveys carried out by Israeli archaeologists in the West Bank—Judea and Samaria—the heartland of early Israel. These data, first synthesized in English by Israel Finkelstein in 1988, revealed a network of hundreds of late-thirteenth- to eleventh-century B.C.E. small, unwalled villages, most of which were in the hill country extending from the lower Galilee to the northern Negev. These sites were not located on the ruins of destroyed Canaanite sites, but were founded de novo. Finkelstein estimates that in the territory west of the Jordan River, the population grew from ca. twenty thousand in the twelfth century B.C.E. to about forty thousand in the eleventh century. Others have interpreted the data as indicating significantly higher numbers. L. Stager, for example, estimates a population of about fifty thousand in the Late Bronze Age that grew to about one hundred fifty thousand in the Iron Age I.[112] In either case, the dramatic increase in numbers represents a demographic change that cannot be attributed to natural birthrates, but must reflect a major influx of new population elements.[113]

Furthermore, the survey data suggest that the phenomenon of a heavy wave of Iron I settlements is not characteristic of the entire central hill-country. Instead, it was most intensive in Ephraim and Manasseh and the eastern part of Benjamin. Settlement during this period was much more sparse in the region of Jerusalem and even more so further south, in Judah. The concentration and distribution of new settlements in the region of the Wadi Far'ah and the Wadi Zerqa, the natural passageways to Transjordan and to the King's Highway, as well as the evidence of width stratigraphy and similarities in material culture, suggest that these earliest settlements were inhabited by a homogeneous nomadic or seminomadic population whose settlement patterns were closely paralleled by those directly east of the Jordan River. The survey data, the traditions in the Hebrew Bible, and the perception of the "Holy Land" as a homogenous unit including both Cisjordan and Transjordan that survived into the post-Mishnaic world (after about 220 C.E.), suggest that we must include parts of Transjordan in the map of the settlement of the southern Levantine hill-country in Iron Age I (**Fig. 19**).

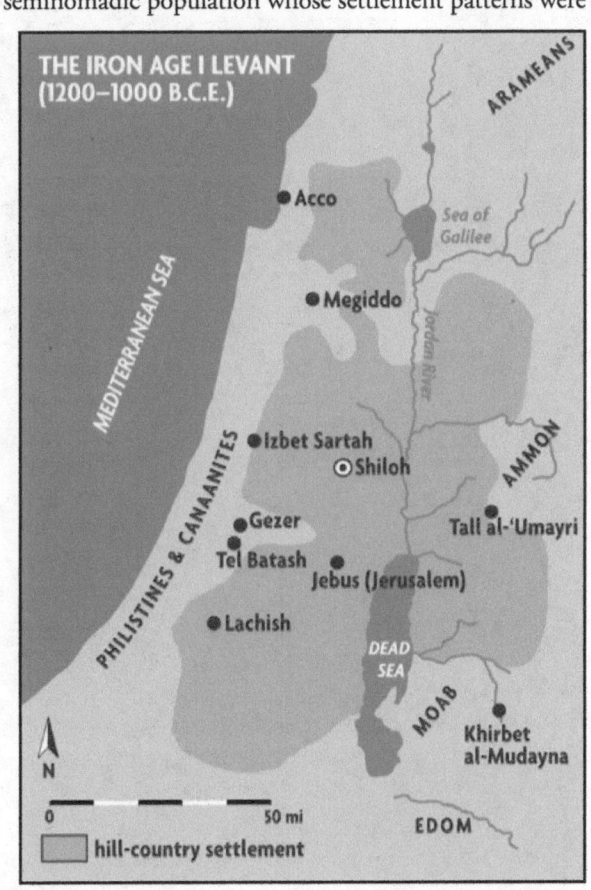

*Fig. 19*

While the evidence in this chapter may seem clear enough to conclude that these highland settlements were Israelite, this conclusion is hotly contested, and their origins and ethnic identity continue to be debated. These are the issues to which we will turn in the next chapter.

CHAPTER 7

# THE MATERIAL CULTURE AND ETHNICITY OF THE HIGHLAND SETTLERS

A clear demographic change occurred in the central hill-country of Canaan during the transition from the Late Bronze Age to the Iron Age I. And the demographic change that occurred was so dramatic that it cannot be attributed to natural birthrates but must instead reflect a major influx of new population elements. The major question then concerns the origins and ethnic identity of these newcomers, the discussion of which has been one of the most intensely debated issues in modern biblical studies. Since the nineteenth century, it has been assumed that specific peoples could be linked with the artifacts they used. The forms these artifacts took, as well as other morphological traits, were understood to be ethnic markers, and they were used in identifying ancient peoples. Specific traits were associated with the ancient Israelites.[1]

## IDENTIFICATION OF THE ISRAELITES

In 1993, Eric Meyers called our attention to the complexity of identifying ethnicity in the material culture in an important survey of the field of biblical archaeology from its early days in which he noted mistakes that had been made in the process of identifying "pots and people," as it were.[2] Meyers's focus was on calling for a greater sensitivity to the problem of pluralism and how it relates to the material culture in all ages in ancient Palestine. He observed that "by calling a site 'Persian,' 'Arab' or even 'Israelite' we are prejudicing the interpretive task," and urged archaeologists to a greater sensitivity to the fact "that ancient Palestine was truly a meeting ground for diverse cultures, and that most of those groups left their mark on its society and material culture."

Archaeologists have come to recognize the complexity of the association of "pots and people," and that it may be very difficult—sometimes even impossible—to determine if a given physical object carried ethnic meaning. Not only is it difficult to identify ethnicity, there are also challenges even to *defining* it. In a recent article discussing this problem, Gloria London has explained that ethnicity

> defies a simple, single definition because ethnic affiliation is not necessarily permanent, nor is it a unilateral designation. An ethnic group may be defined as "a people

with mutual interests, based on common understandings and values." Individuals might belong to one group and call themselves by a certain name, but other people might assign the same individuals to a different group with a different name, in part because ethnicity is neither permanent nor based on one factor alone; it is fluid and changes with time. People shift their allegiances and may belong to more than one ethnic group at any given moment.[3]

As an example of this difficulty, London notes painted Philistine pottery, which is considered a hallmark trait of Philistine sites since it is found in large numbers in eastern Mediterranean coastal sites. However, she warns that one cannot assume that just because it is found at a particular site that its inhabitants must have been Philistines. While Philistines may have been present at the site, it is also possible that the Philistine pottery was brought to the site by people of some other ethnic group who had contact with the Philistines. One cannot conclude a site should be associated with the Philistines unless other elements besides painted pottery are discovered that would somehow distinguish it from sites associated with other ethnic groups. She concludes that, in order to associate a site with a particular ethnic group, one needs more than a single artifact, or even several samples of material culture. Ideally, "one needs behavioral evidence to distinguish among ethnic groups."[4] London gives other cases in which morphological data leads to ambiguous conclusions, and she concludes: "Ethnoarchaeologists might observe and use quantitative data to record the behavior of people of different ethnic groups who live in a single region to determine how each ethnic group behaves, identifies itself, and is identified by others."[5]

In recent years, the pendulum has continued to swing away from the association of "pots and people," and long-held assumptions about using morphological data for Israelite identification have come under heavy criticism, with many scholars arguing that the ethnicity of ancient peoples cannot be identified at all. In an article that seems to reflect a general trend, Diana Edelman argues that, "given the present state of textual and artifactual evidence, nothing definitive can be said about the ethnicity of premonarchic Israel."[6] Her entire paper is about "the reasons for our inability to learn anything about early Israel's ethnic composition and forms of ethnic expression,"[7] and she concludes that any attempt to identify any of the Palestinian peoples of Iron Age I ethnically is to "wish upon a star."[8] Niels Peter Lemche argues that "hardly anything carried an ethnic tag" in the Iron Age,[9] and Thomas L. Thompson goes so far as to argue that ethnicity "is an interpretive historiographical fiction" that was "hardly a common aspect of human existence" during which scholars are searching for early Israel.[10] The quest to identify the ethnicity of ancient peoples, therefore, is an arbitrary task that should be abandoned. According to K. L. Noll, the misguided "pots and people" approach *has* been "largely abandoned," although some still stumble into this "common fallacy" of equating material culture with ethnicity.[11] One of the most outspoken critics of identifying early Israel in the material culture is Israel Finkelstein, who argues that "there was no political entity named Israel before the late-eleventh century."[12] He claims, further, that "any effort to distinguish between 'Israelite' and 'non-Israelite' sites during the twelfth to eleventh centuries B.C.E. according to their finds is doomed to failure."[13] He points to "economic, environmental, and social factors" for any changes in material culture in the central hill-country.[14]

The reason for the modern tendency toward the avoidance of discussions about ethnicity in the archaeological record are nowhere explicitly stated by its adherents, though it may be due to the confusion of the archaeology of ethnicity with racism.[15] Race is a complex subject that has become extremely controversial because of the phenomenon of racism. So what is "race"? Nolan and Lenski define a "race" as some part of the human population in which some combination of genetic differences occur "with a frequency that is appreciably different from that of other parts of the human population."[16] Racism is the "belief that race is the primary determinant of human traits and capacities and that racial differences produce an inherent superiority of a particular race."[17] Ethnicity, on the other hand, refers simply to "a sense of peoplehood," which is not a modern social construct, as the critics claim, but is something that has characterized people throughout human history. "If a certain group thinks itself a distinctive 'people,' then they *are* by that very fact."[18] And that belief is manifested in material correlates of behavior which, although sometimes difficult to identify, are typically present in the archaeological record.[19] Despite the difficulties of using physical data for ethnic identification, not all scholars have abandoned the idea that the ancient Israelites can be identified, and several scholars have continued to argue that certain morphological factors may still be used for this purpose.[20] Here we will consider the following traits and the question of whether they may reflect characteristics that can still be used to identify Israelite sites:

1. Settlement pattern
2. Site layout
3. Four-room house
4. Pottery
5. Foodways

Each of these will be discussed in turn in an effort to determine whether and to what extent it might contribute to discussions about Israelite ethnicity.

## Settlement Pattern

The beginning of Iron I reveals a completely new phenomenon that consists in numerous new settlements in peripheral zones outside the old city-states. These new settlements were responsible for a tremendous population increase in Canaan during the transition from the Late Bronze Age to the Iron Age I.[21] The new settlements that created this demographic change exhibit different characteristics than the settlements of the second millennium: they are typically founded on natural soil or on bedrock, on sites that were previously uninhabited; they are mostly located in marginal areas—such as the central hill-country or the Negev; these sites are typically small, about 2.5 acres; and the principal style of dwelling architecture in these sites is the four-room house. Based on the continuation of these new settlements into Iron Age II, when we know without a doubt that these were Israelites, Volkmar Fritz argues that their predecessors in Iron Age I, who lived in these villages, should be identified as Israelites.[22]

## Site Layout

These sites are arranged with the housing units in a circular enclosure, with the backs of the houses creating a natural city wall, though it does not amount to a fortification wall.

As noted above, courtyard sites such as that of the Stratum II village of 'Izbet Sartah, and most of which date to the Iron Age I, are known from all over Palestine.[23] What characterizes these sites is the comparatively large size of their courtyards, which in most cases occupy 65 to 80 percent of the total area. These sites are typically located in areas that likely provided excellent pasturage, such as the Negev Highlands and the Beersheba valley. It can be deduced that these villages belonged to a people whose economic foundation was animal husbandry, and the large courtyards were for penning herds at night.

A number of scholars argue that this architectural layout reflects the occupational and social background of formerly nomadic inhabitants.[24] The inhabitants of these sites were former tent dwellers who, in their earliest stages of sedentarization, built their permanent settlements in the shape of their former tent encampments. Herzog argues that this interpretation is unreasonable,[25] and other critics argue that "the *hatser*-style layout is a logical approach for any group of any background in a situation where they want to have some measure of defense against hostile outside attack with the minimum amount of investment in materials and labor. . . . It reveals nothing about the origins of the inhabitants of a settlement."[26] D. Edelman concludes that "its use was determined by environmental and ecological factors and concerns, not by socioeconomic or ethnic factors."[27] Finkelstein, however, notes the wide acceptance of the idea "that nomads in the process of sedentarization retain the traditions of their pastoral existence, at least initially."[28] In the case of the Palestinian elliptical sites, they appear to have been founded by sedentarizing pasoralists for whom herding was still the main source of livelihood, and it made sense to them to organize their houses in the shape of the corrals that had typified their nomadic encampments. As the Israelites became more sedentary, the ratio of large, open livestock corral areas to buildings diminishes, although the original elliptical settlement plan continues to form the basis for the general site layout among these newly sedentarized communities.[29] Levy and Holl have demonstrated that this same pattern typified other sedentarizing pastoralist communities.[30]

Research on nomads in Palestine in recent times shows typical circular or elliptical encampments. This arrangement was so common that these encampments were even called *duwwar* ("circle" in Arabic) camps. Finkelstein points to two photographs of such encampments from the beginning of the twentieth century illustrating this phenomenon. The first is of a circular encampment photographed in Transjordan,[31] and the other is of a trapezoidal site that was photographed in the Judean desert.[32] In each of these cases, he notes that the area of the camp and the number of tents is similar, and a large courtyard occupies the center of both encampments, toward which all the openings face.[33] Musil had observed that livestock were protected in the center of such encampments.[34]

The similarity between the elliptical sites of the Iron Age I and the *duwwar* encampments seems clear, on the basis of both their dimensions and overall plan. Finkelstein concludes:

> These sites represent therefore groups that had only recently settled down on the land, who in their dwelling traditions and subsistence economy were still bound to the pastoral way of life that they had practiced prior to their sedentarization. The circular or oval enclosure had definite advantages for such groups—a convenient place for penning their flocks and herds and relative security for their inhabitants.[35]

Regardless of exactly how the site layout is interpreted, however, the settlement pattern and the site layout together do present a clear demographic change in the central hill-country from Late Bronze to Iron Age I. Fritz argues that "this change is probably due to a new population element—either a regrouping within the Canaanite population or an influx of newcomers. It is highly probable that the Israelite population element can be connected to this change in the settlement structure. The hundreds of new Iron Age I villages may have been founded and inhabited by the new Israelite population."[36] Fritz makes this case largely on a principle of continuity of occupation between Iron Age I sites and their Iron Age II inhabitation. Most of the Iron Age II sites were "a direct continuation of the sites of the preceding period."[37] It appears that, in most of these sites, "life continued uninterrupted" from the time of their establishment in the Late Bronze into Iron II. Based on the continuity of material culture from Iron I to Iron II, there seems little doubt that "the Iron Age I settlements were sites of Israelite settlement in the Manasseh Hill-Country."[38] In an independent survey, Robert Miller II has recently reached the same conclusions, that the Iron I highlanders were "the direct antecedents of Iron II Israel." Miller argues that there is "direct continuity from the Iron I highlands to Iron II Israel and Judah in almost every area of material culture: pottery, settlement pattern, architecture, burial customs, and metals."[39] Miller argues that "once archaeology has established the continuity to Iron II, there seems no reason to retain the prefix 'Proto-.'"[40]

## The Four-Room House

As archaeologists studied the new settlements being discovered in the central hill-country, they found these sites tended to contain a particular style of house having no precedent in the settlement history of Canaan. This house style is typified by an entrance at the front that leads into a central space with a floor of beaten earth, which is paralleled on either side by stone-paved aisles bordered by pillars. The fourth room, which usually contains a dirt floor, stretches across the back of the house (**Fig. 20**).

This house style has come to be known as the "four-room house" on the basis of its basic number of areas in the house, although the side aisles and/or the back room are often subdivided, which has led to several variations of the basic form. When four-room houses began to be discovered in the hill-country on both sides of the Jordan River, early excavators proposed that it was a new, specifically "Israelite" form.[41] By 1987, more than 155 examples of this house type had been discovered,[42] and new examples continue to be unearthed at almost every Israelite site. It appears to have been the Israelite equivalent of the two-bedroom "Cape Cod" design that originated in seventeenth-century New England. Studies of the four-room house mainly focus on its function. In L. E. Stager's seminal article on the family, for example, he noted that the four-room house

*Fig. 20*

> was first and foremost a successful adaptation to farm life: the ground floor had space allocated for food processing, small craft production, stabling and storage; the second floor was suitable for dining, sleeping, and other activities. . . . Its longevity attests to its continuing suitability not only to the environment . . . but also for the socioeconomic unit housed in it—for the most part, rural families who farmed and raised livestock.[43]

J. S. Holladay drew essentially the same conclusions,[44] and the focus of the study of the four-room house has since tended to be dominated by functional concerns. Despite functional explanations, the four-room house continued to be regarded as the standard "Israelite" house.[45]

Beginning at least as early as the 1970s, however, structures that were identified as four-room houses began to be discovered in areas that lay outside the territory conventionally associated with the Israelites, including cities on the Canaanite coast, among the Philistine settlements, and in Transjordan. What appeared to be four-room houses were discovered, for example, at 'Afula, Tel Sippor, Tel Keisan, Sahab, Tel Qasile, and many other locations.[46] The discovery of four-room houses outside of areas conventionally thought of as "Israelite," along with the arguments about the functional nature of the dwelling, led many scholars to conclude that it could no longer be identified as the typical "Israelite" house. M. M. Ibrahim, for example, excavated a house at Tell Sahab, southeast of Ammon, that he identified as a "pillared house," the same as those excavated at Palestinian sites.[47] He concluded that his discovery of a house in this style at Tell Sahab contradicted the conclusions of Shiloh.[48] Because of its appearance at other locations, a number of scholars have since argued that the four-room house can no longer be considered an indicator of Israelite ethnicity. N. P. Lemche states that "the argument is false . . . and there is no reason to pay attention to it anymore."[49] Ahlström argues that the four-room house developed out of Late Bronze Age traditions in Canaan, in which a central courtyard was surrounded by two, three, or four rooms.[50] These conclusions have been adopted by archaeologists[51] and biblical scholars[52] alike, and represent what has more or less become a consensus. Diana Edelman summarizes the views of this consensus.

> It has now been acknowledged that the form grew out of the local, LB Palestinian urban architectural tradition and is not a cultural innovation introduced by the arrival of a new ethnic group in the area. Rather, it appears to have been an adaptation of a local urban building style to suit the needs of settlers in the hills who had limited labor power and resources, and multi-use needs.[53]

There are a number of problems with these conclusions. First, the identification of buildings as four-room houses does not appear to always be correct. The premier example that is usually cited for a four-room house found in Transjordan, outside of "Israelite" territory, is that of Sahab, noted above. Excavators did not find any four-room houses at this site; however, an excavation found a one-room divided by columns in a larger complex. While the excavator identified it with the four-room houses discovered west of the Jordan, it clearly lacks the typical characteristics of the four-room house.[54]

Tel Keisan, in the western Galilee, is another example of a site outside of Israelite territory that is heralded as containing four-room houses. Houses built with four units and with pillars were discovered at this site, but the excavators explained that "the rooms formed by the partition of the courtyards were too narrow" for the house to fit the four-room house type. They specifically argued that the structure "cannot be defined as a 'four-room house.'"[55] Buildings with four rooms or with pillars are often identified as four-room houses, but these features by themselves are not enough for such an identification. The four-room house, instead, has a distinctive plan that includes four oblong rooms or spaces, with the central space usually identified as an inner courtyard and the other three arranged on three of its sides.[56] The central space is usually wider than the structure's other spaces, and the entrance is usually opposite the broadroom, at the short end of the central space. Just because a structure has four rooms or pillars should not lead to its confusion with the distinctive floor plan of the four-room house.

Second, the entire argument that houses found in Transjordan are outside "Israelite" territory must be reevaluated. At least parts of Transjordan *were* considered to have been part of the territory in which early Israelites settled.[57] As discussed in chapter 6, the perception of Cisjordan and Transjordan as being sharply divided by the Jordan River is a modern one that does not appear to have been shared in ancient times. The four-room house at Tell el-'Umayri may very well have been associated with Israelite settlement in the Late Bronze-Iron Age I transition, and has been interpreted thus by the excavators.[58] Four-room houses have, however, been discovered in Transjordan at sites that go well beyond what even the most conservative scholars would define as "Israelite" territory. For example, four-room houses have been discovered at Tell Jawa, in Ammonite territory,[59] at Moabite sites, such as Khirbet el-Mudeina el-'Aliya[60] and al-Lahun,[61] and at Edomite sites, such as Ghrareh.[62] Several scholars have noted that, in these and other such cases, four-room houses outside the supposed Israelite territory date primarily to Iron Age I. Daviau noted that at Tall Jawa, Ammonite architects only used the four-room house plan in Iron I.[63] The remains at Khirbet el-Mudeina el-'Aliya seem to be limited to the end of the eleventh century B.C.E.,[64] and al-Lahun appears to have been abandoned at about the same time.[65] The central building at Ghrareh, which appears to have been "pure Palestinian Iron Age,"[66] probably dated from the seventh to sixth century B.C.E.[67] How can the occurrence of the supposed "Israelite" house in these and other locations be accounted for? Are they proof that the four-room house was indeed *not* an Israelite house style?

Rather than being a simple proof that the four-room house could not have been a "type fossil" for the Israelites, its appearance in Ammonite, Moabite, and Edomite sites may reflect the complexities of the Late Bronze-Iron Age transition in the southern Levant. During the Late Bronze Age, the Ammonites, Moabites, and Edomites—and even the Israelites—did not exist as "national" groups. Instead, they were tribal groups who were characterized by "in-group loyalty based on variously fluid notions of common unilineal descent."[68] There appear to have been virtually no walled settlements in the regions of Ammon, Moab, and Edom in the Late Bronze Age.[69] Instead, the tribal inhabitants of these regions appear to have been characterized by a high degree of pastoral nomadism in the Late Bronze and Iron Age I.[70] During periods of nomadization, the social and political allegiances of tribal groups tend to be more fluid.[71] The Bible recalls that the Israelites, Ammonites, Moabites, Edomites, and Arameans had all originally been related.[72] It may have been that, during this early period, the loyalties of the various tribes had not yet crystallized. Faust suggests "it is possible that during the Iron Age I there were people who were Israelite or in the process of becoming so, but due to various reasons their descendants in the Iron Age II became Ammonite, Moabite, etc."[73]

Indeed, in such a milieu, objects or architectural styles could have been used and/or appropriated by people who belonged to different groups. J. R. Kautz had already suggested some years ago that the presence of four-room houses in Moabite (and other) regions "suggests a milieu which cannot be limited to Israel and may indicate that sort of cultural contact between Israel and Moab which the book of Ruth assumes for the period of the Judges."[74] Based on the foregoing discussion, however, it could be that the Iron Age I settlements Tall Jawa, Khirbet el-Mudeina el-'Aliya and al-Lahun, could all have been inhabited by Israelites or those in the process of becoming Israelites. By Iron II, it may be that the "Israelite" inhabitants had left, or decided to become Ammonite or Moabite. In the case of a much later four-room house, such as the one at Ghrareh, in Edom, this is clearly either a case of diffusion or the presence of a mixed population that included Israelite elements.

One example of a four-room house was found far outside of the bounds of the southern Levant, in Egypt. Manfred Bietak discovered a four-room house in the precinct of a temple of Aya and Horemheb at Thebes that dated to sometime between the middle of the twelfth century to the first part of the eleventh century B.C.E.[75] While this may seem like a shocking exception to an understanding of the four-room house as an ethnic marker that would restrict it to the southern Levant, Bietak postulated that the house may have belonged to prisoners of war conscripted from Canaan to work on the deconstruction of the temple, to Shasu prisoners, or to workmen who came from Canaan during a time of drought or war. Bietak concludes that, in any of these three cases, the occupants of this house were likely Israelites.[76]

Despite the criticism of the four-room house as an Israelite "type-fossil," Yigal Shiloh, who had first identified it as an "Israelite" type house, was not deterred in his identification. Shortly before his death, he made some final observations about the four-room house.

> About 95 percent of them, we know now, appear in Israelite settlements and therefore I prefer to call it an Israelite-type house. I am always astonished when people say to me, "Why do you call it an Israelite-type house? I have seen an example of it somewhere else." I say very nice, but 95 percent, statistically, are in Israelite settlements.[77]

Likewise, Dever argues that this house-form has no real predecessors in the prior settlement history of Canaan, and that it appears suddenly on the Late Bronze-Iron Age I horizon. He suggests that this house style "seems to reflect a preference (or nostalgia) for a rural society and economy, and it also reflects the typical Israelite ideal of the 'good life,' based on close-knit families and communal values."[78] He continues to maintain that "these really *are* Israelite houses."

But is it simply the adaptability of this architectural form to an agricultural lifestyle that makes it "Israelite"? Bunimovitz and Faust insist that this "functional explanation" of the four-room house leaves several questions unanswered. They write:

> Attributing the success of the four-room house to its suitability to peasant daily life is a highly compelling argument, yet it falls short of conveying the full story of the structure's exceptional dominance as an architectural form during the Iron Age, and beyond that, as a cultural phenomenon. There were houses typical of other periods that functioned well, but none of them achieved such a dominant position in the architectural landscape of their time. Moreover, none were so uniform in plan.[79]

Bunimovitz and Faust have recently made a convincing case that the four-room house may be understood to be not only an ethnic marker but, more than that, "a symbolic expression of the Israelite mind—that is, their ethos or world-view."[80] Whether houses were urban or rural, rich or poor, they were built according to the same plan. Bunimovitz and Faust suggest that this argues against the functional theory,[81] which they move beyond to explore social aspects of the four-room house. Their conclusion is that the four-room house may reflect ethnic behavior, or that it may even have been designed to communicate ethnicity. They identify four ways in which the four-room house does this.[82]

1. Purity and Space Syntax. Extending a path of thought previously taken by Moshe Weinfeld, Bunimovitz and Faust suggest that the four-room house may have facilitated the separation between purity and impurity. An example of this would be the avoidance of a woman during menstruation. "Indeed, on examining the four-room plan one can immediately recognize its greatest merit, which is maximum privacy. Once the central space of the building, whether an open or roofed courtyard was entered, each of the rooms could be entered directly without going through adjacent spaces."[83] Even if an "unclean" person lived in the house, purity could be strictly maintained, since each room could be entered directly from the central space without passing through other rooms. This special quality does not seem to be present in other ancient Israelite dwelling structures in the Late Bronze Age and Iron Age.

2. Ideology. Another implication of this "access analysis" "is the correspondence between its nonhierarchical configuration and the "democratic" or egalitarian ethos of Israelite society."[84] While houses in many contemporary ethnographic examples often manifest "a hierarchical grading of accessibility and structural depth of spaces within the house related to generational and in some cases gender-based status distinctions (or both)," the four-room house "lacks 'depth' or access hierarchy and expresses a more egalitarian spirit than . . . contemporaneous" examples.[85]

3. Nonverbal Communication. Using the terms "canonical" and "indexical," Bunimovitz and Faust suggest that the four-room house both reminds the occupants of the principles (discussed in points one and two) embodied in the house's architecture, and communicates a message to others—both in and outside the community—that identifies the occupants as part of the community and enhances the coherence of the community.[86]

4. Order and Dominance. Drawing on Mary Douglas's theory that many of the holiness laws were actually about order,[87] Bunimovitz and Faust suggest the same interpretive schema for understanding "the astonishing dominance of the four-room house plan on almost all levels of Israelite architectural design."[88] They explain that "if the Israelites were deeply engaged with unity and 'order' as a negation of separateness and confusion, then these concepts must have percolated through all spheres of daily life, including material culture. Thus, it can be surmised that, once the four-room house took shape and was formalized as *the* container and embodiment of the Israelite lifestyle and symbolic 'order,' it became the 'right' house type and, hence, its great popularity. Building according to other architectural schemes must have been considered a deviation from the norm and possibly a violation of the holy 'order.'"[89]

Whether one agrees with Bunimovitz and Faust's interpretation of the ideology behind the four-room house, their arguments demonstrate the centrality of the four-room house in Israelite society and will, at the least, stimulate further discussion on Israelite ethnicity and ideology.

*The Material Culture and Ethnicity of the Highland Settlers*

## Pottery

The pottery of the Iron Age I highland settlements is distinctive for its limited repertoire.[90] It is characterized primarily by large pithoi, popularly known as collared-rim jars, storage jars, and cooking pots. Other select vessels appear, such as bowls, kraters, chalices, and jugs, but in significantly smaller quantities. Many types of vessels are absent, such as flasks and pyxides, and several types of bowls, juglets, and jugs.[91] Since one of the predominant forms is the collared-rim jar, the discussion begins with this form, and then the repertoire of the highland settlements as a whole.

The collared-rim storage jar (**Fig. 21**) is ubiquitous in the central hill-country. This ceramic type was first identified in 1930 by Hans Kjaer, who described it as a storage jar with a folded rim and a ridge at the base of the neck.[92] W. F. Albright coined the term "collared-rim store jar" during his excavations at Tell el-Fûl, and concluded that this specific ceramic type had appeared during the first half of the twelfth century and was indicative of the Israelites.[93] Y. Aharoni championed this view,[94] and it soon became mainstream. This view was not without objections, however, and as early as 1940 R. Engberg argued that some of Albright's ceramic examples at Megiddo actually represented an older ceramic tradition.[95] During the 1950s and 1960s, scholars observed the presence of collared-rim jars in areas not traditionally thought of as "Israelite,"

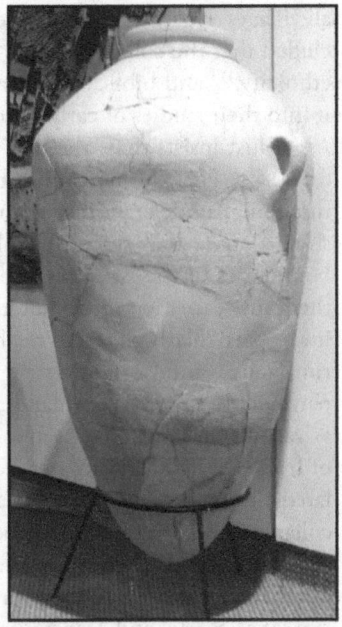

*Fig. 21*

and this began to cast doubt on identifying this ceramic form with the Israelites.[96] In the 1970s and 1980s, collared-rim jars continued to surface both in and out of the territory traditionally understood as "Israelite." Such sites where examples were found included Tel Nami,[97] Hazor,[98] Aphek,[99] Manahat,[100] Gezer,[101] Beth-Shean,[102] Deir 'Alla,[103] and Sahab.[104] At Sahab, a house dating to the second half of Iron Age I contained large numbers of collared-rim jars, a fact that led Ibrahim to argue that this vessel type could no longer be equated with the Israelites.[105] Several archaeologists proposed that the vessel must have originated as the development of the Middle Bronze Age storage jar[106] or the Canaanite storage jar.[107] Kempinski proposed that the vessel was manufactured in Canaanite centers for Israelite use.[108] Yannai has recently argued that collared-rim jars were in use from the Chalcolithic to the early Iron Age throughout Anatolia, Cyprus, western Syria, and Israel, and cannot be used as an indicator of ethnicity.[109]

Archaeologists soon began to seek functional explanations for the distribution of the vessel type, based on its suitability to the local environment. The collared-rim jar may have been essential for water storage for those who did not settle within close proximity to a water source;[110] it could have served as a storage container for a variety of liquid products, including water, olive oil, and wine;[111] or it may have been used for the storage of dry goods.[112] London suggested that the collared-rim jar was simply a type characteristic of rural sites, and that one would expect to find this pottery type wherever rural settlements existed, whether they were inhabited by Israelites, Canaanites, or others. She concludes that "food storage is a requirement in all villages, regardless of their location or residents."[113] Many archaeologists have concluded that the collared-rim jar should not be viewed as a type of vessel that reflects ethnicity,[114] and biblical scholars have generally adopted this view and incorporated it into their studies of early Israel.[115]

Faust insists that "the new consensus is very problematic in the face of the evidence."[116] First, he notes that the claims raised by scholars who argue solely for a functional understanding of the collared-rim jar are contradictory. These scholars should argue that since the collared-rim jar was discovered outside the presumed boundaries of the Israelites, then it must not have been specifically connected with them. Instead, they argue that its appearance in the highlands was due to the fact that it was particularly suited to the highlands in terms of its functionality. If the collared-rim jar is a rural ceramic type used in the highlands because its functionality was particularly suited to highland areas, then why was it found in such large quantities at various lowland sites, such as Megiddo? At 'Afula, just east of Megiddo, hundreds of Iron Age I storage jars were found in Stratum III, but only one of these was a collared-rim jar.[117] Faust argues that this discrepancy disproves London's claim that the collared-rim jar reflects rural society, and he argues that "the same logic used to disprove the ethnic explanation should have been employed for the functional one."[118]

Second, those who have drawn conclusions about the presence of the collared-rim jar at coastal and Transjordanian sites have typically done so without considering the quantitative distribution of the vessels.[119] When one considers the distribution of the collared-rim jars, however, it is very clear that the *primary* users of this ceramic type were the Israelites, whether or not the jar had any ethnic meaning.[120] The largest concentration of collared-rim jars has been found in the central hill-country at sites like Shiloh, Ai, Bethel, Tell el-Ful, Giloah, and 'Izbet Sartah. It is found in medium quantities in Transjordan, in smaller quantities in the Galilee and Jezreel Valleys, and in nearly insignificant quantities on the coastal plain and in the Shephelah.[121] While much has been made of the presence of the collared-rim jar at sites such as the Philistine city of Tel Qasile, only five fragments and one complete vessel were actually found there, a fact that suggested to A. Mazar that they must have been foreign to the site, probably brought there by trade,[122] a possibility which leads to our third point.

Third, the provenience of collared-rim jars must be considered. Where did the vessels found at Canaanite coastal sites originate? Were they manufactured at the sites where they were found? Or might they have originated elsewhere? At lowland sites, where the collared-rim jar has only been found in very small quantities, it has been discovered that they were not locally manufactured. Instead, these vessels were

## The Material Culture and Ethnicity of the Highland Settlers

brought from workshops in neighboring areas.[123] Studies of collared-rim jars at highland sites such as Giloh and Khirbet Raddana, on the other hand, have shown that the large numbers of vessels at these sites were locally produced.[124] Killebrew concludes that the collared-rim jar must have indicated a social boundary between the central hill-country settlement and the lowland sites, and she postulates that itinerant potters may have been responsible for its dispersal.[125]

Fourth, evidence from Jordan that has been accruing in recent years must be taken into consideration. As noted in chapter 6, the thirteenth- to twelfth-century phases at Tell el-'Umayri represent the earliest material culture of the highland sites, making it critical for the study of the development of highland culture. Almost 20 percent of the pottery corpus at Tell el-'Umayri was comprised of collared-rim jars, making them the earliest such vessels discovered thus far. Those at Sahab, mentioned earlier, are more typologically advanced and cannot date any earlier than the late twelfth century.[126] L. G. Herr has found that the collared-rim jar underwent development from its earliest Iron I forms to the forms it took in the earliest Iron II. In early Iron Age I, the collared-rim jar was characterized by a tall neck, flaring rim, a tendency toward a triangular thickening of the rim, and a prominent collar. In the earliest Iron Age II, the vessel came to be characterized by a short neck, a barely thickened rim, a lack of room for any distinctiveness of the rim, and a very short collar.[127] The early Iron Age I collared-rim jars at Tell el-'Umayri seem to represent the earliest appearance of this vessel, and Herr has postulated that the diffusion of the vessel type into Cisjordan may have begun in Transjordan.[128] Killebrew postulates that the vessel type spread from there to the central hill-country of Cisjordan.[129] The distribution of the collared-rim jar in Transjordan, therefore, is not a problem for its association on some level with the Israelites. If Tell el-'Umayri can be identified as an early Reubenite site, then the collared-rim jar appears to have originated among early Israelite settlers east of the Jordan.

The pottery repertoire of the thirteenth- to twelfth-century highland settlements and its relationship to the question of early Israel's ethnic identity has also been the subject of heated controversy. As mentioned above, the pottery of the Iron Age I highland settlements is distinctive for its limited repertoire, which is characterized by a relatively narrow group of utilitarian vessels which, in addition to the collared-rim jar, included storage jars and cooking pots and, in smaller quantities, bowls, kraters, chalices, and jugs. J. A. Callaway, after having spent years excavating both et-Tell and Khirbet Raddana, concluded that the pottery forms all found their parallels at lowland and coastal sites.[130] This conclusion led him to completely change his thinking about early Israel. He concluded that instead of having migrated in from Transjordan, the early Iron I highlanders had their background in Canaanite culture and religion. He wrote, "My conclusion in the light of these discussions is that the Iron I villagers at Ai had their background in Canaanite culture and religion and that this can be documented extensively with artifacts which have their parallels at lowland and coastal sites."[131] This view has led to a consensus that the highland settlers originated from among the Canaanites.[132] Edelman summarizes that ceramic experts consider the generally homogenous repertoire of the Iron I "to be a direct continuation of the Late Bronze 'Canaanite' ceramic tradition," and "should not erroneously be presumed to reflect the presence of a similar, ethnically homogenous population, nor necessarily be an ethnic marker."[133] Dever has been the most outspoken advocate of this view, and has published several charts in which he compares twelfth-century pottery vessels from Shiloh and 'Izbet Sartah with similar thirteenth-century vessels from Gezer, Lachish, and Megiddo in order to demonstrate the supposed Canaanite derivation of the Israelite pottery forms.[134]

Again, as noted in chapter 6, a comprehensive discussion of Israelite origins cannot be carried out without consideration of the evidence from Transjordan. In 2007, A. F. Rainey called attention to the ceramic repertoire of Transjordan and suggested that it should be factored into the study of early Israelite origins. W. G. Dever sardonically replies that "Rainey is an excellent philologian and historical geographer, but he lacks first-hand acquaintance with pottery."[135] He goes on to insist that there "are very few LB sites in the whole region, even fewer well-excavated and published ones," and that "the local pottery is scarcely known, even to specialists." A Late Bronze Age repertoire *does* exist for Transjordan, however, and it has been under study for several decades.[136] Some of the sites associated with it include: Abu al-Kharaz, al-Qasir, Amman, Deir 'Alla, Jarash, Katarat as-Samra, Khirbet Umm ad-Dananir, Quwayliba (Abila), Sahab, Tabaqat Fahl (Pella), Tall al-'Umayri, Tall as-Sa'idiyah, Tall Irbid, and Umm al-Qanafid, as well as some small sites alongside the Wadi Ziqlab. Using this repertoire, as well as other methods for the study of ceramics, the study of ancient ceramic traditions on both sides of the Jordan can indeed be undertaken.[137]

In order to explore the possibility of the derivation of Cisjordanian highland pottery types from Transjordanian prototypes, the same vessels from Shiloh and 'Izbet Sartah used by Dever in his comparative charts can be put side by side with thirteenth-century Transjordanian vessels (**Fig. 22**).[138]

Based on these comparisons, A. F. Rainey concludes that "there is no longer any excuse to look westward for the inspiration of the surviving Iron I pottery shapes," but "the new settlers acquired their pottery traditions from their life on the Transjordanian plateau and the Jordan Valley."[139] Dever argues that what Transjordanian samples are known are all common to the material culture of western Palestine, and

> that is what we would expect, in the aftermath of the collapse of the Late Bronze Age Canaanite culture in the late 13th cent. BCE. In the vacuum, there arose in Syria-Palestine a number of related early Iron Age petty states and peoples—Arameans, Phoenicians, various "Sea Peoples," Israelites, Ammonites, Moabites, Edomites, and others (as well as the surviving nomadic peoples). All these derive from a common Canaanite culture and display related characteristics in language, religion, and material culture like pottery. That fully explains the ceramic "similarities."[140]

Dever insists that "all ceramic experts" agree that the typical Iron Age I ceramic repertoire derives from the Late Bronze Age traditions of western Palestine.[141] Late Bronze Age material certainly did spread into Transjordan, as the recent survey of E. J. van der Steen has shown.[142] But to say that the collapse of Late Bronze Age

## The Material Culture and Ethnicity of the Highland Settlers

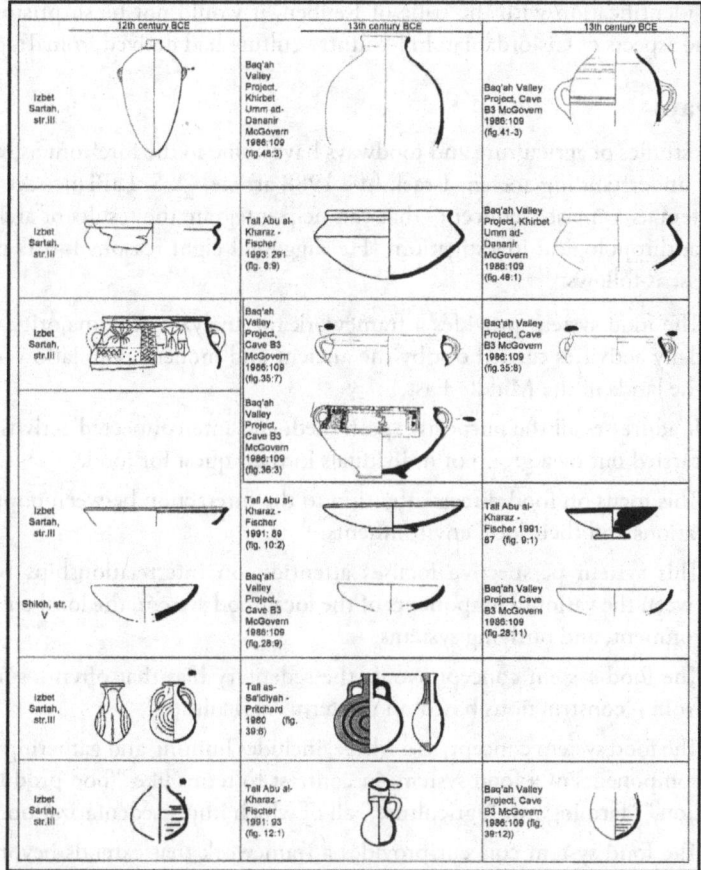

Fig. 22

Canaanite culture in the late thirteenth century B.C.E. resulted in "a sort of early Iron Age *Koine* culture extending throughout Syria, as well as Palestine both east and west,"[143] is an oversimplification of the process of cultural development. Ceramic traditions certainly overlapped, but distinct ceramic traditions also developed in western Palestine and Transjordan. In studying these ceramic traditions, many ceramic experts, contra Dever, have argued for diffusion of various forms from Transjordan to Palestine. H. J. Franken and J. Kalsbeek, for example, suggested that the technique of Iron I cooking pot manufacture started in Jordan before it reached Israel.[144] Herr has also argued that the thirteenth- to twelfth-century pottery corpus from Tell el-'Umayri seems to predate the ceramic assemblages from other Iron Age I sites, such as Ai, Raddana, Shiloh, 'Izbet Sartah, and Sahab, all of which seem to be later in date.[145] In light of the discussion in chapter 6 about the common culture shared at Hesban, Jawa, Jalul, and Tell el-'Umayri during the thirteenth to twelfth centuries and their possible identification with the tribe of Reuben, it would not be surprising to find that some aspects of Cisjordanian hill-country culture had derived from Transjordan.

## Foodways

The studies of agriculture and foodways have come to the forefront as important tools for understanding ancient Israel. In a 1988 article, Ø. S. LaBianca set forth the food system as a "master concept" that can help integrate the results of archaeological and anthropological investigations. He suggested eight reasons for its particular usefulness, as follows:[146]

1. The food system provides a framework for analyzing the majority of daily activities carried out by the ancient and modern populations of the lands of the Middle East.
2. It addresses all the purposive, patterned, and interconnected activities carried out by a group of individuals in their quest for food.
3. This focus on food directs attention to the interaction between populations and their local environments.
4. This system perspective focuses attention on interrelationships between the various components of the local food system, the local environment, and outlying systems.
5. The food system concept avoids the sedentary bias that often results from reconstructions based on the term "agriculture."
6. The food system concept, as a whole, includes hunting and gathering as components of a food system, in contrast to terms like "food production," "farming," or "agriculture," all of which imply sedentarization.
7. The food system concept provides a framework that extends beyond solely human components, i.e., animals found in association with human populations can be accounted for when considered in light of the food system concept.
8. The food system concept facilitates interdisciplinary research.

This final point is of some importance. As scholars from various disciplines—epigraphers, ethnoarchaeologists, ceramic analysts, faunal analysts, paleobotanists, and others—they all, within their respective disciplines, make a contribution toward understanding one or more of the components of the processes in the food system. But, "once the food system is accepted as a master concept for integrating various lines of evidence, members of a multidisciplinary team are in a much better position to relate their data to the overall picture. Without such a master concept, their results will, understandably, be offered as contributions to a particular discipline rather than as contributions to an interdisciplinary project."[147]

Elsewhere, LaBianca notes that there are some important limitations that should be noted in regard to the food system. First, he suggests that "there is no necessary connection between adherence to a food system framework and some form of uniformitarianism or some species of environmental or historical determinism."[148] This is a significant point, in light of the fact that researchers have generally underestimated or dismissed religious factors in favor of materialistic explanations in reconstructing Israelite origins and history.[149] Second, LaBianca notes that the food system approach may not be equally applicable everywhere.[150]

In 1985, David C. Hopkins published his important study of the highland settlements in Israel, entitled *The Highlands of Canaan: Agricultural Life in the Early Iron Age*.[151] He observed that "the absolute increase in the numbers of settlement sites in the early Iron Age is the primary datum of Israel's emergence recognized and accepted on all fronts." In discussing the agricultural situation of the highland settlers, Hopkins gives much credence to N. K. Gottwald's picture of Israel as living on a subsistence economy, and he stresses the "importance [of] the ability, technically and socially, to store foodstuffs as a buffer against the greatly variable yields of Highland agriculture. The large collared-rim pithoi and grain-pits so common on the sites of the early Iron Age Highlands are the concrete attestations of this high priority objective."[152] Oded Borowski, however, has argued to the contrary, pointing out the successes of the Israelites in settling the central hill-country. Their use of terracing, runoff farming, and the use of iron for toolmaking all "led to the creation of agricultural surplus, which, in turn, led to the introduction of new types of storage facilities, such as the pillared storehouses."[153] Firmage clearly illustrates the ways in which the agricultural economy of Israel flourished during the Iron Age:

> It is beyond doubt that certain geographical areas and economic groups enjoyed considerable surpluses. Parts of the Transjordan, for example, were able to export a surplus of wheat to Tyre (Ezek 17.17). The same area provided a tribute of 10,000 kor each of wheat and barley to the Judean king Jotham (2 Chr 27.5). Even small rural communities may have enjoyed substantial surpluses. Finkelstein has suggested that the annual surplus at 'Izbet Sartah (Level II—11$^{th}$ cent.) was on the order of 100 percent (AIS, 268–9).[154] This figure is over and above probable crop losses and seed needed for planting. By way of comparison, Arab villages in the 'Izbet Sartah area . . . on average also produced twice as much grain as they consumed. In general, the specialized horticulture that we find in Iron Age Israel characterizes a society that has developed beyond a meager subsistence economy.[155]

The typical picture of Israel and its villages eking out a subsistence-level existence, therefore, is not only out of accord with the biblical and archaeological data, but also with general settlement patterns. Newer approaches to studying settlement patterns have made clear that sedentarization and nomadization are intimately related to food system intensification and/or abatement, both of which are most fruitfully studied in broad historical and geographical terms.[156] In general, the transition from Late Bronze to Iron I reflects this movement from stabilization to destabilization and, ultimately, back to stabilization. The increase in settlements—flourishing settlements—in the central hill-country accords with this picture.

The role of agriculture has been overlooked in understanding Israel's development as a people and, particularly, their ability to successfully migrate into Canaan. Oded Borowski has recently elucidated the extent of the importance agriculture played in the settlement process. He explains:

> The Canaanite cities, according to the OT, were heavily fortified and possessed war chariots (Jos 17.16, 18; Judg 1.19; 4.3, 13). Most of these cities were situated in areas where they controlled large tracts of agricultural land. The Israelites, who wanted to conquer the land but lacked the military might to do so, were obliged to develop an economic base in the fringe areas which were unoccupied by the Canaanites. In spite of harsh conditions, and with the help of land-use innovations, the Israelites managed to become agriculturalists and created for themselves an economic base from which they could conquer the land. From that time on agriculture dominated Israelite daily life.[157]

Borowski goes on to explain the ways in which the Israelite settlement depended on successful adaptation to natural conditions and available resources. In the process of adapting, Israel employed terracing—"a method heretofore not widely used in Canaan."[158] They also used runoff farming and employed iron in the manufacture of farming tools. All of these approaches, as mentioned earlier, allowed these villages to flourish to the extent that they began to incorporate new types of storage facilities to hold the surplus.[159]

While not all would agree, some anthropologists and archaeologists have concluded that foodways may be one of the few remaining reliable indicators of ethnicity.[160] Noting that certain groups resist change in foodways even in the face of potential assimilation, Finkelstein has argued that foodways "often rival ideology and religion in terms of cultural conservatism [and are] a primary symbol used to maintain cultural identity and group solidarity."[161]

Obviously, the presence or absence of pig bones is one of the clear features of discussions regarding ancient Israelite foodways. In the Late Bronze Age, pigs appear in both the lowlands and the highlands of Palestine. Finkelstein notes that "in the Iron I pigs appear in great numbers in the Shephelah and the southern coastal plain and are quite popular at other lowland sites. But they disappear from the faunal assemblages of the central hill country."[162] Though the faunal assemblage at Hesban included 4.8 percent pig bones, the sites at both Ebal and Khirbet Raddana comprised 0 percent pig bones, and pig bones make up only 0.1 percent of the faunal assemblage at Iron I Shiloh. There was only one pig bone discovered at Shiloh, and it may have been intrusive. Finkelstein reasons that:

> Regardless of the factors that may influence pig distribution, this seems to mean that the taboo on pigs was already practiced in the hill country in the Iron I—pigs were not present in proto-Israelite Iron I sites in the highlands while they were quite popular in a proto-Ammonite site and numerous in Philistine sites. As predicted by Stager several years ago, food taboos, more precisely, pig taboos, are emerging as the main, if not only, avenue that can shed light on ethnic boundaries in the Iron I.[163]

Finkelstein concludes that foodways are the "only" possible indicator of ethnicity in Iron I.[164] While many of Finkelstein's conclusions may be found wanting,[165] foodways must, indeed, be acknowledged as a key factor in the discussion of ethnicity in regard to ancient Israel.

# AN ASCRIPTIVE APPROACH TO ETHNICITY

Despite the complexities, settlement pattern, site layout, the four-room house, pottery, and foodways can all contribute to the identification of the Israelites in the Iron Age I. It is important to remember, however, that material features are not what *create* ethnicity. Instead, material features are simply the material correlates of the ethnic boundaries, which are perceived. Avraham Faust has written an important work in which he explores in great detail the thesis that if Israel can be identified by material features, those material features must be understood in light of Israelite ideology.[166] The early Israelites may or may not have invented the various forms with which we are so preoccupied. It does seem clear, however, that some of them did become reflective of Israelite ethnicity. What is of most importance, however, is not necessarily the first appearance of these traits, but if, when, and why they became ethnically meaningful.

The premises on which Faust's arguments are based are not new. Thirty-five years ago, the pioneering social anthropologist Frederick Barth suggested that, rather than a morphological model that looks for material data that identifies the ethnicity of ancient peoples, researchers should concentrate on social factors.[167] This would enable us to see "ethnic groups as a form of social organization." Barth calls this the "ascriptive" approach to ethnicity. The critical feature in this approach then becomes that of self-ascription and ascription by others.[168] In other words, the determining factor of a people's ethnicity was whatever they and others *perceived* it to be.

These ideas have tremendously important implications for understanding the portrayal of early Israel in the Hebrew Bible. Israel's identity did not imply a racial principle, in the sense that being an Israelite was not a matter of genetics. The Hebrew Bible tells us that a "mixed group" came out of Egypt with the "holy nation" (Exod 12:38; 19:6), without there being any sense of impropriety. Together these groups comprised a loose network of tribes. The "mixed group" and the "holy nation" both formalized their commitment to Yahweh in the covenant ceremony at Sinai (Exod 19–40:38), by which they formed a new society.[169] At Sinai, the disparate families who participated in the covenant-making process accepted Yahweh as their suzerain and bound themselves to live in sacred truce with one another under God's lordship.[170] As a result of this process, the disparate tribes and the "mixed group" of non-Israelites, all of whom had participated in the exodus events, all became unified as a new socioreligious community.[171] As Israel's history progressed, covenant renewal ceremonies continued to integrate new elements into the society (Josh 8:30-35; 24). In sum, social and religious ideology created the unity of Israel as an *ethnos*, and it allowed other tribes and individuals to affiliate themselves with Israel, sharing in its ethnic consciousness.

The issue of how to define an Israelite is one of the main themes of the book of Joshua. Early in the book, at the outset of the "conquest," the narrator recounts the stories of Rahab and Achan, each of whom is the quintessential representative of their *ethnos*, and each of whom becomes the spiritual "other," in order to explore this theme.[172] The story of Rahab is replete with sexual innuendo, which becomes a metaphor for later Israelite spiritual indiscretions. At the beginning of the conquest, she presents a threat. Her sexual promiscuity, which is part of an extended metaphor in which sexual and religious promiscuity are equated, is emphasized by bawdy allusions. In sleeping at Rahab's house, the Israelite spies come precariously close to giving in to idolatry, the same sin that will haunt their future habitation of Canaan. When Rahab went to the roof, however, instead of seducing and compromising the spies, she herself becomes an Israelite and a devotee of Yahweh (Josh 2:9-11).

If Rahab is the quintessential Canaanite who becomes part of Israel, then Achan is the quintessential Israelite who essentially becomes a Canaanite. After the fall of Jericho, Achan stole some of the spoils of war that were supposed to have been "under the ban" (Josh 7:21). His crime is revealed in the context of a long genealogical recounting, which reinforces his status as a representative of Israel. Although he was the only one who stole spoils on this occasion, all Israel was held accountable for his crime, and the nation's next battle, at Ai, was a failure because of it (Josh 7:11). Yahweh made it clear that unless the Israelites got rid of the banned material, they, too, would fall under the ban. This is significant, because it is tantamount to Yahweh telling Israel that, because of Achan's appropriation of banned material, the entire nation now had contracted the status of that banned material. In other words, the people of Israel had become like the Canaanites, who had already been put under the ban and destroyed at Jericho (Josh 6:21).

The misdeeds of the quintessential Israelite threatened to transform Yahweh's people into Canaanites, and if Israel was to act like a Canaanite, then Israel would be treated like a Canaanite. In order for Israel as a whole to avoid being turned into Canaanites, Achan must be destroyed. He was stoned and burned, and his remains were buried under a great heap of stones (Josh 7:24-26). Now that the threat presented by Achan's "conversion" to Canaanitism was eradicated, the conquest could proceed without impediment. Frank Spina noted the dramatic inversion of the Canaanite and the Israelite in this story. While Rahab the Canaanite's family was absorbed into Israel and "has lived in Israel ever since" (Josh 6:25), Achan and his family were reduced to a memorial consisting of a heap of stones. The significance of the inversion is that Rahab was not consigned to her Canaanite status, and Achan did not benefit from his Israelite pedigree. Each became "the other."[173] These important stories in the book of Joshua show that Israel's self-understanding—and the understanding of Israel held by others—may have been more ascriptive than morphological. Just as the tribes were bound into a unified "nation" by their shared religious ideology, others could transfer their ethnic identification through adoption of those ideas—essentially *becoming*

Israelite. Israel did have ethnic boundaries, and those boundaries were reflected by material correlates. Those ethnic boundaries were generated, however, by ideology. And that ideology allowed for the inclusion of foreigners who embraced Yahwism.[174]

# CONCLUSION

In this chapter, we reviewed the theoretical and material issues involved in identifying the ethnicity of the highland settlers discussed in chapter 6. Since the nineteenth century, it has been assumed that specific peoples could be linked with the artifacts they used, and lists of material correlates that could be identified with specific people groups were commonly used in identifying their ethnicity. In recent years, the use of such "trait lists" has fallen out of use, and the approach of associating "pots and people" has come under heavy criticism. The reasons for this are nowhere explicitly stated and appear to be based on confusion of the archaeology of ethnicity with racism. Racism, however, is different from ethnicity, which simply refers to a shared sense of peoplehood. A people's perception of itself as having a distinctive identity usually will be manifested in material correlates of behavior, which, although they may be difficult to identify, are usually present in some way in the archaeological record. We considered five such traits that may still contribute to the identification of a given site as "Israelite," including: settlement pattern, site layout, four-room house, pottery, and foodways. Each of these was discussed in an effort to determine whether and to what extent it might contribute to the discussion about Israelite ethnicity. While these features may still have some value for discussing Israelite ethnicity, material features are not what initially create ethnicity. Instead, material features are simply the correlates of the ethnic boundaries, which are perceived. These conclusions reflect the thinking of the pioneering social anthropologist of the 1960s, Frederick Barth, who understood ethnic groups as a form of social organization. When the story of Israel's emergence in the land of Canaan in the book of Joshua is read with this "ascriptive" understanding of ethnicity in mind, it becomes clear that one of the book's primary concerns is how the emerging Israelites were to define themselves in relation to their Canaanite neighbors. The emerging Israelites had ethnic boundaries reflected in material correlates. Those boundaries, however, were generated by their ideology, in which the Israelites saw themselves as a distinct people. At the same time, however, the Israelites' self-understanding was such that it allowed for the assimilation of foreigners who embraced Yahwism.

CHAPTER 8

# 'IZBET SARTAH: A PROTOTYPICAL ISRAELITE SETTLEMENT SITE

In chapter 6, we reviewed the findings from archaeological surveys, which pointed to a clear demographic change in the central hill-country of Canaan in the thirteenth century B.C.E. Very few of the Iron I sites discovered in these surveys are located on tells. The vast majority are, instead, simple rural villages. In the Manassite territory, these settlements were classified into two groups, of small and medium-sized sites. The smaller sites range from 0.1 to 1.2 acres, while the medium-sized sites range from 1.2 to 2.4 acres.[1] The villages in Manasseh are similar to those excavated at Khirbet Raddana, Ai, Giloh, and 'Izbet Sartah, all of which share similar characteristics. In this chapter, we will focus in on one of these sites, 'Izbet Sartah, in order to get a "close-up" view of a prototypical early Israelite settlement site.

## LOCATION, DISCOVERY, AND SIGNIFICANCE

'Izbet Sartah is a small village dating to the Iron Age I (1200–1000 B.C.E.) located on the western side of the central hill-country (**Fig. 23**). The site is situated on a low spur of the foothills (**Fig. 24**).[2] Tel Aphek, the major biblical site of the region, is located about two miles west of 'Izbet Sartah. South of the site, the Wadi Rabah slopes down from the hills into the plains. There is no natural water supply for the site, and it appears that they relied on cisterns hewn into the limestone slopes.

The site was discovered in 1973 by an archaeological survey team led by the late Moshe Kochavi, which was surveying the area around Tel Aphek on behalf of Tel Aviv University and the Archaeological Survey of Israel. Excavations had already begun at Tel Aphek,[3] and the survey was conducted in an attempt to better understand the settlement history of the region. Two weeks of excavation were carried out in the winter of 1976 and three short excavations of three weeks each in the summers of 1976, 1977, and 1978 were led by Kochavi, with Israel Finkelstein as field director. The final report, published by Finkelstein,[4] is a revised and expanded version

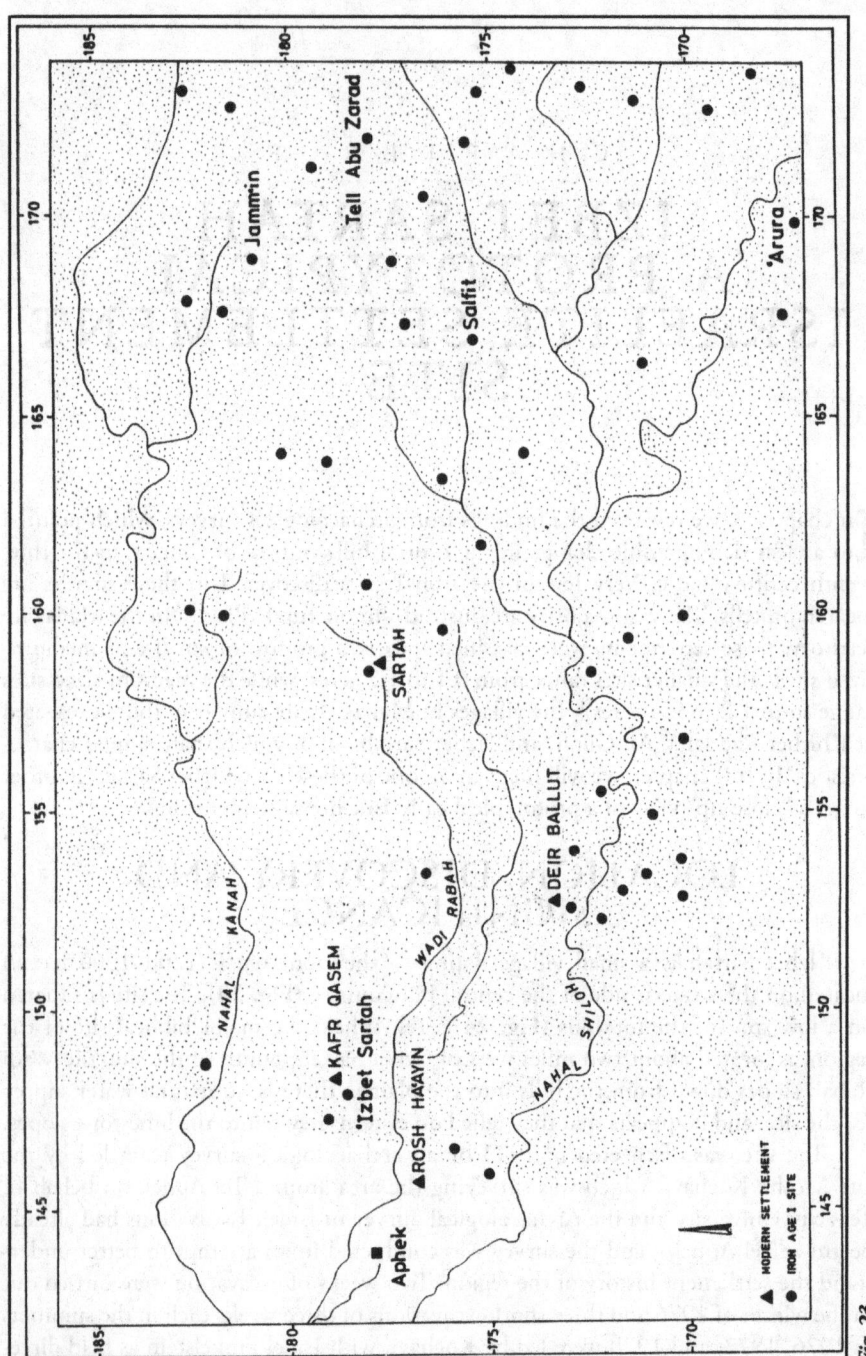

Fig. 23

of the chapters dealing with 'Izbet Sartah in his doctoral dissertation, supplemented with contributions by experts in other disciplines.

The excavation of 'Izbet Sartah uncovered three strata of occupation. The earliest of these, Stratum III, was dated to the time between the end of the thirteenth or the beginning of the twelfth century B.C.E. and the beginning of the eleventh century B.C.E. Stratum II represented a very brief period of occupation at the end of the eleventh century B.C.E. Stratum I, the latest in the series, dated to the beginning of the tenth century B.C.E. The survey also discovered six additional sites dating to this period in the vicinity of 'Izbet Sartah. All of these sites together probably belonged to the influx of hill-country settlers.[5]

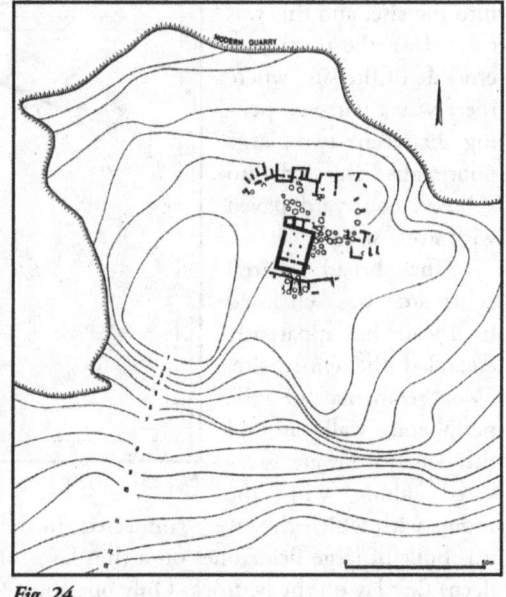

*Fig. 24*

At the outset, we should note that this site has tremendous significance for the study of the early Israelite settlement. Finkelstein enumerated three reasons for 'Izbet Sartah's importance. First, the lack of occupation at the site in later periods made it possible to expose large areas of the site and reconstruct the site-plan of each stratum. Because of this, the excavations at 'Izbet Sartah have been important for understanding how Israelite architecture developed in the Iron I period.[6] Second, 'Izbet Sartah's location near Aphek creates the possibility of studying the relationship between a small Israelite settlement site and a nearby Canaanite city that later became an important Philistine center. Third, 'Izbet Sartah is located in the Shephelah, which was the liminal zone between the coastal plains and the Palestinian highlands. The Shephelah played an important role in the Israelite settlement because it provided a buffer zone between the Canaanites and later the Philistines, both of whom dwelled in the lowlands, while the Israelites confined themselves to the hill-country.[7] The study of 'Izbet Sartah enables us to bring more clarity to the reconstruction of the early Israelite settlement in this vulnerable region.

# THE ARCHAEOLOGICAL REMAINS

## Stratum III

In Stratum III, 'Izbet Sartah was laid out in an elliptical pattern and covered an area of about a half acre (**Fig. 25**). There appears to have been only one entryway into the site, and this was located on the northeastern side of the site, where there was a narrow opening between two large doorjambs. This led into a broad courtyard paved with stone slabs.

The broad central courtyard was enclosed by a wall that apparently encircled the entire site. Two segments of the peripheral wall around the courtyard were excavated, along with the rooms with which they were connected. In the northern sector, the peripheral wall was built of large fieldstones on a thin layer of soil and pebbles (0.7 to 1.1 inches deep) that lay on the bedrock. Only one course of stones survived, and this segment of the wall measured between twenty-four to twenty-seven inches wide. Owing to a combination of stone-robbing and erosion, no Stratum III architectural remains are in the western or eastern sectors. In the southern sector, another segment of the peripheral wall was discovered. Like its northern counterpart, this one had also been built of large and medium-sized fieldstones, and measured twenty to twenty-four inches wide.

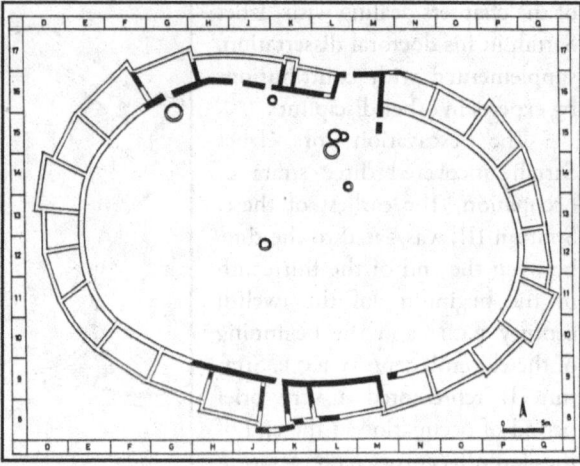

*Fig. 25*

From this wall, other walls projected outward at right angles. These walls clearly divided dwelling units. The walls of these units were not equal in length, which makes it clear that the width of these rooms varied. In these rooms, the flooring was simply the bedrock. There were no doors from one of these units into the others. Instead, they all opened up into the courtyard, where six stone-lined silos were located.

The ceramic repertoire of 'Izbet Sartah was meager. Stratum III was clearly abandoned in a systematic and orderly fashion, and the inhabitants apparently took all of their usable household furnishings with them. The result was that few whole vessels were found. Some of the earliest finds included a small stirrup jar that appears to have been fashioned in the style

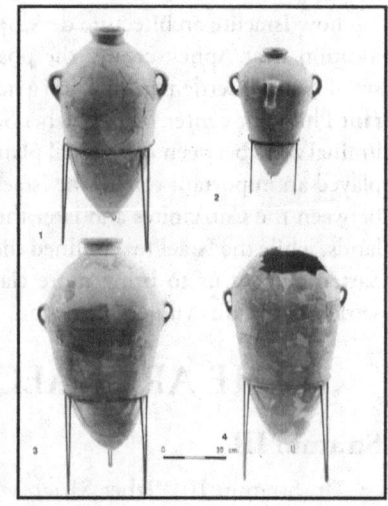

*Fig. 26*

of the Late Mycenaean IIIB,[8] a substantial fragment of a large krater bearing a palm-and-ibex decoration and the sherd of a krater with a "palm" motif in applied relief.

Of special interest are three collared-rim storage jars that were found whole (**Fig. 26**), which echo those of other highland settlements. The bases of several store jars that Finkelstein described as "Canaanite" in style were also found, along with the rims of bowls and cooking pots that were manufactured in the ceramic traditions of the Late Bronze Age.[9] The description of these as "Canaanite" in style should be reevaluated in light of the burgeoning corpus of Transjordanian styles and the similarity of the 'Izbet Sartah repertoire with those east of the Jordan River.[10] The ceramic assemblage did include a few Philistine sherds, which makes it clear that the inhabitants were in some degree of contact with the nearby coastal plain. The pottery repertoire establishes the date of the beginning of activity at the site of 'Izbet Sartah to the end of the thirteenth or the beginning of the twelfth century B.C.E.

## Stratum II

At the end of Stratum III, there was a brief gap before the founding of Stratum II near the end of the twelfth century B.C.E. Stratum II differed in plan from Stratum III and demonstrated some degree of planning. A large four-room house, Building 109, was erected in the site's central courtyard, which was expanded to cover an area of about one acre (**Fig. 27**).

This house was surrounded by dozens of silos, which had been dug into the building remains of Stratum III. These silos were crowded together and, in some cases, touched one another. The outside edge of the site was defined by a chain of small houses. The plans of two of these were reconstructed, and at least two of them appear to have been four-room houses. On the assumption that the layout was similar in the unexcavated areas, it is estimated that about twenty buildings may have surrounded Building 109 on the periphery of the site. These houses did not adjoin one another, however, which meant that the houses did not form a wall, as did those of the Stratum III settlement. The Stratum II settlement at 'Izbet Sartah, therefore, had no defense system.

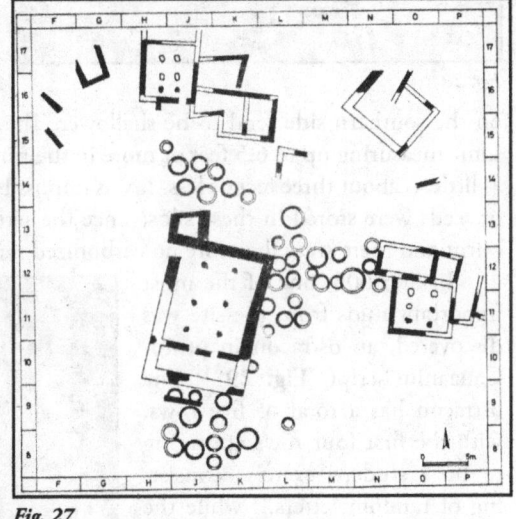

*Fig. 27*

The four-room house in the middle of the central courtyard is the most important building of Stratum II. It measured about 39 by 52 feet, and its outer walls, constructed of large fieldstones, were up to 4.5 feet thick. The entrance to the house was at the end of its western wall, and a small room was attached to the northern side of the building. The house differed slightly from the typical four-room house design in that it had an annex, which was built contemporaneously with the rest of the house, and its entrance was in its northwest corner instead of through the short wall opposite, in what is called the broadroom. The floors of the building were made of bedrock, flagstones, or beaten earth. The eastern and western longitudinal rooms were paved with flagstones, while the central longitudinal room consisted of bedrock at its southern end and beaten earth at its northern end. The central room appears to have served as a courtyard for household industries. It appears that the superstructure of this building had been built of mud-brick, since there were virtually no fallen stones to be found on either side of the surviving lower courses. This building continued to be in use in Stratum I.

Fig. 28

The house was surrounded by forty-three grain silos (**Fig. 28**) with stone-lined walls and floors of either bedrock or a pavement of small stones. Some of these silos abutted the central building, and some of them bordered one another. The depth of the silos varies, with those on the eastern side of the house measuring up to about three feet deep, while those on the southern side tend to be shallower. The size of the silos varies as well, with some measuring up to 6.5 feet or more in their inner diameter, and others measuring as little as about three feet or less. It was impossible to determine what kinds of grains or seeds were stored in these silos, since the settlement of Stratum II had not been burnt and there were therefore no carbonized remains to be found.

In Silo 605, one of the most important finds from the site was discovered, an ostracon in proto-Canaanite script (**Fig. 29**).[11] The ostracon has a total of five rows, with the first four rows appearing to be a student exercise consisting of random letters,[12] while the fifth row contains the entire alphabet, written from left to right. The ostracon contains about eighty to eighty-five characters total, which can be dated paleographically to about 1200 B.C.E.[13] The 'Izbet Sartah ostracon is very significant. Not only does it attest to the

Fig. 29

fact that there was literacy among the inhabitants of the hill-country settlements toward the end of the twelfth century B.C.E., but the ostracon also appears to have been a curricular exercise, which means that writing was being taught, and the use of abecedarium was an important tool for the development of literacy among the hill-country settlers.[14] Outside of the 'Izbet Sartah ostracon, there is no evidence of anything "curricular" in the linear alphabet until the Iron Age IIB. While the corpus of first millennium abecedarian has continued to grow, the 'Izbet Sartah ostracon remains the earliest example of a practice exercise in writing the twenty-two–letter alphabet.[15]

Other finds from Stratum II included a scarab with a sitting line enclosed in a frame. In front of the lion is the Ma'at (feather) sign, and over its back is what appears to be a uraeus. The scarab probably dates to the Twentieth Egyptian Dynasty or slightly later.[16]

Stratum II only existed for a short time after which, like Stratum III, it was systematically abandoned. Its occupants appear to have packed everything up and moved away.

## Stratum I

At the beginning of the tenth century B.C.E., 'Izbet Sartah was reoccupied again for a decade or two. During this phase of occupation, the site was even smaller than before. The four-room house in the center of the site was slightly remodeled with the building of low partition walls between the pillars in each row, two rooms on the north side, and the addition of several installations inside the building (**Fig. 30**). The peripheral buildings went out of use, and about ten new silos were built, using the stones from their walls, in order to replace them. The size of the settlement appears to have been significantly reduced during this phase, and most of the Stratum II silos went unused.

It appears that, after Stratum II, the site was abandoned for several decades. During this period of abandonment, the peripheral buildings collapsed and the silos around the four-room house filled up with debris. When the founders of Stratum I arrived at 'Izbet Sartah, they renovated the four-room house and used stones from the collapsed buildings on the site's periphery to build new silos there.

# THE ARCHITECTURE OF 'IZBET SARTAH

## Stratum III

The Stratum III village of 'Izbet Sartah is oval-shaped and made up of a series of rooms that surround a large central courtyard, where several stone-lined silos were built. The primary architectural unit of the village during this period is its inner peripheral wall. The site's exterior wall is parallel to this inner peripheral wall, but it does not make a continuous, uniform line. Instead, it was formed by linking the outer

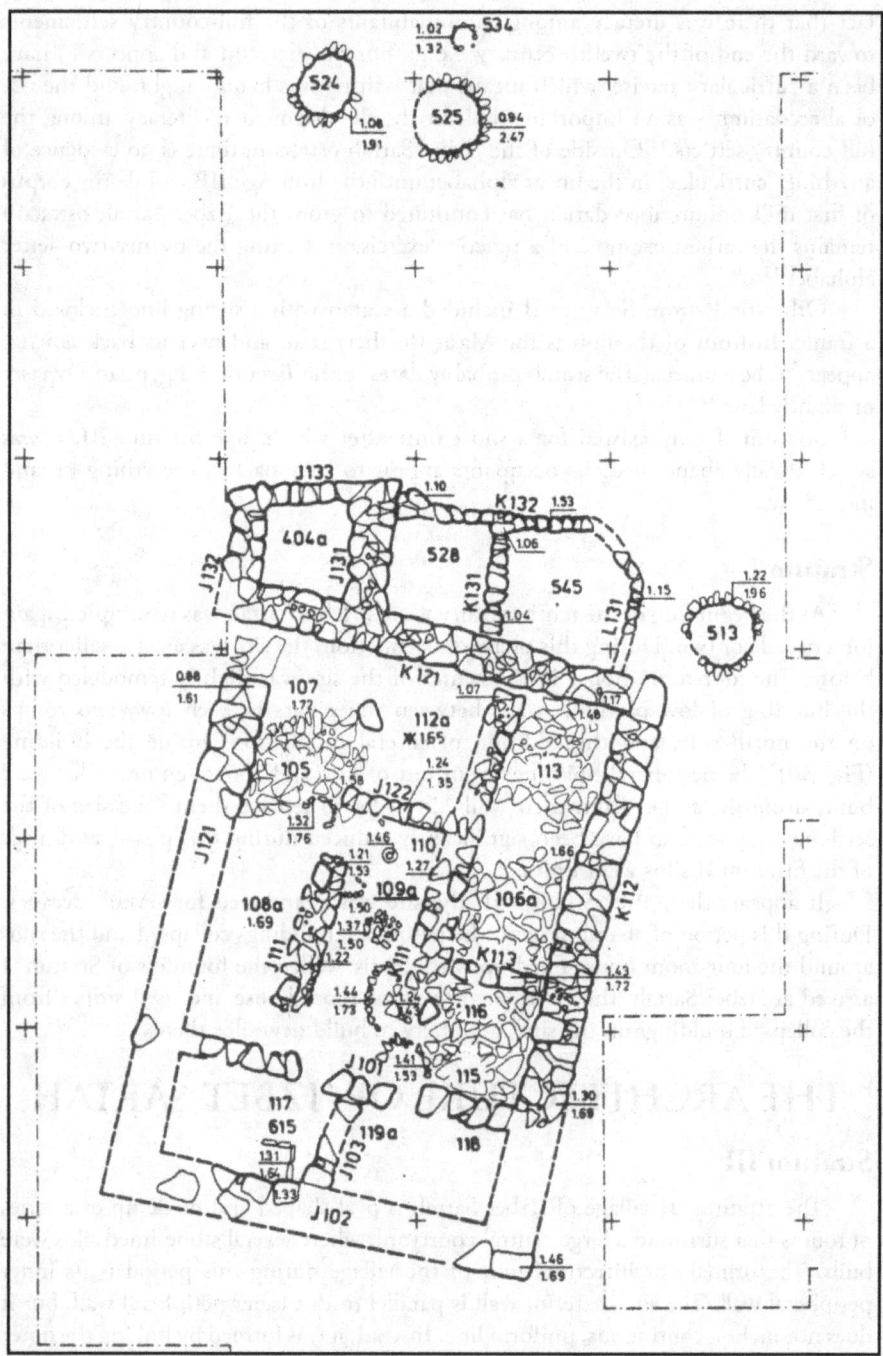

*Fig. 30*

walls of rooms, which had varying widths. Eight of these rooms were uncovered, sharing an average length of about 20 feet. Since the circumference of the peripheral wall appears to have been about 443 to 459 feet, there may have been twenty-two to twenty-four of these rooms along the Stratum III wall. It is estimated, on the basis of the excavation of a few fragmentary remains in the southern and northeastern sectors, they were 16 to 20 feet wide on average. The total size of the settlement was about 154 by 197 feet, producing a total area of about 30,338 square feet. Since the open courtyard occupied about 4,757 feet of this space, it seems clear that the activity of the settlement was concentrated in this area. Sites with similar plans and architectural features have been found throughout Israel, from the Upper Galilee to the highlands of the Negev, typically on the fringes of arable land.[17]

## Stratum II

The architectural plan for 'Izbet Sartah during this period was completely different from that of the preceding phase. The village of Stratum II was well-organized and generally circular in its plan. The core of the site consisted of the four-room house (Building 109b), around which stretched a line of about 110 silos, and a belt of about twenty small buildings that were located around the perimeter of the site. The Stratum II village encompassed a total area of about 41,441 square feet.

The size of the four-room house, the quality of its construction, and its central location in the village suggest that it must have been occupied by a family that held special importance among the residents of Stratum II 'Izbet Sartah. The building was clearly the focal point of the settlement during this period, and it may have been occupied by the patriarchal family head.

A few of the houses that were part of the belt of peripheral buildings were sufficiently well-preserved that their ground plans could be reconstructed. The best preserved structures appear to have been four-room houses. This belt of houses did not form a continuous wall on the outer side of the site. While some of the buildings did join one another, others did not, which left gaps where there were no buildings. In addition, the peripheral buildings were not oriented in the same direction: some faced the slope, while others faced different directions. This is fundamentally different from the site plans at other locations of this period, where the peripheral buildings all faced inwards so that the walls of their rear broadrooms formed a defensive belt around the site.[18] It seems that the peripheral buildings at 'Izbet Sartah were not intended to function this way in Stratum II. Based on the reconstruction of the layout of Stratum II, Finkelstein concludes that there were approximately one hundred inhabitants of Stratum II 'Izbet Sartah.[19]

Another feature of Stratum II of 'Izbet Sartah was the high number of stone-lined silos concentrated in such a small area. Up to five or six silos appeared in excavation squares that measure about 16 by 16 feet.[20]

## Stratum I

The four-room house was the only building that was occupied at the site in Stratum I (Building 109a). From this period, the house yielded 83 sherds from bowls and kraters, 116 from cooking pots, 71 from jugs, 68 from storage jars, 34 from unclassified jars, and 173 from storage vessels. From the distribution of pottery remains throughout the house, it appears that cooking was done in the annexed rooms, the courtyard, and the eastern longitudinal room. The western longitudinal room appears to have been used mainly for storage. Since the broadroom had the fewest vessels of any of the rooms, it may have been the living-sleeping quarters.

# IMPLICATIONS OF THE ARCHITECTURE OF 'IZBET SARTAH

As noted in chapter 7, courtyard sites such as that of the Stratum II village of 'Izbet Sartah, most of which date to the Iron Age I, are known from all over Palestine.[21] These sites are characterized by the comparatively large size of their courtyards, which typically occupy 65 to 80 percent of the total area. It was suggested that this architectural layout of these sites reflects the nomadic origin of their occupants.[22]

The abundance of silos may also reinforce the identity of 'Izbet Sartah's inhabitants as a people early in the process of sedentarization. Silos are not unique to early Israelite sites, and have been found in the Late Bronze Age, for example, at Tel Halif[23] and Beth Shemesh.[24] A profusion of silos, however, is one of the clearest characteristics of the early hill-country settlement sites.[25] Over fifty silos were found at Tell en-Nasbeh; dozens were discovered at Tell Beit Mirsim; about fifteen were excavated at Shiloh; several were found in the first Israelite level at Tel Aphek; numerous silos were discovered at Tel Zeror; more than twenty-two pits were found in Stratum XII Hazor; in Area B of Stratum VI at Tel Dan, twenty-five silos were excavated; large, rock-hewn pits that may have been used as silos were found at Beer-sheba and also at Tell el-Ful. The number of silos at Late Bronze Age sites was insignificant, and they are virtually unknown in Iron Age II.

The plethora of silos in Iron Age I beg the question of why there were so many required in the highlands of this period. Finkelstein suggests that "a proliferation of silos generally characterizes groups in the process of sedentarization or societies organized in local rural frameworks."[26] Finkelstein points to contemporary Bedouin settlements, where the Bedouin have only recently sedentarized, and notes that the first structures built were for grain storage.[27] Small silos are typically not found in urban societies or under governmental organization, where better storage solutions have been implemented. In societies in the process of sedentarization, however, "silage is the first problem for which such societies must find a permanent architectural solution."[28]

There were several crude, rock-cut cisterns also found at 'Izbet Sartah, which suggest that the inhabitants may not have had access to the Yarkon River to its south but had to rely instead on stored rainwater.

## THE ECONOMY OF 'IZBET SARTAH

The foregoing discussion of silos at 'Izbet Sartah makes it clear that the inhabitants of the site practiced agriculture, a fact that is reinforced by the numerous grinding stones and sickle blades that were found during the excavations. The total capacity of the silos of Stratum II can be estimated, since its excavation exposed most of the inhabited area. The excavator estimated the number of silos of Stratum II at about 110, which, based on the average silo as having a volume of 49.4 cubic feet, would have provided a total storage capacity of about 5,297 cubic feet. While there is no direct evidence regarding the kind of material stored in these silos, it has been assumed that grain was the primary commodity. Since wheat and barley are the traditional crops in the vicinity of 'Izbet Sartah, they would be the most likely kinds of grain to have been cultivated by its inhabitants.[29] The total amount of plowable land required for supplying the average amount of grain stored on the site would be about 544 acres. This amount of land would, in a good year, fill the silos to the brim. Estimating that 70 percent of the cereals harvested would have been available for consumption, 'Izbet Sartah's silos may have held 83,180 pounds of wheat and 32,948 pounds of barley annually.

In addition to agriculture, the villagers also practiced animal husbandry. Sheep and goats, whose bone remains made up 52.7 percent of the faunal assemblage, were clearly the most common domesticates. Cattle, with a bone representation of 34.3 percent, were also important to the economy of 'Izbet Sartah. Camels also played a role and comprised 8.4 percent of the faunal assemblage. Hunting played a very minor role in the economy, as attested by the fact that only 3 percent of the remains came from hunted animals, such as fallow deer and gazelle. The inhabitants of 'Izbet Sartah used their mature animals for milk, wool, labor, and, occasionally, meat. Young animals were kept for reproduction and growth, and they mainly slaughtered adult sheep and goats. Interestingly, in Stratum III, there were considerably more bones from sheep/goat foreparts than from the hindquarters.[30] The analysts of the faunal remains note that "this forepart preponderance... may reflect a certain dietary preference of the inhabitants."[31] This higher proportion may be related to the biblical traditions that the Israelites were to sacrifice the right foreleg of the animal and give the right hind leg to the priests.[32] Five pig bones were found in mixed loci, but these may have come from the Byzantine occupation of the site. Pig remains are completely absent in the pure strata of 'Izbet Sartah, and their absence may be attributed to their having been perceived as unclean.[33]

The foregoing data about land and animal usage make it possible to estimate the size of the population. Assuming that an individual would consume about 330 to 551 pounds of cereal products per year, anywhere from 150 to 250 people could have been fed by the aforementioned amounts of wheat. The excavator had estimated that Stratum II probably had a population of about one hundred persons, who were probably organized into about twenty family units, each of which consisted of four or five persons. If this was the case, then the available cereals and animal products at the site would have provided each person at the site with about 0.8 to 0.95 ounces of high grade protein and 0.98 to 1 ounce of animal fat, which would have provided a total of about 330 to 350 K (calories) per day. In a good year, therefore, the caloric needs of the population were met with no problem. The foregoing numbers related to cereals would mean that ʿIzbet Sartah likely had a surplus of wheat and barley, which they could have traded for other foodstuffs, olive oil, wine, and other products, such as clothing or tools.[34]

# ETHNIC IDENTITY OF THE INHABITANTS OF ʿIZBET SARTAH

Finkelstein understood the ethnic identity of the inhabitants of ʿIzbet Sartah to be Israelite, but this has been disputed. William Dever has for many years argued that the pottery repertoire of the early highland settlers was continuous with that of the Canaanites in the Late Bronze Age,[35] and has argued specifically that there is nothing in the material culture of ʿIzbet Sartah "that would indicate anything other than the resettling of local, indigenous Canaanite elements of the population at the end of the Late Bronze Age."[36] In a recent article, Amihai Mazar has suggested specifically that the pottery and other artifacts from ʿIzbet Sartah are closer to that of Tel Qasile than to the material culture of the highland settlers.[37] This leads him to conclude that the site should probably be understood as a peripheral site of the coastal plain instead of as an "Israelite" site. Ahlström implied that the site may have been Philistine.[38]

There are other possibilities for the ethnic identity of the inhabitants of ʿIzbet Sartah rather than Israelite. They may have been remnants of the Canaanite population from nearby Aphek after its destruction in the second half of the thirteenth century B.C.E. Another possibility is that ʿIzbet Sartah may have been a "daughter" village of Philistine Aphek during its heyday. There are a number of factors, however, that reinforce the identification of ʿIzbet Sartah as an Israelite site.

**1. Geographical Location.** The village of ʿIzbet Sartah is located on the western slopes of the Ephraimite hill-country near five other sites, all of which are thought to have been Israelite, situated in the lower foothills overlooking the coastal plain.[39] The region allotted to Ephraim[40] was sparsely populated during the Late Bronze Age, but underwent a dramatic increase in the Iron Age I, when scores of new villages were established, many of which were concentrated around Shiloh.[41] This settlement pattern corresponds with that of the Israelite settlement surveyed in chapter 6.

**2. Site Layout.** As discussed above, the plan of the Stratum III village of ʿIzbet Sartah—a band of broadrooms arranged in an ellipse with a courtyard in the center—typifies a pastoral society that is in the earliest stages of sedentarization. This site layout, which mirrors those of the early Israelite settlement sites in the highlands, is not found on the coastal plain or among known Philistine sites.

**3. Four-Room House.** The Stratum II village focuses on a four-room house in the center of its courtyard. As seen in chapter 6, while the four-room house does appear in non-Israelite regions, in Iron I it appears primarily in the central hill-country. It does not appear at Aphek until the ninth century.

**4. Silos.** As discussed above, while silos are not completely unique to early Israelite settlement sites, a proliferation of silos is one of their clearest characteristics.[42] The stone-lined silo does not appear at nearby Aphek until the tenth century.

**5. Material Culture.** When the simple material culture of 'Izbet Sartah is compared with that of nearby Aphek, which was a Canaanite city under Egyptian hegemony in the Late Bronze Age and under Philistine control in the twelfth to eleventh centuries,[43] it becomes clear that they do not share the same ethnic identity. Canaanite Aphek had palaces, temples, and inscriptions in multiple ancient Near Eastern languages. Above the debris of the Canaanite town of Aphek, beautiful Philistine pottery was found in great quantities. At 'Izbet Sartah, on the other hand, there is only one substantial building, a typical four-room house, which is surrounded by much less substantial farm buildings that form a protective belt around it. Stone-lined silos dot the area. The simple, rustic material culture of 'Izbet Sartah corresponds with that of the Israelites discussed in chapter 7.

**6. Pottery.** Decorated Philistine ware was scarce at 'Izbet Sartah, while it was abundant at Tel Qasile. This would seem to mitigate against an identification of the inhabitants of 'Izbet Sartah as Philistines. In addition, collared-rim storage jars, which are abundant in early Israelite highland sites, may point to an Israelite identity for 'Izbet Sartah. As discussed in chapter 6, while the collared-rim jar cannot be woodenly used as an ethnic marker, its appearance regionally and quantitatively may have ethnic implications. Few collared-rim jars were found in the contemporary levels at Tel Qasile, Aphek, or Gezer, while they were found in relative abundance in 'Izbet Sartah Stratum III.

**7. The 'Izbet Sartah Ostracon.** One peculiarity of the tablet is that some of its letters are transposed. The ה comes before the ז and the פ precedes the ע. While one might blame this on the sloppiness of the inscription's author, the same ז-ה sequence is duplicated on the Tel Zayit abecedary,[44] and the פ-ע sequence is used in the alphabetic acrostics of Lamentations 2, 3, and 4. Some nineteenth century scholars supposed that later copyists of Lamentations had accidentally transposed the verses. Keil, however, had already observed the unlikelihood of this argument on the basis that the irregularity appears in all three poems.[45] The פ-ע sequence has also been found in the triple abecedary contained in the Hebrew script found at Kuntillet Ajrud.[46] This suggests that a contemporary secondary Israelite tradition of ordering the letters existed.[47] The use of this letter order suggests that the sherd was written by an Israelite.[48]

In sum, the village of 'Izbet Sartah is dissimilar to those of its neighbors in the coastal plain in a number of respects, and similar to those of the earliest Israelites.

# HISTORICAL CONNECTIONS

The occupational history of 'Izbet Sartah reflects the difficulties of establishing settlements in the border area between the foothills and the coastal plain during the

Iron Age I. The Israelites sought to settle near the margin of the coastal plains, but at other times they retreated back into the hill-country.

The date of the first settlement at 'Izbet Sartah is unclear. The site may have been founded either just before or after the destruction of Egypto-Canaanite Aphek, but before the Philistines established themselves there.[49] Some of the other sites along the edge of the foothills discovered by the survey may have also been settled at this time. Stratum III was probably abandoned in the face of increasing conflict between the Israelites and the Philistines at the beginning of the eleventh century B.C.E., which culminated in the crucial battle at Ebenezer (1 Sam. 4:1-11).[50] After this major defeat, the Israelites apparently withdrew back into the highlands and did not resettle 'Izbet Sartah until the end of the eleventh century, during the time of Saul (Stratum II). After only a brief period of occupation, however, the Israelites abandoned the site again, probably because the Philistines had regained the advantage. At the beginning of the tenth century, the Israelites resettled 'Izbet Sartah yet a third time (Stratum I). This westward expansion can probably be associated with the reign of David. Not long after this, the Yarkon basin became available for settlement. The Israelites took advantage of the availability of this very fertile plain and immediately began to settle there.[51] Evidence of Israelite occupation also appears at Aphek at this time.[52]

## IMPLICATIONS FOR RESEARCH ON THE ISRAELITE SETTLEMENT

The site of 'Izbet Sartah holds tremendous importance for the study of the early Israelite settlement in Canaan for at least five reasons. First, 'Izbet Sartah Stratum III, founded at the end of the thirteenth century or the beginning of the twelfth, remains as one of the earliest of the Israelite settlement sites discovered so far. Its date reinforces our reconstruction of the Israelite settlement as having begun in the mid-thirteenth century B.C.E. and as having been connected in some way to the destruction of at least some major Canaanite cities.[53]

Second, its location in the lower foothills overlooking the Canaanite plain and the Aphek pass also reinforces our reconstruction of Israel's emergence as a complex process that also involved peaceful settlement. While not in alignment with Finkelstein's overall view of the settlement as basically peaceful in nature, it does appear that the Israelites attempted to settle this region without conflict and that, "as long as the new elements did not pose a threat to the masters of the plain, their presence was unopposed."[54] Both the biblical and archaeological evidence make it clear that, at least in certain regions, the Israelites settled in close proximity to—and sometimes even in the midst of—Canaanite centers. Finkelstein notes that "not only were the Israelites not hesitant about living close to the Canaanite plain but that they may have even been attracted to Aphek, perhaps for economic reasons."[55] This would not be out of accordance with the biblical account, which observes that the Israelites depended on the Philistines for iron during the period of the judges.[56] This does not, however, imply an entirely complementary existence. The presence of rock-cut cisterns at 'Izbet Sartah, for example, may imply that its Israelite inhabitants did not have access to the nearby Yarkon River but had to rely on stored rainwater. It may have been that the Yarkon River was controlled by the Canaanites and, later, the Philistines, both of whom may have refused to allow the Israelites to use it, hence their need to rely on rock-cut cisterns.

Third, the pottery assemblage may reinforce the idea that the inhabitants of 'Izbet Sartah had contact with their neighbors on the coastal plain. The ceramic assemblage is somewhat more complex than that of the hill-country sites in Iron I. While 'Izbet Sartah's pottery assemblage most closely resembles that of the hill-country, its comparative complexity points to at least some contact with the coastal plains.

Fourth, 'Izbet Sartah's location accords with and illustrates the pattern of settlement of the early Israelite settlers, who established their villages in areas suitable for cereal cultivation and pasturage. The inhabitants of 'Izbet Sartah survived on cereals and animal products. Because of its location in a fertile area of the foothills, it was able to produce a surplus of wheat and barley that they probably traded with the villages to their east and, Finkelstein speculates, possibly also with those on the plain.[57]

Fifth, the layout of the two main strata at 'Izbet Sartah clearly reflect the socio-ethnic background of the Late Bronze-Iron Age I settlers as having had a pastoral background. Finkelstein concludes that "the regional surveys and the material culture of the settlement sites confirm that the majority of the population that settled the land during Iron Age I came from a pastoral background and not directly from any urban or rural framework of the Canaanite society."[58]

## CONCLUSIONS

'Izbet Sartah is a prototypical settlement site. Its date, location, pottery assemblage, and site layout all comport with what we have seen to be true of the early Israelite settlement sites as a whole. While it appears that there was a military dimension to the immigration of earliest Israel into Canaan, the largest percentage of the population lived in the kinds of small, unwalled agricultural settlements that were characteristic of village life in western Asia since the inception of settled life in the region.[59] Life in these villages revolved around agricultural work and the maintenance of herds of sheep and goats. The bulk of the villager's day would have been occupied by working the fields that adjoined the settlement or shepherding the flocks,[60] the same tasks that would have occupied the inhabitants of 'Izbet Sartah. Life among the earliest Israelites was not, however, solely focused on agricultural and pastoral pursuits. Like most peoples in the ancient world, the earliest Israelites were a religious people. We will now turn to a discussion of the role played by religion in the life of early Israel and the development of its national consciousness.

CHAPTER 9

# EARLY ISRAELITE SANCTUARIES AND THE BIRTH OF A NATION

In the previous chapter, the discussion centered on 'Izbet Sartah, a prototypical Israelite village, and on the village life of the earliest Israelites. In this chapter, we will seek to discover what there is to learn about the religion of earliest Israel and what role it played in the formation of Israel's national consciousness at this stage of its history. Current scholarship emphasizes the diversity and localization of Yahweh worship in early Israel and, accordingly, assumes that early Israel would not have had a central sanctuary. B. D. Bibb, for example, suggests that, "rather than cooperating to move their sanctuary from place to place, it is more likely that particular groups developed their own regional shrines."[1]

The view that earliest Israel did not have a central sanctuary has become almost axiomatic. F. S. Frick, for example, asserts that "there is no evidence, biblical or archaeological, for a central sanctuary in Palestine of the period of the judges."[2] This tendency probably goes back to the interpretation of Deut 12 articulated by W. M. L. de Wette in his 1805 dissertation, which established the foundations of literary criticism of the Pentateuch for the nineteenth century. De Wette identified the scroll "found" by the priests during the renovation of the Jerusalem Temple (2 Kgs 23) with the book of Deuteronomy.[3] He interpreted Deut 12:5, which commands the Israelites to "seek the place that the LORD your God will choose out of all your tribes as his habitation to put his name there," as an "altar law" that called for the centralization of the cult, which Josiah made one of the key platforms of his reforms.

According to de Wette, this was the *raison d'être* of the book of Deuteronomy, which was essentially an apologetic for exclusive worship at a single site chosen by Yahweh, which he identified as Jerusalem. According to this reconstruction, centralization was only a seventh-century B.C.E. phenomenon in Israel. Variations of this thesis have dominated the study of Deuteronomy and of Israelite religion in mainstream scholarship until the present time.[4] Even among conservative scholars, who tend to date the book of Deuteronomy much earlier, Deut 12 is regarded as setting forth an ideal of centralization. Pekka Pitkänen, for example, concludes that "Deuteronomy sees centralization as an ideal, to be attained after settlement is complete and conditions are ideal, with Israel dwelling in peace."[5] Earl Kalland accepts that centralization was to be part of Israel's settled life in Canaan, and notes that having one specified place would provide a contrast to the multiplicity of sites where the Canaanites worshiped their gods, as well as provide the political and social benefits of unifying the people.[6] Peter Vogt also sees centralization as explicitly commanded in this passage, although he argues that the focus of the unit is not on centralization of all worship at a single sanctuary *per se*, but on emphasizing "the supremacy of Yahweh by his choice of where and how he is to be worshiped."[7]

While the general understanding of Deut 12 as commanding centralization of Israelite worship predominates, there have always been those who have questioned it. C. F. Keil and F. Delitzsch, in the latter part of the nineteenth century, said the place where Yahweh "put his name" varied. They argued that "the presence of the Lord was not, and was not intended, to be exclusively confined to the tabernacle (or the temple). As God of the whole earth, wherever it might be necessary, for the preservation and promotion of God's kingdom, he could make known his presence, and accept the sacrifices of his people in other places, independently of this sanctuary; and there were times when this was really done."[8] Deut 12 does instruct that there be a unity of worship, but it was not necessarily to consist primarily in the bringing of sacrificial offerings to one location. Instead, the unity of worship was to consist in their bringing their offerings wherever Yahweh made his presence known.

In a paper presented at the annual meeting of the Society of Biblical Literature in 2008, Ziony Zevit examined several occurrences of the phrase אֶת־פְּנֵי יְהוָה לִרְאוֹת, which is used in the Hebrew Bible in contexts where people travel somewhere for worship.[9] The phrase is typically translated as "to appear before the Lord,"[10] but Zevit makes a convincing case that it should be translated "to see the face of the Lord." Ziony considers several extrabiblical cult sites, including the Tabernacle, the Bull Site, Mount Ebal, and the sacred precinct at Tel Dan, and argues that when Israelites would have gathered at these places לִרְאוֹת אֶת־פְּנֵי יְהוָה, it would have meant Yahweh would have been "seen" or "encountered" at each of them. Jacob Milgrom translates the divine name יהוה as "I am/will be present," and insists that the divine name is itself explicitly a קֹדֶשׁ, "a sanctum."[11] Yahweh's immanent presence was at these various sanctuaries.

It seems that Deut 12:5 may allow for a main central sanctuary, but does not necessarily imply a sole sanctuary. There are numerous passages, for example, that clearly present the use of *bāmôt* as an acceptable way to worship Yahweh prior to the construction of the Jerusalem temple. Samuel regularly carried out sacrificial rituals at a *bāmāh* located at Ramah.[12] The prophet told Saul that a band of prophets made use of a *bāmāh* located at Gibeah-Elohim.[13] Solomon carried out sacrifices at a *bāmāh* at Gibeon, which is referred to as "the principal high place."[14] It appears that the use of *bāmôt* to worship Yahweh was widespread throughout Judah prior to the building of the temple.[15] The Chronicler explains that the tabernacle and the Tent of Meeting were installed at the *bāmāh* at Gibeon and that the Aaronide priests presided over the sacrifices there prior to the construction of the temple.[16]

The Chronicler also notes that, even after the construction of the temple, some *bāmôt* continued to be used, but only for the worship of Yahweh.[17] Worship at various local altars was not opposed until the reigns of Hezekiah[18] and Josiah,[19] and it appears that the only reason even then was because they had become corrupt. There was an effort in the eighth and seventh centuries B.C.E. to purge the land of *bāmôt*, but it does not appear to have been because of a fanatical interest in centralization. Instead, the national political and/or spiritual leadership perceived that worship at the *bāmôt* had become idolatrous.

The idea that Deuteronomy alters conceptions of God found in earlier sources through a revolutionary program of demythologization, centralization, and secularization has come under close scrutiny and reevaluation by a number of recent authors and will no doubt not be resolved any time soon.[20] Regardless of the date and compositional history of the book of Deuteronomy, however, it is clear that sanctuaries existed before, alongside, and after the existence of the Jerusalem temple, and scholarly efforts to identify these have been under way for some time.

## THE AMPHICTYONY HYPOTHESIS

One of the efforts to reconstruct early Israel's cultus was that by Martin Noth, who proposed what has come to be known as the "amphictyony hypothesis" in a highly influential study in 1930.[21] The amphictyony hypothesis had a wide subscription for over fifty years, until it began to fall out of favor in the 1960s and 1970s.[22] The meaning of the term *amphictyony* is unclear and may be either the name of a tribe[23] or a compound expression meaning "a community of those who dwell around" a sanctuary.[24] In the fourth century B.C.E., the term was used by Demosthenes for a sacrosanct league which had been oriented around the shrine of Apollo at Delphi since at least the beginning of the sixth century B.C.E.

Throughout its history, while political events would sometimes lead to changes in the identity of the members, the Delphi amphictyony maintained a constant number of twelve member cities. Later classical writers use the term, but they apply it to groups that do not always correspond exactly with the Delphi amphictyony. Mayes suggests, therefore, that "it is to this league that the term originally belongs, and only by analogy is it later applied to other leagues."[25] Mayes suggests that the Delphi league is the only one to which the term *amphictyony* can be properly applied and that it is "the model against which the appropriateness of any analogous use of the term is to be tested."

The Delphi league was a sacrosanct consortium of twelve cities organized around a central religious shrine for the purpose of its maintenance and defense. The amphictyony established a set of rules by which they managed the finances of the amphictyony and maintained the sanctuary and its access roads on a rotating basis. The amphictyony chose delegates, called *hieromnemones*, who were charged with organizing these tasks and who assembled during festivals to do so. Mayes notes that though the focus of the amphictyony was cultic, its purposes were more comprehensive. He explains that "the members undertook not to destroy any of the towns of the league and not to cut off their water supplies, within the framework of attempting to preserve a state of political equilibrium between the members. Thus, it was not simply for the purpose of maintaining a sanctuary that the amphictyony came into existence, but rather in order to give cultic expression to an agreed state of mutual relations which had already been achieved."[26] Leagues of Greek cities, also oriented around a sanctuary, can be found in the Greek cities of Asia Minor, the most important of which was the league of Ten Ionic Cities founded in the eighth century B.C.E. Similar leagues are found in Italy as well as in other regions and time periods.

The concept of Greek and Italian groupings being reflected in ancient Israel had been explored as early as the nineteenth century.[27] In the twentieth century, Albrecht Alt applied the term *amphictyony* to pre-monarchic Israel, followed by the sociologist Max Weber in 1930, but it was Martin Noth who developed a comprehensive theory of an Israelite amphictyony.[28] Noth found the following elements of the Greek amphictyony in Israel during the period prior to the monarchy:

1. "Israel" was the name of a league of twelve tribes that consistently maintained the number of its tribes as twelve.

2. This tribal league had a central sanctuary in which the Ark of the Covenant was the focus of worship. The Ark did not have a permanent resting place prior to the monarchy (2 Sam 7:6), but "it was set up in one place for a more or less prolonged period and this place then formed the central place of worship, the geographical center of the ancient Israelite amphictyony."

3. The ark was first at Shechem, then at Bethel, Gilgal, and finally at Shiloh.

4. The tribes recognized Yahweh as their God at Shechem in a covenant ceremony that included the making of a pact and the adoption of statutes and laws.

5. Delegates of the twelve tribes, called *nesi'im*, who corresponded to the Greek *hieromnemones*, assembled at the annual religious festivals to discuss amphictyonic affairs.

6. The amphictyonic law is reflected in part in the Covenant Code (Exod 21–23).

7. Breaches of the amphictyonic law would be punished, an example of which can be found in the tribal action taken against Benjamin following the Gibeah crime (Judg 19–20).

The amphictyony hypothesis was heavily criticized in the 1960s and especially the 1970s, with criticism focusing on Noth's understanding of the Hebrew Bible's tribal lists, the existence of a central sanctuary, and the function of the amphictyony.[29] One of the key arguments against the amphictyony hypothesis of special relevance for this study is that it depended on the acknowledgment of a central sanctuary by its constituent members. Whereas the Greek amphictyony of the sixth century B.C.E. was formed around the shrine of Apollo at Delphi, the current view, as we noted above, is "there is no unequivocal support for an analogous structure in pre-monarchic Israel."[30]

## MULTIPLE SANCTUARY SITES

While all the details of the Greek amphictyony may not apply, the biblical materials do suggest that there were a number of early sites where the sanctuary had been located. Long ago, Benjamin Mazar suggested that 'Adam (Tell ed-Dāmiyeh), near Jisr ed-Dāmiyeh, one of the important fords of the Jordan, had been an early Israelite cultic site.³¹ Mazar based this identification on a number of passages of early Hebrew poetry, which, he suggested had been mistranslated. In Psalm 68, a victory song similar to the song of Deborah, the writer proclaims that לָקַחְתָּ מַתָּנוֹת בָּאָדָם (v. 19). In accordance with its policy for the usage of gender-neutral language, the NRSV translates the phrase as "receiving gifts from people" (v. 18). Other translations read, "you have received gifts [from] men" (e.g., NASB). Mazar suggested, however, that אָדָם instead of being translated as "from men," should be translated as a preposition with a proper noun, "in Adam." In this case, the text would read, "you have taken tribute in Adam." In Psalm 78:60, which reviews YHWH's historical guidance of Israel, the writer recounts YHWH's abandonment of the sanctuary as follows: בָּאָדָם וַיִּטֹּשׁ מִשְׁכַּן שִׁלוֹ אֹהֶל שִׁכֵּן. English translations have typically taken both lines of this couplet to be referring to the same sanctuary at Shiloh, as in the NRSV's rendering, "He abandoned his dwelling at Shiloh, /the tent where he dwelt among mortals." It may be, however, that while the first line names the sanctuary at Shiloh, the second line names another city called 'Adam.

The final passage discussed by Mazar is Hosea 6, in which YHWH laments the faithlessness of the nation of Israel. Verse 6 reports that וְהֵמָּה כְּאָדָם עָבְרוּ בְרִית, which the NASB renders, "Like Adam, they have transgressed the covenant." While this has often been understood as a reference to the primal human of Genesis 1–2, this seems to run counter to the overall context of the passage. Hosea 6:7–7:16 traces Israel's covenant violation backward through the nation's history, and finds that it had already begun during the earliest stages of the conquest. Since verse 8 deals with Gilead, where the Transjordanian tribes dwelled who threatened to revolt against the Israelites who lived in the hill-country (Josh 22), and verse 9 deals with Shechem, the site of Joshua's great covenant-renewal ceremony in Joshua 24, it seems to make more sense that אָדָם in verse 7 refers to a site. The NRSV, following this line of reasoning, translates the line, "But at Adam they transgressed the covenant." If these translations are correct, this confluence of references to 'Adam may suggest that it was an early Israelite cult site, preceding those at Shechem and Shiloh.³²

## GILGALIM

Mazar suggested the existence of cultic sites in the east. Beginning in 1983, the survey of Manasseh began discovering sites, all in the Jordan Valley, whose enclosures are designed in the shape of a "sandal," the shape of which is not directed by the topography (**Fig. 31**). These sites include el-'Unuq, Bedhat esh-Sha'ab, Masua, and Yafit (three), all of which have been typed by the survey as "enclosures" (**Fig. 32**).³³ The first of these sites to be published was el-'Unuq.³⁴ This site is a large enclosure,

*Fig. 31*

about four acres, on an isolated hilltop in the Wadi el-Far'ah valley. The enclosure is elliptical in shape, measuring 272 yards long and 76 yards wide. It is surrounded by a well-built wall of large unworked fieldstones, constructed in a double row. The enclosure is subdivided into two unequal parts, with the smaller division in the north and the larger one in the south. While other structures may have been built on the inside, no buildings have been discerned. There is, however, a round stone pile 16 feet in diameter located in the southern tip. Zertal suggests that this heap probably covered a round structure. The enclosure is not a village, town, or settlement, as it does not seem to have had any permanent residential structures inside it, and the wall seems too monumental for the site to have been designed for the corralling of sheep or for other agricultural purposes. However, large amounts of pottery were found at the site, and the repertoire was very similar to that of Stratum 2 at Mt. Ebal (below): 70 percent Iron IA, 20 percent "Einun," and 10 percent Iron II. Many of the shards bore the indentations common among Manassite and Ephraimite pottery.[35]

Bedhat esh-Sha'ab, located east of el-'Unuq and near the Jordan River Road, was explored by the survey in 1989 and excavated over two seasons during 2002–2003.[36] The site is 3 acres in area and is elliptical or "sandal"-shaped, with a larger quadrant in the top part of the site (Area A) and a smaller quadrant in the lower area (Area B) (**Fig. 33**). These two areas are partially separated by two subdivided spaces between them (Areas D and E), though there is an open space, which also includes an entrance into the site, that connects them (Area C).

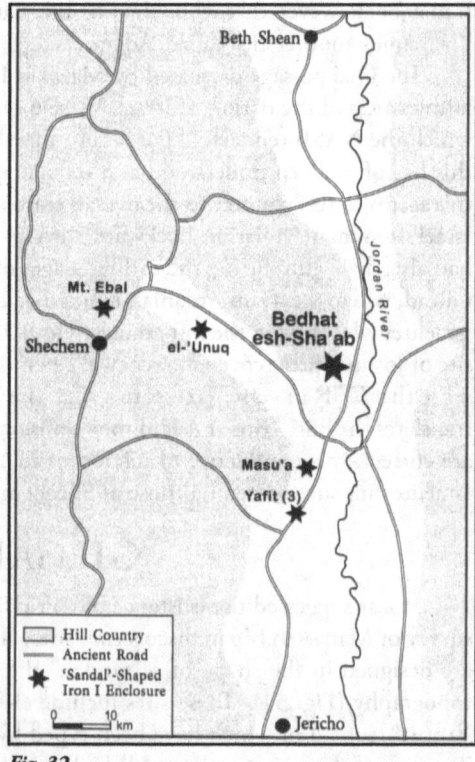

*Fig. 32*

A round structure is located in the top right quadrant of the site (section A4) that has been dubbed a *bāmāh* (**Fig. 34**). The *bāmāh* has a floor around most of it, which was covered with a concentration of animal bones, as well as pottery and cooking vessels. A cut was made next to the *bāmāh*, revealing early Iron Age I pottery under the floor. The pottery was a homogeneous assemblage dating to the late thirteenth and early twelfth centuries B.C.E. Aside from the *bāmāh*, no other structures are located in the site.

*Fig. 33*

Bedhat esh-Sha'ab is surrounded by a wall, over 1210 feet long, made of two lines of stones built in a single course. The section of the wall in Area B, which is the "heel" of the "sandal," is very unusual. In this section, the wall is not solid. Instead, beginning at the entrance in Area C, it consists of two rows of stones situated six to eight feet apart, with what appears to be the remains of a rough pavement raised about eight to eleven inches in above the surface of the ground between them (**Fig. 35**).

*Fig. 34*

*Fig. 35*

This special construction created a kind of passage or "road," which runs around the "heel" of the "sandal" for some 279 feet. This kind of construction has no known parallels. It could not have been used for defense, since it is an open construction with relatively large spaces between the stones. In addition, since the special construction was not accidental but was built as part of the enclosure wall, it must have served a purpose within the context of the entire site. We will return to the question of its function below. The site as a whole is located under a slope that partially encircles the complex, forming something like a huge amphitheatre. The slopes around and above Bedhat esh-Sha'ab would have made ideal places for a large assembly to see and hear proceedings.

El-'Unuq, Bedhat esh-Sha'ab, and the other enclosures are all located in the low ground of the plains, some of them have internal divisions, and all contain Iron Age I and, in some cases Iron Age II, pottery sherds, although these are scarce. The scarcity of pottery, along with a complete lack of buildings inside the enclosures, suggests they were not designed as dwelling places. On the other hand, the structures are too large and well-built to have served as animal pens. These structures seem to be completely unique in the Mediterranean region in this period and appear to have been built by seminomads who utilized a pottery repertoire similar to that of the new population group that entered Canaan from the east.[37] These "sandal-shaped" enclosures may have served to tie the nomadic populations to a well-known public center.[38] Zertal has suggested calling these sites *gilgalim*, a term that connotes gathering places.[39] It has long been recognized that "Gilgal" is not a place name but, more probably, a type of fortified encampment. Rather than identifying it as a site name, Waltke simply defines it as "a circle of stones" (though with a question mark).[40] The name seems to mean something like "circle (of stones)," a meaning apparently derived from a duplication of the root גָּלַל (*galal*) "to roll" (cf. Josh 5:9). The MT refers to at least three, and possibly five, different locations identified as "Gilgal" in both the north and the south. Most of these *gilgalim* appear to have had a cultic function. A Gilgal served as the site of the circumcision of the generation of Hebrews born during the wilderness wanderings as well as their celebration of the Passover (Josh 5:2-11). A Gilgal was located near Mounts Ebal and Gerizim, where the Israelites renewed the covenant with Yahweh in the midst of the settlement.[41] A Gilgal served as the site where the Israelites camped and from which they launched their sorties during the period of the settlement, and where the tribal territories were allotted.[42] A Gilgal became an important cultic center during the time of Samuel, and a Gilgal was the site where some men of Judah welcomed David back from exile following his son Absalom's death.[43] Gilgal is not mentioned again until it appears in the Minor Prophets. Although Micah cites Gilgal positively in a rehearsal of Yahweh's deliverance of the early Hebrews, it features in Hosea and Amos as a site of apostate worship.[44]

In addition to the usage of the term in the Hebrew Bible, the interpretation of the sites in the Jordan Valley as *gilgalim* and the idea that *gilgalim* served cultic purposes may be reinforced by the etymology of certain cultic terms.[45] The Hebrew word for festival, חַג, is from the verb חוּג, which means to "encircle" or "circumvent."[46] The term חַג, therefore, in addition to its basic meaning of "festival," carries the connotation of a "procession" around, or even a "round dance."[47] Encircling a sacred area in a procession was an important ritual element in the ancient Near East. The Arabic term *hajj*, related to the Hebrew חַג, is the term for the pilgrimage to Mecca and is understood to describe the circumambulation of the Ka'aba.[48] This may help explain the unusual feature at the passage or "road" in the heel of the "sandal" at Bedhat esh-Sha'ab. Zertal and Ben-Yosef have dubbed it the "procession road," and suggest that it may have been used for some kind of ritual encirclement of part of the site.[49] Based on the importance of Gilgal in the conquest traditions and

## Early Israelite Sanctuaries and the Birth of a Nation

in the cultic life of the tribal confederacy, scholars have long postulated that Gilgal may have been a central sanctuary of the early Yahwists.[50] It may be that the *gilgalim* underlie this tradition.

The Hebrew word for "foot," רֶגֶל, can also mean "festival." The festivals mentioned in the Pentateuch as feasts are the Passover, the Festival of Weeks, and the Feast of Tabernacles.[51] All three of these festivals required a pilgrimage to Jerusalem, and therefore came to be known as the שָׁלֹשׁ רְגָלִים, or the "three pilgrim festivals." The three festivals are described as רְגָלִים because of the journey to Jerusalem that would be undertaken on foot.[52] Interestingly, רֶגֶל can also symbolize control over an enemy or ownership of territory.[53]

Prior to entering the land of Canaan, Yahweh promised that he would give to them "every place on which you set foot" (Deut 11:24). This promise was reaffirmed to Joshua as he assumed the leadership of Israel and prepared to enter Canaan (Josh 1:3). Treading on the territory symbolized ownership of it. Treading on land as a symbol of ownership apparently evolved into the idea of the foot or the sandal on one's foot as a symbol of ownership. When Ruth's next-of-kin transferred his right of redemption to Boaz, he took off his sandal to show that he was relinquishing it. The text states that "this was the custom in former times in Israel concerning redeeming and exchanging: to confirm a transaction, the one took off a sandal and gave it to the other" (Ruth 4:7).[54] In battle, victors would often place their feet on the necks of those they vanquished. For example, when Adoni-zedek's coalition of five kings is defeated, Joshua called the chiefs of the Israelite warriors to "put your feet on the necks of these kings" in order to symbolize that they had subjugated them (Josh 10:24). Based on these meanings of רֶגֶל and on the design of the Jordan Valley *gilgalim*, Zertal suggests that their shape symbolized the migrants' belief that they owned the territory on which they built these new enclosures. An interesting comparison are the massive footprints, each three-foot long, carved into the limestone slabs lining the floor of the temple portico at 'Ain Dara, in northern Syria (**Fig. 36**).[55] Two of these giant footprints are located on the first slab, and the left footprint is imprinted on the second slab. These footprints are very delicate, and were apparently designed to look as if they had been made by a large figure walking into the temple. Since temples in the ancient Near East were considered to be the dwelling places of the gods, the footprints at 'Ain Dara were probably intended to symbolize the deity entering her abode.[56] Could

*Fig. 36*

it be that the *gilgalim*, constructed in the shape of sandals, may have been intended to symbolize Yahweh, the deity of the new migrants, striding into his land? The Hebrew

Bible certainly contains an elaborate theology of the land and views it as Yahweh's to give.[57] In the least, the *gilgalim* attest to early cultic activities of the nomadic or seminomadic migrants who were entering into Canaan from Transjordan.

# THE MOUNT EBAL ENCLOSURE

The westernmost "sandal"-shaped enclosure is the Late Bronze-Iron Age I site on Mount Ebal, discovered in 1980 during the early days of the survey (**Fig. 37**).[58] The site, known in Arabic as el-Burnat, lies on a mountain ridge high above sea level and far from any roads. Excavated over eight seasons, from 1982 to 1989, the site consists of two strata. In Stratum II, the earliest stratum, two Egyptianized scarabs were found that clearly establish a *terminus post quem* of the mid-to-late thirteenth century B.C.E. for the founding of the site.[59]

Stratum II consisted of a structure, subdivided into smaller sections by two thin walls, built on bedrock on the ridge of the mountain. East of the center of this structure was a depression in the floor in which a six-foot-wide circular depression containing a layer of ash and charred animal bones was located.

*Fig. 37*

The discovery of a chalice nearby, along with scattered hearths, excessive ash, potsherds, and animal bones in the area outside the building suggest this was a small cultic site where offerings were made. A four-room house is located just to the northwest, and may have been used by those who serviced the site. The site was significantly modified in Stratum IB, which dates to the end of the thirteenth or the beginning of the twelfth century B.C.E. In this period a monumental rectilinear structure built of unhewn stones was built above the earlier construction of Stratum II (**Fig. 38**). This structure, measuring about 29.5 by 23 feet, has no floor or entrance and seems to have been deliberately filled with layers of the bones of male bulls, caprovids,[60] and fallow deer; ash; and Iron I pottery, including one whole collared-rim jar. Many of the bones had been butchered at the joints and roasted in an open flame. A small ledge partially encircles the structure, and a ramp, about five feet wide, is located on the southeast side. Paved courtyards are on either side of this ramp, each of which includes numerous stone installations that were filled with bones, ash, jars, jugs, juglets, and pyxides.

The area of the four-room house was paved over to make a paved court in front of the main complex, and a gate descending into this courtyard was added. A thin retaining wall separates the area of the central structure from the larger area to its east. A thin enclosure wall, about 3 feet high and 820 feet long, and designed in

Fig. 38

the shape of a "sandal," surrounds the entire site. The site was interpreted as cultic in nature, with its central structure being a *bāmāh* on which ritual ceremonies took place. The site appears to have been deliberately covered with stones sometime around 1140 B.C.E. in order to protect it. In 1985, Zertal suggested that the main structure of Stratum IB at Mount Ebal may be associated with the altar of Josh 8:30-35 and that it may have served as a central sanctuary among the early Israelites,[61] but critics dismissed it as either a watchtower,[62] a house,[63] or a barbecue site.[64]

Some scholars object that the Ebal structure could not have served as an altar for the Israelites during the settlement period because of its date in the thirteenth to twelfth centuries. B. G. Wood, for example, rejects the possibility that this may have been the altar of Josh 8:30-35 for this reason and notes the late date of the structure "is later than most evangelicals who favor a late date would place the event."[65] The notes in the recently published *Archaeological Study Bible* explain that "the current dating of the site does not fit with Biblical chronology, which suggests an earlier, fourteenth-century (ca. 1400 B.C.E.) date for Joshua and the Conquest."[66] If one holds to an early date exodus-conquest, then the late date of the Ebal structure is indeed a problem. Pitkänen raised the possibility that the Stratum IB structure could have served as a monument and, as such, was an improved version of the Stratum II structure.[67] There are biblical texts describing structures built as monuments without a functional purpose,[68] and Pitkänen suggests that the lack of living quarters in association with Stratum IB could support the interpretation of the Ebal altar as a monument. However, animal bones were not only found in Stratum II but were also found in Stratum IB, which seems to indicate a continuing cultic usage, which Pitkänen recognizes.

With regard to the issue of location, some scholars object that the site could not be the altar described in Josh 8:30-35 because it is not on the very peak of Mount Ebal but is located instead on the second of four terraces descending the eastern side of the mountain. Mount Gerizim cannot even be seen from the site. This may seem to be in contradiction to the injunction of Deut 11:29-30 and 27:2-8. However, as Zertal noted, while Deut 11:29 does state that the curses are to be read הַר־עֵיבָל עַל, or "*on* Mount Ebal," Deut 27:4 and Josh 8:30 state that the structure is to be built בְּהַר עֵיבָל or "*in* Mount Ebal."[69] Zertal suggested that the use of the ב rather than עַל may hint "that Joshua's altar was not at the top of the mountain."[70] Along this line, Pitkänen suggested that the ceremony need not have taken place at the site of the altar.[71]

Another factor that may have a bearing on the issue of the location of the Ebal structure in relation to Mount Gerizim is the possibility that the traditional location of Mount Gerizim may be incorrect. This is not a new suggestion, but is connected with the ancient debate about the Samaritan Pentateuch's version of Deut 27:4, which reads "Mt. Gerizim" in place of the Masoretic Text's "Mt. Ebal."[72] Eusebius believed that the Samaritan identification of Jebel et-Tor as Mount Gerizim was incorrect.[73] Indeed, no Iron Age remains have been discovered on Jebel et-Tor.[74] Zertal has recently proposed an alternative identification of Mount Gerizim with Jebel Kebir, the mountain adjacent to Ebal on its eastern side, in the direction of the Jordan River (**Fig. 39**).[75] If this identification is correct, then the Ebal structure would be visible to parties standing both on Mount Ebal and on Mount Gerizim.

*Fig. 39*

With regard to the size and shape of the Ebal structure, Wood and Young in particular object that the Ebal structure is "monumental" in proportion and rectangular in shape, "not square as prescribed by Mosaic law."[76] Wood and Young overlook the fact, however, that Mosaic law mentions and gives legislation for multiple kinds of altars, including an earthen altar (Exod 20:24), an altar of unworked stones (Exod 20:25), and the tabernacle altar (Exod 27:1-8). With respect to the altar of unworked stones, completely lacking are "any specifications concerning the dimensions of the altar, its length, width, and height, whether it was round, square or oblong, whether its base and the top were equal or there was a gradual decrease of its size, and whether there were horns."[77] The only concern the text does specify is the height of the stone altars, which would preclude the maintenance of modesty during their ascent. In order to address this problem, the text stipulates that steps not be used (Exod 20:26). This explicit prohibition "implies that another means such as a ramp would be acceptable."[78] The Mount Ebal structure is most evocative of the altar of unworked stones.[79] The command for the building of the Ebal altar in Deut 27:5-6 repeats the prohibition of Exod 20:25 against working the stones to be used in its construction. Likewise, Josh 8:31 specifically cites Exod 20:24-25 in its account of Joshua's fulfillment of that command. Zevit concluded that the Ebal structure "may be considered a most elaborate example of the stone field altar."[80]

Wood and Young seek to compare the Ebal structure with two "contemporary" Israelite altars, the tabernacle altar and the altar at the Arad sanctuary. Neither of these, however, is contemporary. The tabernacle altar only survives in the literary record, which places it in the Mosaic period, which would date to the Late

Bronze Age I (1550–1400 B.C.E.) or the Late Bronze Age II (1400–1200 B.C.E.), depending on whether one followed the early or late date for the exodus. The Arad altar, which dates to Iron Age II (1000–586 B.C.E.),[81] is similar to the Ebal structure in terms of its construction. It is built of unhewn stones with a fill. The Arad construction, however, is a medium-sized altar and does not have the special characteristics of the larger structure at Mount Ebal.[82] Wood and Young state that the Ebal structure "would have been totally out of keeping with known Israelite altars of the period." The fact is, however, that there are no known Israelite altars contemporary with the Ebal structure.[83] The site is essentially anomalous in terms of physical parallels. However, when one compares the Ebal structure with the literary traditions of the Hebrew Bible and extrabiblical Second Temple sources which include descriptions of ancient Israelite altar sites, it appears that the central structure conforms to most of the biblical principles of Israelite altar architecture.[84] Based on the altar typology outlined by Robert Haak,[85] the construction on Mount Ebal most closely resembles the type Ib open-air altar in that it is unassociated with a sacred building, though it was constructed of unworked stones instead of carved from the natural rock.[86]

The reason for the monumental size and elaborate construction of the Ebal altar was its function in early Israelite society. As the Hebrew people migrated into the land of Canaan, it appears they had a number of sanctuaries, including the ones at 'Adam, Bedhat esh-Sha'ab, Masua, Yafit (3), and el-'Unuq, that may have been used by different tribes or families within the larger homogeneous population. These enclosures appear to have been public structures that tied the nomadic populations to well-known public centers, a feature common in enclosed nomadism.[87] In the earliest sites, the settlers built simple *bāmôt* to serve the needs of local groups. When they began to sedentarize in the central hill-country of Manasseh, they then constructed a cultic site that could function in a more central capacity. The existence of a cultic center is an indicator of social organization, and suggests that these migrants were characterized by a common cultural identity with possible nationalistic overtones.[88] According to Josh 8:30-35, a cultic site on Mount Ebal did play a central role in crystallizing ancient Israel's national consciousness early in their history.[89]

It seems that the resistance to an identification of the site as such from both nonconfessional and evangelical scholars is based on ideology rather than on the archaeological data. For nonconfessional scholars, an early Israelite central sanctuary could not have existed because there was no emphasis on centralization until the eighth or seventh centuries B.C.E. Any early sanctuaries should simply be local or domestic in nature rather than monumental. For evangelicals, the site goes against the "biblical" chronology and therefore cannot be the altar associated with Josh 8:30-35. When all the data are taken together, however, it seems to me that the Iron Age I structure on Mount Ebal is very likely to have been the site that lay behind the traditions contained in Josh 8:30-35.[90]

# CONCLUSION

If the fortified encampments of the Jordan Valley, located among the earliest sites of the Israelite settlement, are understood as *gilgalim*, then they may represent either the movement of early Israel's cultic center, or the use of multiple cultic centers, as they migrated westward. When the Hebrews first encamped beside the Jordan, it appears that they set up the sanctuary at 'Adam, near Tell ed-Dāmyieh. From there, it appears that they established similar sites at Masua, Yafit (3), el-'Unuq, and finally Mount Ebal. In the earliest sites, the settlers constructed simple *bāmôt*, whereas when they began to sedentarize in the central hill-country of Manasseh, they then constructed a cultic site that could function in a more central capacity. This massive structure reflects the important role altars played in centralizing peoples in the ancient world.[91] According to the traditions reflected in Deut 27:1-10 and Josh 8:30-35, the cultic site on Mount Ebal and the rituals carried out there played a central role in crystallizing ancient Israel's national consciousness at this early stage in their history.[92] A monumental altar was warranted by these momentous events.

CHAPTER 10

# A CULTURE-SCALE MODEL OF THE EARLY ISRAELITE SETTLEMENT

By building on the foregoing data we can begin to articulate a theory of Israelite emergence in Canaan. A scientific theory is a structured system of interrelated ideas that explains some aspect of the phenomenal world. Whether a theory is conceived of as an idealized but true approximation of the reality under study or as a construct that simply helps us make sense of our observations, it is considered the natural *sine qua non*—the end product—of science. If we cannot take the data we have gathered in the foregoing study and use it to articulate a theory, then we have not engaged in a scientific study. In other words, "No theory, no science."[1]

This is important because doing so is a worthy goal of archaeologists and social scientists. Guy Gibbon suggests that theories help us tell a better, more coherent story in relation to the data, as well as eliminate or reduce logical inconsistencies, along with "metaphysical fluff" that can neither be verified nor falsified.[2] He notes further:

> More positively, scientific theories organize seemingly undifferentiated masses of information, establish law-like regularities between phenomena, expose gaps in our narratives, provide explanations of recognized empirical regularities, predict other possible regularities that hold between observable phenomena, and suggest tests and other research activities. Formal systematic theories perform these tasks by being explanatorily forceful, economical of thought, and heuristically fertile. If these arguments are valid, it is fair to conclude that without integrating theories, archaeological knowledge will continue to be a thing of "shreds and patches."[3]

There is not, however, a commonly agreed upon view among the social sciences of what a scientific theory is, how it should be characterized, or what the criteria for its terms are.[4] Gibbon suggests Jerald Hage's *Techniques and Problems of Theory Construction in Sociology* as a useful introduction to theory construction in sociology and suggests that while there are certainly differences between the data provided by sociology and that provided by archaeology, Hage's scheme is both simple and general enough to be adapted by archaeologists.[5]

Hage outlines six components of a theory: (1) concept names; (2) verbal statements; (3) theoretical/operational definitions; (4) theoretical/operational linkages; (5) ordering into primitive and derived terms; (6) ordering into premises and equations.[6] We will focus on the first four of Hage's parts, since these provide the basic ingredients of a well-formed theory. The goal will be to develop a theoretical concept that can describe or make the archaeological data available to us more comprehensible.

In the end, a theory must be evaluated by others. Gibbon reviews a number of criteria that may be used for such an evaluation,[7] but I'll mention only a few of them here. A theory may be rejected because it lacks *simplicity*; it contains too many axioms and qualifying assumptions to be easily adopted by others. A theory may be rejected because it lacks *comprehensiveness*, in that it fails to explain all the data. A theory is said to have *fertility* if it suggests avenues of research that have not been previously explored or relationship between variables that had formerly gone unnoticed. A theory's *plausibility* has to do with whether it coheres with what is thought to be feasible in the "real world." A theory may be rejected because it lacks *logical consistency*, or contains ambiguities in logic. The *elegance* of a theory refers to its gracefulness, to whether or not the component parts of the theory cohere.

My goal in the following pages is to articulate a theory that meets the foregoing criteria, and explains as much of the data as possible, both biblically and archaeologically. I do not claim that this model is empirically correct. Instead, it is heuristic, and it provides an alternate route to the generalizing that has characterized so much of the recent writing about early Israelite history. I will begin by defining the overall schema that will be used, that of culture scale, and then focus in two levels of that scale, the domestic and political scales. I will then show how Israel progressed through two distinct stages of domestic-scale culture, and then developed into a political-scale culture. I will then seek to show how this illuminates early Israel's settlement in Canaan.

## CULTURE SCALE

As discussed in chapter 1, one of the major emphases in the New Archaeology is the study of culture, which W. G. Dever defines as a specific people group's adaptation to the environment, their patterned individual and social responses, and the recognition that these features of culture are ever-changing.[8] This has been a standard feature of anthropological study since at least the middle of the twentieth century. One of the most widely adopted strategies for the study of culture has been to measure the complexity of cultures and divide them into culture types. These are then grouped into a continuum of progressive stages often known in anthropology as levels of sociocultural integration. Many anthropologists have sought to define and/or measure these levels of complexity.[9] Measuring societal complexity is not an end in and of itself, but serves the purpose of understanding a given social group, since cultures at different levels of sociocultural integration are different by definition.[10] Cultures at different levels of integration organize socially, implement varying political controls, and adapt to their environment technologically and economically all in different ways. The study of societal complexity is one method for seeking to understand these differences.

John H. Bodley has used culture scale as a lens through which to view and interpret cultures.[11] His scale is organized according to power systems: domestic, political, or commercial (**Fig. 40**). In each of these types of societies, power is organized differently. Domestic-scale cultures are small-scale societies in which social power is maintained and dispersed at the household level. The focus in a domestic-scale culture is on the well-being of the household. The organization of a society domestically enables its members to focus on the sapienization process. The term *sapienization*, which derives from the Latin *sapiens* (as in *homo sapiens*), refers to the development of a people group and its culture. When family groups in a society do not have to worry about producing a taxable surplus to send to a government, then each household is able to control its own material resources, and production and distribution are managed in the domestic sphere. In a domestic-scale culture, systems of social support for households are provided by networks of kin. This means that while social power may vary based on the size and shape of individual families and their kinship support networks, the households in the community have roughly equal social power.

Political-scale cultures are larger-scale societies led by a ruler instead of by household heads. In a political-scale culture, production systems are centrally managed and are geared to the wants and needs of this ruler or a ruling class. When a society transitions into a political-scale culture, its primary culture process ceases to be sapienization and becomes, instead, politicization, which refers to the production and maintenance of the political apparatus. At this level, taxes are imposed, specialization occurs, a military is built, and urbanization arises. Households must become involved in all of these processes, and their own interests must be subordinated to the interests of political rulers.

Commercial-scale cultures are not led by an individual ruler, but by those who control the production and distribution of goods and services by means of the business enterprises they own and the financial capital they control. In commercial-scale cultures, power is basically commercial, and it is driven by cultural institutions such as private property, contractual agreements, and monetary systems, all of which are validated, controlled, and protected by the centralized political power. Food production, labor, and various goods and services once managed by households are all converted into commercial products and brought under the purview of business enterprises, into which societies are incorporated. At this level of culture scale, national societies the world over are involved in mass-industrialized production and distribution systems, and they participate in a global culture characterized by common cultural understandings.

Sociocultural growth and the changes that accompany it in the culture scale have not been consistent and do not seem to be predictable. Early humankind lived almost exclusively in small-scale, self-sufficient local societies based initially on mobile foraging and later on sedentary village life. Every significant domestic technology was invented and disseminated during this time, including ceramics, textiles, farming, and herding. And these technologies improved the quality of daily life for everyone, because in the domestic-scale cultures, they were equally available to every household. While domestic-scale cultures persisted in various parts of the world, some even into modern times, the politicization process began in others, and chiefdoms, small agrarian kingdoms, and even empires began to develop. How this process occurs has been a subject of speculation among anthropologists since at least the beginning of the twentieth century.

| Culture Scale | Culture Process | Food Objective | Cost/Benefit |
|---|---|---|---|
| Domestic | Sapienization | Nutrition | Stability<br>Equality |
| Political | Politicization | Taxable surplus | Instability<br>Inequality |
| Commercial | Commercialization | Profit-making commodity | Inequality<br>Instability<br>Poverty |

*Fig. 40. Culture scale and its features (adapted from J. H. Bodley,* Cultural Anthropology, *20). Used by permission.*

## A CULTURE-SCALE MODEL OF THE EARLY ISRAELITE SETTLEMENT

As discussed in chapter 2, variations of the Mendenhall-Gottwald hypothesis, with its focus on Canaanite origins for the highland settlers, have come to predominate today.[12] In the previous chapters, however, I have sought to show that the textual and archaeological evidence militate against it. The Alt-Noth hypothesis comports much more closely with the evidence. In its fully articulated form, the Alt-Noth hypothesis proposed a two-phased process of settlement. In the first phase, the Israelites settled in the highlands, and in the second phase, they sought to carry out a "conquest" for the purpose of expanding their territory.[13]

In later variations of the Alt-Noth hypothesis, the conflicts with the indigenous inhabitants were not because of Israelite attempts at "conquest" at all, but were a response to offensive measures taken by the indigenous inhabitants who did not want them settling in their land. M. Weinfeld explains that, while the book of Joshua may describe the Israelites as seeking to invade, "Yet it seems that on their arrival in the promised land the migrating tribes intended to settle in unoccupied territory rather than in the cities which were already inhabited, and only after confrontation with the inhabitants of the cities were they forced to resort to warfare and military conquest."[14]

While this two-phased process of settlement consisting of a peaceful settlement followed later by military entanglements not instigated by the Hebrews themselves may appeal to modern post-colonialist sensibilities, I do not believe it comports with a close reading of the biblical texts, the archaeological data, or the ethnographic evidence about pastoral nomads, all of which have led us to this point in our study. The data seem to point to a modified version of the Alt-Noth hypothesis that focuses on culture scale. In this model, Israel's emergence occurs as a natural progression through the culture scale. In the first two stages, the Hebrew tribes exist as a domestic-scale culture that was originally transhumant but, in a subsequent stage, sedentarized in highland villages. In the third stage, the sedentarized Israelite village culture developed into a political-scale culture. This process of development may be reconstructed as follows:

## 1. Transhumance (Domestic-Scale Culture—Phase 1)

As seen in chapter 6, archaeological survey data that has been gathered over the last several decades has shown a gradual process of geographic expansion of the early Israelite tribes. The settlement process began in the Jordan Valley and eastern Manasseh. In this region, sites were discovered mainly along the Wadi Far'ah and Malih.[15] During this stage, dating to approximately the middle of the thirteenth to the middle of the twelfth centuries B.C.E., the settlers were seminomads, with an economy based on sheep husbandry.

During this period, several of the Hebrew tribes coalesced into a unified group and made military incursions into the land of Canaan, events that are echoed in the ritual conquest tradition.[16] This is not to say that the Israelites occupied the land, which the book of Joshua does not claim, but that they made sorties into the land and planned its apportionment.[17] These Hebrew invaders did not settle at the sites they attacked, but instead made a site called Gilgal their home base from which they launched their attacks and to which they would return.[18] Merling has written at length about Gilgal and its role in early Israel.[19] Gilgal had been the place where the Israelites camped after having crossed the Jordan, where they circumcised the new generation, and celebrated the Passover.[20] After each circumambulation of Jericho, the Israelites returned to Gilgal, where the Gibeonites sought Joshua out in order to establish a covenant with him.[21] After defeating a coalition of the kings of five key southern city-states that had formed in response to the consorting of the Gibeonites with the Israelites, "Joshua returned, and all Israel with him, to the camp at Gilgal."[22] Even after the southern and northern campaigns (chs. 9–11), and after the Israelites are said to have "possessed" the land (ch. 12), they are also still said to have been residing in Gilgal (Josh 14:6). In addition to other purposes, these may have served as military staging grounds.[23]

While the Hebrews undertook some military campaigns, these campaigns were essentially sorties; they were not territorial conquests with immediate Hebrew occupation. When closely read, the book of Joshua does not actually describe a sweeping, instant conquest-with-occupation. The text only claims burning at Jericho, Ai, and Hazor, which makes the search for extensive conflagration levels at other Late

Bronze Age sites in order to connect them with the Israelites a moot effort. When this is understood, the portrayal of Judges follows directly and easily, with no inherent contradiction.[24]

## 2. Sedentarization (Domestic-Scale Culture—Phase 2)

The book of Joshua recognizes that Israel's "infiltration" was incomplete, and during this stage, the tribes that had previously banded together in order to effect a "conquest" in Canaan now telescoped back to their original sizes and began to settle in the highlands as separate units. Judges recounts that, on numerous occasions, the Israelites lived in a symbiotic relationship with the autochthonous peoples.[25] During the twelfth century B.C.E., the Hebrews began to sedentarize in the desert fringes and eastern valleys of Manasseh. Consequently, in the initial stages of sedentarization, many of the sites in the eastern valleys of Manasseh were founded opposite Late Bronze Age sites, which suggests a complementary existence between the Israelites and the indigenous inhabitants of these Late Bronze sites.

During this phase, the settlers moved to an economy based on a mixture of sheep-raising, wheat and barley farming, and possibly cultivation of some olive groves and vineyards. Since the older Canaanite towns would have had control over the perennial water sources, the new settlers had to reach agreement with the local Canaanites on the usage of their water sources. Zertal has noted that "such agreements today typify the relationships between the *fellahin*—the owners of the water sources—and the Bedouin—the consumer. The second stage of the settlement of the region—that in the inner valleys—was fully dependent on such agreements."[26]

As the Hebrews continued to sedentarize in the eleventh and tenth centuries B.C.E., they penetrated into the western and northern hill-country. They were not, however, able to gain complete control over this territory, and the Canaanites apparently continued to occupy Hebron, Jerusalem, Beth-shean, Ibleam, Dor, Endor, Taanach, Megiddo, and Napheth.[27] The book of Joshua includes numerous accounts of partial and unsuccessful settlement by the Israelites. Judah, Ephraim, Manasseh, and several other tribes were unable to settle the land allotted to them, and several tribes were given land from Ephraim, Manasseh, and Judah for the same reason.[28] Josh 18 reports that only four tribes had actually received their inheritance.

The difficulty in undertaking a "conquest" of the lowlands was that the Canaanite cities were located there and that "all the Canaanites who live in the plain have chariots of iron, both those in Beth-shean and its villages and those in the Valley of Jezreel" (Josh 17:16). The Israelites, therefore, settled primarily in the hill-country (Josh 17:14ff.). The central hill-country was sparsely populated, with entire wood-covered areas uninhabited, where the Israelites could clear land and "switch over from a semi-nomadic existence based mainly on the breeding and growing of flocks to agriculture and permanent settlement."[29] The settlers utilized terrace agriculture and cultivated crops well-suited for the terra rossa, such as olive trees and vineyards.

This stage of Israel's existence in the highlands was crucial because, as a domestic-scale culture, it allowed them to focus on the process of sapienization for almost two centuries. During this time, Israel developed as a distinct culture, and we can identify at least nine salient features of this early Israelite domestic-scale culture, as follows:

## Environment

The earliest environment the Israelites would have occupied in the land of Canaan would have been the eastern Jordan Valley in the territory of East Manasseh. This large area is characterized by four types of climate.[30] East Manasseh in general is characterized by Mediterranean fringes, semiarid, and tropical environments, while its valleys have a Mediterranean environment. In the eastern valleys, the climate is Mediterranean, while it becomes more arid further east, where precipitation drops in the direction of the Jordan Valley. These climatic conditions make agricultural cultivation difficult.

## Cattle and Agricultural Complex

The Israelites reacted to these difficult environmental circumstances in a variety of ways. In the earliest stages of Israel's emergence in Canaan, the Hebrews wandered in the eastern Jordan Valley. The Bible attests that they traversed the desert with their flocks,[31] and it contains a rich vocabulary related to their cattle complex.[32] In the Hebrew Bible, *cattle* is a collective term for domesticated quadrupeds, particularly bovines, which is used to translate a variety of Hebrew terms. Small cattle (מִקְנֶה, צֹאן), including sheep (כֶּבֶשׂ) and goats (עֵז, תַּיִשׁ), were the most common domesticated animals during the Iron Age. The Awassi sheep, with its fat tail (Exod 29:22) and coat similar to that of a goat, was the most familiar breed of sheep in Israel, and was raised primarily for its flesh, fat, and milk. It is clear from the variety and specificity of terminology for this animal in the Bible that it played a key role in ancient Israelite society. The typical term for a sheep is כֶּבֶשׂ (e.g., Exod 29:39); for a young sheep, שֶׂה (e.g., Exod 12:5), a ewe, רָחֵל (e.g., Isa 53:7); and a ram, אַיִל (e.g., Gen 15:9). With respect to goats, two main types were in the region: the black, or Bedouin, goat, concentrated in the Negev and Sinai, and the Damascene, or hill-country, goat. The black-haired Bedouin goat could go without water for up to four days, which made it ideal for use in arid and semiarid areas, while the Damascene goat needed to be watered twice a day.

The majority of a herd would be comprised of goats wherever harsh conditions existed since they were more adapted to such settings. The Bible includes several terms for goats: the doe is עֵז (e.g., Gen 15:9); the male goat, תַּיִשׁ (Prov 30:31) and עַתּוּד (Gen 31:10). Sheep and goats were raised for wool or hair, milk and its byproducts, meat, skins, and dung. Sheep husbandry typifies the desert fringe, since these animals are more efficient suppliers of wool, milk, and meat. As the tribes traveled further west, they lived as seminomadic or transhumant pastoralists. Shepherds established sedentarized bases in the semiarid zones contiguous with the arable land of the Canaanite hill-country, while moving their herds in rather confined and regular patterns to exploit seasonal pasturage.[33]

When the Israelites began to settle in the highlands, they practiced a mixed agricultural economy that combined the cultivation of grains with the herding of sheep and goats.[34] Large cattle, from בָּקָר (Gen 12:16), include cows, bulls, and oxen and were used mainly as plow animals. Their presence at Mount Ebal attests to the existence of plow agriculture as early as the twelfth century in the eastern valleys of Manasseh. The Israelites built their initial villages in fringe areas largely unoccupied by the Canaanites. These regions had been left uninhabited because they were heavily wooded and lacked suitable agricultural land. The scarcity of water sources also contributed to making Palestine's central hill-country an inhospitable area for agricultural settlement.

In order to develop an agricultural society, they began by clearing the forests and building terraces in order to create agricultural land.[35] The Israelites cultivated cereals and a variety of fruit trees.[36] Wheat was cultivated,[37] but in the early stages of the settlement the most important cereal was barley, which was used for making bread and beer.[38] Israel's settlement, therefore, depended heavily on its successful adaptation to the environment and its use of available resources.[39]

## Egalitarian Society

As discussed in chapter 6, the highland culture of Iron Age I was characterized by small, unwalled villages averaging about 1.7 to 2.5 acres in size, with populations that probably did not exceed seventy-five to one hundred persons.[40] Ethnographic evidence suggests that in societies organized on a domestic scale, all adults can participate in decision making so long as the group remains below about 150 people.[41] As seen in chapter 8, on 'Izbet Sartah, the Iron I villages appear to have been economically self-sufficient and independent. Each family was autonomous and produced its own economic necessities, cultivated its own fields and, if there was any surplus, chose whether to sell any of it. It seems that the highland villages generally had equal access to resources, although this was surely not always the case.[42] In the sense of there being no clear evidence of a division of labor, the Hebrew villages are thought to have been at least relatively egalitarian societies.[43]

## Flexible Marriage

The ordinary Hebrew marriage created a simple nuclear family household based on husband, wife, and child. Similar to those of other domestic-scale cultures, however, the marriage arrangement was flexible, depending on the needs of the family. Similar to the "ghost marriage" among the African cattle people,[44] the ancient Hebrews had a provision called Levirite marriage in which a brother was obligated to marry the widow of his childless deceased brother (Deut 25:5-6). The firstborn child of this marriage would be legally regarded as that of the deceased brother rather than that of the genetic father. Like the practices of the female "husband" and the "ghost marriage," Levirite marrage was a means for providing for the security and even survival of a member of the מִשְׁפָּחָה, or household.⁴⁵

## Segmentary Lineage

Tribes are made up of kinship systems, which are expressed through genealogies. The kinship systems are important for bringing people together, many of whom may be related, but some of whom may not. Kinship relations were an important organizing principle for a people's understanding of economic, political, and social relationships, including those with outsiders. The property of a village or family, for example, as well as the formation of political and economic alliances among families and among villages, would all have been kinship-based. Kinship seems to have served as a convention within which relationships of power were defined.[46] "The primary function of genealogies, then, is not to produce and transmit accurate lists of biological relationships through time, but to define social, political, and economic relations, which are always open to revision, thus representing a fluid mixture of genuine and fictitious connections."[47]

In the Hebrew Bible, most genealogies are segmented.[48] In segmented systems, genealogies could serve as memory devices for managing relationships among individuals and groups, regulating inheritance rights, and maintaining succession rights. When relationships or statuses changed, genealogies could fluctuate. If the influence of individuals or groups declined, their names may have been dropped. Omissions from genealogical lists, therefore, may or may not be conclusive in evaluating either the biological or social relatedness of certain people groups and, in and of itself, may become an important factor for understanding the dynamics of their social relationship. In any case, McNutt points out that "as a result of such omissions, contrasting genealogies may exist that derive either from different times in a group's life or from different spheres of social life. . . . Variants of written genealogies such as those in the Hebrew Bible, therefore, may not necessarily be the result of copyist error or textual corruption, but signs of the ongoing life of the genealogy."[49] These segmented systems made it possible for people groups to continually change over time.

## Age Sets

Although it is nowhere explicitly stated in the Hebrew Bible, one might infer the existence of age sets on the basis of analogy from other domestic-scale cultures, such as those of the Australian Aborigines, the African cattle people, and others.[50] It would appear that domestic-scale cultures, with their emphasis on sapienization, share this characteristic, whether it is articulated or not. In addition, numerous passages in the Hebrew Bible suggest that the ancient Israelites recognized a system of age sets. I propose that the early Iron Age village society may have recognized five age sets, as follows:[51]

a) **Housechildren** (ages 0–4). The child was nurtured in the household, which was the basic social unit for transmitting values.[52] Children were believed to require firm correction,⁵³ since they are born with an inherent foolishness⁵⁴ that can only be removed by strict corporal discipline. Foolishness is such an ingrained characteristic of children that failure to discipline a child is said to be the same as hatred for the child, since that would allow their foolish nature to shape the child's character and identity.⁵⁵ Childhood was a time for instruction, during which children could be taught so that they might outgrow their foolishness and ignorance in order to fulfill their roles.⁵⁶

b) **Youth** (ages 5–12). As early as five or six, boys and girls both may have been assigned simple tasks, such as gathering fuel, caring for younger children, watering and picking garden vegetables, and helping with the preparation of food. Children within this age set would likely have worked with the women, where they could be kept within or close to the family compound. By the age of seven or eight, children may have worked up to about four hours per day.

c) **Young Adult** (age 13–marriage). As children grew older, they would gravitate toward gender-specific tasks and begin to work with adults of the same gender. In agrarian economies, children typically reach nearly full adult labor input by about the age of thirteen and are often assigned workloads upwards of nine hours per day.⁵⁷ Young men in this age set apprentice with their fathers and begin to learn their trade, and young women would be instructed by older women in all the various aspects of their own specialized domestic and economic domain.⁵⁸ For most girls, marriage would occur in the early teens, while boys may have been slightly older.⁵⁹

d) **Adult**. When a young man became a father (אָב), he became the head of a household unit, known as the "house of the father" (בֵּית אָב),which included the senior male, his wife and children, as well as any other dependents, including unmarried daughters, daughters-in-law, or grandchildren. The house of the father comprised a unit that lived together in a single home or cluster of homes. A number of such families living together in a village made up a clan (מִשְׁפָּחָה). The men and women of these social groups had clearly delineated roles.⁶⁰ Men cleared new fields of undergrowth or trees and carried out the plow agriculture necessary for growing field crops. They would also hew out cisterns, build houses, and make terraces. Women kept the home in order, cared for small children, tended the small animals and the garden, prepared and preserved food, and made textiles.⁶¹

When a man and a woman had children, the childen would be put to work in order to help the family make its living. As a family eking out a living as subsistence farmers in the highland village economy, there would be little room for the children to waste time or resist authority. Young people and adults all had to provide labor and learn how to carry out the tasks necessary for the family to subsist.⁶² In this setting, parental guidance was considerable, and legal strictures reflect the importance of parental authority in such a setting.⁶³

e) **Elder**. The primary term for an elder in the Hebrew Bible is זָקֵן, which is derived from זָקָן, the Hebrew word for "beard." The term זָקֵן therefore refers to someone with a full beard and implies maturity. Elders ( זְקֵנִים ) bore the pride of white hair (e.g., Prov 20:29), were old and would typically have grandchildren (e.g.,

Prov 17:6). The "elders" were recognized as constituting a particular social class in Hebrew society (e.g., Exod 19:7). Senior parents over a multigenerational household of more than a dozen people gave a jural dimension to their role.

The age-set system facilitates the socialization of Hebrew children into the life of the society. This ensured family household continuity. In other words, it ensured that the skills, values, and resources necessary for survival would be transmitted across the generations. In many ways, the age-set system in Hebrew society was determined by the economic functions of the household. The diversity and technical nature of the various subsistence activities that had to be carried out in the early Israelite villages meant that parents had to be closely involved with teaching their children the tasks they would assume as they grew up.[64]

The age-class system would have been especially important in the early Israelite highland villages because they constituted an acephalous society. The age sets facilitate an egalitarian society by regulating the rights, privileges, and responsibilities of men who might otherwise find themselves in frequent conflict. The age-class system would have ensured that every male enjoyed the same potential to learn how to make a contribution to his community, marry, raise a family, receive respect within the community, and eventually become an elder. All of these potential experiences were realized in orderly sequence because each male was a member of an age set in which these rights were jointly shared. While the portrayal of the highland culture in the book of Judges portrays the tribes as often at odds with one another, the fact that it persisted for two hundred years may attest to a certain level of cohesion that may have existed at least in the villages and that may have been aided by such a device as the age-set system.

## Law

The Book of the Covenant, composed of the laws found in Exod 20:22–23:33, is generally recognized as the oldest law code in the Pentateuch.[65] While the date of its composition is debated, some vestiges of traditional laws may be detected within these texts, including theft controls, two marriage customs, conditions for liability, regulations for the treatment of draught animals, prohibitions against violence, instructions for the use of simple materials in religious worship, and benefits for both the poor and slaves. These topics are not treated comprehensively enough for the ordering of life in the villages and may be selective representation of the kinds of legal traditions that may have been operative in certain villages.[66] Based on ethnographic analogies, D. A. Knight suggests that Israelite villages would likely have had traditional laws that reflected and promoted the social customs and traditions of the community, recognized the social and political hierarchy basic to the village life and its kinship groups, sought to ensure cooperation and eliminate discord, resolved conflicts among members of the community, regulated family life, managed pastoral and agricultural livelihoods, were responsive to conditions of vulnerability among the lower classes, and generally fostered the interests of a given village.[67]

## Elders

In ancient Israel, the זְקֵנִים, or "elders," referred to a particular social class. The term זְקֵנִים therefore refers to men with a full beard, and implies age and maturity.[68] The term זְקֵנִים often refers to the totality of men of mature years with legal competence in a community.[69] Within the village context of early Israel, the fathers of the households served as its elders.[70] Because of the age-set system, the elders were venerated as having attained an award for their experience, and their age was considered an emblem of wisdom. The elders were considered wise, in contrast to the young, who were considered foolish. The old were considered to have something to teach, and the young should be their learners.[71] The aged were considered to have the wisdom necessary to counsel and to provide direction to a community. The assembly of elders met at the gate of the city, where they conducted public meetings and trials for both the inhabitants of the village, as well as those dwelling there without a household, such as orphans, widows, and aliens.[72]

## Yahwism

A common devotion to Yahweh brings coherence to this entire system. The belief of the people in Yahweh and the Yahwistic covenant gives authority to the tribal leaders, the village elders, and those who would mediate the covenant. It is not known precisely when Yahwism originated. However, a consensus seems to have grown among scholars that the poetry of ancient Israel constitutes a prime source for early Israel's history and theology.[73] The Testament of Jacob (Gen 49), the Song of the Sea (Exod 15), the Oracles of Balaam (Num 23–24), the Testament of Moses (Deut 33), and the Song of Deborah (Judg 5) are all generally agreed to have been pre-monarchic in composition and as such attest to the early existence of Yahwism.

Albright had dated the Song of the Sea even earlier, to the early part of the thirteenth century B.C.E.,[74] though Freedman has insisted it should be dated a century later, in the early twelfth century, and all of the aforementioned poems may be confidently dated to the twelfth and eleventh centuries B.C.E.[75] In any case, these early poems attest that Yahwism bound the Hebrew people together at least as early as the late thirteenth or early twelfth centuries B.C.E.,[76] if not earlier.

The importance of Yahwism has often been underestimated or dismissed in favor of materialistic explanations for the origins of Israel's tribal unity.[77] Positivism and reductionism have generally seen religion as dependent upon social processes rather than causing them, and religion has generally been seen as but one aspect of the culture of early Israel, "the expression of a particular cultural identity rather than its sole foundation."[78] Our ethnographic studies, however, suggest that religion tends to play a much more central role in domestic-scale cultures.

Indeed, among the Australian aborigines[79] and the African cattle people,[80] for example, religion provides the foundation on which the rest of the system is based and in which it all coheres. D. M. Merling writes that "religion, for good or bad, is a powerful motivator. Some may suppose that much YHWHism was a late development; even so, the peoples of earlier times had religion and it did affect their lives and history."[81] Benjamin Mazar stressed this point:

> It should be remembered that during that period religious and national sentiments were strong among the tribes of Israel. The belief in the God of the Fathers, not solely as Israel's only God, protecting His people and His Messiah, but as the only God of all peoples, ruler of beings, watching over the fate of men and nations, served as a tremendous motivating force in the creation of the Israelite state and in the evolvement of its political and social order. This process explains the adoption of the spiritual life of Israel by non-Israelites and quasi-Israelites in the service of David and Solomon, one of the expressions of which was the Hebraization of personal names.[82]

The Hebrew Bible attests to Yahwism as a key factor in the formation of early Israel. The most prominent example is that of Rahab, already discussed, who is assimilated, along with her house, into the Israelite community. When the Hebrew spies first entered the land of Canaan, Rahab confessed her faith in Yahweh and asked that the house of her father (בֵּית אָב), including "my father and mother, my brothers and sisters, and all who belong to them" (Josh 2:12-13), might be admitted into the covenant community. When the Israelites took the city of Jericho, Rahab and her entire מִשְׁפָּחָה are spared, and "her family has lived in Israel ever since" (Josh 6:25). Likewise, the Gibeonites were assimilated among the people of Israel (Josh 9:1). These and other people groups were consequently grafted into the covenant community at covenant renewal ceremonies, such as in Josh 8:30-35 and Josh 24.

This second phase of Israel's existence in the highlands was vital. As a domestic-scale culture, Israel's focus was on sapienization, their development as a distinct culture. The salient features of that culture were built on and cohered in their Yahwistic faith. During this time, non-Israelites became Israelites both through adherence to the Yahwistic covenant as well as through the mundane social process of symbiotic coexistence and eventual assimilation. The growth of the people Israel, along with other external factors, led to the next stage of their cultural development.

## 3. Politicization (Political-Scale Culture)

In the final stage of the early Israelite settlement, the tribes of Israel developed into a state-level society and came to dominate the region. Reconstructing this process by which Israel transitioned from a loose network of tribes to a state-level society, however, has been controversial. Since the 1960s, the rise of the state has been seen by many anthropologists as an inevitable stage in the evolutionary process,[83] commonly described as a cultural process called "politicization" by anthropologists. In the process of politicization, social power is concentrated in the hands of a few, and the needs of individual households are subordinated to the needs of the ruling class. This process has typically been seen as having been accompanied by at least four cultural subprocesses: taxation, specialization, militarization, and urbanization.[84]

Anthropologists have generally seen this process as a negative development. Describing how the process occurs, Bodley writes:

> The great divide in human cultural development between a world totally controlled by domestically organized cultures and a world dominated by politically and commercially organized cultures occurred when the first villagers surrendered their political autonomy to chiefs from other villages. This created a second level of political authority, with villages aggregated under a paramount chief to form a chiefdom. Adding a third administrative level to form a state and a fourth to form an empire are logical steps in the growth process.[85]

The key to the politicization process, according to this view, is the concentration of social power in the hands of a political elite. This is a "coercive" process with an "inherent" inequity. Bodley explains:

> The power inequity inherent in the politicization process means that rulers must devise and transmit new cultural beliefs and behaviors that will coerce or persuade people to accept their authority. This is not an easy task because politicization competes directly with the sapienization process and the interests of individual households.[86]

In this view, politicization is "a maladaptive evolutionary process that rewards a powerful, self-interested minority for promoting cultural ideas that support runaway growth harmful to others."[87] This view of the politicization process has predominated since the 1960s, and continues to predominate today.[88]

In approaching the study of state-level societies, anthropologists and archaeologists have typically turned to trait lists. W. G. Dever has suggested that a trait list for a political-scale society would include at least the following five elements: (1) A topographical unit with a fortification wall; (2) dense occupation; (3) reflection of great social differentiation and centralized administration; (4) evidence of economic accumulation (surplus) and distribution; and (5) constitution of a "central place."[89] The study of the "archaeology of the state" has tended to rely on comparisons of these types of material remains. However, new inroads have been made in understanding the politicization process in ancient Israel that call the foregoing assumptions into question. D. M. Master notes that material approaches may not be the best for understanding "politicization" in ancient Israel.[90]

In contrast to the dominant tribe-chiefdom-state taxonomy, the sociologist Max Weber first divided societies not on the basis of material destruction, clustering of wealth, or size, as had Engels, but on how individual societies view the nature of law, authority, and legitimacy. In his scheme, societies can be large or small and have the same view of authority and legitimacy. The society can fluctuate between sedentary and pastoralist with little change in the way that the relationship between ruler and ruled is conceived.[91]

In the late 1970s, the sociologist Max Weber made a pioneering study of early Israel and proposed a patrimonial model, in which the forces of tradition and personal association, natural forces apparent in the ancient household, appear to have shaped the concept of authority.[92] He proposed that societies such as that of ancient Israel expressed authority primarily in terms of kinship. Weber applies this logic to larger, more centralized societies, deducing the idea of a "patrimonial state." Stager reconstructs this patrimonial state as a series of "nested households," at the base of which is the בֵּית אָב, the "house of the father."[93] The material evidence of this symbol is found in the architecture of the four-room houses and the way they are clustered throughout the Iron Age. The "state" is organized along similar lines, with the king functioning as the head of the household. His subjects still depend on personal relationships with and loyalty to him and, in return, they expected to receive security and support. Just like the father ( אָב ) of a household, therefore, the king "presides over his own" house (בַּיִת ) that includes all the families and households under his province. The Tel Dan Stela refers to this kind of understanding when it refers to the בֵּית דָּוִד ("House of David"), as do Assyrian inscriptions that refer to the בֵּית עָמְרִי ("House of Omri"). Stager argues that "these two 9th-century references to Judah are enough evidence in themselves to demonstrate that Judah was a 'full-fledged state' in the eyes of its neighbors long before the end of the 8th century."[94]

This patrimonial state may have had some important differences from some other ancient understandings of the state, however. Stager concludes that, in Israelite society, the king does not represent the height of authority in this three-tiered arrangement. This position is held by Yahweh, who reigns as the ultimate patrimonial master, who holds the highest authority over the king and the "children of Israel," who are closely connected to him by covenant as his kindred (עַם) or kindred-in-law.[95] Human kingship and divine kingship, then, are more-inclusive forms of patrimonial domination. Households are nested within households, with each tier becoming more comprehensive as one moves from domestic to royal to divine levels.[96] The older approaches saw the Israelite monarchy as some kind of "alien" urban institution grafted onto a reluctant, egalitarian, kin-based tribal society. Through external and internal conflict, it evolved into a class-driven society dominated by an oppressive urban elite. "Seen through the lens of the patrimonial model . . . [however], Israelite kingship is simply a higher level of kinship."[97]

Based on this more emic understanding of Israelite patrimonialism, "it is not so difficult to imagine a farmer such as Saul or a shepherd such as David becoming king."[98] The politicization process in ancient Israel "does not imply any increase in technology or administrative capacity. Literacy, international trade, and extensive mobilization of resources are all found in the Late Bronze Age, a time of lower population and fewer urban centers."[99] Understanding Israelite "politicization," rather, requires an abandonment of the etic approaches to a more emic approach. Building on Weber's work, Master, King, and Lawrence have reconstructed the concept of a patrimonial state in which the king was not originally perceived as an oppressive dictator taking advantage of his people, but a kinsman who was caring for them. In this paradigm, politicization could certainly be said to have occurred with the election of Saul to the place of king.

## SYNTHESIS

In this discussion we have seen that the Israelites migrated into Canaan from the east, and because of the Canaanite presence in the lowlands, they concentrated their settlements in the hill-country. But despite the fact that Israel's process of settlement was such that they confined themselves to the hill-country for some time, this turned out to be propitious, for it was there, in relative isolation, that they were able to focus on the sapienization process, which led to the development of Israelite culture. It was in the highlands that the specific traits of the culture developed (four-room house, austere pottery, and so forth), by which the Israelites defined themselves in contrast to other people groups around them.

During this time, the belief in Yahweh, not solely as Israel's God, but as the God of all peoples, provided the basis for Israelite identity and also attracted non-Israelites to adopt Israel's spiritual life. Richard Hess observes that the emergence of early Israel was clearly a multiplex phenomenon characterized by features from virtually all of the hypotheses of Israelite origins.[100] He notes that some of the early Israelites may have entered the land and been involved in the destruction of select sites such as Hazor; nomadic and other peoples forced to flee for economic and/or political reasons could have become Israelite at any time during its appearance and growth in Canaan (Alt); dissatisfied elements from Canaanite city-states could have become Israelites (Mendenhall and Gottwald); Egyptian "buffer groups" in northern Palestine (Coote) or *habiru* groups (de Moor) could have become Israelite; settlers who had adopted an enclosed nomadic existence during the Late Bronze Age could have re-sedentarized in the succeeding periods and become Israelites (Finkelstein).[101]

What is significant is that it was the salient features of early Israel as a domestic-scale culture that allowed for the incorporation of these new population elements. The segmentary lineage system and Yahwistic theology allowed for foreign elements to be grafted into Israelite society, as in the cases of Rahab and the Gibeonites, mentioned above. Rahab and the Gibeonites were both fully assimilated into early Israel, with Rahab appearing in later biblical genealogies (Matt 1:5) and Gibeon as a sacred site where the tabernacle and the altar of burnt offering were temporarily housed.[102] During the postexilic period, the men of Gibeon assisted in the rebuilding of the Old Gate and the restoration of Jerusalem as far as the Broad Wall (Neh 3:7-8). The entire book of Ruth, which features a Moabite heroine, is a voice for the inclusiveness of Yahwism in early Israel. Ruth, who immigrates from Moab to Israel, is ultimately woven into a ten-generation genealogy in which she appears as the great-grandmother of King David (Ruth 4:17-22).

Numerous other examples could be cited, but these are enough to make the point that Israel's origin resulted from a coalescence of peoples with widely differing backgrounds and experiences and their coming to embrace the decentralized, nonhierarchical social form of early Israel's domestic-scale culture, along with its cult of Yahweh.[103] Herein is the genius of Israel's settlement in the highlands. With their settlement in the relative isolation of the central hill-country, they lived as a domestic-scale culture. Since the most distinctive feature of domestic-scale cultures is the sapienization process, this means they were able to focus exclusively on the production and maintenance of their families, their society, and their culture for almost two hundred years. As people from various groups sought to become a part of Israel, the highlanders had the societal mechanisms to assimilate them and socialize them into Israelite culture. The population of Israel increased, therefore, both by natural birth but also by conversion or assimilation. Hence the Israelites increased in number during these years in the highlands.

Yahwism also served as a strong motivating force in the creation of the Israelite state and in the development of its political and social order. As the Israelites underwent politicization, they gradually attained dominance in the region. Yohanan Aharoni's observations, written over thirty years ago, describe the long-term ramifications of their initial geographic location in the highlands:

> It is true that during the achievement of the settlement process the blocks of tribes became separated and non-Israelite elements existed in various localities. But in the final analysis, there emerged a continuous settlement over the entire country, in the plains as well as in the hill-country, and the conditions so created made for the political and demographical unity of the land of Israel.[104]

The settlement in the hill-country, which began as a necessity, ultimately became the means by which Israel arose to prominence in the region. "The necessity to settle in the mountain areas was responsible for the fact that the Israelite occupation became, in the end, more than a conquest. For the first time, the center of gravity of the country moved to the mountain districts, creating conditions propitious for the establishment of an independent and strong monarchy.

# CONCLUSION

The "conquest" was not a blitzkrieg. There seems to be no doubt that the process of the settlement of early Israel included the military actions of an element of its population. This kind of activity is indeed the fastest moving current among Braudel's three "speeds" of history, and it may be for this reason that it tends to attract the focus of those who reflect on historical events—including Dtr. Israel's emergence in Canaan was not, however, comprised solely of events that occurred in this "speed." In the long run, Israel's emergence was the movement of a people through the culture scale. According to Braudel's schema, while military events may tend to preoccupy historians, it is the everyday material life, the labors and exchanges of countless forgotten village folk, that make up the *deepest* undercurrents of history. These undercurrents are anchored in people's quest for food, clothing, and shelter, and in their efforts to coexist with their environment and others who occupy it.[105] For the ancient Israelites, this whole process of their progression through the culture scale was the "conquest" by which they emerged as the dominant force in the region (**Fig. 41**).

| Culture Scale | Tribal Organization | Tribal Activity | Tribal Leadership | Food Objective |
|---|---|---|---|---|
| Domestic: Phase I | Clans that have banded together | Migration/ Conquest/ Sorties | Joshua/tribal leaders/elders | Nutrition |
| Domestic: Phase II | Clans that have disbanded | Sedentarization/ Assimilation/ Establishment of villages averaging 1.5 acres occupied by ca. 100 people | Acephalous/ elders/occasional charismatic leaders (judges) | Nutrition |
| Political | Tribal Kingdom | Politicization/ Rise of cities/ Eventual domination in the region | The King, or Paterfamilias | Taxable surplus |

*Fig. 41. Ancient Israel's Progression through the Culture Scale*

# AFTERWORD

Interest in ethnic and national origins seems to be a human universal. People of every tribe and nation throughout human history have wanted to know who they are and where they come from, and most cultures have stories of origins that answer such questions.[1] The book of Joshua recounts such a story of origins for the ancient Israelites, claiming they originated outside the land of Canaan and entered it in a process of conquest. Ever since the Enlightenment, scholars have been fixated on the book of Joshua and the issue of Israelite origins. In recent times, the focus of research has been on the extent to which the historiography in the book of Joshua coheres with the archaeological remains of earliest Israel that have been discovered thus far. Harmonizing the biblical and archaeological data, however, is beset with challenges, and scholars have often concluded the two data sets are in opposition to one another. *How Israel Became a People* seeks to respond to this apparent conundrum in two ways. First, it asks whether we can reconstruct the Israelite settlement in Canaan from the book of Joshua alone. Second, it utilizes biblical, extrabiblical, and archaeological data in an attempt to reconstruct the Israelite settlement in Canaan.

Chapter 1 is devoted to the question of whether an adequate picture of the Israelite settlement can be derived solely from the biblical book of Joshua. Because of the tension between the biblical account and the current archaeological data related to early Israel, the academy has generally concluded that the book of Joshua yields little actual historical information about the early history of Israel. These negative conclusions about the historical value of the book of Joshua, however, are a result of an inaccurate perception of ancient historiography. The academy has tended to view ancient historiography as akin to modern journalism. Just as a journalist interviews a number of eyewitnesses in an attempt to reconstruct an event or a series of events with complete accuracy, so it is assumed that the ancient historiographer sought to make an objective account of events. Ancient historiographers were not journalists or objective historians, however, and they had completely different goals than modern academic historians. All across the ancient Near East, historiographers were seeking *to interpret what their gods were doing*, rather than trying to write objective history about secular events. In ancient Israel, the prophets served this function and, tellingly, the book of Joshua has historically been included in the "Former Prophets," which should attest to the idea that it contains material authored by those who sought to interpret what Israel's own national god, Yahweh, was doing on behalf of Yahweh's people.

## Afterword

People in the ancient Near East *were* interested in the past; they found it to be interesting and important, but not for its own sake. The idea that history is important for its own sake is a modern academic chimera and, as we have seen, no one—ancient or modern—seems to have been interested in "history for history's sake." Just as in modern times, ancients considered the past to be interesting and important because they found within it a key to social coherence, which lent meaning to life in the present. The author of the book of Joshua was not trying to write a scientific account of the early Israelite settlement, with explanations of what kinds of pottery the earliest Israelites used, what kinds of houses they built, and how they organized their villages in the highlands. Instead, he was "preaching" about what Yahweh could and would do if Israel were faithful to the covenant and if they carried through with the "conquest" of Canaan. At the conclusion of his own discussion of historiography, John Walton concludes that "critical scholarship needs to rethink its imperialistic and anachronistic imposition of modern standards and values on ancient texts [and] confessional scholars need to rethink precisely what constitutes the truth of the text that they seek to defend in light of the text's own poetics and perspectives."[2] While the site destructions attributed to the Israelites in the book of Joshua should certainly be studied, my point is that the most fruitful avenues of study in this book may lie in literary and theological directions.[3]

The second and longest part of the book, consisting of chapters 2 through 10, is a scientific account of the early Israelite settlement. These chapters are concerned with questions about when the exodus-conquest occurred, whether the Israelites evolved from the indigenous population or migrated into the land from the outside, where their earliest settlements were located, the kinds of villages they established, how they ordered their domestic lives, what kinds of pottery they used, what types of houses they built, and what role their religion played in the entire process. In order to try to answer these questions, relevant biblical texts and pertinent extrabiblical texts and archaeological data were surveyed. I concluded that most of the early Israelites entered Canaan from the east as transhumant pastoralists. Several of the tribes coalesced into a unified group and made military incursions into the land of Canaan, which are echoed in the book of Joshua. Rather than settling in the cities they attacked, however, they disbanded and sedentarized in the highlands as separate units, where they often lived in a symbiotic relationship with the indigenous population. Gradually, they fanned out over a period of two centuries, during which time they evolved from a domestic-scale culture to a political-scale culture and eventually emerged as the dominant force in the region. In this culture-scale model, the "conquest" was a process that began in the late thirteenth century and reached its fruition with the institution of the monarchy in the late twelfth to early eleventh centuries B.C.E.

I would like to highlight some comments made by Mark Smith in his presidential address at the Seventy-fourth International Meeting of the Catholic Biblical Association of America, held at Assumption College, in Worcester, Massachusetts, August 6–9, 2011. After considering certain data related to the possibility that Yahweh may have been known outside of Israel as early as the fifteenth century B.C.E., Smith concluded that "it is clear that there is much here about which we are ignorant," but he went on to suggest that

> our ignorance is an important datum. In this respect, Israel's God—and ours—is something of a mystery to us. Like modern scholars, the Israelites who composed these relatively early pieces worked with a certain ignorance of their own about the original profile of their God. In fact, their understanding of God, which may have included a lack of knowledge of the old profile of their God, was sufficient for them. It may have been the very mystery about these old depictions that made them all the more attractive to later tradition.[4]

In the same way that the early Israelite authors may have been attracted to the stories of Yahweh because of the mystery inherent within them, modern scholars continue to be attracted to the quest for early Israelite origins because there are so many tantalizing mysteries inherent to the search. However, just as "the truth of God for the religious tradition of Israel did not depend on full knowledge of origins,"[5] modern scholars must not mistake the human quest for clarity about Israelite origins with the reality of God for humanity. The real importance of the story of Israel's emergence in Canaan does not lie in settlement patterns, site layouts, architecture, pottery forms, or foodways, but in the power of Yahweh to create a people.

# GLOSSARY

**Abecedary:** An inscription in which the alphabet is written out in order.
**Altar:** An elevated platform or surface on which sacrifices or other offerings are made to a deity.
**Amphictyony:** An alliance of states established around a central religious sanctuary.
**Bāmāh, pl. bāmôt:** The root of the term is obscure. It may refer to an altar or an elevated cultic installation with an altar. Usually translated as "high place(s)."
**Caprovids:** A category that includes both sheep and goats, the bones of which are often not distinguished from one another in faunal analysis.
**Commercial-Scale Culture:** A culture in which power is essentially commercial and is driven by cultural institutions such as private property, contractual agreements, and monetary systems, all of which are organized by a centralized political power.
**Cult:** A system of religious worship or ritual.
**Culture Scale:** Differences in the size of a given culture, based on varying ways of organizing social power.
**Deuteronomic:** Pertaining to Deuteronomy, found in the book of Deuteronomy.
**Deuteronomistic:** Expressing ideas similar to those found in Deuteronomy, but derivative in character.
**Deuteronomistic History:** A hypothetical historical work comprised of the books of Deuteronomy, Joshua, Judges, Samuel, and Kings, constituting a single work.
**DtrH:** The Deuteronomistic History.
**Domestic-Scale Culture:** A culture in which social power is centered in the family or in kinship groups, who control production and distribution. Domestic-scale cultures are typically small, with only about five hundred people.
**Dtr:** The Deuteronomistic Historian.
**Ethnic Markers:** Physical symbols that indicate identification with a specific ethnic group, such as certain markings on the body, pottery styles, house designs, and so forth.
**Ethnicity:** A shared sense of identity or peoplehood.
**Ethnogenesis:** The process by which an ethnic identity is developed or an ethnic group is formed.
**Ethnos:** From the Greek *ethnos*, which refers to a community of people.
**Faunal Remains:** The remains of any form of animal life.

*Glossary*

**Fiction:** (1) A nonfactual genre of literature characterized by its depiction of events that, by definition, did not happen; (2) an element of artistry or craft; e.g., representations of the past, inasmuch as they are not literally the past, may contain a "fictionalizing" aspect.

**Fictional narrative:** A narrative that portrays events that never happened, although they may be described as being "true-to-life."

**Food System:** The various patterned and interconnected activities carried out by a group of individuals in their quest for food.

**Fortification:** A defensive earthwork, such as a fort or a wall.

**Four-Room House:** A type of domestic building characteristic of the Iron Age. Its basic plan consists of an entrance at the front that leads into a central space with a floor of beaten earth, paralleled on either side by stone-paved aisles bordered by pillars. The fourth room, which usually contains a dirt floor, stretches across the back of the house.

**Functionalism:** An anthropological approach that interprets cultural traits in terms of their contribution to the maintenance of the culture.

**Glacis:** A sloping bank, typically plastered, below an outer fortification wall, designed to make it more difficult for invaders to approach or undermine the city wall.

**Habiru/ʿApiru:** A population group on the social and political margins of the ancient Near East from about 1850 to 1150 B.C.E. The term ʿapiru may have been a pejorative for refugees, runaways, or anyone who had "hit the road."

**Hebrew:** An ethnicon applied to Abraham and his descendants in the Hebrew Bible. The term is probably either derived from ʿever, in which case it would mean something like "the man from beyond," or from ʿibrum, in which case it would mean something like "the one from the back country."

**Historical Books:** The books that contain the history of Israel from its entry into Canaan to its exile in Babylonia and its life in Persia, including Joshua, Judges, Ruth, Samuel, Kings, Chronicles, Ezra-Nehemiah, and Esther.

**Historical Narrative:** a narrative that claims to tell readers what really happened.

**Historiography:** the giving of an account of the past; the interpretation of the past. Historiography may be defined as a kind of verbal representational art.

**History:** An account of what has happened in the life of a people, country, or institution.

**Late Mycenaean IIIB:** A period that corresponds with Palestine's Late Bronze Age, and tends to be found specifically in Late Bronze IIB strata (1300–1200 B.C.E.).

**LXX:** The abbreviation for the Koine Greek version of the Hebrew Bible. Its name is derived from the Talmudic tradition that it was translated by seventy-two elders commissioned for the task by King Ptolemy.

**MT:** The abbreviation for the Masoretic Text, the version of the Hebrew Bible copied and edited by the Masoretes between the seventh and tenth centuries C.E. The MT is almost universally regarded as the official version of the Hebrew Bible.

*Glossary*

**Nomad:** A wanderer with no fixed home, but who moves about constantly in search of food or pasture.
**Nomadization:** The process by which a sedentary family or people group transitions to a nomadic lifestyle.
**Political-Scale Culture:** A cultural system led by a ruler rather than by household heads. In political-scale cultures, production systems are centrally managed and geared toward the support of the political apparatus.
**Politicization:** The process of producing and maintaining political power.
**Positivism:** A philosophical system, originating with August Comte, based on the scientific observation of facts. Positivism emphasizes the testability or provability of statements.
**Pottery:** Earthenware, such as pots, bowls, and dishes, fashioned from clay by a potter.
**Provenance (provenience):** Place of origin.
**Redactor:** Editor.
**Sapienization:** The process of humanization, or the development of people.
**Sedentarization:** The process by which nomads or seminomads settle down into a sedentary lifestyle.
**Shasu:** A generic term for desert dwellers used in Egyptian texts beginning in the early Eighteenth Dynasty. The term refers to a social class rather than an ethnic unity and is equivalent to the modern term *Bedouin*.
**Shephelah:** The Hebrew term for the sloped hills and fertile valleys that separate the Judean hill-country from the western coastal plain.
**Sherd(s):** A piece or pieces of broken pottery.
**Silo:** A stone-lined or plastered pit used to store large quantities of grain. Silos are usually located near public areas and structures.
**Socialization:** The process by which culture is transmitted to children or to newcomers seeking to assimilate into a new social group.
**Strata (pl.), stratum (sing.):** A layer of occupational debris distinct from earlier and later layers. The strata represent the occupational history of a tell.
**Stratigraphy:** The sequence of strata of a tell. The excavation and analysis of one occupational layer at a time is known as the stratigraphic method.
**Subsistence Economy:** An economy in which production and distribution are carried out by the local community for its own consumption.
**Survey, Archaeological:** The examination of the features and artifacts that lie exposed on the surface of the ground in order to discover attributes of human culture.
**Tell:** The Hebrew term (sometimes *tel*) for an artificial mound created by the accumulation of ruined cities, one on top of the other. In Arabic, the term is *tall*.
**Temenos**: The sacred area of a temple or other cultic site.
**Temple:** A public building that houses the statue of a god and in which the rites of his or her cult are carried out. The temple is understood as the abode of the deity.

*Glossary*

**Trait List:** An enumeration of artifacts or characteristics identified with a specific ethnic group.
**Transhumance:** The relocation of livestock herds according to season in order to follow the most favorable grazing conditions.
**Tribe:** A group of people, families, or clans, identified with a common ancestor, who comprise a close community under a local leader or chief.

# NOTES

## Pharaohs of Egypt's Eighteenth and Nineteenth Dynasties

1. Adapted from M. Van De Mieroop, *The Eastern Mediterranean in the Age of Ramesses II* (Malden, Mass.: Blackwell, 2007), 255–56.

## 1. Why Must We Reconstruct the History of the Israelite Settlement?

1. L. L. Grabbe, ed., *Can a "History of Israel" Be Written?* (JSOTSup 245; Sheffield: Sheffield Academic Press, 1997).

2. G. F. Hasel, "Biblical Theology Movement," *The Concise Evangelical Dictionary of Theology* (ed. W. A. Elwell; Grand Rapids: Baker, 1991), 64–65.

3. C. G. Bartholomew, "Biblical Theology and Biblical Interpretation: Introduction," in *Out of Egypt: Biblical Theology and Biblical Interpretation* (ed. C. Bartholomew et al.; vol. 5, The Scripture and Hermeneutics Series, ed. C. Bartholomew and A. Thiselton; Grand Rapids: Zondervan, 2004), 4–6. For the development of biblical theology since Gabler, see G. Hasel, *Old Testament Theology: Basic Issues in the Current Debate* (rev. ed.; Grand Rapids: Eerdmans, 1972), esp. ch. 1.

4. G. Ernest Wright, *God Who Acts: Biblical Theology as Recital* (London: SCM Press, 1952; SBT 8).

5. Ibid., 126–27.

6. G. E. Wright, *Biblical Archaeology* (Philadelphia: Westminster, 1957), 17.

7. Ibid., 17.

8. J. Bright, *The Authority of the Old Testament* (Grand Rapids: Baker, 1967), 42.

9. Z. Zevit, "The Biblical Archaeology versus Syro-Palestinian Archaeology Debate in Its American Institutional and Intellectual Contexts," in *The Future of Biblical Archaeology: Reassessing Methodologies and Assumptions* (ed. J. K. Hoffmeier and A. Millard; Grand Rapids: Eerdmans, 2004), 14.

10. W. G. Dever, "Syro-Palestinian and Biblical Archaeology," in *The Hebrew Bible and Its Modern Interpreters* (ed. D. A. Knight and G. M. Tucker; Minneapolis: Fortress, 1985), 59–60. Dever has commented at length on the work of G. E. Wright in his "Biblical Theology and Biblical Archaeology: An Appreciation of G. Ernest Wright," *HTR* 73 (1980): 1–15. Walter Rast took issue with Dever's attribution of the motivation of Wright's archaeological efforts to biblical theology. He explained, "I am more inclined to see Wright's contribution as an effort in hermeneutics, affecting his preoccupation with the relation of the historical-archaeological ambience of the ancient Near East and the biblical texts." W. E. Rast, "A Response to Professor

Dever," in *A Symposium on the Relationship between Bible, Oriental Studies, and Archaeology*, Occasional Papers of the Horn Archaeological Museum, Andrews University, no. 3 (Berrien Springs, Mich.: Siegfriend H. Horn Archaeological Museum, 1984), 47.

11. W. F. Albright, "Archaeology and the Date of the Hebrew Conquest of Palestine," *BASOR* 58 (1935): 10–18.

12. W. F. Albright, "Further Light on the History of Israel from Lachish and Megiddo," *BASOR* 68 (1937): 22–26.

13. G. E. Wright, "Epic of Conquest," *BA* 3:25–40.

14. See the vast bibliography in *IJH*, 213–284.

15. E.g., Y. Kaufman, *The Biblical Account of the Conquest of Canaan* (Jerusalem: Magnes, 1953).

16. E.g., L. Wood, *A Survey of Israel's History* (Grand Rapids: Zondervan, 1986), 141–53; J. P. Free, *Archaeology and Bible History* (rev. and exp.; Grand Rapids: Zondervan, 1992), 111–16.

17. This issue will be discussed in detail in ch. 2. For an initial overview, see W. G. Dever, "Israel, History of Archaeology and the Conquest," in *ABD* 3:547–48.

18. G. E. Wright, "Is Glueck's Aim to Prove That the Bible Is True?" *BA* 22 (1959): 16.

19. Cf. B. S. Childs, *Biblical Theology in Crisis* (Philadelphia: Westminster, 1970).

20. E.g., J. B. Pritchard, "Culture and History," in *The Bible in Modern Scholarship* (ed. J. P. Hyatt; Nashville: Abingdon, 1965), 313–24; R. de Vaux, "Method in the Study of Early Hebrew History," in *The Bible in Modern Scholarship* (ed. J. P. Hyatt; Nashville: Abingdon, 1965), 15–29; idem., "On Right and Wrong Uses of Archaeology," in *Near Eastern Archaeology in the Twentieth Century: Essays in Honor of Nelson Glueck* (ed. J. A. Sanders; New York: Doubleday, 1970), 64–80; B. Mazar, "The Historical Background of the Book of Genesis," *JNES* 24 (1969): 73–83; P. W. Lapp, *Biblical Archaeology and History* (Cleveland: World, 1969).

21. James Barr, however, denied that there really was a crisis of biblical theology which, indeed, continues to flourish in many ways. Cf. J. Barr, "The Theological Case against Biblical Theology," in *Canon, Theology and Old Testament Interpretation* (ed. G. M. Tucker, D. L. Petersen, and R. R. Wilson; Philadelphia: Fortress, 1988), 3–19, esp. 3–4.

22. E.g., M. Weippert, *The Settlement of the Israelite Tribes in Palestine: A Critical Survey of Recent Scholarly Debate* (London: SCM, 1971); T. L. Thompson, *The Historicity of the Patriarchal Narratives: The Quest for the Historical Abraham* (New York: Walter de Gruyter, 1974).

23. B. T. Arnold, "History and Historiography, OT," *NIDB* 2:833.

24. A. K. Grayson, "Historiography," *ABD* 3:205–6.

25. Arnold, "History and Historiography, OT."

26. R. G. Collingwood, *The Idea of History* (Oxford: Oxford University Press, 1956), 9–10.

27. M. Z. Brettler, *The Creation of History in Ancient Israel* (London: Routledge, 1995), 10.

28. J. Huizinga, "A Definition of the Concept of History," in *Philosophy and History: Essays Presented to Ernst Cassirer* (ed. R. Klibansky and H. J. Paton; New York: Harper Torchbooks, 1963), 9.

29. J. Huizinga, *Geschichte und Kulture* (Stuttgart: Kroner, 1954), 13.

30. John Van Seters, *In Search of History: Historiography in the Ancient World and the Origins of Biblical History* (New Haven: Yale University Press, 1983).

31. Arnold, "History and Historiography, OT."

32. A. K. Grayson, *Assyrian and Babylonian Chronicles* (Winona Lake, Ind.: Eisenbrauns, 2000), 43–44.

33. "Texts from Hammurabi to the Downfall of the Assyrian Empire," trans. A. L. Oppenheim (*ANET* 274–301); "Neo-Assyrian Inscriptions," trans. K. L. Younger (*COS* 2.261–306).

34. K. L. Sparks, *Ancient Texts for the Study of the Hebrew Bible: A Guide to the Background Literature* (Peabody, Mass.: Hendrickson, 2005), 369.

35. J. H. Breasted, *Ancient Records of Egypt* 1:51–72. See also T. A. H. Wilkinson, *Royal Annals of Ancient Egypt: The Palermo Stone and Its Associated Fragments* (New York: Kegan Paul, 2000).

36. (*COS* 2.3:19–23).

37. Partial translations can be found in *AEL* 2:29–35; *ANET* 234–41; J. H. Breasted, *Ancient Records of Egypt*, 2.163–217; *COS* 2.2A: 7.13. See also J. K. Hoffmeier, "The Structure of Joshua 1–11 and the Annals of Thutmose III," in *Faith, Tradition, and History* (ed. Millard et al.), 165–79; P. F. O'Mara, "The Birth of Egyptian Historiography," *DE* 46 (2000): 49–64.

38. "The Victory Stela of King Piye (Piankhy)," translated M. Lichtheim (*COS* 2.7:42–51).

39. *Manetho* (trans. W. G. Waddell; Loeb Classical Library, Cambridge: Harvard University Press, 1940).

40. W. K. Simpson et al., eds., *The Literature of Ancient Egypt: An Anthology of Stories, Instructions, Stelae, Autobiographies, and Poetry* (3d ed.; New Haven: Yale, 2003), 69–71.

41. T. Bryce, *The Major Historical Texts of Early Hittite History* (Australia: University of Queensland, 1982), 21–48; *COS* 1.72.

42. Bryce, *The Major Historical Texts of Early Hittite History*, 49–98.

43. E. von Schuler, *Die Kaskäer: Ein Beitrag zur Ethnographie des alten Kleinasien* (Berlin: Walter de Gruyter, 1965), 185–87 (partial); Van Seters, *In Search of History*, 108.

44. "The Ten Year Annals of Great King Mursili II of Hatti" (*COS* 2.16:82–90); Sparks, *Ancient Texts for the Study of the Hebrew Bible*, 393–94.

45. "The Apology of Hattusili III," translated by Th. P. J. van den Hout (*COS* 1.77:199–204).

46. K. L. Sparks, *Ethnicity and Identity in Ancient Israel: Prolegomna to the Study of Ethnic Sentiments and Their Expression in the Hebrew Bible* (Winona Lake, Ind.: Eisenbrauns, 1998), 58.

47. Cf. Aristotle, *Poetica* 23; Cicero, *de Legibus* 1.1.5; Josephus, *Contra Apion* 1.3; Libanius, *Against Herodotus*; Manetho, *Against Herodotus*; Plutarch, *On the Malignity of Herodotus*; Thucydides, *History of the Peloponnesian War* 1.20–21. Cited in Sparks, *Ethnicity and Identity in Ancient Israel*, 58.

48. Sparks, *Ancient Texts for the Study of the Hebrew Bible*, 404.

49. Ibid., 405.

50. Thucydides, *Historiae* 1.21.

51. Ibid., 1.22.

52. K. Sacks, *Polybius on the Writing of History* (University of California Publications in Classical Studies 24; Berkeley: University of California Press, 1981), 79–95.

53. Thucydides, *Historiae* 1.20–21.

54. W. W. Hallo, "Biblical History in Its Near Eastern Setting: The Contextual Approach," in *Scripture in Context* (ed. C. D. Evans, W. W. Hallo, and J. B. White; Pittsburgh: Pickwick, 1980), 6.

55. Possibly pronounced "genut," the *gnwt* were early Egyptian annalistic records that predated the Palermo Stone. The *gnwt* contained lists of major events of each year and provided year names for the purpose of dating. See D. B. Redford, "Historical Sources: Textual Evidence," *OEAE* 2:104–8.

56. E.g., B. T. Arnold, "The Weidner Chronicle and the Idea of History," in *Faith, Tradition and History* (ed. A. R. Millard, J. K. Hoffmeier, and D. W. Baker; Winona Lake, Ind.:

Eisenbrauns, 1994), 143; M. Burrows, "Ancient Israel," in *The Idea of History in the Ancient Near East* (ed. R. C. Dentan; New Haven: American Oriental Society, 1983), 101–31; J. Licht, "Biblical Historicism," in *History, Historiography, and Interpretation: Studies in Biblical and Cuneiform Literatures* (ed. H. Tadmor and M. Weinfeld; Jerusalem: Magnes, 1983), 109; Sparks, *Ancient Texts for the Study of the Hebrew Bible*, 408–14; J. H. Walton, *Ancient Israelite Literature in Its Cultural Context: A Survey of Parallels Between Biblical and Ancient Near Eastern Texts* (2nd ed.; Grand Rapids: Zondervan, 1990), 115; idem., *Ancient Near Eastern Thought and the Old Testament: Introducing the Conceptual World of the Hebrew Bible* (Grand Rapids: Baker, 2006), 228.

57. Walton, *Ancient Near Eastern Thought and the Old Testament*, 228.

58. Licht, "Biblical Historicism," 109.

59. P. Satterthwaite and G. McConnville, *Exploring the Old Testament: A Guide to the Historical Books* (Downers Grove, Ill.: InterVarsity, 2007), 12.

60. Licht, "Biblical Historicism," 109.

61. Sparks, *Ancient Texts for the Study of the Hebrew Bible*, 408–9.

62. E.g., no. 1, line 8: "The battle with Nabu-nasir waged against Borsippa is not written."

63. Sparks, *Ancient Texts for the Study of the Hebrew Bible*, 408.

64. E. A. Knauf, "From History to Interpretation," in *The Fabric of History: Text, Artifact and Israel's Past* (ed. D. V. Edelman; JSOT 127; Sheffield: JSOT Press, 1991), 26–64.

65. Noth articulated these ideas in *The History of Israel* (trans. P. R. Ackroyd from the 2d ed. of *Geschichte Israels*; New York: Harper, 1960); *A History of Pentateuchal Traditions* (trans. and intro. B. W. Anderson; Englewood Cliffs, N.J.: Prentice-Hall, 1972); and *The Deuteronomistic History* ( JSOTSup 15; Sheffield: JSOTS, 1991).

66. R. D. Nelson, *Joshua* (OTL; Louisville: Westminster John Knox, 1997), 2–3.

67. Ibid., 22.

68. I. Finkelstein, *The Bible Unearthed: Archaeology's New Vision of Ancient Israel and the Origin of Its Sacred Texts* (New York: Free Press, 2001), 90–96; idem., "Patriarchs, Exodus, Conquest: Fact or Fiction?" in I. Finkelstein and A. Mazar, *The Quest for the Historical Israel: Debating Archaeology and the History of Early Israel* (ed. B. B. Schmidt; Atlanta: Society of Biblical Literature, 2007), 54.

69. Cf. the discussions in R. L. Hubbard Jr., *Joshua* (NIVAC; Grand Rapids: Zondervan, 2009) and in A. E. Hill and J. H. Walton, *A Survey of the Old Testament* (2d ed.; Grand Rapids: Zondervan, 2000), 169–71.

70. Cf. the discussion in R. S. Hess, *Joshua: An Introduction and Commentary* (TOTC; Leicester: InterVarsity, 1996), 26–31.

71. Cf. P. Satterthwaite and G. McConville, *Exploring the Old Testament: A Guide to the Historical Books* (Downers Grove, Ill.: InterVarsity, 2007), 209.

72. E. Yamauchi, "The Current State of Old Testament Historiography," in *Faith, Tradition and History: Old Testament Historiography in Its Near Eastern Context* (ed. A. R. Millard, J. K. Hoffmeier, and D. W. Baker; Winona Lake, Ind.: Eisenbrauns, 1994), 26.

73. Cf. also the discussion of the formation of the book of Joshua in T. C. Butler, *Joshua* (WBC 7; Waco, Tex.: Word, 1983), xx–xxiii.

74. M. Van De Mieroop, *Cuneiform Texts and the Writing of History* (London: Routledge, 1999), 84. Cited in Walton, *Ancient Near Eastern Thought*, 229.

75. R. Alter, *The Art of Biblical Narrative* (New York: Basic, 1981), 23, 25.

76. P. R. Davies, *In Search of "Ancient Israel"* (Sheffield: Sheffield Academic Press, 1992), 13.

77. Ibid., 17.

78. M. Sternberg, *The Poetics of Biblical Narrative: Ideological Literature and the Drama of Reading* (Bloomington: Indiana University Press, 1987), 25.
79. Brettler, *The Creation of History in Ancient Israel*, 1.
80. Sternberg, *The Poetics of Biblical Narrative*, 25.
81. V. P. Long, *The Art of Biblical History* (Grand Rapids: Zondervan, 1994), 63.
82. Walton, *Ancient Near Eastern Thought and the Old Testament*, 228.
83. H. White, *Metahistory: The Historical Imagination in Nineteenth-Century Europe* (Baltimore: Johns Hopkins University Press, 1973).
84. For example, G. Garbini, *History and Ideology in Ancient Israel* (New York: Crossroad, 1988), has disparaged nearly all histories of ancient Israel as theologically biased and ideologically driven.
85. T. L. Thompson, *Early History of the Israelite People: From the Written and Archaeological Sources* (New York: Brill, 1992), 61.
86. See Thompson, ibid.; idem., "Text, Context and Referent in Israelite Historiography," in *The Fabric of History: Text, Artifact and Israel's Past* (ed. D. Edelman; JSOTSup 127; Sheffield: JSOT Press, 1991), 65–92; idem., "Some Exegetical and Theological Implications of Understanding Exodus as a Collected Tradition," in *Fra Dybet* (John Strange Festschrift); (ed. N. P. Lemche and M. Müller; Copenhagen: Museum Tusculanum, 1994), 233–42; idem., "A Neo-Albrightean School in History and Biblical Scholarship?" in *JBL* 114/4 (1995): 683–705.
87. J. J. Collins, *The Bible after Babel: Historical Criticism in a Postmodern Age* (Grand Rapids: Eerdmans, 2005), 32. See N. P. Lemche, *The Israelites in History and Tradition* (Louisville: Westminster John Knox, 1998), 20.
88. I. Provan, "Ideologies, Literary and Critical: Reflections on Recent History Writing on the History of Israel," *JBL* 114 (1995): 595.
89. Grayson, *Assyrian and Babylonian Chronicles*, 52.
90. G. W. Ahlström, *The History of Ancient Palestine from the Paleolithic Period to Alexander's Conquest* (ed. D. V. Edelman; JSOTSup 146; Sheffield: JSOT Press, 1992), 29.
91. K. A. D. Smelik, *Converting the Past: Studies in Ancient Israelite and Moabite Historiography* (OTS 28, 1992), 15.
92. Knauf, "From History to Interpretation," 46 n1.
93. W. G. Dever, "How to Tell a Canaanite from an Israelite," in *The Rise of Ancient Israel* (ed. H. Shanks; Washington, D.C.: Biblical Archaeology Society, 1992), 28.
94. K. L. Younger Jr., "Judges 1 in Its Near Eastern Context," in *Faith, Tradition, and History: Old Testament Historiography in Its Near Eastern Context* (ed. A. R. Millard, J. K. Hoffmeier, and D. W. Baker; Winona Lake, Ind.: Eisenbrauns, 1994), 207.
95. G. von Rad, "Typological Interpretation of the Old Testament," *Interpretation* 15 (1961): 181.
96. M. Liverani, "Propaganda," *ABD* 5:476.
97. Liverani, "Propaganda," 475.
98. Mark Chavalas, "Genealogical History as 'Charter': A Study of Old Babylonian Period Historiography and the Old Testament," in *Faith, Tradition, and History: Old Testament Historiography in Its Near Eastern Context*, ed. A. R. Millard, James K. Hoffmeier, David W. Baker (Winona Lake, Ind.: Eisenbrauns, 1994), 125.
99. Chavalas, "Geneaological History as Charter," 107.
100. Walton, *Ancient Israelite Literature in Its Cultural Context*, 115.
101. R. Dillard and T. Longman III, *An Introduction to the Old Testament* (Grand Rapids: Zondervan, 1994), 23–25.
102. Ibid., 23.
103. Ibid.

104. Walton, *Ancient Israelite Literature in Its Cultural Context*, 119.
105. Cf. Walton, *Ancient Israelite Literature in Its Cultural Context*, 120–22.
106. Grayson, *Assyrian and Babylonian Chronicles*, 51–56, 157–69.
107. B. Albrektson, *History and the Gods* (ConBOT 1; Lund: Gleerup, 1967), 14, 100.
108. Walton, *Ancient Near Eastern Thought and the Old Testament*, 221.
109. E.g., Deut 5:15; 7:18; 8:2; 9:7; 15:15; 16:3, 12; 24:18, 22; Josh 1:13; Ps 105; 106.
110. Licht, "Biblical Historicism," 109.
111. Brettler, *The Creation of History in Ancient Israel*, 137.
112. Halpern, *The First Historians*, 8.
113. Collins, *The Bible after Babel*, 38.
114. S. Niditch, "Historiography, 'Hazards,' and Study of Ancient Israel," *Int* 57 (2003): 138–50, esp. 140.
115. Brettler, *The Creation of History in Ancient Israel*, 12.
116. W. M. L. de Wette, *Auffoderung zum Studium der Hebräischen Sprache und Litteratur* (Jena and Leipzig: Gabler, 1805).
117. Ahlström, *The History of Ancient Palestine*, 50 (italics mine).
118. Polybius 1.1.
119. Ibid.
120. Ibid., 31.22.
121. Livy, *The Early History of Rome: Books I–V of The History of Rome from Its Foundations* (trans. A. De Sélincourt; New York: Penguin Books, 1960; repr., 2002), 29.
122. Ibid.
123. Ibid., 30.
124. Halpern, *The First Historians*, 138.
125. T. Butler, *Joshua* (WBC; Waco, Tex.: Word, 1983), xxiii.
126. G. Mitchell, *Together in the Land: A Reading of the Book of Joshua* (Sheffield: JSOT Press, 1993), 52.
127. W. G. Dever, *Recent Archaeological Discoveries and Biblical Research* (Seattle: University of Washington Press, 1990), 40–41.
128. E.g., I. Finkelstein, *The Archaeology of the Israelite Settlement* (Jerusalem: Israel Exploration Society, 1988), 22; N. P. Lemche, *Early Israel: Anthropological and Historical Studies on the Israelite Society Before the Monarchy* (Leiden: E. J. Brill, 1985), 174; N. Na'aman, "The 'Conquest of Canaan' in the Book of Joshua and in History," in *From Nomadism to Monarchy: Archaeological and Historical Aspects of Early Israel* (ed. I. Finkelstein and N. Na'aman; Washington, D.C.: Biblical Archaeological Society, 1994), 223.
129. M. Noth, *The Deuteronomistic History* (ed. D. J. A. Clines, P. R. Davies, and D. M. Gunn; JSOTSup 15; Sheffield: Department of Biblical Studies, 1981), 4–5.
130. R. Polzin, *Moses and the Deuteronomist: A Literary Study of the Deuteronomistic History*, Part One: *Deuteronomy, Joshua, Judges* (Bloomington: Indiana University Press, 1993), 85.
131. M. Sternberg, *The Poetics of Biblical Narrative: Ideological Literature and the Drama of Reading* (Bloomington: Indiana University Press, 1987), 187.
132. Ibid., 186–88.
133. Cf. the discussion in I. Kalimi, *The Reshaping of Ancient Israelite History in Chronicles* (Winona Lake, Ind.: Eisenbrauns, 2005), 18.
134. In study Bible notes, for example.
135. Cf. the discussion in J. A. Fitzmyer, *The Acts of the Apostles: A New Translation with Introduction and Commentary* (AB 31; New York: Doubleday, 1998), 442ff.

136. D. Merling Sr., *The Book of Joshua: Its Theme and Role in Archaeological Discussions* (AUSDDS 23; Berrien Springs, Mich.: Andrews University Press, 1997), 155–70.

137. D. Merling Sr., "The Book of Joshua: Its Structure and Meaning," in *To Understand the Scriptures: Essays in Honor of William H. Shea* (ed. D. Merling; Berrien Springs, Mich.: Institute of Archaeology, Siegfried H. Horn Archaeological Museum, Andrews University, 1997), 199–205.

138. For the relationship between Joshua and Judges 1, see D. Merling, *The Book of Joshua: Its Theme and Role in Archaeological Discussions*, 171–77 ; G. E. Wright, "The Literary and Historical Problem of Joshua 10 and Judges 1," *JNES* 5 (1946), 105–14; K. L. Younger Jr., "Judges 1 in Its Near Eastern Literary Context," in *Faith, Tradition and History: Old Testament Historiography in Its Near Eastern Context* (ed. A. R. Millard, J. K. Hoffmeier, and D. W. Baker; Winona Lake, Ind.: Eisenbrauns, 1994), 207–27.

139. G. von Rad, *Old Testament Theology* (trans. D. M. G. Stalker; New York: Harper & Row, 1962), 107.

140. Ibid., 108.

141. F. Braudel, *On History* (trans. Sarah Matthews; Chicago: University of Chicago Press, 1992), 38, 53n21.

142. F. Braudel, *The Structures of Everyday Life* (trans. S. Reynolds; vol. 1; New York: Harper & Row, 1981), 24.

143. F. Braudel, *Capitalism and Material Life 1400–1800* (trans. M. Kochan; New York: Harper & Row, 1973), xii; idem., *The Structures of Everyday Life*, 23–26.

144. As per W. G. Dever, "Archaeology and the Current Crisis in Israelite Historiography," in *Eretz-Israel* 25 (Jerusalem: Israel Exploration Society, 1996), 18–27.

145. R. Kessler, *The Social History of Ancient Israel: An Introduction* (trans. L. M. Maloney; Minneapolis: Fortress, 2008), 27.

146. Ibid., 28 (italics mine).

147. W. G. Dever, "Syro-Palestinian and Biblical Archaeology," 59–63. For the rise and fall of "biblical archaeology," see also T. W. Davis, *Shifting Sands: The Rise and Fall of Biblical Archaeology* (New York: Oxford University Press, 2004).

148. E.g., G. Gibbon, *Anthropological Archaeology* (New York: Columbia University Press, 1984).

149. W. G. Dever, "Impact of the 'New Archaeology,'" in *Benchmarks in Time and Culture: Essays in Honor of Joseph A. Callaway* (ed. J. F. Drinkard Jr., G. L. Mattingly, and J. M. Miller; Atlanta: Scholars Press, 1988), 341.

150. Ibid., 344–45.

151. J. W. Rogerson, "Anthropology and the Old Testament," *ABD* 1:258.

152. Oystein S. LaBianca, "Sociocultural Anthropology and Syro-Palestinian Archaeology," in *Benchmarks in Time and Culture: An Introduction to Palestinian Archaeology. Essays in Honor of Joseph A. Callaway* (ed. Joel F. Drinkard Jr., Gerald L. Mattingly, and J. Maxwell Miller; Atlanta: Scholars Press, 1988), 369.

153. S. A. Rosen, "The Tyranny of Texts: A Rebellion against the Primacy of Written Documents in Defining Archaeological Agendas," in *"I Will Speak the Riddles of Ancient Times": Archaeological and Historical Studies in Honor of Amihai Mazar on the Occasion of His Sixtieth Birthday* (ed. A. M. Maeir and P. de Miroschedji; Winona Lake, Ind.: Eisenbrauns, 2006), 881.

154. Ibid., 881–85.

155. Ibid., 893.

156. See the criticism of the supposed archaeological reconstruction of "original matriarchy" in R. R. Ruether, *Goddesses and the Divine Feminine: A Western Religious History* (Berkeley, Calif.: University of California Press, 2005).

157. T. L. Thompson, *The Early History of the Israelite People from the Written and Archaeological Sources*; G. W. Ahlström, *The History of Ancient Palestine*; R. B. Coote and K. W. Whitelam, *The Emergence of Israel in Historical Perspective* (SWBA 5; Sheffield: Almond Press, 1987).

158. Dever, "Archaeology and the Current Crisis in Israelite Historiography," 19.

159. R. L. Zettler, "Written Documents as Excavated Artifacts and the Holistic Interpretation of the Mesopotamian Archaeological Record," in *The Study of the Ancient Near East in the Twenty-First Century* (ed. J. S. Cooper and G. M. Schwartz; Winona Lake, Ind.: Eisenbrauns, 1996), 81–102; Dever, "Archaeology and the Current Crisis in Israelite Historiography," 20; see also Dever, "Archaeology, Material Culture, and the Early Monarchial Period in Israel," in *The Fabric of History: Text, Artifact and Israel's Past* (ed. D. V. Edelman; Sheffield: JSOT Press, 1991), 101–15; idem., "Unresolved Issues in the Early History of Israel: Toward a Synthesis of Archaeological and Textual Reconstructions," in *The Bible and the Politics of Exegesis: Essays in Honor of Norman K. Gottwald on His Sixty-Fifth Birthday* (ed. D. Jobling, P. L. Day, and G. T. Sheppard; Cleveland: Pilgrim, 1991), 195–208; idem., "Archaeology, Texts, and History Writing: Toward an Epistemology," in *Uncovering Ancient Stones: Essays in Memory of H. Neil Richardson* (ed. L. M. Hopfe; Winona Lake, Ind.: Eisenbrauns, 1994), 105–17.

## 2. CLASSICAL AND RECENT MODELS OF THE ISRAELITE SETTLEMENT

1. N. P. Lemche, "Early Israel Revisited," *Currents in Research: Biblical Studies* 4 (1996): 9–34.

2. E.g., Exod 12:38; Josh 2; 6; 9.

3. For example, a partial list of publications just since 1990: J. A. Callaway, rev. J. M. Miller, "The Settlement in Canaan: The Period of the Judges," in *Ancient Israel* (rev. and enl. ed.: Washington, D.C.: Biblical Archaeology Society, 1999), 55–89; W. G. Dever, "Israel, History of (Archaeology and the Israelite 'Conquest')," *ABD* 3:545–58; idem., "Archaeology and the Emergence of Early Israel," in *Archaeology and Biblical Interpretation* (ed. J. R. Bartlett; London: Routledge, 1997), 20–50; R. Gnuse, "BTB Review of Current Scholarship: Israelite Settlement of Canaan: A Peaceful Internal Process—Part 2," *BTB* 21 (1991): 109–17; N. K. Gottwald, "Israel, Origins of," *NIDB* 3:132–38; idem., *The Hebrew Bible: A Brief Socio-Literary Introduction* (Minneapolis: Fortress, 2009), 150–64; idem., "Recent Studies of the Social World of Premonarchic Israel," *CR:BS* 4 (1996): 9–34; B. Halpern, "Settlement of Canaan," *ABD* 5:1120–43; R. S. Hess, "Early Israel in Canaan: A Survey of Some Recent Evidence and Interpretations," *PEQ* 125 (1993): 125–42; A. E. Killebrew, *Biblical Peoples and Ethnicity: An Archaeological Study of Egyptians, Canaanites, Philistines, and Early Israel, 1300–1100 B.C.E.* (Atlanta: Society of Biblical Literature, 2005), 181–85; J. J. McDermott, *What Are They Saying about the Formation of Israel?* (New York: Paulist, 1998), 36–45; P. M. McNutt, *Reconstructing the Society of Ancient Israel* (Library of Ancient Israel; ed. D. A. Knight; Louisville: Westminster John Knox, 1999), 53–63; S. A. Meier, "History of Israel 1: Settlement Period," in *Dictionary of the Old Testament: Historical Books* (ed. B. T. Arnold and H. G. M. Williamson; Downers Grove, Ill.: InterVarsity, 2005), 425–34; D. Merling Sr., *The Book of Joshua: Its Theme and Role in Archaeological Discussions*, Andrews University Seminary Doctoral Dissertation Series 23 (Berrien Springs, Mich.: Andrews University Press, 1997), 1-20-105; E. H. Merrill, "The Late Bronze Early Iron Age Transition and the Emergence of Israel," *BSac* 152 (1995): 145–62; P. J. Ray Jr., "Classical Models for the Appearance of Israel in Palestine," in *Critical Issues in Early Israelite History* (ed. R. S. Hess, G. A. Klingbeil, and P. J. Ray Jr.; Winona Lake, Ind.: Eisenbrauns, 2008), 79–93; C. G. Rasmussen, "Conquest, Infiltration, Revolt,

or Resettlement? What Really Happened During the Exodus-Judges Period?" in *Giving the Sense: Understanding and Using Old Testament Historical Texts* (ed. D. M. Howard and M. A. Grisanti; Grand Rapids: Kregel, 2003), 138–59; K. L. Younger, "Early Israel in Recent Biblical Scholarship," in *The Face of Old Testament Studies: A Survey of Contemporary Approaches* (ed. D. W. Baker and B. T. Arnold; Grand Rapids: Baker, 1999), 176–206.

4. See the collection of articles published under the theme of "The House that Albright Built," *NEA* 65.1 (2002): 5–86.

5. W. F. Albright, *The Biblical Period from Abraham to Ezra: An Historical Survey* (New York: Harper, 1963), 26.

6. E.g., T. P. Peet, *Egypt and the Old Testament* (Liverpool: University of Liverpool Press, 1922); J. W. Jack, *The Date of the Exodus* (Edinburgh: T&T Clark, 1925).

7. W. F. Albright, "The Israelite Conquest in the Light of Archaeology," *BASOR* 74 (1939): 11–23.

8. Albright, *The Biblical Period from Abraham to Ezra*, 27.

9. G. E. Wright, *Biblical Archaeology* (Philadelphia: Westminster, 1957), 84.

10. Ibid., 84. The issue of the symbolic interpretation of biblical numbers will be discussed in greater detail later in ch. 2.

11. These issues will be discussed in later chapters.

12. W. F. Albright, *Archaeology and the Religion of Israel: The Ayer Lectures of the Colgate-Rochester Divinity School 1941* (Baltimore: Johns Hopkins, 1965), 95.

13. Wright, *Biblical Archaeology*, 69–70.

14. J. Bright, *A History of Israel* (3d ed.; Philadelphia: Westminster, 1981), 129–30.

15. Ibid., 132.

16. Y. Yadin, "Is the Biblical Account of the Israelite Conquest of Canaan Historically Reliable?" *BAR* 7 (1982): 19.

17. E.g., P. Lapp, "The Conquest of Palestine in the Light of Archaeology," *CTM* 38 (1967): 283–300; J. A. Soggin, "Ancient Biblical Traditions and Modern Archaeological Discoveries," *BA* 23 (1960): 95–100.

18. E.g., J. P. Free, *Archaeology and Bible History* (rev. and enl. ed. by H. F. Vos; Grand Rapids: Zondervan, 1992); A. Hoerth, *Archaeology and the Old Testament* (Grand Rapids: Baker, 1998), 205–16; L. Wood, *A Survey of Israel's History* (rev. by D. O'Brien; Grand Rapids: Zondervan, 1986).

19. See the survey of scholarship up to that point in J. M. Miller, "The Israelite Occupation of Canaan," in *Israelite and Judaean History* (ed. J. H. Hayes and J. M. Miller; London: SCM Press, 1977), 213–84.

20. SBT 8; London: SCM, 1952.

21. G. E. Wright, *God Who Acts*, 126–27.

22. J. Bright, *The Authority of the Old Testament* (Grand Rapids: Baker, 1967), 42.

23. W. G. Dever, "Syro-Palestinian and Biblical Archaeology," in *The Hebrew Bible and Its Modern Interpreters* (ed. D. A. Knight and G. M. Tucker; Minneapolis: Fortress, 1985), 59–60.

24. E.g., J. M. Miller, "The Israelite Occupation of Canaan," in *Israelite and Judaean History* (ed. J. H. Hayes and J. M. Miller; Philadelphia: Trinity Press International, 1977), 256.

25. Ibid., 236–37.

26. E.g., W. G. Dever, "The Relationship Between Bible, Oriental Studies, and Archaeology from the Perspective of an Archaeologist," in *A Symposium on the Relationship between Bible, Oriental Studies, and Archaeology*, Occasional Papers of the Horn Archaeological Museum, Andrews University, no. 3 (ed. P. Perkins, M. Liverani, and W. G. Dever; Berrien Springs, Mich.: Siegfried H. Horn Archaeological Museum, 1984), 31–45; idem., *Recent Archaeological Discoveries and Biblical Research* (Seattle: University of Washington Press, 1990), 37–84; idem.,

"Israel, History of (Archaeology and the Israelite 'Conquest')," 546–48; idem., "How To Tell a Canaanite from an Israelite," in *The Rise of Ancient Israel* (ed. H. Shanks; Washington, D.C.: Biblical Archaeology Society, 1992), 26–56; idem., "Archaeology and the Emergence of Early Israel," 20–50; idem., *Who Were the Early Israelites and Where Did They Come From?* 23–74.

27. W. G. Dever, "Israel, History of (Archaeology and the 'Conquest')," *ABD* 3:548. For some reason, Dever did not include many of the cities listed in Josh 12:94. Stager published a more comprehensive chart in 1998. Cf. L. E. Stager, "Forging an Identity: The Emergence of Ancient Israel," in *The Oxford History of the Biblical World* (ed. M. D. Coogan; New York: Oxford University Press, 1998), 132–33.

28. For discussion of Dan, see ch. 5.

29. Dever, "Israel, History of (Archaeology and the 'Conquest')," 548.

30. K. L. Younger, "Early Israel in Recent Biblical Scholarship," in *The Face of the Old Testament: A Survey of Contemporary Approaches* (Grand Rapids: Baker, 1999), 178–91.

31. Provan, Long, and Longman, *A Biblical History of Israel*, 140.

32. More on this in ch. 5.

33. Theological reasons for the rejection of the Conquest Theory will be discussed in ch. 5.

34. D. Merling Sr., *The Book of Joshua*, 26–28. I have used Merling's observations on Albright as starting points for the following discussion, which differs substantially from that of Merling.

35. See J. A. Miles Jr., "Understanding Albright: A Revolutionary Etude," *HTR* 69 (1976): 155–57.

36. B. O. Long, "Mythic Trope in the Autobiography of William Foxwell Albright," *BA* 56 (1993): 36–45. Long makes this argument at greater length in *Planting and Reaping Albright: Politics, Ideology, and Interpreting the Bible* (University Park, Penn.: Pennsylvania State University, 1997).

37. L. G. Running and D. N. Freedman, *William Foxwell Albright: A Twentieth-Century Genius* (New York: Two Continents, 1975), 355–56.

38. J. D. Wright, "W. F. Albright's Vision of Israelite Religion," *NEA* 65.1 (2002): 66.

39. Albright, *The Biblical Period from Abraham to Ezra*, 27.

40. Ibid.

41. Albright, *Archaeology and the Religion of Israel*, 95.

42. See the discussion in Albright, *The Biblical Period from Abraham to Ezra*, 29–30.

43. R. V. Schnucker, "Neo-Orthodoxy," in *The Concise Evangelical Dictionary of Theology* (ed. W. A. Elwell; Grand Rapids: Baker, 1991), 331–33.

44. W. L. Grant, "Neo-Orthodoxy," *NCE* 10:332–34.

45. J. D. Schloen has argued that Albright's approach to Israelite origins was laudable in that it attempted to provide a "sweeping typological synthesis" of cultural developments in ancient Canaan and Israel. Schloen sees this approach as still having merit and argues that it should not be discarded. He argues this kind of approach is necessary in the current radical postmodern era that is overly critical of large-scale historical synthesis. See J. D. Schloen, "W. F. Albright and the Origins of Israel," *NEA* 65.1 (2002): 60–62.

46. Albright, "The Israelite Conquest in the Light of Archaeology," 13.

47. See the overview in J. C. H. Laughlin, "Archaeology," *NIDB* 1:232–47.

48. Walter Brueggemann, *Theology of the Old Testament: Testimony, Dispute, Advocacy* (Minneapolis: Fortress, 1997), 61. See also idem., *Texts under Negotiation: The Bible and Postmodern Imagination* (Minneapolis: Fortress, 1993), ch. 1.

49. A. Comte, *Cours de Philosophie Positive* (6 vols.; Paris, 1830–1842), in *Auguste Comte and Positivism: The Essential Writings* (ed. G. Lenzer; New York: Harper Torchbooks, 1975), 71.

50. Ibid., 72.

51. "Positivism," in *The Concise Oxford Dictionary of Archaeology* (ed., T. Darvill; Oxford: Oxford University Press, 2002), 335.

52. R. Jameson, "Positivism," in *A Dictionary of Archaeology* (ed. I. Shaw and R. Jameson; Oxford: Blackwell, 1999), 475.

53. W. G. Dever, "Biblical Theology and Biblical Archaeology: An Appreciation of G. Ernest Wright," in *HTR* 73 (1980): 1–15.

54. "Positivism," in *The Penguin Archaeology Guide* (ed. P. Bahn; London: Penguin, 2001), 365. Cf. also Thomas Kuhn, *The Structure of Scientific Revolutions* (Chicago: University of Chicago Press, 1962); M. Polanyi, *Personal Knowledge: Toward a Post-critical Philosophy* (Chicago: University of Chicago Press, 1974). Both of these works are thought to have effectively undermined positivism as a system of epistemology.

55. Cf. L. G. Perdue, *Reconstructing Old Testament Theology: After the Collapse of History* (Minneapolis: Augsburg Fortress, 2005).

56. For a discussion of these and other new emphases, see Walter Brueggemann, *Theology of the Old Testament*, 84–102.

57. E.g., P. R. Davies, *In Search of "Ancient Israel"* (JSOTSup 148; Sheffield: Sheffield Academic Press, 1995), 47; idem., "Method and Madness: Some Remarks on Doing History with the Bible," *JBL* 114 (1995): 669–705; idem., "Whose History? Whose Israel? Whose Bible? Biblical Histories, Ancient and Modern," in *Can a "History of Israel" Be Written?* (ed. L. L. Grabbe; JSOTSup 245; Sheffield: Sheffield Academic Press, 1997), 104–22; T. L. Thompson, "A Neo-Albrightean School in History and Biblical Scholarship?" *JBL* 114 (1995): 683–98; idem., "Historiography of Ancient Palestine and Early Jewish Historiography: W. G. Dever and the Not So New Biblical Archaeology," in *The Origins of the Ancient Israelite States* (ed. V. Fritz and P. R. Davies; JSOTSup 228; Sheffield: Sheffield Academic Press, 1996), 26–43.

58. J. C. H. Laughlin, "Archaeology," *NIDB*, 1:242–46.

59. In a 1995 article, Iaian W. Provan pointed out the indebtedness of even minimalists to positivism. Cf. I. W. Provan, "Ideologies, Literary and Critical: Reflections on Recent Writing on the History of Israel," *JBL* 114.4 (1995): 585–606. This article launched a flurry of exchanges. Cf. Philip R. Davies, "Method and Madness: Some Remarks on Doing History with the Bible," in *JBL* 114.4 (1995): 699–705; T. L. Thompson, "A Neo-Albrightean School in History and Biblical Scholarship?" in *JBL* 114.4 (1995), 683–98; I. W. Provan, "In the Stable with the Dwarves: Testimony, Interpretation, Faith, and the History of Israel," in *Windows into Old Testament History: Evidence, Argument, and the Crisis of "Biblical Israel"* (ed. V. P. Long, D. W. Baker, and G. J. Wenham; Grand Rapids: Eerdmans, 2002), 167–87.

60. Merling, *The Book of Joshua*, 26.

61. A. Alt, *Die Landnahme der Israeliten in Palästina: Territorialgeschichtliche Studien* (Leipzig: Druckerei der Werkgemeinschaft, 1925).

62. Alt believed this was attested by the different names used for God in the stories of the patriarchs. See Alt, "The God of the Fathers," in *Essays on Old Testament History and Religion* (trans. R. A. Wilson; Sheffield: JSOT Press, 1989), 15–86.

63. A. Alt, *Essays on Old Testament History and Religion* (trans. R. A. Wilson; Sheffield: JSOT Press, 1989), 175.

64. M. Noth, *The History of Israel* (2d ed.; New York: Harper, 1960), 69.

65. Ibid., 80–81.

66. Ibid., 53.

67. Jerusalem: Magnes, 1957.

68. Y. Aharoni, *The Archaeology of the Land of Israel: From the Prehistoric Beginnings to the End of the First Temple Period* (ed. M. Aharoni and trans. A. F. Rainey; Philadelphia: Westminster, 1982), 159–72.

69. Y. Aharoni, "The Settlement of Canaan," in *Judges* (ed. B. Mazar; vol. 3 of *The World History of the Jewish People*; New Jersey: Rutgers University Press, 1971), 94–128.

70. W. F. Albright, *From the Stone Age to Christianity: Monotheism and the Historical Process* (New York: Doubleday, 1957).

71. E. C. Rust, "Biographical Sketch of Joseph A. Callaway: Christian Minister, Old Testament Professor, and Field Archaeologist," in *Benchmarks in Time and Culture: Essays in Honor of Joseph A. Callaway* (ed. J. F. Drinkard Jr., G. L. Mattingly, and J. M. Miller; Atlanta: Scholars Press, 1988), 457–58.

72. J. A. Callaway, "Ai (et-Tell): Problem Site for Biblical Archaeologists," in *Archaeology and Biblical Interpretation: Essays in Memory of D. Glenn Rose* (ed. L. G. Perdue, L. E. Toombs, and G. L. Johnson; Atlanta: John Knox, 1987), 87–99.

73. J. A. Callaway, "Village Subsistence at Ai and Raddana in Iron Age I," in *The Answers Lie Below: Essays in Honor of Lawrence Edmund Toombs* (ed. H. O. Thompson; Lanham, Md.: University Press of America, 1984), 51–66.

74. J. A. Callaway, "A New Perspective on the Hill Country Settlement of Canaan in Iron Age I," in *Palestine in the Bronze and Iron Ages: Papers in Honor of Olga Tufnell* (ed. J. N. Tubb; London: Institute of Archaeology, 1985), 32.

75. J. A. Callaway, "A New Perspective on the Hill Country Settlement of Canaan in Iron Age I," 33–46.

76. Ibid., 46.

77. Ibid., 33.

78. Ibid., 33 (emphasis mine).

79. Callaway, "Ai (et-Tell): Problem Site for Biblical Archaeologists," 97.

80. M. Weippert, *The Settlement of the Israelite Tribes in Palestine: A Critical Study of Recent Scholarly Debate* (Studies in Biblical Theology 21; Naperville: Alec R. Allenson, 1971), 145.

81. Cf. Ø. S. LaBianca, *Sedentarization and Nomadization: Food System Cycles at Hesban and Vicinity in Transjordan* (Hesban 1; Berrien Springs, Mich.: Institute of Archaeology and Andrews University Press, 1990), 33–49.

82. Ø. S. LaBianca, *Sedentarization and Nomadization*, 42.

83. G. E. Mendenhall, "The Hebrew Conquest of Palestine," *BA* 25 (1962): 66–87.

84. Ibid., 71.

85. G. E. Mendenhall, *The Tenth Generation: The Origins of the Biblical Tradition* (Baltimore: Johns Hopkins University Press, 1973), 216.

86. Ibid., 216–17.

87. N. K. Gottwald, *The Tribes of Yahweh: A Sociology of the Religion of Liberated Israel, 1250–1050 B.C.E.* (Maryknoll, N.Y.: Orbis, 1985).

88. Ibid., xxv.

89. Ibid., 475.

90. Ibid., 489.

91. G. E. Mendenhall, "Ancient Israel's Hyphenated History," in *Palestine in Transition: The Emergence of Ancient Israel* (ed. D. N. Freedman and D. F. Graff; Sheffield: Almond Press, 1983), 92, 102.

92. Ibid., 92. Cf. idem., *The Tenth Generation*, 24–26.

Notes to Pages 42–46

93. E.g., N. K. Gottwald, "Rethinking the Origins of Ancient Israel," in *"Imagining" Biblical Worlds: Studies in Spatial, Social and Historical Constructs in Honor of James W. Flanagan* (ed. D. M. Gunn and P. M. McNutt; Sheffield: Sheffield Academic Press, 2002), 190–201.

94. Gottwald, "Israel, Origins of."

95. Mary-Louise Mussell, "An Archaeological Evaluation of the Social Revolution Model of the Israelite Settlement in Canaan" (Ph.D. diss., Drew University Graduate School, 1993), 273–74.

96. A. F. Rainey, review of N. K. Gottwald, *The Tribes of Yahweh, JAOS* 107.3 (1987): 543.

97. As acknowledged in Dever, *Who Were the Early Israelites and Where Did They Come From?* 212.

98. Mussell, "An Archaeological Evaluation of the Social Revolution Model of the Israelite Settlement in Canaan," 5–9.

99. G. E. Mendenhall, "The Hebrew Conquest of Palestine," 87.

100. Ibid.

101. Ibid.

102. B. Halpern, *The Emergence of Israel in Canaan* (Chico, Calif.: Scholars Press, 1983).

103. B. Halpern, "Settlement of Canaan," *ABD* 5:1132–35.

104. Ibid., *ABD* 5:1134.

105. B. Halpern, *The Emergence of Israel in Canaan*, 88–89.

106. B. Halpern, "Settlement of Canaan," *ABD* 5:1139.

107. B. Halpern, "The Exodus from Egypt: Myth or Reality?" in *The Rise of Ancient Israel* (ed. H. Shanks; Washington, D.C.: Biblical Archaeology Society, 1992), 104–6. This theory will be discussed in some detail in ch. 4.

108. Ibid., 107.

109. D. B. Redford, *Egypt, Canaan, and Israel in Ancient Times* (Princeton, N.J.: Princeton University Press, 1992).

110. Ibid., 275–79.

111. Ibid., 280.

112. D. B. Redford, *Egypt, Canaan, and Israel in Ancient Times*, 272–73. This issue will be discussed in some detail in ch. 4.

113. E.g., Gen 19:30-38; 36.

114. R. W. Younker, "The Emergence of the Ammonites," in *Ancient Ammon* (ed. B. McDonald and R. W. Younker; Leiden: Brill, 1999), 189–218; idem., "The Emergence of Ammon: A View of the Rise of Iron Age Polities from the Other Side of the Jordan," in *The Near East in the Southwest: Essays in Honor of William G. Dever* (ed. B. A. Nakhai; AASOR, vol. 58; Boston: American Schools of Oriental Research, 2004), 153–76.

115. Similar to the process described in G. E. Mendenhall, *The Tenth Generation*, 186–87.

116. R. W. Younker, "The Emergence of Ammon," 170.

117. T. E. Levy and A. F. C. Holl, "Migrations, Ethnogenesis, and Settlement Dynamics: Israelites in Iron Age Canaan and Shuwa-Arabs in the Chad Basin," *JAA* 21 (2002): 835–118.

118. Ibid., 96.

119. Ibid., 96–97.

120. Ibid., 112–13.

121. V. Fritz, "Conquest or Settlement? The Early Iron Age in Palestine," *BA* 50 (1987): 84–100.

122. V. Fritz, "Conquest or Settlement?" 97. See ch. 8.

123. Ibid., 92–96.

124. T. L. Thompson, *Early History of the Israelite People: From the Written and Archaeological Sources* (Leiden: Brill, 1994), 112.

125. E.g., G. Ahlström, *Who Were the Israelites?* (Winona Lake, Ind.: Eisenbrauns, 1986); idem., *The History of Ancient Palestine* (Minneapolis: Fortress, 1993); R. B. Coote, *Early Israel: A New Horizon* (Minneapolis: Fortress, 1990); R. B. Coote and K. W. Whitelam, *The Emergence of Early Israel in Historical Perspective* (2d ed; Sheffield: Sheffield Phoenix Press, 2010); P. R. Davies, *The Origins of Biblical Israel* (London: T&T Clark, 2007); I. Finkelstein and N. A. Silberman, *The Bible Unearthed: Archaeology's New Vision of Ancient Israel and the Origin of Its Sacred Texts* (New York: Free Press, 2001), 97–122; N. P. Lemche, *Early Israel: Anthropological and Historical Studies on the Israelite Society Before the Monarchy* (Leiden: Brill, 1985); idem., *Ancient Israel: A New History of Israelite Society* (Sheffield: Sheffield Academic Press, 1990); E. Pfoh, *The Emergence of Israel in Palestine: Historical and Anthropological Perspectives* (London: Equinox, 2009).

126. An excellent introduction, overview, and analysis can be found in M. B. Moore, *Philosophy and Practice in Writing a History of Israel* (Library of Hebrew Bible/Old Testament Studies 435; London: T&T Clark, 2006). A cogent analysis and criticism of minimalism from philosophical, epistemological, and archaeological perspectives can also be found in W. G. Dever, *What Did The Biblical Writers Know and When Did They Know It?* (Grand Rapids: Eerdmans, 2001).

127. W. G. Dever, *Who Were the Early Israelites and Where Did They Come From?* 191–21.

128. Ibid., 178.

129. Ibid., 188.

130. Ibid., 189.

131. Ibid., 167.

132. K. J. R. Arndt, *A Documentary History of the Indiana Decade of the Harmony Society*, vol. 1: 1814–1819 (Indianapolis: Indiana Historical Society, 1971), xi.

133. K. J. R. Arndt, *A Documentary History of the Indiana Decade of the Harmony Society*, 1814–1824, vol. 2: 1820–1824 (Indianapolis: Indiana Historical Society, 1978), 513.

134. Ibid., 2:514–15.

135. For example, some kibbutzim were secular, even staunchly atheistic, proudly trying to be "monasteries without God." See D. Gavron, *The Kibbutz: Awakening from Utopia* (Lanham, Md.: Rowman & Littlefield, 2000); H. Near, *The Kibbutz Movement: A History, Origins and Growth, 1909–1939*, vol. 1 (Oxford: Oxford University Press, 1992).

136. See the discussions in E. R. Curtis, *A Season in Utopia: The Story of Brook Farm* (New York: Thomas Nelson. 1961); K. Melville, *Communes in the Counter Culture: Origins, Theories, Styles of Life* (New York: William Morrow, 1972); D. E. Pitzer, *America's Communal Utopias* (Chapel Hill: University of North Carolina Press, 1997); M. Marchand Ross, *Child of Icaria* (Corning: Gauthier, 1938); B. Shenker, *Intentional Communities: Ideology and Alienation in Communal Living* (London: Routledge & Kegan Paul, 1986); E. and D. Schwieder, *A Peculiar People: Iowa's Old Order Amish* (Ames: Iowa State University Press, 1975); R. Sutton, *Les Icariens: The Utopian Dream in Europe and America* (Champaign: University of Illinois Press, 1994); M. Tyldesley, *No Heavenly Delusion? A Comparative Study of Three Communal Movements* (United Kingdom: Liverpool University Press, 2003; B. Yambura, *A Change and a Parting* (Ames: Iowa State University Press, 1960).

137. E.g., I. Finkelstein, "The Emergence of Israel in Canaan: Consensus, Mainstream and Dispute," *SJOT* 5.2 (1991): 47–59.

138. W. G. Dever, "Earliest Israel: God's Warriors, Revolting Peasants, or Nomadic Hordes?" in *Eretz-Israel* 30 (Jerusalem: Israel Exploration Society, 2011), 4.

139. Gottwald, "Recent Studies of the Social World of Premonarchic Israel," 165.

## 3. THE DATE OF THE EXODUS-CONQUEST
## PART I: BIBLICAL EVIDENCE

1. This chapter adapts material that was originally published as "The Date of the Exodus-Conquest Is Still an Open Question: A Response to Rodger Young and Bryant Wood" and is used by permission. *JETS* 5/12 (2008): 245–66.

2. Random examples of scholarly works by evangelicals that defend the early date are Gleason L. Archer, *A Survey of Old Testament Introduction* (rev. ed., Chicago: Moody, 1994), 239–52; Raymond B. Dillard and Tremper Longman III, *An Introduction to the Old Testament* (Grand Rapids: Zondervan, 1994), 59–62; Andrew E. Hill and John H. Walton, *A Survey of the Old Testament* (2d ed., Grand Rapids: Zondervan, 2000), 83–84; Alfred J. Hoerth, *Archaeology and the Old Testament* (Grand Rapids: Baker 1998), 178–81; Walter C. Kaiser, Jr., "Exodus," in *The EBC*, vol. 2 (ed. Frank E. Gaebelein; Grand Rapids: Zondervan, 1990), 288–91; idem., *A History of Israel: From the Bronze Age Through the Jewish Wars* (Nashville: Broadman & Holman, 1998), 104–9; William H. Shea, "Exodus, Date of," in *ISBE* 2 (ed. G. W. Bromiley et al.; Grand Rapids: Eerdmans, 1982), 230–38; Leon J. Wood, *A Survey of Israel's History* (rev. ed., Grand Rapids: Zondervan, 1986), 20, 69–86.

3. Bryant G. Wood, "The Rise and Fall of the 13th-Century Exodus-Conquest Theory," *JETS* 48/3 (Sept 2005): 475, attributes the idea of a thirteenth-century exodus-conquest to Albright. While it is true that what has come to be known as the formal "Conquest Model" essentially originated with Albright, the identification of Ramesses II as the pharaoh of the oppression and his son Merneptah with the exodus had been common long before the time of Albright. Kittel, Maspéro, Wiedemann et al., date the exodus near the close of the Nineteenth Dynasty. MacCurdy, Eerdmans et al., even go as far as locating it in the Twentieth Dynasty. James Jack called this position—the association of the exodus with these later dynasties—"the traditional school." Cf. James Jack, *The Date of the Exodus in the Light of External Evidence* (Edinburgh: T&T Clark, 1925), 18.

4. Jack, *The Date of the Exodus*, 199–202.

5. See, for example, the discussion by John J. Bimson, *Redating the Exodus and Conquest* (JSOTSup 5; Sheffield: The University of Sheffield, 1978), 92–93.

6. For example, a chronological chart listing the exodus as having occurred in 1446 B.C.E. appears in the *Life Application Bible*, NIV (Wheaton, Ill.: Tyndale, 1991), xvi.

7. D. C. Browning Jr., "The Hill Country Is Not Enough for Us: Recent Archaeology and the Book of Joshua," *SJT* 41/1 (1998): 25–43.

8. D. C. Browning Jr., "'Why Have You Brought Us Up Out of Egypt to Die in the Wilderness?' Murmurings Against a 15th-Century Date for the Exodus" (paper presented at the annual meeting of ASOR, Cambridge, Mass., November 18, 1999).

9. Eugene Merrill, review of *On the Reliability of the Old Testament*, in *JETS* 48, no. 1 (March 2005): 119.

10. "Propositions for Evangelical Acceptance of a Late-Date Exodus-Conquest: Biblical Data and the Royal Scarabs from Mt. Ebal," *JETS* 50 (2007): 31–46.

11. Cf. R. C. Young and B. G. Wood, "A Critical Analysis of the Evidence from Ralph Hawkins for a Late-Date Exodus-Conquest," *JETS* 51, no. 2 (2008): 225–43. Young is the author of the sections dealing with textual arguments and Wood of the material that treats archaeological arguments.

12. Ibid., 225–26.

13. A point I implied in "Propositions," 35.

14. Robert G. Boling, *Judges: Introduction, Translation, and Commentary* (AB; New York: Doubleday, 1975), 23.

15. R. K. Hawkins, "Propositions," 35; J. K. Hoffmeier, "What Is the Biblical Date for the Exodus? A Response to Bryant Wood," *JETS* 50 (2007): 227–29.
16. Wood, "The Rise and Fall of the 13th-Century Exodus," 475.
17. J. K. Hoffmeier, "What Is the Biblical Date for the Exodus? A Response to Bryant Wood," *JETS* 50 (2007): 226.
18. Hawkins, "Propositions," 35.
19. Daniel I. Block, *Judges, Ruth* (NAC 6; Nashville: Broadman & Holman, 1999), 61.
20. Hoffmeier, "Response to Wood," 228.
21. 8.3.1.
22. 2.2.19.
23. Paul J. Ray, "Another Look at the Period of the Judges," in *Beyond the Jordan* (ed. Glenn A. Carnagey Sr.; Eugene, Oreg.: Wipf & Stock, 2005), 93–104.
24. A. E. Steinmann, "The Mysterious Numbers of the Book of Judges," *JETS* 48 (2005): 491–500.
25. Ibid., 498–500.
26. K. L. Younger, Jr., *Judges, Ruth* (NIVC; Grand Rapids: Zondervan, 2002), 24–25.
27. Younger notes that 1 Sam 12:11 makes Samuel's judgeship explicit.
28. Cited by Rabbi Yehuda Felix, "Hannah, the Mother of Prayer," in *The Tanakh Companion to the Book of Samuel* (ed. Nathaniel Helfgot; Teaneck, N.J., Ben Yehuda Press, 2006), 26–27.
29. Younger Jr., *Judges, Ruth*, 25.
30. G. E. Wright, *Biblical Archaeology* (Philadelphia: Westminster, 1957), 83–84.
31. Hoffmeier, "Response to Wood," 237.
32. Richard S. Hess, *Israelite Religions: An Archaeological and Biblical Survey* (Grand Rapids: Baker, 2007), 275.
33. Cf. S. R. Driver, "Notes and Studies," in *JTS* 36 (1935): 403; W. F. Albright, "Abram the Hebrew: A New Archaeological Interpretation," *BASOR* 163 (1961): 50–51.
34. Cf. D. N. Freedman, J. Lundbom, and G. J. Botterweck, "דּוֹר," *TDOT* 3:174.
35. Ibid.
36. Additionally, "generations" are interpreted in *1 Enoch* and in *Jubilees* as a series of weeks. See 1 En. 10:12; Jub. 5:10.
37. Nahum M. Sarna and Hershel Shanks, "Israel in Egypt: The Egyptian Sojourn and the Exodus," in *Ancient Israel: From Abraham to the Roman Destruction of the Temple* (ed. Hershel Shanks; Washington, D.C.: Biblical Archaeology Society, 1999), 41.
38. Young and Wood, "A Critical Analysis of the Evidence from Ralph Hawkins," 228–30.
39. J. Wellhausen, *Prolegomena to the History of Israel* (G. Reimer, German original, 1879; trans. J. Southerland Black and Allan Menzies; New York: Meridian, 1957), 272ff.
40. E.g., R. Kittel, *A History of the Hebrews* 2 (Oxford: Williams & Norgate, 1896; German original Gotha, Germany: Perthes, 1892; trans. John Taylor), 234; C. F. Burney, *Notes on the Hebrew Text of the Book of Kings* (London: Oxford, 1903), 60–61.
41. Noth also rejected the view that the 480 years had to do with the period from the construction of Solomon's temple to the return from exile. Cf. M. Noth, *Überlieferungsgeschichtliche Studien* (Darmstadt: Halle M. Niemeyer, 1943), 18–27.
42. E.g., S. J. De Vries, "Chronology, OT," *NIDB* Supp. (Nashville: Abingdon, 1976), 162.
43. Clyde M. Miller, *First and Second Kings* (vol. 7, The Living Word Commentary on the Old Testament; Abilene, Tex.: ACU Press, 1991), 140.
44. See his note 14.
45. Isaac Abravanel, *Peyrush 'al Neviy 'iym ri'honiym* (Jerusalem: [s.n.], 1969), 484ff.

46. David L. Lieber, ed., *Etz Hayim: Torah and Commentary* (New York: Rabbinical Assembly and United Synagogue of Conservative Judaism, 2001), 500; Michael Fishbane, *JPS Bible Commentary: Haftarot* (Philadelphia: Jewish Publication Society, 2002), 121.

47. Cf. N. M. Sarna, *Exploring Exodus: The Origins of Biblical Israel* (New York: Schocken Books, 1986), 9.

48. מעשה אבות סימן לבנים (Bereishit Rabba 40).

49. See, for example, Rabbi David Cohen, *Templates for the Ages: Historical Perspectives through the Torah's Lenses* (Brooklyn, N.Y.: Mesorah, 1999).

50. These numbers are viewed as approximations.

51. Cf. Rabbi Hersh Goldwurn, *History of the Jewish People: The Second Temple Era* (Brooklyn, N.Y.: Mesorah, 1982); Meir Holder, *History of the Jewish People: From Yavneh to Pumbedisa* (Brooklyn, N.Y.: Mesorah, 1986).

52. Cf. Jack Finegan, *Handbook of Biblical Chronology: Principles of Time Reckoning in the Ancient World and Problems of Chronology in the Bible* (rev. ed.; Peabody, Mass.: Hendrickson, 1998), 92–116.

53. The patristic period is generally dated from about c.e. 100 to either c.e. 451 or to the eighth century c.e.

54. See G. Bray, *Biblical Interpretation: Past and Present* (Downers Grove, Ill.: InterVarsity, 2000).

55. Bede, *On the Temple*, trans. with notes by S. Connolly (Translated Texts for Historians 21; Liverpool: Liverpool University Press, 1995).

56. Cf. Deut 34:7.

57. Cf. Acts 1:15.

58. Bede, *On the Temple*, 1.5.1.

59. R. C. Young, "Tables of Reign Lengths from the Hebrew Court Recorders," *JETS* 48 (2005): 225–48; idem., "The Talmud's Two Jubilees and their Relevance to the Date of the Exodus," *WTJ* 68 (2006): 71–83; idem., "Seder Olam and the Sabbaticals Associated with the Two Destructions of Jerusalem (Part I)," *JBQ* 34 (2006): 173–79; idem., "Seder Olam and the Sabbaticals Associated with the Two Destructions of Jerusalem (Part 2)," *JBQ* 34 (2006): 252–59.

60. For discussion of the Jubilee years and the Sabbatical cycles, see R. K. Harrison, *Leviticus: An Introduction and Commentary* (TOTC; Downers Grove, Ill.: InterVarsity, 1980); John E. Hartley, *Leviticus* (WBC 4; Dallas, Tex.: Word, 1992); Baruch Levine, *Leviticus* (JPS Torah Commentary; Philadelphia: The Jewish Publication Society, 1989; Jacob Milgrom, *Leviticus 23–27* (AB; New York: Doubleday, 2001).

61. S. Olam 11; b. Arak. 12a.

62. Following *Arak.* 12a.

63. E.g., Keith W. Carley, *The Book of the Prophet Ezekiel* (London: Cambridge, 1974), 268.

64. See the citations in the following four points.

65. As observed by C. F. Keil, *Ezekiel, Commentary on the Old Testament*, vol. 9 (trans. James Martin; Edinburgh: T&T Clark, 1865–1892), 343–44.

66. James C. Vanderkam, "Calender," *NIDB* 1:524.

67. Ralph H. Alexander, "Ezekiel," *The Expositor's Bible Commentary* (ed. Frank E. Gaebelein; Grand Rapids: Zondervan, 1986), 953.

68. Horace D. Hummel, *Ezekiel 21–8* (Concordia Commentary; Saint Louis: Concordia, 2007), 1194.

69. Keil, *Ezekiel*, 344.

70. As observed in Walter Eichrodt, *Ezekiel: A Commentary* (OTL; Philadelphia: Westminster, 1970), 540.
71. Cf. Exod 12:3; Lev 23:27; 25:9; Num 29:7.
72. Eichrodt, *Ezekiel,* 540.
73. Herbert G. May, "Exegesis of the Book of Ezekiel" (IB 6; ed. G. A. Buttrick; New York: Abingdon, 1956), 284.
74. Keil, *Ezekiel,* 344.
75. Michael Fishbane, letter to author, March 25, 2008. Cf. Eleazar De Beaugency, *Peyrush 'al Neviy'iym 'achroniym.*
76. *S. Olam* 24; *b. Meg.* 14b.
77. Young has already noted the spurious nature of the rabbinic traditions on which this is based. See R. C. Young, "The Talmud's Two Jubilees and Their Relevance to the Date of the Exodus," 72–73.
78. J. P. Hyatt, "The Book of Jeremiah: Exegesis" (IB 5; ed. G. A. Buttrick; New York: Abingdon, 1956), 1056.
79. Gerald L. Keown, Pamela J. Scalise, and Thomas G. Smothers, *Jeremiah 26–52* (WBC 27; Dallas, Tex.: Word, 1995), 185.
80. Ibid.
81. John Bright, *Jeremiah* (AB; New York: Doubleday, 1965), 224.
82. H. Wildberger, *Isaiah 28–39* (A Continental Commentary; Minneapolis: Fortress, 2002), 430.
83. Most commentators subscribe to this view. E.g., F. Delitzsch, *Isaiah, Commentary on the Old Testament,* vol. 7 (trans. James Martin; Edinburgh: T&T Clark, 1865–1892), 367–68; O. Kaiser, *Isaiah 13–39: A Commentary* (OTL; Philadelphia: Westminster, 1974), 396–97; J. N. Oswalt, *The Book of Isaiah: Chapters 1–39* (NIC; Grand Rapids: Eerdmans, 1986), 664–65; E. J. Young, *The Book of Isaiah* (NICOT; Grand Rapids: Eerdmans, 1969), 498–501.
84. Or, if they had implemented it at all, they had failed to follow it for very long.
85. E.g., T. R. Hobbs, *2 Kings* (WBC 13; Waco, Tex.: Word, 1985), 332; Paul R. House, *1, 2 Kings* (NAC 8; Nashville: Broadman & Holman, 1995), 387; Volkmar Fritz, *1 & 2 Kings* (ACC; Minneapolis: Fortress, 2003), 402–3; Donald J. Wiseman, *1 & 2 Kings: An Introduction and Commentary* (TOTC; Downers Grove, Ill.: InterVarsity, 1993), 299–300.
86. G. E. Mendenhall and G. Herion, "Covenant," *ABD* 1:1179–1202; P. R. Williamson, "Covenant," in *Dictionary of the Old Testament: Pentateuch* (ed. T. Desmond Alexander and David W. Baker; Downers Grove, Ill.: InterVarsity, 2003), 139–55.
87. Walter Brueggemann, *1 & 2 Kings* (Smyth & Helwys Bible Commentary; Macon, Ga.: Smyth & Helwys, 2000), 554.
88. Wright, "Sabbatical Year," *ABD* 5:860.
89. Young and Wood, "Critical Analysis," 15.
90. Young argues that the Jubilee cycle was forty-nine years in length, rather than the fifty years that is typically assumed. See Young, "The Talmud's Two Jubilees," 75.
91. H. W. Guggenheimer, *Seder 'Olam: The Rabbinic View of Biblical Chronology* (Lanham, Md.: Rowan & Littlefield, 2005), 116–17.
92. Milgrom, *Leviticus 23–27,* 2152.
93. Ibid.
94. Harrison, *Leviticus,* 224.
95. R. T. Beckwith, *Calendar and Chronology, Jewish and Christian: Biblical, Intertestamental and Patristic Studies* (Leiden: Brill, 2001), 257.
96. J. Finegan, *Handbook of Biblical Chronology* (rev. ed.; Peabody, Mass.: Hendrickson, 1998), 111.

97. E. Frank, *Talmudic and Rabbinical Chronology: The Systems of Counting Years in Jewish Literature* (New York: Philipp Feldheim, 1956), 19.

98. Neither Young nor Keil take the 70 weeks, or 490 years, mathematically. See C. F. Keil, *Daniel, Commentary on the Old Testament*, vol. 9 (trans. M. G. Easton; Edinburgh: T&T Clark, 1865–1892), 725–60; E. J. Young, *The Prophecy of Daniel: A Commentary* (Grand Rapids: Eerdmans, 1978), 201–21.

99. Cf. J. M. Rosenthal, "Seder Olam," *Encyclopedia Judaica* 2d ed., vol. 18 (ed. Fred Skolnik; Jerusalem: Keter, 2007), 235–36.

100. R. C. Young, "When Did Solomon Die?" *JETS* 46 (2003): 601.

101. Young appears to want to regard the rabbinic traditions the same way archaeologists and biblical scholars would regard a material or inscriptional discovery contemporaneous with some biblical event as providing a contemporary, independent witness to that event. The Talmudic materials, however, are not contemporaneous with the events under discussion here (the exodus and conquest), but are removed from them by about a millennium and a half. They are the product of another age and culture, and their purposes for writing and their understanding of history and its uses are all different from those of the biblical authors. See J. Neusner, *The Idea of History in Rabbinic Judaism* (Brill Reference Library of Judaism, vol. 12; Leiden: Brill, 2004).

102. Marc Brettler, letter to author, March 23, 2008.

103. C. J. H. Wright, "Jubilee, Year of," *ABD* 3:1028.

104. Cf. J. Barton, "Form Criticism (OT)," *ABD* 2:838–41.

105. Cf. R. S. Hess, "Asking Historical Questions of Joshua 13–19: Recent Discussion Concerning the Date of the Boundary Lists," in *Faith, Tradition & History: Old Testament Historiography in Its Near Eastern Context* (ed. A. R. Millard, J. K. Hoffmeier, and D. W. Baker; Winona Lake, Ind.: Eisenbrauns, 1994), 191–205; Z. Kallai, *Historical Geography of the Bible: The Tribal Territories of Israel* (Jerusalem: Magnes/Leiden: Brill, 1986), 277–325.

106. B. Chilton, "Genre," *NIDB* 2:556.

107. As suggested in Hoffmeier, "Response to Wood," 237–39. Cf. also Wiseman, *1 & 2 Kings*, 104; K. A. Kitchen, *On the Reliability of the Old Testament* (Grand Rapids: Eerdmans, 2003), 307–8; idem., "Chronology," in *Dictionary of the Old Testament: Historical Books* (ed. Bill T. Arnold and H. G. M. Williamson; Downers Grove, Ill.: 2005), 181–82.

108. J. Reade, "Assyrian Kinglists, The Royal Tombs of Ur, and Indus Origins," *JNES* 60 (2001): 3–4, cited in Hoffmeier, "Response to Wood," 238. Read also discusses other examples of *Distanzangabe*.

109. Hoffmeier, "Response to Wood," 239.

110. Cf. D. Manor, "Joshua," in *Old Testament Introduction* (ed. Mark Mangano; Joplin, Mo.: College Press, 2005), 216–18. Manor points to 1 Chr 6:3–10 and Exod 6:16–25, which imply that Phineas was alive when the exodus commenced.

111. M. Lichtheim, *Ancient Egyptian Literature*, vol. 3: *The Late Period* (Berkeley: University of California, 1980), 168.

112. Manor, *Joshua*, 217.

113. A. H. Gardiner, "The Delta Residence of the Ramessides pt. 1," *JEA* 5 (1918): 127–271.

114. L. Habachi, "Khatana-Qantir: Importance," *ASAE* 52 (1954): 443–559.

115. See M. Bietak and E. Czerny, eds., *Tell El-Dab'a I: Tell El-Daba and Qantir, The Site and Its Connections with Avaris and Piramesse* (Wienna: Verlag der Österreichischen Adademie Der Wissenschaften, 2001).

116. J. W. Jack, *The Date of the Exodus* (Edinburgh: T&T Clark, 1925), 25–28.

117. C. Aling, "The Biblical City of Ramses," *JETS* 25:2 (1982): 129–38; G. L. Archer, *A Survey of Old Testament Introduction* (rev. ed.; Chicago: Moody, 1994), 231–33; E. H. Merrill, *Kingdom of Priests: A History of Old Testament Israel* (rev. ed.; Grand Rapids: Baker, 2008), 26–88 (Merrill only considers this a possibility, while he is inclined toward other solutions); M. F. Unger, *Archaeology and the Old Testament* (4th ed.; Grand Rapids: Zondervan, 1960), 149; B. G. Wood, "The Rise and Fall of the 13th-Century Exodus-Conquest Theory," *JETS* 48 (2005): 479; L. J. Wood, *A Survey of Israel's History* (rev. and enl. ed. by D. O'Brien; Grand Rapids: Zondervan, 1986), 73–74.

118. Hoffmeier, "Response to Wood," 233.

119. Additional examples cited by Hoffmeier include Gen 14:3, 7, 17; 23:2.

120. B. K. Waltke and M. O'Connor, *An Introduction to Biblical Hebrew Syntax* (Winona Lake, Ind.: Eisenbrauns, 1990), §8.4.1.

121. Hoffmeier, "Response to Wood," 234.

122. J. K. Hoffmeier, *Ancient Israel in Sinai: The Evidence for the Authenticity of the Wilderness Tradition* (Oxford: Oxford University Press, 2005), chs. 4 and 5.

123. E.g., W. C. Kaiser, Jr., *A History of Israel: From the Bronze Age Through the Jewish Wars* (Nashville: Broadman & Holman, 1998), 85–86; R. Vasholz, "On the Dating of the Exodus," *Presbyterion: Covenant Seminary Review* 32/2 (2006): 112; L. J. Wood, *Israel's History*, 73–74.

124. R. Dalman, "Egypt and Early Israel's Cultural Setting: A Quest for Evidential Possibilities," *JETS* 51/3 (2008): 464.

125. J. K. Hoffmeier, "Rameses of the Exodus Narratives is the 13th Century B.C. Royal Ramesside Residence," *TRINJ* 28 (2007), 7.

126. R. K. Hawkins, "Zoan," *NIDB* 5:990.

127. J. K. Hoffmeier, "Ramesses of the Exodus Narratives," 8–9. Hoffmeier argues that the use of the name Ramesses in Gen 47:11 and Exod 1:11 suggests a compositional date for these passages during the time which Pi-Ramesses flourished (1270–1120 B.C.E.), since after this the Twenty-First Dynasty ruler, Smendes, built Zoan out of the ruins of the abandoned city of Pi-Ramesses, a name forgotten in subsequent centuries. The author of Ps 78, probably writing in the first millennium B.C.E., referred to the events of plagues and the exodus as having occurred on the Fields of Zoan (78:12, 43). The original name of Pi-Ramesses may have no longer been known in his day, since it had not existed for centuries. The fact that Genesis and Exodus refer to "Rameses" instead of Zoan suggests that they may have been written by the same author during the period when Ramesses was still known.

# 4. The Date of the Exodus-Conquest Part II: Extrabiblical Evidence

1. N. Na'aman, "Amarna Letters," *ABD* I:174–81. For translations, see *ANET* 483–90; *COS* 3:237–42; W. L. Moran, *The Amarna Letters* (Baltimore: Johns Hopkins University Press, 1992).

2. See the essays collected in R. Cohen and R. Westbrook, eds., *Amarna Diplomacy: The Beginnings of International Relations* (Baltimore: The Johns Hopkins University Press, 2000).

3. See N. Na'aman, "The Egyptian-Canaanite Correspondence," in *Amarna Diplomacy: The Beginnings of International Relations* (ed. R. Cohen and R. Westbrook; Baltimore: Johns Hopkins University Press, 2000), 125–38.

4. E. Yamauchi, "Habiru," *NIDBA*, 223–24.

5. Cf. R. S. Hess, *Amarna Personal Names* (American Schools of Oriental Research Dissertation Series 9; Winona Lake, Ind.: Eisenbrauns, 1993), 102–3.

6. N. Na'aman, "*Habiru* and Hebrews: The Transfer of a Social Term to the Literary Sphere," *JNES* 45 (1986): 271–88; cf. also M. Greenberg, *The Hab/piru* (New Haven, Conn.: American Oriental Society, 1955), 3–12.

7. B. G. Wood, "From Ramesses to Shiloh: Archaeological Discoveries Bearing on the Exodus-Judges Period," in *Giving the Sense: Understanding and Using Old Testament Historical Texts* (ed. D. M. Howard and M. A. Grisanti; Grand Rapids: Kregel, 2003), 270.

8. Ibid., 270.

9. F. M. Cross, *From Epic to Canon: History and Literature in Ancient Israel* (Baltimore, Md.: Johns Hopkins University Press, 1998), 69n57; N. K. Gottwald, "Habiru, Hapiru," *NIDB* 2:710; M. D. Hiebert, *The Historical Conquest: Historical Events of the Amarna Age in Canaan and Their Preservation in the Biblical Narrative* (Gladstone, Canada: Westbourne Study Center, 2004); G. E. Mendenhall, *Ancient Israel's Faith and History: An Introduction to the Bible in Context* (ed. G. A. Herion; Louisville: Westminster John Knox, 2001), 30–33; S. D. Waterhouse, "Who Were the Habiru of the Amarna Letters?" *JATS* 12 (2001): 31–42.

10. G. Van Groningen, *TWOT* II:643.

11. N. K. Gottwald, "Habiru, Hapiru," *NIDB* 2:710; N. P. Lemche, "Hebrew," *ABD* 3:95.

12. N. P. Lemche, "Habiru, Hapiru," *ABD* 3:7. See, however, F. M. Cross, who argues that "the development follows known patterns of linguistic change," in *From Epic to Canon*, 69n57.

13. See A. F. Rainey, review of O. Loretz, *Habiru-Hebräer: Eine sozio-linguistische Studie über die Herkunft des Gentiliziums 'ibrî vom Appelativum habiru*, *JAOS* 101 (1987): 539–41.

14. Van Groningen, *TWOT* II: 643.

15. P. K. McCarter, *1 Samuel: A New Translation with Introduction and Commentary*. AB 8. (New York: Doubleday, 1980), 240–41; R. K. Hawkins, "Paddan-Aram," *NIDB* 4:355.

16. D. E. Fleming, "Genesis in History and Tradition: The Syrian Background of Israel's Ancestors, Reprise," in *The Future of Biblical Archaeology: Reassessing Methodologies and Assumptions* (ed. J. K. Hoffmeier and A. Millard; Grand Rapids: Eerdmans, 2004), 193–232, esp. 220–21.

17. A. F. Rainey, "Unruly Elements in Late Bronze Canaanite Society," in *Pomegranates and Golden Bells: Studies in Biblical, Jewish, and Near Eastern Ritual, Law, and Literature in Honor of Jacob Milgrom* (ed. D. P. Wright, D. N. Freedman, and A. Hurvitz; Winona Lake, Ind.: Eisenbrauns, 1995), 482.

18. In Exodus 14–15, after crossing the Red Sea, the Hebrews set out for the wilderness of Shur, which marks the beginning of the wilderness period. The remainder of the Pentateuch is set "in the wilderness" (e.g., Deut 1:1). The wilderness period is repeatedly recalled and invoked throughout the historical books, the prophets, and the Psalms. See ch. 1, "The Wilderness Period," in James K. Hoffmeier, *Ancient Israel in Sinai: The Evidence for the Authenticity of the Wilderness Tradition* (New York: Oxford University Press, 2005), 3–22.

19. Gen 39:14, 17; 40:15; 41:12; 43:32.

20. Chs. 4, 13, 14, 29.

21. N. P. Lemche, "Habiru, Hapiru," *ABD 3:7*.

22. While the Amarna archive consists primarily of letters *to* the Egyptian pharaoh from others, it does contain seven letters sent from the pharaoh to his vassals in Canaan.

23. R. Giveon, *Les Bédouins Shosou des Documents Égyptiens* (Documenta et Monumenta Orientis Antiqui 18; Leiden: Brill, 1971), 261–63; D. B. Redford, *Egypt, Canaan, and Israel in Ancient Times* (Princeton, N.J.: Princeton University Press, 1992), 271; W. A. Ward, "The Shasu 'Bedouin.' Notes on a Recent Publication," *Journal of the Economic and Social History of*

*the Orient* 15 (1972): 56–59; M. Weippert, "Semitische Nomaden des zweiten Jahrtausends. Über die Šzsw der ägyptischen Quellen," *Biblica* 55 (1974): 433.

24. "The Craft of the Scribe (Papyrus Anastasi I)," translated by James P. Allen (*COS* 3.2.13).

25. Epigraphic Survey, *The Battle Reliefs of King Sety I*, vol. 4, *Reliefs and Inscriptions at Karnak* (Chicago: Oriental Institute, 1986), pls. 2–6.

26. "The Report of a Frontier Official (Papyrus Anastasi VI)," translated by John A. Wilson (*ANET*, 259).

27. Gen 25:19–34. Cf. also J. A. Dearman, "Edom, Edomites," *NIDB* 2:188–91.

28. B. Grdseloff, "Édôm, d'après les sources egyptiennes," *Revue de l'histoire juive d'Egypte* 1 (1947): 69–99, cited in Astour, "Yahweh in Egyptian Topographic Lists," 18n11. Astour notes that this article was originally published in a short-lived journal no longer available in most libraries and that he is working from a Xerox provided to him by M. Görg.

29. Grdseloff, "*Édôm, d'après les sources egyptiennes*," 82, cited in Astour, "Yahweh in Egyptian Topographic Lists," 21.

30. Redford, *Egypt, Canaan, and Israel in Ancient Times*, 203.

31. G. W. Ahlström, *Who Were the Israelites?* (Winona Lake, Ind.: Eisenbrauns, 1986), 57–60.

32. C. F. Aling and C. E. Billington, "The Name Yahweh in Egyptian Hieroglyphic Texts," *Artifax* 24/4 (2009): 18.

33. Astour, "Yahweh in Egyptian Topographic Lists," 22. Gemination occurs when a letter is doubled, as in "Assur" or "Arrapha."

34. R. K. Hawkins, "Paddan-Aram," *NIDB* 4:355.

35. Y. Aharoni, *The Land of the Bible* (trans. A. F. Rainey; Philadelphia: Westminster, 1979), 44, 139, 290, 334.

36. Astour, "Yahweh in Egyptian Topographic Lists," 23–24.

37. Hoffmeier, *Ancient Israel in Sinai*, 243.

38. See the references in R. Giveon, "The Shosu of the Late XXth Dynasty," *Journal of the American Research Center in Egypt* 8 (1969–1970): 51–53; Ward, "The Shasu 'Bedouin,'" 35–60.

39. Cf. Gen 39:14, 17; 41:12; Exod 1:15, 16, 19; 2:7.

40. The Merneptah Stele, to be discussed later.

41. T. E. Levy, R. B. Adams, and R. Shafiq, "The Jabal Hamrat Fidan Project: Excavations at the Wadi Fidan 40 Cemetery, Jordan (1997)," *Levant* 31 (1999): 293–308.

42. Levy, Adams, and Shafiq, "The Jabal Hamrat Fidan Project," 299–302, 305–6.

43. T. E. Levy, R. B. Adams, and A. Muniz, "Archaeology and the Shasu Nomads: Recent Excavations in the Jabal Hamrat Fidan, Jordan," in *Le-David Maskil: A Birthday Tribute for David Noel Freedman* (ed. D. N. Freedman and W. H. C. Propp; Biblical and Judaic Studies, vol. 9; Winona Lake, Ind.: Eisenbrauns, 2004), 63–89.

44. T. E. Levy, "'You Shall Make for Yourself No Molten Gods': Some Thoughts on Archaeology and Edomite Ethnic Identity," in *Sacred History, Sacred Literature: Essays on Ancient Israel, the Bible, and Religion in Honor of R. E. Friedman on His Sixtieth Birthday* (ed. S. Dolansky; Winona Lake, Ind.: Eisenbrauns, 2008), 239–55.

45. Levy, Adams, and Muniz, "Archaeology and the Shasu Nomads," 80.

46. Ibid., 89.

47. M. Van De Mieroop, *The Eastern Mediterranean in the Age of Ramesses II* (Malden, Mass.: Blackwell, 2007), 54.

48. Ibid., 54–55.

49. Ibid.

50. Ibid., 57.

51. N. K. Gottwald, "Habiru, Hapiru," *NIDB* 2:710. This view is shared by H. Cazelles, *POTT*, 22; G. J. Wenham, *Genesis 1–15* (WBC 1; Waco, Tex.: Word Books, 1987), 313.

52. Ø. S. LaBianca, *Sedentarization and Nomadization: Food System Cycles at Hesban and Vicinity in Transjordan* (Hesban 1; Berrien Springs, Mich.: Andrews University Press), 42.

53. A. M. Khazanov, *Nomads and the Outside World* (2d ed.; Madison, Wis.: The University of Wisconsin Press, 1994), 152. Cf. also the recent study of E. Van Der Steen, "Tribal Societies in the Nineteenth Century: A Model," in *Nomads, Tribes, and the State in the Ancient Near East: Cross-Disciplinary Perspectives* (ed. J. Szuchman; Chicago: The Oriental Institute of the University of Chicago, 2009), 105–17.

54. See LaBianca, *Sedentarization and Nomadization*.

55. P. C. Salzman, *Pastoralists: Equality, Hierarchy, and the State* (Boulder, Colo.: Westview, 2004), 129.

56. Ibid.

57. Cf. P. Spencer, *The Maasai of Matapato: A Study of Rituals of Rebellion* (Bloomington: Indiana University Press, 1988).

58. J. Wellhausen, *The Arab Kingdom and Its Fall* (London: Curzon, 1927), 85–86.

59. Salzman, *Pastoralists*, 129.

60. Abraham's behavior in general does not comport with the behavior of *'apiru*: he keeps livestock and avoids the cities of Sodom and Gomorrah in favor of a rural existence, while the *'apiru* preferred urban areas and avoided sheepherding; he only becomes militarily active when Lot is taken captive, while the *'apiru* regularly hired themselves out as mercenaries or lived as robbers and plunderers.

61. M. Görg, "Israel in Hieroglyphen," *BN* 106 (2001) 21–27. Cf. also P. van der Veen, C. Theis, and M. Görg, "Israel in Canaan (Long) before Pharaoh Merneptah? A Fresh Look at Berlin Statue Pedestal Relief 21687," *JAEI* 2/4 (2010): 15–25.

62. B. G. Wood, "The Rise and Fall of the 13th-Century Exodus-Conquest Theory," *JETS* 48 (2005): 21–27; idem., "The Biblical Date for the Exodus is 1446 B.C.E.: A Response to James Hoffmeier," *JETS* 50/2 (2007): 254–55.

63. Hoffmeier enumerates four objections based on Egyptian linguistic and orthographical features, all of which go beyond the scope of this work. For the details, see Hoffmeier, "Response to Wood," 241.

64. W. M. F. Petrie, *Six Temples in Thebes in 1896* (London: Egyptian Research Account, 1897), Pls. XIII–XIV.

65. "The (Israel) Stele of Merneptah," translated by James K. Hoffmeier (COS 2.6.41).

66. Ibid.

67. The stele was first published by W. Spiegelberg, in "Der Siegeshymnus des Merneptah auf der Flinders-Petrie Stele," Zeitschrift für Ägyptologie 34 (1896): 1–25. See also M. G. Hasel, *Domination and Resistance: Egyptian Military Activity in the Southern Levant, ca. 1300–1185 B.C.* Probleme der Ägyptologie 11 (Leiden: Brill, 1988), 195–96.

68. M. Noth, *The History of Israel* (London: Adam & Charles Black, 1960), 3.

69. O. Eissfeldt, "Palestine in the Time of the Nineteenth Dynasty," *CAH*, vol. 2, pt. 2 (1965) 26a, 14.

70. K. A. Kitchen, *Ancient Orient and Old Testament* (Downers Grove, Ill.: InterVarsity, 1966), 91.

71. P. R. Davies, *Memories of Ancient Israel: An Introduction to Biblical History: Ancient and Modern* (Louisville: Westminster John Knox, 2008), 90–91; D. V. Edelman, "Ethnicity in Early Israel," in *Ethnicity in the Bible* (ed. M. G. Brett; Leiden: Brill, 1996), 35; O. Margalith, "On the Origin and Antiquity of the Name 'Israel,'" *ZAW* 102 (1990), 225–37; T. L.

Thompson, "Defining History and Ethnicity in the South Levant," in *Can a "History of Israel" Be Written?* (ed. L. L. Grabbe; JSOTSup 245; Sheffield: Sheffield Academic Press, 1997), 12.

72. I. Hjelm and T. L. Thompson, "The Victory Song of Merenptah, Israel and the People of Palestine," *JSOT* 27 (2002): 13ff.

73. M. G. Hasel, *Domination and Resistance*; idem., "Merneptah's Reference to Israel: Critical Issues for the Origin of Israel," in *Critical Issues in Early Israelite History* (ed. R. S. Hess, G. A. Klingbeil, and P. J. Ray Jr.; BBRSup 3; Winona Lake, Ind.: Eisenbrauns, 2008), 47–59; Kitchen, *Ancient Orient and Old Testament*; idem., "The Victories of Merenptah, and the Nature of Their Record," *JSOT* 28 (2004): 259–72.

74. Cf. Kitchen, "The Victories of Merenptah and the Nature of Their Record," 270ff.

75. Davies, *Memories of Ancient Israel*, 91.

76. G. W. Ahlström, *The History of Ancient Palestine* (ed. D. Edelman; Minneapolis: Fortress, 1993), 60, 286, 387. See also G. W. Ahlström and D. V. Edelman, "Merneptah's Israel," *JNES* 44 (1985): 59–61; G. W. Ahlström, *Who Were the Israelites?* (Winona Lake, Ind.: Eisenbrauns, 1986), 37–39.

77. Ahlström, *Who Were the Israelites?* 40; cf. also idem., *The History of Ancient Palestine*, 285n2.

78. N. P. Lemche, *The Israelites in History and Tradition*, 37. Lemche's only source for this claim is G. W. Ahlström, *The History of Palestine*, 285n2, cited above.

79. K. A. Kitchen, "The Physical Text of Mernneptah's Victory Hymn (The 'Israel' Stela)," *JSSEA* 24 (1997): 75.

80. M. G. Hasel, "The Egyptian Name Equation in New Kingdom Texts: Country, Territory, or People?" (paper presented at the annual meeting of the Society of Biblical Literature, Nashville, Tenn., 2000); idem., "A Statistical Analysis of Foreign Name Determinatives in the 'Battle of Kadesh' Accounts" (paper presented at the annual meeting of the American Oriental Society, Nashville, Tenn., 2003); idem., "The Structure of the Final Hymnic-Poetic Unit on the Merenptah Stela," *ZAW* 116 (2004).

81. W. G. Dever, "Unresolved Issues in the Early History of Israel: How to Tell a Canaanite from an Israelite," in *The Rise of Ancient Israel* (ed. H. Shanks; Washington, D.C.: Biblical Archaeology Society, 1992), 26–60; idem., "Ceramics, Ethnicity, and the Question of Israelite Origins," *BA* 58 (1995): 200–213; idem., "Archaeology, Ideology and the Quest for an 'Ancient' or 'Biblical' Israel," *NEA* 61 (1998): 39–52; idem., "Iron Age Kernoi and the Israelite Cult," in *Studies in the Archaeology of Israel and Neighboring Lands in Memory of Douglas L. Esse* (ed. S. R. Wolff; SAOC 59/ASOR Books 5; Chicago: Oriental Institute of the University of Chicago/Atlanta: American Schools of Oriental Research, 2001), 119–33; idem., *Who Were the Early Israelites and Where Did They Come From?* (Grand Rapids: Eerdmans, 2003); idem., "Merneptah's 'Israel,' The Bible's, and Ours," in *Exploring the Longue Durée: Essays in Honor of Lawrence E. Stager* (ed. J. D. Schloen; Winona Lake, Ind.: Eisenbrauns, 2009), 89–96; R. K. Hawkins, "The Survey of Manasseh and the Origin of the Central Hill Country Settlers," in *Critical Issues in Early Israelite History* (ed. R. S. Hess, G. A. Klingbeil, and P. J. Ray Jr.; BBRS 3; Winona Lake, Ind. Eisenbrauns, 2008), 165–79.

82. M. Hasel, "Merneptah's Reference to Israel: Critical Issues for the Origin of Israel," in *Critical Issues in Early Israelite History* (ed. R. S. Hess, G. A. Klingbeil, and P. J. Ray Jr.; BBRS 3; Winona Lake, Ind.: Eisenbrauns, 2008), 47–59. For an earlier version, with some variation, see J. J. Bimson, "Merneptah's Israel and Recent Theories of Israelite Origins," *JSOT* 49 (1991): 21.

83. R. de Vaux, *The Early History of Israel* (trans. D. Smith; Philadelphia: Westminster, 1978), 390–91.

84. E.g., Hasel, "The Structure of the Final Hymnic Poetic Unit on the Merneptah Stela"; J. K. Hoffmeier, *Israel in Egypt: The Evidence for the Authenticity of the Exodus Tradition* (New York: Oxford University Press, 1997), 29; K. A. Kitchen, *On the Reliability of the Old Testament* (Grand Rapids: Eerdmans, 2003), 460; A. F. Rainey, "Israel in Merenptah's Inscription and Reliefs," *IEJ* 51 (2001): 63–64.

85. Noth, *The History of Israel*, 3.

86. T. L. Thompson, "Defining History and Ethnicity in the South Levant," 12.

87. Hjelm and Thompson, "The Victory Song of Merenptah, Israel and the People of Palestine," 16.

88. K. A. Kitchen, "The Victories of Merenptah, and the Nature of Their Record," 271ff.

89. For the collected materials and resources for their study, see S. Ahituv, *Canaanite Toponyms in Ancient Egyptian Documents* (Jerusalem: Magnes, 1984).

90. It has been suggested that the term צִרְעָה (*sir'â*), which appears in passages dealing with the conquest (Exod 23:28; Deut 7:20; Josh 24:12) and is usually translated as "hornets," may be a symbol for Egypt. Based on his identification of the hornet as the symbol of Lower Egypt, John Garstang suggested that the hornet was a reference to the continual campaigns of Thutmoses III (ca. 1475 B.C.E.) that weakened the strength of the Canaanite city-states, thereby preparing the way for an Israelite invasion. Yadin accepted this interpretation of the צִרְעָה, but argued that it would have also been appropriate to the thirteenth century B.C.E. due to continued Egyptian campaigns in the latter part of the Late Bronze Age. For references and discussion, see O. Borowski, "The Identity of the Biblical *sir'â*," in *The Word of the Lord Shall Go Forth: Essays in Honor of David Noel Freedman in Celebration of His Sixtieth Birthday* (ed. C. L. Meyers and M. O'Connor; Winona Lake, Ind.: Eisenbrauns, 1983), 315–19.

91. A. J. Frendo, "Two Long-Lost Phoenician Inscriptions and the Emergence of Ancient Israel," *PEQ* 134/1 (2002): 37–43.

92. C. R. Krahmalkov, "Languages (Phoenician)," *ABD* 4:222.

93. R. Browning, "Procopius," in *The Oxford Classical Dictionary* (3d ed.; New York: Oxford University Press, 1996), 881.

94. P. C. Schmitz, "Procopius' Phoenician Inscriptions: Never Lost, Not Found," in *PEQ* 139/2 (2007): 101.

95. F. Dahn, *Prokopius von Cäsarea: ein Beitrag zur Historiographie der Völkerwanderung und des sinkenden Römerthums* (Berlin, 1865), 193–94.

96. Browning, "Procopius," 881.

97. Frendo, "The Emergence of Ancient Israel," 38.

98. F. C. Movers, *Das Phönizische Alterthum*, vol. 2.2., *Geshichte der Colonien* (Berlin, 1850), 429–30 and references there.

99. Schmitz, "Procopius' Phoenician Inscriptions," 102.

100. As noted in A. J. Frendo, "Back to the Bare Essentials, Procopius' Phoenician Inscriptions: Never Lost, Not Found—A Response," in *PEQ* 139/2 (2007): 105–6.

101. L. M. Whitby, "Chronicon Paschale," in *The Oxford Classical Dictionary* (3d ed.; New York: Oxford University Press, 1996), 328.

102. P. Schröder, *Die Phönizische Sprache: Entwurf einer Grammatik nebst Sprach-und Schriftproben. Mit einem Anhang, enthaltend eine Erklärung der Punischen Stellen im Pönulus des Plautus* (Halle: 1869; 1979 repr. Liechtenstein), 3n2, and references there. Cited in Frendo, "The Emergence of Ancient Israel," 40.

103. P. Schröder, *Die Phönizische Sprache*, 3n3.

104. A. J. Frendo, "The Emergence of Ancient Israel," 40.

105. M. Van De Mieroop, *The Eastern Mediterranean in the Age of Ramesses II*, 42–43.

106. Ibid., 238–39.

107. Ibid., 241.
108. "The War against the Sea Peoples," translated by J. A. Wilson (*ANET*, 262–63).
109. Van De Mieroop, *The Eastern Mediterranean in the Age of Ramesses II*, 243.
110. Ibid., 245.
111. Ibid., 246–47.
112. Ibid., 248.
113. W. A. Ward and M. S. Joukowsky, eds., *The Crisis Years: The 12th Century B.C. from Beyond the Danube to the Tigris* (Dubuque, Iowa: Kendall/Hunt, 1992).
114. W. G. Dever and S. Gitin, eds., *Symbiosis, Symbolism, and the Power of the Past: Canaan, Ancient Israel, and Their Neighbors from the Late Bronze Age through Roman Palaestina. Proceedings of the Centennial Symposium, W. F. Albright Institute of Archaeological Research and American Schools of Oriental Research, Jerusalem, May 29–May 31, 2000* (Winona Lake, Ind.: Eisenbrauns, 2003).
115. Van De Mieroop, *The Eastern Mediterranean in the Age of Ramesses II*, 250.
116. F. Braudel, *Memory and the Mediterranean* (trans. Siân Reynolds; New York: Knopf, 2001), 146.
117. Van De Mieroop, *The Eastern Mediterranean in the Age of Ramesses II*, 251.
118. Ibid., 252.
119. Ibid., 253.
120. S. Bunimovitz, "Socio-Political Transformations in the Central Hill Country in the Late Bronze-Iron I Transition," in *From Nomadism to Monarchy: Archaeological and Historical Aspects of Early Israel* (ed. I. Finkelstein and N. Na'aman; Jerusalem: Israel Exploration Society, 1994), 179–202.
121. M. W. Chavalas and M. R. Adamthwaite, "Archaeological Light on the Old Testament," in *The Face of Old Testament Studies: A Survey of Contemporary Approaches* (ed. D. W. Baker and B. T. Arnold; Grand Rapids: Baker Books, 1999), 79–81.
122. B. M. Bryan, "Art, Empire, and the End of the Bronze Age," in *The Study of the Ancient Near East in the 21st Century: The William Foxwell Albright Centennial Conference* (ed. J. S. Cooper and G. M. Schwartz; Winona Lake, Ind.: Eisenbrauns, 1996), 33–79.
123. Cf. e.g., E. D. Oren, "An Egyptian Marsh Scene on Pottery from Tel Seraʿ: A Case of Egyptianization in Late Bronze Age III Canaan," in *"I Will Speak the Riddles of Ancient Times": Archaeological and Historical Studies in Honor of Amihai Mazar on the Occasion of His Sixtieth Birthday* (ed. A. M. Maeir and P. de Miroschedji; Winona Lake, Ind.: Eisenbrauns, 2006), 273.
124. A. E. Killebrew, "New Kingdom Egyptian-Style and Egyptian Pottery in Canaan: Implications for Egyptian Rule in Canaan During the 19th and Early 20th Dynasties," in *Egypt, Israel, and the Ancient Mediterranean World: Studies in Honor of Donald B. Redford* (ed. G. N. Knoppers and A. Hirsch; Leiden: Brill, 2004), 309–43; R. A. Mullins, "A Corpus of Eighteenth Dynasty Egyptian-Style Pottery from Tel Beth-Shean," in *"I Will Speak the Riddles of Ancient Times": Archaeological and Historical Studies in Honor of Amihai Mazar on the Occasion of His Sixtieth Birthday* (ed. A. M. Maeir and P. de Miroschedji; Winona Lake, Ind.: Eisenbrauns, 2006), 259; J. Weinstein, "The Egyptian Empire in Palestine: A Reassessment," *BASOR* 241 (1981): 1–28; idem., "The Collapse of the Egyptian Empire in the Southern Levant," in *The Crisis Years: The 12th Century B.C. from Beyond the Danube to the Tigris* (ed. W. A. Ward and M. S. Joukowsky; Dubuque, Iowa: Kendall/Hunt, 1992), 142–50.
125. C. R. Higginbotham, "Elite Emulation and Egyptian Governance in Ramesside Canaan," *Tel Aviv* 23 (1996): 154–69; idem., "The Egyptianizing of Canaan: How Iron-Fisted was Pharaonic Rule in the City-States of Syria-Palestine?" *BAR* 24/3 (May/June 1998): 37–43, 69; idem., *Egyptianization and Elite Emulation in Ramesside Palestine: Governance and Accomodation on the Imperial Periphery*. CHANE 2 (Leiden: Brill, 2000), see esp. 129–42.

126. R. W. Younker, "The Emergence of Ammon: A View of the Rise of Iron Age Polities from the Other Side of the Jordan," in *The Near East in the Southwest: Essays in Honor of William G. Dever* (ed. B. A. Nakhai; Boston, Mass.: American Schools of Oriental Research, 2007), 153–76; L. E. Stager, "The Impact of the Sea Peoples in Canaan (1185–1050 B.C.E.)," in *The Archaeology of Society in the Holy Land* (ed. T. E. Levy; London: Leicester University, 1995), 332–48; idem., "Forging an Identity: The Emergence of Ancient Israel," in *The Oxford History of the Biblical World* (ed. M. D. Coogan; New York: Oxford University Press, 1998), 123–75.

127. A. Zertal, "An Early Iron Age Cultic Site on Mount Ebal: Excavation Seasons 1982–1987," Tel Aviv 13–14 (1986–1987): 137.

128. See ch. 5.

129. E. Bloch-Smith and B. A. Nakhai, "A Landscape Comes to Life: The Iron Age I," *NEA* 62 (1999): 62–92, 101–27.

130. Y. Aharoni, *The Land of the Bible*, 165.

131. K. A. Kitchen, "Some New Light on the Asiatic Wars of Ramesses II," *EJA* 50 (1964): 47, 65–66.

132. "An Egyptian Letter," translated by John A. Wilson (*ANET*, 475–79).

## 5. Major Cities of the Conquest

1. G. S. P. Freeman-Grenville, "The *Onomasticon* of Eusebius of Caesarea and the *Liber Locorum* of Jerome," in G. S. P. Freeman-Grenville, Rupert L. Chapman III, and Joan E. Taylor, *The Onomasticon by Eusebius of Caesarea* (Jerusalem: Carta, 2003), 61.

2. Ibid.

3. J. Wilkinson, J. Hill, and W. F. Ryan, "Jerusalem Pilgrims" in *Jerusalem Pilgrimage 1099–1185*. The Hakluyt Society, Second Series, 167 (London, 1988), 4.

4. See J. R. Franke, *Joshua, Judges, Samuel, Ruth, 1–2 Samuel* (ACCS IV; Downers Grove, Ill.: InterVarsity, 2005), 32–41.

5. Rabbi N. Scherman, ed., *Joshua, Judges. The Early Prophets with a Commentary Anthologized from the Rabbinic Writings* (ed. Rabbi N. Scherman and Rabbi M. Zlotowitz; New York: Mesorah, 2000), 26–31.

6. E. Robinson and E. Smith, *Biblical Researches in Palestine, and in the Adjacent Regions. A Journal of Travels in the Year 1838*, vol. 1 (Boston: Crocker and Brewster, 1856; repr., Ann Arbor: The University of Michigan University Library, n.d.), 552.

7. Ibid., 557.

8. C. Warren, "Mounds at Ain es-Sultan," *PEFQS* (1869): 14–16; idem., "Tell es-Sultân," in *Survey of Western Palestine* 3 (1883): 222–26.

9. F. B. Meyer, *Joshua and the Land of Promise* (New York: Revell, 1893).

10. C. F. Keil and F. Delitzsch, *The Book of Joshua* (vol. 2, Commentary on the Old Testament; trans. James Martin; Edinburgh: T&T Clark, 1865–1892), 47–54. Since their work does not carry an exact date, it may be that it postdates Warren's work at Tell es-Sultan.

11. E. Sellin and C. Watzinger, *Jericho, die Ergebnisse der Ausgrabungen, 1913* (Leipzig: Hinrichs, 1913).

12. C. Watzinger, "Zur Chronologie der Schichten von Jericho," *ZDMG* 80 (1926): 131–36.

13. J. Garstang, "Jericho: City and Necropolis," in *Liverpool Annals of Archaeology and Anthropology* 21 (1934): 99–136.

14. Ibid., 67–76.

15. J. Garstang and J. B. E. Garstang, *The Story of Jericho* (London: Hodder & Stoughton, 1940), 125, 140.

16. J. Garstang, *Joshua-Judges* (London: Constable, 1931), 54–61.

17. J. Garstang, "Jericho: Sir Charles Marston's Expedition of 1930," *The Palestine Exploration Fund Quarterly Statement* 62 (1930): 131–32.

18. W. F. Albright, "The Israelite Conquest of Canaan in the Light of Archaeology," *BASOR* 74 (1939): 18–20.

19. A. Rowe and J. Garstang, "The Ruins of Jericho," *Palestine Exploration Fund Quarterly Statement* 68 (1936): 170.

20. W. F. Albright, *The Archaeology of Palestine* (Gloucester, Mass.: Peter Smith, 1971), 108.

21. R. P. L.-H. Vincent, "A Travers les Fouilles Palestiniennes. II, Jéricho et Sa Chronologie," *RB* 4 (1935): 599–600.

22. C. F. A. Schaeffer, *Stratigraphie compare et chronologie de l'Asie occidentale (IIIe et IIe millenaires): Syria, Palestine, Asie Mineure, Chypre, Perse et Caucase* (London: Oxford University Press, 1948), 129ff; R. de Vaux, incompletely cited in R. K. Harrison, Introduction to the Old Testament (Grand Rapids: Eerdmans, 1969), 176n62.

23. K. M. Kenyon, "Excavations at Jericho," *PEQ* 84.2 (1952): 64–72.

24. K. M. Kenyon, "Some Notes on the History of Jericho in the Second Millennium B.C.," *PEQ* 83 (1951): 101–38.

25. K. M. Kenyon, "Excavations at Jericho, 1954," *PEQ* 86 (1954): 45–63.

26. K. M. Kenyon, *Excavations at Jericho* (vol. 3, *The Architecture and Stratigraphy of the Tell* [Text]; London: British School of Archaeology in Jerusalem, 1981), 371.

27. Cf. K. M. Kenyon and T. A. Holland, *Excavations at Jericho*, vol. 5 of *The Pottery Phases of the Tell and Other Finds* (London: British School of Archaeology in Jerusalem, 1983), 467.

28. K. M. Kenyon, *Digging Up Jericho: The Results of the Jericho Excavations, 1952–1956* (New York: Praeger, 1957), 263.

29. Ibid., 262.

30. E.g., M. D. Coogan, "Archaeology and Biblical Studies: The Book of Joshua," in *The Hebrew Bible and Its Interpreters* (ed. W. H. Propp, B. Halpern, and D. N. Freedman; Winona Lake, Ind.: Eisenbrauns, 1990), 21. Coogan characterizes the argument that Late Bronze Age remains may have been eroded as one of *parti pris*, or extreme prejudice or bias.

31. Kenyon, *Digging Up Jericho*, 261–62.

32. A. A. Burke, *"Walled Up to Heaven": The Evolution of Middle Bronze Age Fortification Strategies in the Levant* (Studies in the Archaeology and History of the Levant 4; Winona Lake, Ind.: Eisenbrauns, 2008), 282.

33. A. Kempinski, "Middle and Late Bronze Age Fortifications," in *The Architecture of Ancient Israel: From the Prehistoric to the Persian Periods* (ed. A. Kempinski and R. Reich; Jerusalem: Israel Exploration Society, 1992), 136.

34. A. Mazar, *Archaeology of the Land of the Bible*, 10,000–586 B.C.E. (New York: Doubleday, 1990), 331.

35. K. M. Kenyon, "Jericho," in *Encyclopedia of Archaeological Excavations in the Holy Land* (ed. M. Avi-Yonah; London: Prentice Hall, 1976), 563–64.

36. J. Garstang, "Jericho: City and Necropolis," pl. XV, rooms 80 and 81.

37. P. Bienkowski, *Jericho in the Late Bronze Age* (England: Aris and Phillips, 1986), 112.

38. J. Garstang, "Jericho: City and Necropolis," 105–16; J. Garstang and J. B. E. Garstang, *The Story of Jericho* (London: Marshall, Morgan & Scott, 1948), 123ff.

39. Bienkowski, *Jericho in the Late Bronze Age*, 112–13.

40. Ibid., 113.
41. Ibid., 124-25.
42. See R. Gonen, "Urban Canaan in the Late Bronze Period," *BASOR* 253 (1984): 61-73.
43. Ibid., 69-70.
44. K. M. Kenyon, *Excavations at Jericho, The Architecture and Stratigraphy of the Tell,* 371.
45. Kenyon, *Digging Up Jericho,* 258.
46. K. M. Kenyon, *The Bible and Recent Archaeology* (London: British Museum Publications, 1978), 43.
47. N. Marchetti and L. Nigro, *Excavations at Jericho, 1998; Preliminary Report on the Second Season of Archaeological Excavations and Surveys at Tell es-Sultan, Palestine* (Rome: Università di Roma, 2000); L. Nigro and H. Taha, *Tell es-Sultan/Jericho in the Context of the Jordan Valley: Site Management, Conservation and Sustainable Development* (Rome: Università di Roma, 2006).
48. M. Noth, *Überlieferungsgeschichtliche Studien I* (Tübingen: Niemeyer Verlag, 1943).
49. For an overview, see S. L. McKenzie, "Deuteronomistic History," *AB* 2:160-68; idem., "Deuteronomistic History," *NIDB* 106-8; S. L. Richter, "Deuteronomistic History," in *Dictionary of the Old Testament: Historical Books* (ed. B. T. Arnold and H. G. M. Williamson; Downers Grove, Ill.: InterVarsity, 2005), 219-30.
50. M. Noth, *The Deuteronomistic History* (JSOTSup 15; Sheffield: JSOT Press, [1943], 1981), 89 (italics mine).
51. S. L. McKenzie, "Historiography, Old Testament," in *Dictionary of the Old Testament: Historical Books* (ed. B. T. Arnold and H. G. M. Williamson; Downers Grove, Ill.: InterVarsity, 2005), 420.
52. M. Noth, *The History of Israel* (2d ed.; New York: Harper & Row, 1958), 42-50.
53. Ibid., 149.
54. Ibid.
55. M. Noth, *Das Buch Josua* (Handbuch zum Alten Testament 7; Tübingen: J. C. B. Mohr, 1938), 16-17.
56. M. Noth, "Hat Die Bibel Doch Recht?" in *Festschrift für Günther Dehn, zum 75 Geburtstag am 18 April 1957* (ed. W. Schneemelcher; Neukirchen: Verlag der Buchhandlung des Erziehungsvereins, 1957), 13ff.
57. Cf. M. D. Coogan, "Archaeology and Biblical Studies: The Book of Joshua," in *The Hebrew Bible and Its Interpreters* (BJSUCSD 1; ed. W. H. Propp, B. Halpern, and D. N. Freedman; Winona Lake, Ind.: Eisenbrauns, 1990), 19-32.
58. J. A. Soggin, *Joshua: A Commentary* (OTL; Philadelphia: Westminster, 1972), 83.
59. Ibid., 84.
60. Ibid.
61. Ibid., 86.
62. J. Gray, *Joshua, Judges, Ruth* (NCBC; Grand Rapids: Eerdmans, 1986), 80-81.
63. Ibid., 81.
64. R. D. Nelson, *Joshua: A Commentary* (OTL; Louisville: Westminster John Knox, 1997), 3.
65. Ibid., 4-5.
66. Ibid., 5.
67. R. B. Coote, "Joshua" NIB 2:555.
68. Ibid., 556.
69. Ibid., 560.

70. Ibid., 560.
71. Ibid., 577.
72. L. L. Rowlett, "Inclusion, Exclusion and Marginality in the Book of Joshua," *JSOT* 55 (1992), 23. Cited in Coote, "Joshua" in NIB 2:577. Coote's reconstruction also includes other stages, including post-exilic priestly additions to Joshua. For the full discussion, see Coote, *Joshua*, 556–80.
73. Coote, *Joshua*, 578.
74. Ibid., 615.
75. Ibid.
76. C. Pressler, *Joshua, Judges, and Ruth* (WBC; Louisville: Westminster John Knox, 2002), 44–45.
77. Ibid., 45.
78. Ibid.
79. Ibid., 51.
80. J. F. D. Creach, *Joshua* (Interpretation; Louisville: John Knox Press, 2003), 5.
81. Ibid., 6.
82. E.g., A. G. Auld, *Joshua, Judges, and Ruth* (Lousiville: Westminster John Knox, 1984), 2–4, 42–45; R. G. Boling, *Joshua: A New Translation with Notes and Commentary* (AB 6; New York: Doubleday, 1982), 41–51, 211–15; E. J. Hamlin, *Inheriting the Land: A Commentary on the Book of Joshua* (Grand Rapids: Eerdmans, 1983), 46–47; L. Hoppe, *Joshua, Judges with an Excursus on Charismatic Leadership in Israel* (Wilmington, Del.: Michael Glazier, 1982), 15–16, 18–20.
83. M. H. Woudstra, *The Book of Joshua* (NICOT; Grand Rapids: Eerdmans, 1981), 69n6.
84. B. G. Wood, "Did the Israelites Conquer Jericho? A New Look at the Archaeological Evidence," *BARev* 16.2 (1990): 44–58.
85. P. Bienkowski, "Jericho Was Destroyed in the Middle Bronze Age, Not the Late Bronze Age," *BARev* 16.5 (1990): 45–46, 69.
86. B. Wood, "Dating Jericho's Destruction: Bienkowski Is Wrong on All Counts," *BARev* 16.5 (1990): 45, 47–49, 68–69.
87. D. M. Howard Jr., *Joshua* (NAC 5; Nashville: Broadman & Holman, 1998), 178. Cf. also A. L. Harstad, *Joshua* (Concordia Commentary; Saint Louis: Concordia, 2004), 122–23.
88. L. G. Herr, letter to author, July 2, 2010.
89. Kenyon and Holland, "Excavations at Jericho," 736.
90. Coogan, "Archaeology and Biblical Studies: The Book of Joshua," 27–29.
91. D. Merling, "The Relationship between Archaeology and the Bible: Expectations and Reality," in *The Future of Biblical Archaeology: Reassessing Methodologies and Assumptions* (ed. J. K. Hoffmeier and A. Millard; Grand Rapids: Eerdmans, 2004), 33.
92. Ibid., 33.
93. E.g., reductionism, relativism, and determinism.
94. G. A. Herion, "The Impact of Modern and Social Science Assumptions on the Reconstruction of Israelite History," *JSOT* 34 (1986): 22.
95. B. Halpern, "Text and Artifact: Two Monologues?" in *The Archaeology of Israel: Constructing the Past, Interpreting the Present* (JSOTSup 237; ed. N. A. Silberman and D. Small; Sheffield: Sheffield Academic Press, 1997), 313. In n. 7, Halpern states that "it would of course be invidious to cite examples," but, to see the general principle sketched out, he points readers to R. J. Collingwood, *An Autobiography* (Oxford: Oxford University Press, 1939), 29–43.
96. S. A. Rosen, "The Tyranny of Texts: A Rebellion against the Primacy of Written Documents in Defining Archaeological Agendas," in *"I Will Speak the Riddles of Ancient Times":*

*Archaeological and Historical Studies in Honor of Amihai Mazar on the Occasion of His Sixtieth Birthday* (ed. A. M. Maeir and P. de Miroschedji; Winona Lake, Ind.: Eisenbrauns, 2006), 881.

97. J. M. Miller, "Is It Possible to Write a History of Israel Without Relying on the Hebrew Bible?" in *The Fabric of History: Text, Artifact and Israel's Past* (JSOTSup 127; ed. D. V. Edelman; Sheffield: JSOT Press, 1991), 94.

98. B. Halpern, "Erasing History: The Minimalist Assault on Ancient Israel," in *BARev* 11.6 (1995): 29.

99. R. L. Zettler, "Written Documents as Excavated Artifacts and the Holistic Interpretation of the Mesopotamian Archaeological Record," in *The Study of the Ancient Near East in the 21st Century: The William Foxwell Albright Centennial Conference* (ed. J. S. Cooper and G. M. Schwartz; Winona Lake, Ind.: Eisenbrauns, 1996; cf. also Halpern, "Text and Artifact: Two Monologues?" 330–40. For an extensive discussion of the philosophy of history writing, as well as the relationship between text and artifact in historiography, see M. B. Moore, *Philosophy and Practice in Writing a History of Ancient Israel* (LHB/OT S 435; London: T&T Clark, 2006).

100. K. M. Kenyon, "Jericho: Tell es-Sultan," 2:680. Kenyon also observed the difficulties erosion on the site had created for reaching definitive conclusions about settlement at Tell es-Sultan in the Late Bronze Age. After devoting several pages to discussing the erosion and its effects, she explains: "It is a sad fact that of the town walls of the Late Bronze Age, within which period the attack by the Israelites must fall by any dating, not a trace remains. The erosion which has destroyed much of the defenses has already been described." See K. M. Kenyon, *Digging Up Jericho: The Results of the Jericho Excavations 1952–1956* (New York: Frederick A. Praeger, 1957), 262.

101. D. Merling, "The Book of Joshua, Part I: Its Evaluation by Nonevidence," *AUSS* 39 (2001): 61–72; "The Book of Joshua, Part II: Expectations of Archaeology," *AUSS* 39 (2001): 209–221.

102. R. S. Hess, "The Jericho and Ai of the Book of Joshua," in *Critical Issues in Early Israelite History* (BBRSup 3; ed. R. S. Hess, G. A. Klingbeil, and P. J. Ray Jr.; Winona Lake, Ind.: Eisenbrauns, 2008), 33–46.

103. J. A. Dearman, "City," *NIDB* 1:671.

104. Ibid., 671.

105. T. M. Willis, "City Gate," *NIDB* 1:677.

106. Keil and Delitzsch, *The Book of Joshua*, 50.

107. S. L. McKenzie, "Historiography, Old Testament," 421. It is true that Jericho was one of the oldest cities in Canaan, dating back to the Mesolithic (10,000–8,000 B.C.E.) and Neolithic (ca. 8000–4000) periods.

108. L. F. DeVries, *Cities of the Biblical World: An Introduction to the Archaeology, Geography, and History of Biblical Sites* (Peabody, Mass.: Hendrickson, 1997), 191.

109. R. G. Boling, *Joshua*, 213–14.

110. Hess, "The Jericho and Ai of the Book of Joshua," 36.

111. Ibid.

112. Ibid.

113. G. E. Wright, *Biblical Archaeology*, 80.

114. Nelson, *Joshua*, 91.

115. K. M. Kenyon, *Archaeology in the Holy Land* (New York: Norton, 1979), 208.

116. D. Merling, "The Book of Joshua, Part II: Expectations of Archaeology," *AUSS* 39.2 (2001): 214.

117. Hess, "The Jericho and Ai of the Book of Joshua," 39.

118. Ibid., 40–41.

119. Ibid., 41.

120. Merling, "The Book of Joshua, Part II: Expectations of Archaeology," 214–15; Hess, "The Jericho and Ai of the Book of Joshua," 36.

121. Hess, "The Jericho and Ai of the Book of Joshua," 36.

122. G. W. Ramsey, *The Quest for the Historical Israel* (Atlanta: John Knox, 1981), 107–24.

123. See, for example, W. W. Willis Jr., "The Archaeology of Palestine and the Archaeology of Faith: Between a Rock and a Hard Place," in *What Has Archaeology to Do with Faith?* (ed. J. H. Charlesworth and W. P. Weaver; Philadelphia: Trinity Press International, 1992), 75–111.

124. I use these terms cautiously and with trepidation. For caveats, definitions, and other terminological alternatives, see M. B. Moore, *Philosophy and Practice in Writing a History of Ancient Israel*, 75–78, 108–9.

125. Merling, "The Book of Joshua, Part II: Expectations of Archaeology," 221.

126. Freeman-Grenville, *The Onomasticon by Eusebius of Caesarea*, 13.

127. E. Robinson, *Biblical Researches in Palestine, Mount Sinai and Arabia Petraea: A Journal of Travels in the Year 1838*, vol. I (Boston: Crocker and Brewster, 1856), 448, 574–75.

128. C. Wilson, "On the Site of Ai and the Position of the Altar which Abraham Built between Bethel and Ai," *PEFQS* 1 (1869–70): 123–26; idem., "Account of et-Tell," in *The Survey of Western Palestine* (ed. C. R. Conder and H. H. Kitchener; vol. 2; London: Palestine Exploration Fund, 1882), 372–74.

129. See the review in B. G. Wood, "The Search for Joshua's Ai," in *Critical Issues in Early Israelite History* (ed. R. S. Hess, G. A. Klingbeil, and P. J. Ray Jr.; Winona Lake, Ind.: Eisenbrauns, 2008), 207–9.

130. W. F. Albright, "Ai and Beth-Aven," in *Excavations and Results at Tell el-Fûl (Gibeah of Saul)* (ed. B. W. Bacon; AASOR 4; New Haven, Conn.: American Schools of Oriental Research, 1924), 141–49.

131. E.g., W. F. Albright, "The Israelite Conquest of Canaan in the Light of Archaeology," *BASOR* 74 (1939): 1–23.

132. Garstang, *Joshua, Judges*, 356.

133. J. Marquet-Krause, *Les fouilles d'Ay, 1933–1935: Le resurrection d'une grande cité biblique*. Bibliothèque Archéologique et Historique 45 (Paris: Paul Geuthner, 1949).

134. M. R. Dussaud, "Note additionnelle," *Syria* 16 (1935): 346–52; J. Marquet-Krause, "La deuxième champagne de fouilles à 'Ai (1934). Rapport sommaire," *Syria* 16 (1935): 325–45.

135. Noth, *The History of Israel*, 149n2.

136. Albright, "The Israelite Conquest in the Light of Archaeology," 16.

137. J. A. Callaway, "Ai (et-Tell): Problem Site for Biblical Archaeologists," in *Archaeology and Biblical Interpretation: Essays in Memory of D. Glenn Rose* (ed. L. G. Perdue, L. E. Toombs, and G. L. Johnson; Atlanta: John Knox, 1987), 90.

138. See the summary in J. A. Callaway, *The Early Bronze Age Sanctuary at Ai (et-Tell)* (London: Bernard Quaritch, 1971), 4–5.

139. J. A. Callaway, "New Evidence on the Conquest of 'Ai," *JBL* 87 (1968): 315.

140. Ibid., 316.

141. Ibid., 316–17.

142. Ibid., 320.

143. J. A. Callaway, "Was My Excavation of Ai Worthwhile?" *BAR* 11.2 (1985): 68–69.

144. Callaway, "Ai (et-Tell) Problem Site," 93–96.

145. E.g., D. P. Livingston, "Location of Bethel and Ai Reconsidered," *WTJ* 33 (1970): 20–44; W. W. Winter, "Biblical and Archaeological Data on Ai Reappraised," *Review of the Cincinnati Bible College and Seminary* 16.4 (1970): 73–83.

146. See ch. 2.

147. See the helpful review in B. G. Wood, "The Search for Joshua's Ai," 207–9.

148. E. Robinson, *Biblical Researches in Palestine, Mount Sinai and Arabia Petraea*, vol. I, 448.

149. E. Sellin, "Mittheilungen von meiner Palästinareise 1899," *Mittheilungen und Nachrichten des Deutschen Palaestina-Vereins* 6 (1900): 1. Cited in B. Wood, "The Search for Joshua's Ai," 229–30.

150. I. Finkelstein and Y. Magen, eds., *Archaeological Survey of the Hill Country of Benjamin* (Jerusalem: Israel Antiquities Authority Publications, 1993), 22, 81.

151. B. G. Wood, "Kh. el-Maqatir 1995–1998," *IEJ* 50 (2000): 123–30; idem., "Khirbet el-Maqatir, 1999," *IEJ* 50 (2000): 249–54; idem., "Khirbet el-Maqatir, 2000" *IEJ* 51 (2001): 246–52.

152. R. K. Hawkins, "Luz," *NIDB* 3:734.

153. Wood, "The Search for Joshua's Ai," 214–21.

154. See A. F. Rainey, "Bethel is Still Beitîn," *WTJ* 33 (1971): 175–88; idem., "Looking for Bethel: An Exercise in Historical Geography," in *Confronting the Past: Archaeological and Historical Essays on Ancient Israel in Honor of William G. Dever* (ed. S. Gitin, J. E. Wright, J. P. Dessel; Winona Lake, Ind.: Eisenbrauns, 2006), 269–73.

155. E.g., Wood, "The Search for Joshua's Ai," 237, fig. 13.

156. P. Briggs, *Testing the Factuality of the Conquest of Ai Narrative in the Book of Joshua*. Academic Monograph No. AR-1 (Albuquerque, N. Mex.: Daystar Systems, 2007), 110.

157. R. S. Hess, *Joshua: An Introduction and Commentary* (Leicester: InterVarsity, 1996), 188.

158. *HALOT* 1:296.

159. The translators of the LXX inadvertently modified the Hebrew of the MT when they often imposed urban understandings on the text in their translations. By the time the LXX translators carried out their work, the Hebrew Bible was already "old" and "foreign." For example, for an urban Jew in Alexandria, "tents" as a dwelling place was an anachronism. Instead of translating Deut 5:30, therefore, as "return to your tents," it made more sense to the LXX translators to render it as "return to your houses." It is this kind of urban predisposition that conditions our reading of the kinds of passages under discussion in Joshua. See the insightful essay of L. Greenspoon, "Text and the City," in *Cities through the Looking Glass: Essays on the History and Archaeology of Biblical Urbanism* (ed. R. Arav; Winona Lake, Ind.: Eisenbrauns, 2008), 39–52.

160. D. Merling, *The Book of Joshua: Its Theme and Role in Archaeological Discussions*. Andrews University Seminary Doctoral Dissertation Series, vol. 23 (Berrien Springs, Mich.: Andrews University Press, 1996), 257–58.

161. 1 Macc. 11:67; *Ant.* 5.199.

162. Cf. D. A. Dorsey, *The Roads and Highways of Ancient Israel* (Baltimore: Johns Hopkins University Press, 1991), 93–97, 101, 157, 159–61.

163. "The Craft of the Scribe (Papyrus Anastasi I)," translated by J. P. Allen (*COS* 3.2.12).

164. Yearly reports can be accessed via www.unixware.mscc.huji.ac.il/~hatsor/hazor.html.

165. A. Ben-Tor and S. Zuckerman, "Hazor at the End of the Late Bronze Age: Back to Basics," *BASOR* 350 (2008): 1–6.

166. E.g., J. J. Bimson, *Redating the Exodus and Conquest* (Sheffield: JSOT Press, 1978), 185–200; K. Freiling, "When Did Joshua Destroy Hazor?" *Artifax* 20/3 (2005): 17–21;

E. H. Merrill, *A Kingdom of Priests: A History of Old Testament Israel* (2d ed.; Grand Rapids: Baker, 2008), 137; D. Petrovich, "The Dating of Hazor's Destruction in Joshua 11 via Biblical, Archaeological, and Epigraphic Evidence," *JETS* 51/3 (2008): 489–512.

167. B. G. Wood, "The Rise and Fall of the 13th-Century Exodus-Conquest Theory," *JETS* 48 (2005): 487–88.

168. Cf. M. Hunt, "Harosheth-Hagoiim," *ABD* 3:62–63.

169. J. K. Hoffmeier, "What Is the Biblical Date for the Exodus? A Response to Bryant Wood," *JETS* 50/2 (2007): 244.

170. W. L. Moran, *The Amarna Letters* (Baltimore: Johns Hopkins University Press, 1992), 235, 362.

171. W. L. Moran, *The Amarna Letters*, 289–90.

172. "The Craft of the Scribe (Papyrus Anastasi I)," translated by J. P. Allen (*COS* 3.2.12).

173. *HALOT* 1:553–54.

174. Cf. e.g., M. Dahood, *Psalms I* (New York: Doubleday, 1966), 271; F. Delitzsch, "Psalms" (Commentary on the Old Testament, vol. 5; trans. F. Bolton; Edinburgh: T&T Clark, 1865–1892), 328.

175. J. D. Smoak, "Scribe," *NIDB* 5:136–38.

176. See Yadin, *Hazor: The Head of All Those Kingdoms (Joshua 11:10). The Schweich Lectures of the British Academy, 1970* (London: Oxford University Press, 1972), 108–9.

177. J. P. Allen, "A Hieroglyphic Fragment from Hazor," *BES* 15 (2001): 13–15.

178. K. A. Kitchen, "An Egyptian Inscribed Fragment from Late Bronze Hazor," *IEJ* 53 (2003) 20.

179. Ibid., 24–25.

180. Y. Aharoni, "New Aspects of the Israelite Occupation in the North," in *Near Eastern Archaeology in the Twentieth Century* (ed. J. A. Sanders; Garden City: Doubleday, 1970), 254–67.

181. V. Fritz, "Das Ende der Spätbronzenzeitlichen Stadt Hazor Stratum XIII und die Biblische Überlieferung im Joshua 11 und Richter 4," *UF* 5 (1973): 123–39.

182. I. Finkelstein, "Hazor at the End of the Late Bronze Age: A Reassessment," *Ugarit-Forschungen* 37 (2005): 341–49.

183. S. Zuckerman, "Anatomy of a Destruction: Crisis Architecture, Termination Rituals and the Fall of Canaanite Hazor," *JMA* 20/1 (2007): 3–32.

184. Ibid., 25.

185. S. Zuckerman, "The Last Days of a Canaanite Kingdom: A View from Hazor," in *Forces of Transformation: The End of the Bronze Age in the Mediterranean* (ed. C. Bachhuber and R. G. Roberts; Oxford: Oxbow, 2009), 101.

186. Ibid., 102.

187. As observed in Petrovich, "The Dating of Joshua's Destruction in Joshua 11," 3n15.

188. A. Ben-Tor, "The Sad Fate of Statues and the Mutilated Statues of Hazor," in *Confronting the Past: Archaeological and Historical Essays on Ancient Israel in Honor of William G. Dever* (ed. S. Gitin, J. E. Wright, and J. P. Dessel; Winona Lake, Ind.: Eisenbrauns, 2006), 3–16.

189. A. Ben-Tor, "The Fall of Canaanite Hazor: The 'Who' and 'When' Questions," in *Mediterranean Peoples in Transition: Thirteenth to Early Tenth Centuries BCE: In Honor of Trude Dothan* (ed. S. Gitin, A. Mazar, and E. Stern; Jerusalem: Israel Exploration Society, 1998), 456–67.

190. "The Execration of Asiatic Princes," translated by J. A. Wilson (*ANET*, 328–29); "Execration Texts," translated by R. K. Ritner (*COS*, 1.32:50–52).

191. A. Malamat, "Syro-Palestinian Destinations in a Mari Tin Inventory," *IEJ* 21 (1971): 31–38.

192. "List of Asiatic Countries Under the Egyptian Empire," translated by J. A. Wilson (*ANET*, 242–43).

193. Robinson, *Biblical Researches in Palestine*, vol. 3 (Boston: Crocker and Brewster, 1871), 392.

194. A. Biran, "To the God Who Is in Dan," in *Temples and High Places in Biblical Times* (ed. A. Biran; Jerusalem: The Nelson Glueck School of Biblical Archaeology of Hebrew Union College-Jewish Institute of Religion, 1981), 142–51.

195. A. Biran, ed., *Dan I: A Chronicle of the Excavations, the Pottery Neolithic, the Early Bronze Age and the Middle Bronze Age Tombs* (Jerusalem: Nelson Glueck School of Biblical Archaeology, Hebrew Union College-Jewish Institute of Religion, 1996).

196. A. Biran, ed., *Dan II: A Chronicle of the Excavations and the Late Bronze Age "Mycenaean" Tomb* (Jerusalem: Nelson Glueck School of Biblical Archaeology, Hebrew Union College-Jewish Institute of Religion, 2002).

197. E.g., I. Provan, V. P. Long, and T. Longman, III, *A Biblical History of Israel* (Louisville: Westminster John Knox, 2003), 181–83.

198. J. C. H. Laughlin, "Dan, Tell," *NIDB* 2:11.

199. A. Biran, "Dan," in *Archaeology and Biblical Interpretation: Essays in Memory of D. Glenn Rose* (ed. L. G. Perdue, L. E. Toombs, and G. L. Johnson; Atlanta: John Knox Press, 1987), 105.

200. See ch. 8, where pits/silos are discussed extensively with regard to the site of ʿIzbet Sartah.

201. A. Biran, "The Collared-rim Jars and the Settlement of the Tribe of Dan," in *Recent Excavations in Israel: Studies in Iron Age Archaeology* (ed. S. Gitin and W. G. Dever; AASOR 49; Winona Lake, Ind.: Eisenbrauns, 1989), 83.

202. There are pithoi of the "Galilean" type found in Stratum VI at Tel Dan, which does have precedent in Canaanite culture. In addition, Canaanite influence can be seen in the cooking pots and other vessels found in Stratum VI. Clearly, the new settlers absorbed some features of the material culture of their Canaanite predecessors. For discussion about the origin of the collared-rim jar and its possible association with Israelite ethnicity, see chs. 7 and 8.

203. A. Biran, "The Collared-rim Jars and the Settlement of the Tribe of Dan," 81.

204. D. W. Manor, "Laish (Place)," *ABD* 4:130–31.

205. A. Biran, *Biblical Dan* (Jerusalem: Israel Exploration Society, 1994), 125–26.

206. A. Biran, "Dan," 101.

207. A. Malamat, "The Danite Migration and the Pan-Israelite Conquest: A Biblical Narrative Pattern," in *History of Biblical Israel: Major Problems and Minor Issues* (Leiden: Brill, 2004), 171–85.

208. A. Biran, "Dan," 105–6.

209. L. E. Stager, "Forging an Identity: The Emergence of Ancient Israel," in *The Oxford History of the Biblical World* (ed. M. D. Coogan; New York: Oxford, 1998), 167.

# 6. Reconstructing the Israelite Settlement Archaeologically

1. G. L. Kelm, *Escape to Conflict: A Biblical and Archaeological Approach to the Hebrew Exodus and Settlement in Canaan* (Fort Worth, Tex.: IAR Publications, 1991), 141–56.

2. I. Finkelstein, *The Archaeology of the Israelite Settlement* (Jerusalem: Israel Exploration Society, 1988).

3. W. E. Arnal, "Galilee, Galileans," *NIDB* 2: 514; R. Frankel, "Galilee (Prehellenistic)," *ABD* 2:879-95.

4. Y. Aharoni, "The Settlement of the Israelite Tribes in Upper Galilee" (Ph.D. diss., Hebrew University, 1957) (Hebrew).

5. R. Frankel, "Preliminary Report of the Archaeological Survey of Western Galilee, 1976-1979," in *The Western Galilee Antiquities* (ed. M. Yedaya; Israel: Mateh Asher, 1986), 304-17 (Hebrew); idem., *Settlement Dynamics and the Regional Diversity in Ancient Upper Galilee: Archaeological Survey of Upper Galilee* (IAAR 14; Jerusalem: Israel Antiquities Authority, 2001).

6. Frankel, "Galilee (Prehellenistic)," 882-83.

7. For the new, small settlements, see Aharoni, "The Settlement of the Israelite Tribes in Upper Galilee"; for Hazor, see A. Ben-Tor, "The Yigal Yadin Memorial Excavations at Hazor, 1990-93: Aims and Preliminary Results," in *The Archaeology of Israel: Constructing the Past, Interpreting the Present* (ed. N. A. Silberman and D. B. Small; JSOTSS 237; Sheffield: Sheffield Academic Press, 1997), 107-27; A. Ben-Tor and R. Bonfils, eds., *Hazor V: An Account of the Fifth Season of Excavation, 1968* (Jerusalem: Israel Exploration Society and Hebrew University of Jerusalem, 1997); for Dan, see A. Biran, *Biblical Dan* (Jerusalem: Israel Exploration Society, 1994), 125-42.

8. J. Pakkala, S. Münger, and J. Zangenberg, *Kinneret Regional Project: Tel Kinrot Excavations, Report 2* (ed. S. AroValjus; Vantaa: Tummavuoren kirjapaino Oy, 2004), 17-24.

9. R. Frankel, "Upper Galilee in the Late Bronze-Iron I Transition," in *From Nomadism to Monarchy: Archaeological and Historical Aspects of Early Israel* (ed. I. Finkelstein and N. Na'aman; Jerusalem: Israel Exploration Society, 1994), 25-34.

10. Z. Gal, *Lower Galilee during the Iron Age* (ASOR Dissertation Series 8; ed. B. Halpern; Winona Lake, Ind.: Eisenbrauns, 1992), 56.

11. Gal, "Iron I in Lower Galilee and the Margins of the Jezreel Valley," in *From Nomadism to Monarchy: Archaeological and Historical Aspects of Early Israel* (ed. I. Finkelstein and N. Na'aman; Jerusalem: Israel Exploration Society, 1994), 38.

12. Gal, *Lower Galilee during the Iron Age*, 84.

13. Z. Gal, "Iron I in Lower Galilee and the Margins of the Jezreel Valley," 40-42.

14. For Megiddo, see D. Ussishkin, "Megiddo," *NIDB* 4:17-27; for Jokneam, see S. Zuckerman, "Jokneam," *NIDB* 3:374.

15. For Beth-Shean, see A. Mazar, *Excavations at Beth-Shean 1989-1996, Vol. I: From the Late Bronze Age IIB to the Medieval Period* (Jerusalem: Israel Exploration Society and Institute of Archaeology, 2006); for Rehov, see A. Mazar, "Rehov, Tel," *NIDB* 4:759.

16. I. Singer, "Egyptians, Canaanites and Philistines in the Period of the Emergence of Israel," in *From Nomadism to Monarchy: Archaeological and Historical Aspects of Early Israel* (ed. I. Finkelstein and N. Na'aman; Jerusalem: Israel Exploration Society, 1994), 309.

17. For Taanach, see W. Rast, *Taanach I: Studies in the Iron Age Pottery* (Cambridge, Mass: American Schools of Oriental Research, 1978), 3-8; for Afula, see M. Dothan, "'Afula," *NEAEHL* 1:37-39.

18. M. D. Green, "Hill, Hill Country," *NIDB* 2:825-26.

19. Finkelstein, *The Archaeology of the Israelite Settlement*, 353.

20. R. Gophnah and Y. Porat, "The Land of Ephraim and Manasseh," in *Judea, Samaria, and the Golan* (ed. C. Epstein, M. Kochavi, and P. Bar-Adon; Jerusalem: Hotsaat ha-Agudah le-seker arkheologiy shel Yisrael 'al-yede Karta, 1972), 196-242 (Hebrew).

21. I. Finkelstein, S. Bunimovits, and Z. Lederman, *Shiloh: The Archaeology of a Biblical Site* (Tel Aviv University Sonia and Marco Institute of Archaeology Monograph Series Number 10; ed. I. Finkelstein; Tel Aviv: Institute of Archaeology of Tel Aviv University, 1993).

22. Finkelstein, *The Archaeology of the Israelite Settlement*, incorporates data from the survey; the first two volumes of the survey appear in vol. 1. Finkelstein, Z. Lederman, and S. Bunimovitz, *Highlands of Many Cultures: The Southern Samaria Survey* (2 vols.; Tel Aviv University Sonia and Marco Nadler Institute of Archaeology Monograph Series 14; Tel Aviv: Institute of Archaeology of Tel Aviv University, 1997).

23. Finkelstein, *The Archaeology of the Israelite Settlement*, 72–73; I. Finkelstein et al., "Description of Sites," in *Highlands of Many Cultures*, 1:518, 893.

24. Finkelstein, *The Archaeology of the Israelite Settlement*, 187.

25. I. Finkelstein, Z. Lederman, and S. Bunimovitz, *Highlands of Many Cultures*, vol. 2, 893–96.

26. For the territory to the south, see I. Finkelstein and Y. Magen, *Archaeological Survey of the Hill Country of Benjamin* (Jerusalem: Israel Exploration Society, 1993); for the foothills to the west, see M. Kochavi and I. Beit-Arieh, *Archaeological Survey of Israel, Map of Rosh Ha'Ayin* (Jerusalem: Israel Antiquities Authority, 1994); and A. Shavit, "The Ayalon Valley and Its Vicinity during the Bronze and Iron Ages" (M.A. thesis, Tel Aviv University, 1992) (Hebrew); for the area to the east, see Y. Spanier, "Eastern Samaria in the Hellenistic, Roman and Byzantine Periods" (M.A. thesis, Bar-Ilan University, Ramat-Gan, 1992) (Hebrew).

27. J. Murphy-O'Connor, "Jerusalem," *NIDB* 3:246–59.

28. See J. M. Cahill, "Jerusalem in the Time of the United Monarchy: The Archaeological Evidence," in *Jerusalem in Bible and Archaeology: The First Temple Period* (ed. A. G. Vaughn and A. E. Killebrew; Atlanta: Society of Biblical Literature, 2003), 13–80.

29. R. K. Hawkins, "Millo," *NIDB* 4:88.

30. See A. Mazar, "Jerusalem and Its Vicinity in Iron Age I," in *From Nomadism to Monarchy: Archaeological and Historical Aspects of Early Israel* (ed. I. Finkelstein and N. Na'aman; Jerusalem: Israel Exploration Society, 1994), 72–73.

31. A. Mazar, "Remarks on Biblical Traditions and Archaeological Evidence Concerning Early Israel," in *Symbiosis, Symbolism and the Power of the Past: Canaan, Ancient Israel, and Their Neighbors from the Late Bronze Age through Roman Palestina* (ed. W. G. Dever and S. Gitin; Winona Lake, Ind.: Eisenbrauns, 2003), 92.

32. Z. Kallai, "The Land of Benjamin and Mt. Ephraim," in *Judea, Samaria, and the Golan* (ed. C. Epstein, M. Kochavi, and P. Bar-Adon; Jerusalem: Hotsaat-Agudah le-seker arkheologi shel Yisrael 'al-yede Karta, 1972), 151–93 (Hebrew).

33. See Finkelstein and Magen, *Archaeological Survey of the Hill Country of Benjamin*.

34. Finkelstein, *The Archaeology of the Israelite Settlement*, 56–60; Mazar, "Jerusalem and Its Vicinity in Iron Age I," 76–78.

35. Finkelstein, *The Archaeology of the Israelite Settlement*, 48–50; Mazar, "Jerusalem and Its Vicinity in Iron Age I," 78–91.

36. M. Kochavi, "The Land of Judah," in *Judaea, Samaria, and the Golan: Archaeological Survey, 1967–1968* (ed. M. Kochavi; Jerusalem: Carta, 1972), 19–89; A. Ofer, "'All the Hill Country of Judah': From a Settlement Fringe to a Prosperous Monarchy," in *From Nomadism to Monarchy: Archaeological and Historical Aspects of Early Israel* (ed. I. Finkelstein and N. Na'aman; Jerusalem: Israel Exploration Society, 1994), 118–19.

37. I. Finkelstein, *Living on the Fringe: The Archaeology and History of the Negev, Sinai and Neighbouring Regions in the Bronze and Iron Ages* (Sheffield: Sheffield Academic Press, 1995), 101.

38. A. Kempinski, "Masos, Tel," in *NEAEHL* 3:986.

39. A. Kempinski et al., "Excavations at Tel Masos: 1972, 1974, 1975," *EI* 15 (1981): 175.

40. Finkelstein, *Living on the Fringe*, 117–18.

41. Finkelstein, *Living on the Fringe*, 118; Z. Herzog, "The Beer-sheba Valley: From Nomadism to Monarchy," in *From Nomadism to Monarchy*, 146.

42. Z. Herzog, "Tell Beersheba," *NEAEHL* 1:68–70.

43. Herzog, "The Beer-sheba Valley," 148.

44. E.g., A. Alt, "The Settlement of the Israelites in Palestine," in *Essays on Old Testament History and Religion* (Garden City: Doubleday, 1967), 175–221; C. H. J. De Gues, "Manasseh," *ABD* 4:494–96; B. Mazar, "The Early Israelite Settlement in the Hill Country," in *The Early Biblical Period: Historical Studies* (ed. S. Ahituv and B. A. Levine; Jerusalem: Israel Exploration Society, 1986), 25–49.

45. I. Finkelstein, *The Archaeology of the Israelite Settlement* (Jerusalem: Israel Exploration Society, 1988), 65–91, 353–56.

46. M. Kochavi, "The Israelite Settlement in Canaan in the Light of Archaeological Surveys," in *Biblical Archaeology Today: Proceedings of the International Congress on Biblical Archaeology, Jerusalem, 1984* (ed. J. Amitai; Jerusalem: Israel Exploration Society, 1985), 56.

47. E.g., W. F. Albright, "The Site of Tirzah and the Topography of Western Manasseh," *JPOS* 11 (1931): 241–51.

48. A. Zertal, "The Mount Manasseh (Northern Samaria Hills) Survey," in *NEAEHL* 4:1311–12.

49. By processing these sites, a computer-generated profile of an Iron Age I site was created using a seven-point methodology. An Iron I site is defined as one yielding Iron Age I pottery, in some cases also exhibiting a characteristic architecture and settlement pattern, based upon past excavations of hill-country sites with remains dated to 1250–1000 B.C.E. A. Zertal, "The Iron Age I Culture in the Hill-Country of Canaan: A Manassite Perspective," in *Mediterranean Peoples in Transition: Thirteenth to Early Tenth Centuries BCE* (ed. S. Gitin, A. Mazar, and E. Stern; Jerusalem: Israel Exploration Society, 1998), 240.

50. Finkelstein, *The Archaeology of the Israelite Settlement*, 89.

51. A. Zertal, *The Manasseh Hill Country Survey*, vol. 1: *The Shechem Syncline* (Leiden: Brill, 2004), 53.

52. R. Gonen, "The Late Bronze Age," in *The Archaeology of Ancient Israel* (ed. A. Ben-Tor; New Haven, Conn.: Yale University Press, 1992), 212–57.

53. A. Faust (2003: 147–50), followed by E. Bloch-Smith (2003: 410–11), has recently argued that many Iron Age I rural sites were either abandoned, destroyed, or deserted about fifty years after having been founded. Faust argues that, following this highland abandonment, the concentration of the population then shifted to larger urban settlements (Faust 2003: 147–50), a demographic change he associates with the process of state formation. Faust's study cites the surveys in Judah and Samaria but not, however, those of sorthern Samaria and the highlands of Benjamin, and thus will not be dealt with in this discussion (see the detailed critique in Finkelstein 2005: 202–8).

54. Zertal, "The Iron Age I Culture in the Hill-Country of Canaan: A Manassite Perspective," in *Mediterranean Peoples in Transition: Thirteenth to Early Tenth Centuries BCE*, 242.

55. A. Zertal, *The Manasseh Hill Country Survey* (vol. II, The Eastern Valleys and the Fringes of the Desert (Tel Aviv: University of Haifa and the Ministry of Defense, 1996) (Hebrew). This volume has recently been published in English translation as *The Manasseh Hill Country Survey* (vol. 2, The Eastern Valleys and the Fringes of the Desert; CHANE 21/2; Leiden: Brill, 2007).

56. Zertal, *The Eastern Valleys and the Fringes of the Desert*, 115–642.

57. Ibid., 81–85.

58. D. Ben-Yosef, "The Jordan Valley during Iron Age I: Aspects of Its History and the Archaeological Evidence for Its Settlement" (Ph.D. diss., University of Haifa, 2007) (Hebrew).

59. On enclosed nomadism, see M. Rowton, "Enclosed Nomadism," *JESHO* 17:1 (1974): 1–30. See also R. Cribb, *Nomads in Archaeology* (Cambridge: Cambridge University Press, 1991).

60. A. Mazar, "Giloh: An Early Israelite Site in the Vicinity of Jerusalem," *IEJ* 31 (1981): 21.

61. A. Zertal, "Israel Enters Canaan: Following the Pottery Trail," *BAR* 17 (1991): 42.

62. A. Zertal, "The Iron Age I Culture in the Hill-Country of Canaan: A Manassite Perspective," 242–43.

63. Mazar, "Giloh: An Early Israelite Site in the Vicinity of Jerusalem," 21–22.

64. Zertal, "Israel Enters Canaan: Following the Pottery Trail," 43.

65. A. Zertal, "To the Land of the Perizzites and the Giants: On the Israelite Settlement in the Hill Country of Manasseh," in *From Nomadism to Monarchy: Archaeological and Historical Aspects of Early Israel* (ed. I. Finkelstein and N. Na'aman; Washington, D.C.: Biblical Archaeology Society, 1994), 52–53.

66. Eleven points are marshaled from the survey data to argue for a distinction between the Manasseh population and the other central-hill and Galilean populations. These are: settlement pattern, site size, architecture, continuity from Late Bronze into Iron II, limited pottery inventory, size and inner division, diet, metallurgical finds, cult and possible cult sites, place names, population size, and cultural connections.

67. A. Zertal, "To the Land of the Perizzites and the Giants," 58–59; idem., "The Iron Age I Culture in the Hill-Country of Canaan," 242–43.

68. L. E. Stager, "Forging an Identity: The Emergence of Ancient Israel," in *The Oxford History of the Biblical World* (ed. M. D. Coogan; New York: Oxford University Press, 1998), 134–35.

69. W. G. Dever, "Cultural Continuity, Ethnicity in the Archaeological Record and the Question of Israelite Origins," *Eretz Israel* 24 (1993), 32.

70. W. G. Dever, "Israelite Origins and the 'Nomadic Ideal': Can Archaeology Separate Fact from Fiction?" in *Mediterranean Peoples in Transition: Thirteenth to Early Tenth Centuries BCE* (ed. S. Gitin, A. Mazar, and E. Stern; Jerusalem: Israel Exploration Society, 1998), 227.

71. E.g., E. B. Banning, "Archaeological Survey in the Southern Levant," in *Near Eastern Archaeology: A Reader* (ed. S. Richard; Winona Lake, Ind.: Eisenbrauns, 2003), 164–67; J. S. Holladay, "Method and Theory in Syro-Palestinian Archaeology," in *Near Eastern Archaeology: A Reader* (ed. S. Richard; Winona Lake, Ind.: Eisenbrauns, 2003), 33–47; J. R. Kautz, III, "Archaeological Surveys," in *Benchmarks in Time and Culture: Essays in Honor of Joseph A. Callaway* (ed. J. F. Drinkard, Jr., G. L. Mattingly, and J. M. Miller; Atlanta: Scholars Press, 1988), 209–22).

72. W. G. Dever, *Who Were the Early Israelites and Where Did They Come From?* (Grand Rapids: Eerdmans, 2003), 94–95. I first noticed this contradiction in Dever's writings about archaeological surveys in Mark Ziese, *Joshua* (Joplin, Mo.: College Press, 2008), n. 4.

73. W. G. Dever, "How To Tell a Canaanite from an Israelite," in *The Rise of Ancient Israel* (ed. H. Shanks; Washington, D.C.: The Biblical Archaeology Society, 1992), 51.

74. W. G. Dever, "Cultural Continuity, Ethnicity in the Archaeological Record and the Question of Israelite Origins," 27.

75. A. Zertal, "Using Pottery Forms and Width Stratigraphy to Trace Population Movements," *BAR* 17 (1991): 39–41.

76. N. Lapp, "Pottery Chronology of Palestine," *ABD* 5:433–4.

77. Z. Zevit, *Religions of Ancient Israel: A Synthesis of Parallactic Approaches* (London: Continuum, 2001), 103n35.

78. E.g., R. D. Nelson, "Tribes, Territories of," *NIDB* 5:668–76; W. B. Nelson Jr., "Promised Land," in *The Oxford Companion to the Bible* (ed. B. M. Metzger and M. D. Coogan; New York: Oxford University Press, 1993), 619–20. This tradition seems to reflect Egyptian imperial definitions of Canaan, as well as perceptions of its boundaries reflected in second millennium B.C.E. documents. Cf. N. Na'aman, "The Canaanites and Their Land," *UF* 26 (1994): 397–418; idem., "Four Notes on the Size of Late Bronze Age Canaan," *BASOR* 313 (1999): 31–37. Additional biblical texts that seem to exclude Transjordan include Num 13:21; Josh 13:2-6; Ezek 47:13–21; 48:1.

79. Cf. the summary of the academic discussions in J. Milgrom, *Numbers* (JPS Torah Commentary; Philadelphia: The Jewish Publication Society, 1989), 494–96. W. G. Dever takes this view in his recent article, "Earliest Israel: God's Warriors, Revolting Peasants, or Nomadic Hordes?" in *Eretz Israel* 30 (Jerusalem: Israel Exploration Society, 2011), 4–12.

80. Milgrom, *Numbers*, 496.

81. E.g., K. W. Whitelam, *The Invention of Ancient Israel: The Silencing of Palestinian History* (London: Routledge, 1996). Whitelam argues extensively that the biblical accounts provide a foundation narrative for modern Zionism and the modern state of Israel. In his most recent publication, Whitelam argues that the maps in our atlases, general textbooks, and scholarly articles do not represent historical reality, but are constructions of contested knowledge. K. W. Whitelam, "Lines of Power: Mapping Ancient Israel," in *To Break Every Yoke: Essays in Honor of Marvin L. Chaney* (ed. R. B. Coote and N. K. Gottwald; Sheffield: Sheffield Phoenix Press, 2007), 40–79. For a different view on the origin of the lists of tribal allotments, see R. S. Hess, "Asking Historical Questions of Joshua 13–19: Recent Discussion Concerning the Date of the Boundary Lists," in *Faith, Tradition, and History: Old Testament Historiography in Its Near Eastern Context* (ed. A. R. Millard, J. K. Hoffmeier, and D. W. Baker; Winona Lake, Ind.: Eisenbrauns, 1994), 191–205; idem., "A Typology of West Semitic Place Name Lists with Special Reference to Joshua 13–21," *BA* 59:3 (1996): 160–70.

82. See the discussion in ch. 7.

83. W. G. Dever, "Is There Any Archaeological Evidence for the Exodus?" in *Exodus: The Egyptian Evidence* (ed. E. S. Frerichs and L. H. Lesko; Winona Lake, Ind.: Eisenbrauns, 1997), 75.

84. W. G. Dever, "Archaeological Data on the Israelite Settlement: A Review of Two Recent Works," *BASOR* 184 (1991): 88n7 (emphasis mine).

85. E.g., Num 21:25-35; 32:1-2; Deut 2–3; 4:41-49; 29:7-8.

86. Josh 12:1-6; 13:8-32; 17:1-6; Judg 11:19-26; 2 Kgs 3; 1 Chr 7:14.

87. "The Inscription of King Mesha," translated by K. A. D. Smelik (*COS* 2.23.137–38).

88. Num 21:21-31.

89. J. A. Dearman, "Historical Reconstruction and the Mesha Inscription," in *Studies in the Mesha Inscription and Moab* (ed. A. Dearman; Atlanta: Scholars Press, 1989), 208–10. The study of Transjordan has begun to burgeon in recent years. For two excellent introductions, see P. Bienkowski, *Early Edom and Moab* (London: Equinox, 1992); B. MacDonald, *East of the Jordan: Territories and Sites of the Hebrew Scriptures* (Boston: ASOR, 2000).

90. A. Alt, "The Settlement of the Israelites in Palestine," in *Essays on Old Testament History and Religion* (Garden City: Doubleday, 1967), 175–221.

91. Chang-Ho C. Ji, "Settlement Patterns in the Region of Hesban and 'Umeiri, Jordan: A Review of 1973–1992," *NEASB* 43 (1998): 1–21; Ø. S. LaBianca and R. W. Younker, "The Kingdoms of Ammon, Moab and Edom: The Archaeology of Society in Late Bronze/Iron Age Transjordan (ca. 1400–500 BCE)," in *The Archaeology of Society in the Holy Land* (ed. T. E.

Levy; London: Leicester University, 1995), 399–411; E. J. van der Steen, "Aspects of Nomadism and Settlement in the Central Jordan Valley," *PEQ* 127 (1995): 141–58.

92. Chang-Ho C. Ji, "Israelite Settlement in Transjordan: The Relation between the Biblical and Archaeological Evidence," *NEASB* 41 (1996): 61–67.

93. Chang-Ho C. Ji, "Israelite Settlement in Transjordan," 65; E. J. van der Steen, "Survival and Adaptation: Life East of the Jordan in the Transition from the Late Bronze Age to the Early Iron Age," *PEQ* 131 (1999): 176–92.

94. Chang-Ho C. Ji, "The East Jordan Valley during Iron Age I," *PEQ* 129 (1997): 19–32.

95. L. G. Herr, "Tell el-'Umayri and the Madaba Plains Region During the Late Bronze-Iron Age I Transition," in *Mediterranean Peoples in Transition: Thirteenth to Early Tenth Centuries BCE* (ed. S. Gitin, A. Mazar, and E. Stern; Jerusalem: Israel Exploration Society, 1998), 251–64; idem., "The Settlement and Fortification of Tell al-'Umayri in Jordan During the LB/Iron I Transition," in *The Archaeology of Jordan and Beyond: Essays in Honor of James A. Sauer* (ed. L. E. Stager, J. A. Greene, and M. D. Coogan; Studies in the Archaeology and History of the Levant 1; Winona Lake, Ind.: Eisenbrauns, 2000), 167–79.

96. Herr, "The Settlement and Fortification of Tell al-'Umayri in Jordan During the LB/Iron I Transition," 177.

97. F. M. Cross, "Reuben, the Firstborn of Jacob: Sacral Traditions and Early Israelite History," in *From Epic to Canon: History and Literature in Ancient Israel* (Baltimore: Johns Hopkins University Press, 1998), 53–70.

98. L. G. Herr, "Tall al-Umayri and the Reubenite Hypothesis," in *Eretz Israel, Frank Moore Cross Volume* (Jerusalem: Israel Exploration Society, 1999), 64–77. I. Finkelstein has recently challenged this interpretation, arguing that Tell al-'Umayri is a proto-Ammonite site, "Tall al-Umayri in the Iron Age I," in *The Fire Signals of Lachish: Studies in the Archaeology and History of Israel in the Late Bronze Age, Iron Age, and Persian Period in Honor of David Ussishkin* (ed. I. Finkelstein and N. Na'aman; Winona Lake, Ind.: Eisenbrauns, 2011), 113–28. His arguments, however, are based on an adjustment of the chronology of Tell el-'Umayri by over a century, a functionalist interpretation of the architecture at the site, and a hypercritical reading of the biblical evidence, and are not convincing.

99. P. J. Ray Jr., *Tell Hesban and Vicinity in the Iron Age* (Hesban 6; Berrien Springs, Mich.: Andrews University Press and the Institute of Archaeology, 2001), 79–80.

100. R. W. Younker, Constance Clark Gane, and Reem Al-Shqour, "The Madaba Plains Project: Excavations at Tall Jalul," in *The Madaba Plains Project: Forty Years of Archaeological Research in Jordan's Past* (ed. D. R. Clark et al.; London: Equinox, 2011), 58–65.

101. See P. M. Daviau et al., *Excavations at Tall Jawa, Jordan: The Iron Age Town* (CHANE; Leiden: Brill, 2003).

102. A. F. Rainey, "Whence Came the Israelites and Their Language?" *IEJ* 57:1 (2007): 50.

103. J. A. Callaway, "A New Perspective on the Hill Country Settlement of Canaan in Iron Age I," in *Palestine in the Bronze and Iron Ages: Papers in Honour of Olga Tufnell* (ed. J. N. Tubb; London: Institute of Archaeology, 1985), 33–46.

104. On the perception of the Jordan River, see N. Glueck, *The River Jordan* (New York: McGraw-Hill, 1968).

105. See the introduction and bibliography in H. Donner, *The Mosaic Map of Madaba: An Introductory Guide* (Kampen: Kok Pharos, 1992).

106. See the treatment and bibliography in G. W. Bowersock, *Mosaics as History: The Near East from Late Antiquity to Islam* (Cambridge: Belknap Press of Harvard University Press, 2006).

107. Bowersock, *Mosaics as History*, 75.
108. As attested, for example, in Augustine. See G. Bonner, *St. Augustine of Hippo: Life and Controversies* (2d ed.; Norwich, UK: Canterbury Press, 1986); A. W. Matthews, *The Development of St. Augustine from Neoplatonism to Christianity 386–391 A.D.* (Washington, D.C.: University Press of America, 1980).
109. N. Boudraa and J. Krause, *North African Mosaic: A Cultural Reappraisal of Ethnic and Religious Minorities* (London: Cambridge Scholars Publishing, 2007); K. M. D. Dunbabin, *The Mosaics of Roman North Africa: Studies in Iconography and Patronage* (London: Oxford University Press, 1979).
110. See the last three chapters in H. Shanks, ed., *Christianity and Rabbinic Judaism: A Parallel History of Their Origins and Early Development* (Washington, D.C.: Biblical Archaeology Society, 1992).
111. A. F. Rainey and R. S. Notley, *The Sacred Bridge: Carta's Atlas of the Biblical World* (Jerusalem: Carta, 2006), 111–12.
112. L. Stager, "Forging an Identity: The Emergence of Ancient Israel," in *The Oxford History of the Biblical World* (ed. M. D. Coogan; New York: OUP, 1998), 134. M. Broshi, although he estimates the population for the entirety of Iron Age Palestine, including the coastal zones, proposes even higher numbers. He postulates a population of about sixty to seventy thousand in 1200 B.C.E., about one hundred fifty thousand in 1000 B.C.E., and about four hundred thousand by the mid eighth century B.C.E. See M. Broshi, "The Population of Iron Age Palestine," in *Biblical Archaeology Today, 1990, Proceedings of the Second International Congress on Biblical Archaeology; Supplement: Pre-Congress Symposium: Population, Production and Power* (ed. A. Biran and J. Aviram; Jerusalem: Ketepress Enterprises, Ltd., 1993), 14–18.
113. Stager, ibid.

# 7. The Material Culture and Ethnicity of the Highland Settlers

1. Such as pottery forms, architecture, site layout, aniconism, social organization, and burial practices.
2. E. M. Meyers, "Identifying Religious and Ethnic Groups through Archaeology," in *Biblical Archaeology Today, 1990: Proceedings of the Second International Congress on Biblical Jerusalem, June 1990* (ed. J. Aviram and A. Biran; Jerusalem: Israel Exploration Society, 1993) 738–45.
3. G. London, "Ethnicity and Material Culture," in *Near Eastern Archaeology: A Reader* (ed. S. Richard; Winona Lake, Ind.: Eisenbrauns, 2003), 146.
4. Ibid.
5. Ibid., 149.
6. Cf. D. Edelman, "Ethnicity and Early Israel," in *Ethnicity and the Bible* (ed. M. G. Brett: Leiden: Brill, 1996), 25.
7. Ibid.
8. Ibid., 55.
9. N. P. Lemche, *The Israelites in History and Tradition* (Library of Ancient Israel; ed. D. A. Knight; Louisville: Westminster John Knox, 1998), 166.
10. T. L. Thompson, "Defining History and Ethnicity in the South Levant," in *Can a "History of Israel" Be Written?* (ed. L. L. Grabbe; Sheffield: Sheffield Academic Press, 1997), 175.

Notes to Pages 138–40

11. K. L. Noll, *Canaan and Israel in Antiquity: An Introduction* (London: T&T Clark, 2001), 162.

12. I. Finkelstein, "The Emergence of Israel in Canaan: Consensus, Mainstream and Dispute," *SJOT* 2 (1991): 56.

13. I. Finkelstein, "The Emergence of Israel: A Phase in the Cyclic History of Canaan in the Third and Second Millennia BCE," in *From Nomadism to Monarchy: Archaeological and Historical Aspects of Early Israel* (ed. I. Finkelstein and N. Na'aman: Washington, D.C.: Biblical Archaeology Society, 1994), 17.

14. I. Finkelstein, "Pots and People Revisited: Ethnic Boundaries in the Iron Age I," in *The Archaeology of Israel: Constructing the Past, Interpreting the Present* (ed. N. A. Silberman and D. Small; England: Sheffield Academic Press, 1997), 275–85.

15. S. Jones, *The Archaeology of Ethnicity: Constructing Identities in the Past and Present* (London and New York: Routledge, 1997), 40–105.

16. P. Nolan and G. Lenski, *Human Societies: An Introduction to Macrosociology* (11th ed.; Boulder, Colo.: Paradigm, 2009), 29.

17. "Racism," as defined in Merriam-Webster's Collegiate Dictionary, 11th ed.

18. W. G. Dever, "Ethnicity and the Archaeological Record: The Case of Early Israel," in *The Archaeology of Difference: Gender, Ethnicity, Class and the "Other" in Antiquity* (ed. D. R. Edwards and C. T. McCollough; AASOR 60/61, ed. N. Serwint; Boston: American Schools of Oriental Research, 2007), 52.

19. W. G. Dever, "Ethnicity and the Archaeological Record," 52. Cf. Jones, *The Archaeology of Ethnicity*, 106–27.

20. E.g., W. G. Dever, *Who Were the Early Israelites and Where Did They Come From?* (Grand Rapids: Eerdmans, 2003), 101–28; idem., "Ethnicity and the Archaeological Record," 49–66; A. Faust, *Israel's Ethnogenesis: Settlement, Interaction, Expansion and Resistance* (London: Equinox, 2006), 33–107; S. Jones, *The Archaeology of Ethnicity*.

21. See Chapter 6 for data regarding this population increase.

22. V. Fritz, "Israelites and Canaanites: You Can Tell Them Apart," in *Biblical Archaeology Review* 28, No. 4 (July/August 2002): 28–31, 63.

23. See Z. Herzog, "Settlement and Fortification Planning in the Iron Age," in *The Architecture of Ancient Israel: From the Prehistoric to the Persian Periods* (ed. A. Kempinski and R. Reich; Jerusalem: Israel Exploration Society, 1992), 233.

24. E.g., D. H. K. Amiran and Y. Ben-Arieh, "Sedentarization of Bedouin in Israel," *IEJ* 13 (1963): 161–81; A. Faust, *Israel's Ethnogenesis: Settlement, Interaction, Expansion and Resistance* (London: Equinox, 2006), 182; I. Finkelstein, "The Iron Age 'Fortresses' of the Negev Highlands: Sedentarization of the Nomads," *Tel Aviv* 11 (1984): 189–209; idem., *Living on the Fringe: The Archaeology and History of the Negev, Sinai and Neighbouring Regions in the Bronze and Iron Ages* (Sheffield: Sheffield Academic Press, 1995), 46–49; T. E. Levy and A. F. C. Holl, "Migrations, Ethnogenesis, and Settlement Dynamics: Israelites in iron Age Canaan and Shuwa-Arabs in the Chad Basin," *JAA* 21 (2002): 83–118; A. Shmueli, *Nomadism about to Cease* (Tel Aviv: Reshafim, 1980 [Hebrew]), 83, 154–55. Roger Cribb has discussed this same phenomenon in the context of the settlement sites of Iranian nomads. Cf. R. Cribb, *Nomads in Archaeology* (Cambridge: Cambridge University Press, 1991), 149–51.

25. Z. Herzog, "Settlement and Fortification Planning in the Iron Age," 233.

26. D. Edelman, "Ethnicity and Early Israel," in *Ethnicity and the Bible* (ed. M. G. Brett; Leiden: Brill, 1996), 47.

27. Ibid.

28. Finkelstein, *Living on the Fringe*, 46.

29. Herzog, "Settlement and Fortification Planning in the Iron Age," 233.

30. T. E. Levy and A. F. C. Holl, "Migrations, Ethnogenesis, and Settlement Dynamics," 113.

31. A. Musil, *Arabia Petraea III* (Wien: A Hölder, 1908), 131.

32. G. Dalman, *Arbeit und Sitte in Palästina*, VI (Gütersloh: C. Bertelsmann, 1939), ab. 12.

33. Finkelstein, *Living on the Fringe*, 47–48.

34. Musil, *Arabia Petraea III*, 130.

35. I. Finkelstein, *'Izbet Sartah: An Early Iron Age Site near Rosh Ha'ayin, Israel* (BAR International Series 299; Oxford: Oxford University Press, 1986), 121.

36. Fritz, "Israelites and Canaanites: You Can Tell Them Apart," 30.

37. A. Zertal, *The Manasseh Hill Country Survey*, vol. 1: *The Shechem Syncline*. Culture and History of the Ancient Near East, vol. 21 (Leiden: Brill, 2004), 56.

38. Zertal, *The Manasseh Hill Country Survey*, 56.

39. R. D. Miller, III, "A Gazetteer of Iron I Sites in the North-Central Highlands of Palestine," in *Preliminary Excavation Reports and Other Archaeological Investigations: Tell Qarqur, Iron I Sites in the North-Central Highlands of Palestine*. Annual of the American Schools of Oriental Research 56 (ed. Nancy Lapp; Boston: American Schools of Oriental Research, 1999), 55–68.

40. Ibid., 68.

41. Cf. esp. Y. Shiloh, "The Four-Room House: Its Situation and Function in the Israelite City," *IEJ* 20 (1970): 180–90.

42. Y. Shiloh, "The Casemate Wall, the Four Room House, and Early Planning in the Israelite City," *BASOR* 268 (1987): 3.

43. L. E. Stager, "The Archaeology of the Family in Ancient Israel," in *BASOR* 260 (1985): 17.

44. J. S. Holladay Jr., "House, Israelite," in *ABD* 3:308–318. Holladay's study also made a "socioeconomic analysis," in which the author also noted ideological factors in the structure of the four-room house, pp. 316–17.

45. E.g., J. S. Holladay, "Four Room House," *OEANE* 2:337–41; G. E. Wright, "A Characteristic North Israelite House," in *Archaeology in the Levant: Essays for Kathleen Kenyon* (Warminster: Aris & Philips, 1978), 149–54.

46. For additional examples and further discussion, see A. Mazar, "The Iron Age Dwellings at Tell Qasile," in *Exploring the Longue Durée: Essays in Honor of Lawrence E. Stager* (ed. J. D. Schloen; Winona Lake, Ind.: Eisenbrauns, 2009), 319–36.

47. M. M. Ibrahim, "Third Season of Excavation at Sahab, 1975 (Preliminary Report)," *ADAJ* 20 (1975): 72.

48. Ibid., 73.

49. N. P. Lemche, *The Israelites in History and Tradition* (ed. D. A. Knight; Louisville: Westminster John Knox, 1998), 32.

50. G. W. Ahlström, "Giloh: A Judahite or Canaanite Settlement," *IEJ* 34 (1984): 171.

51. E.g., E. Bloch-Smith, "Israelite Ethnicity in Iron I: Archaeology Preserves What Is Remembered and What Is Forgotten in Israel's History," *JBL* 122/3 (2003): 408–409.

52. E.g., R. B. Coote and K. W. Whitelam, *The Emergence of Early Israel in Historical Perspective* (2d ed.; Sheffield: Sheffield Phoenix Press, 2010), 125–26; N. P. Lemche, *The Israelites in History and Tradition*, 32; R. D. Nelson, *Joshua* (Louisville: Westminster John Knox, 1997), 4; K. L. Noll, *Canaan and Israel in Antiquity: An Introduction* (London: T&T Clark, 2001), 162.

53. D. Edelman, "Ethnicity and Early Israel," in *Ethnicity and the Bible* (ed. M. G. Brett; Leiden: Brill, 1996), 44.

54. See M. M. Ibrahim, "Third Season of Excavation at Sahab, 1975 (Preliminary Report)," figs. 1–2.

55. J. B. Humbert, "Keisan, Tell," *NEAEHL* 3:865–66.

56. E. Netzer, "Domestic Architecture in the Iron Age," in *The Architecture of Ancient Israel: From the Prehistoric to the Persian Periods* (ed. A. Kempinski and R. Reich; Jerusalem: Israel Exploration Society, 1992), 193–99.

57. Cf. L. G. Herr, "The Settlement and Fortification of Tell al-'Umayri in Jordan during the LB/Iron I Transition," in *The Archaeology of Jordan and Beyond: Essays in Honor of James A. Sauer* (ed. L. E. Stager, J. A. Greene, and M. D. Coogan; Winona Lake, Ind.: Eisenbrauns, 2000), 178; Chang-Ho C. Ji, "The Iron I in Central and Northern Transjordan: An Interim Summary of Archaeological Data," *PEQ* 127 (1995): 122–40; idem., "A Note on the Four-Room House in Palestine," *Orientalia* 66 (1997): 387–413; idem., "The East Jordan Valley during Iron Age I," *PEQ* 129 (1997): 19–37.

58. L. G. Herr and D. R. Clark, "Excavating the Tribe of Reuben: A Four-Room House Provides a Clue to Where the Oldest Israelite Tribe Settled," *BAR* 27.2 (2001): 36–47, 64–66.

59. P. M. M. Daviau, *Excavations at Tall Jawa, Jordan: The Iron Age Town* (Culture and History of the Ancient Near East; Leiden: Brill, 2003).

60. L. G. Herr, "Mudeina el-'Aliya, Khirbet el," *NEAEHL* 5:1846.

61. I. M. Swinnen, "The Iron Age I Settlement and Its Residential Houses at al-Lahun in Moab, Jordan," *BASOR* 354 (2009): 29–53.

62. S. Hart, "Excavations at Ghrareh, 1986: Preliminary Report," *Levant* 20 (1988): 98.

63. P. M. M. Daviau, "Domestic Architecture in Iron Age Ammon: Building Materials, Construction Techniques, and Room Arrangement," in *Ancient Ammon* (ed. B. Macdonald and R. W. Younker; Leiden: Brill, 1999), 132.

64. L. G. Herr, "Mudeina el-'Aliya, Khirbet el," *NEAEHL* 5:1846.

65. D. Homès-Fredericq, "Late Bronze and Iron Age Evidence from Lehun in Moab," in *Early Edom and Moab: The Beginning of the Iron Age in Southern Jordan* (ed. P. Bienkowski; Sheffield Archaeological Monographs 7; Sheffield: Sheffield Academic Press, 1992), 187–202.

66. Hart, "Excavations at Ghrareh, 1986: Preliminary Report," fig. 3.

67. Ibid., 98.

68. Ø. S. LaBianca and R. W. Younker, "The Kingdoms of Ammon, Moab and Edom: The Archaeology of Society in Late Bronze/Iron Age Transjordan (ca. 1400–500 BCE)," in *The Archaeology of Society in the Holy Land* (ed. T. E. Levy; New York: Facts on File, 1995), 406–7.

69. A. Dearman, "Settlement Patterns and the Beginning of the Iron Age in Moab," in *Early Edom and Moab: The Beginning of the Iron Age in Southern Jordan* (ed. P. Bienkowski; Sheffield: J. R. Collis, 1992), 65–76.

70. LaBianca and Younker, "The Kingdoms of Ammon, Moab and Edom," 406–8.

71. Ø. S. LaBianca, *Sedentarization and Nomadization: Food System Cycles at Hesban and Vicinity in Transjordan* (Hesban 1; Berrien Springs, Mich.: Institute of Archaeology and Andrews University Press, 1990), 38–43. This phenomenon will be discussed in greater detail in ch. 10.

72. B. Halpern, "The Exodus from Egypt: Myth or Reality?" in *The Rise of Ancient Israel* (ed. H. Shanks; Washington, D.C.: Biblical Archaeology Society, 1992), 103–4.

73. Faust, *Israel's Ethnogenesis*, 224.

74. J. R. Kautz, "Tracking the Ancient Moabites," *BA* 44 (1981): 33.

75. M. Bietak, "An Iron Age Four-Room House in Ramesside Egypt," *Eretz-Israel* 23 (1992): 10–12.

76. In the case of the house having belonged to Shasu prisoners, Bietak supposes that the Israelites may have coalesced from the Shasu.

77. "Yigal Shiloh: Last Thoughts," Part 2, *BAR* 14.2 (1988): 42.
78. W. G. Dever, *Who Were the Early Israelites and Where Did They Come From?* (Grand Rapids: Eerdmans, 2003), 105.
79. A. Faust and S. Bunimovitz, "The Four Room House: Embodying Iron Age Israelite Society," *NEA* 66.1–2 (2003): 25.
80. S. Bunimovitz and A. Faust, "Ideology in Stone: Understanding the Four-Room House," *BAR* 28.4 (2002): 36.
81. Ibid.
82. S. Bunimovitz and A. Faust, "Building Identity: The Four-Room House and the Israelite Mind," in *Symbiosis, Symbolism, and the Power of the Past: Canaan, Ancient Israel, and Their Neighbors from the Late Bronze Age through Roman Palestina* (William G. Dever and Seymour Gitin, eds.; Winona Lake, Ind.: Eisenbrauns, 2003), 415–19.
83. Ibid., 415.
84. Ibid., 416.
85. Ibid., 417.
86. Ibid., 417–18.
87. M. Douglas, *Purity and Danger: An Analysis of the Concept of Pollution and Taboo* (London: Routledge, 2002).
88. Bunimovitz and Faust, "Building Identity: The Four-Room House and the Israelite Mind," 419.
89. Ibid.
90. A. E. Killebrew, *Biblical Peoples and Ethnicity: An Archaeological Study of Egyptians, Canaanites, Philistines, and Early Israel, 1300–1100 B.C.E.* (Atlanta: Society of Biblical Literature, 2005), 177.
91. For illustrations of these vessel types, cf. Killebrew, *Biblical Peoples and Ethnicity*, 177.
92. H. Kjaer, "The Excavation of Shiloh 1929," *JPOS* 10 (1930): 87–174.
93. W. F. Albright, "Further Light on the History of Israel from Lachish and Megiddo," *BASOR* 68 (1937): 22–25; idem., "Book Reviews," *AJA* 44 (1940): 548; idem., *The Archaeology of Palestine* (Gloucester, Mass.: Peter Smith, 1971), 118.
94. Y. Aharoni, "New Aspects of the Israelite Occupation in the North," in *Near Eastern Archaeology in the Twentieth Century: Essays in Honor of Nelson Glueck* (ed. J. A. Sanders; New York: Doubleday, 1970), 263–64.
95. R. Engberg, "Historical Analysis of Archaeological Evidence: Megiddo and the Song of Deborah," *BASOR* 78 (1940): 4–9.
96. D. L. Esse, "The Collared Store Jar: Scholarly Ideology and Ceramic Typology," *SJOT* 2 (1991): 103–4.
97. M. Artzy, "Nami, Tel," in *NEAEHL* 3:1097; idem., *IEJ* 40 (1990): 76. At Tel Nami the vessel is used as a burial jar.
98. Y. Yadin, *Hazor I: The First Season, 1955* (Jerusalem: Magnes, 1958), pl. 130:2.
99. P. Beck and M. Kochavi, "A Dated Assemblage of the Late 13th Century B.C.E. from the Egyptian Residency at Aphek," *Tel Aviv* 12 (1985): 40.
100. G. Edelstein and I. Milevski, "The Rural Settlement of Jerusalem Reevaluated: Surveys and Excavations in the Reph'aim Valley and Mevasseret Yerushalayim," *PEQ* 126 (1994): 15.
101. J. Seger, *Gezer V: The Field I Caves* (ed. J. D. Seger and H. D. Lance; Jerusalem: Hebrew Union College, 1988), pls. 16:1; 25:1; 29:1.
102. F. W. James and P. E. McGovern, *The Late Bronze Egyptian Garrison at Beth Shan: A Study of Levels VII and VIII* (Philadelphia: University of Pennsylvania Museum of Archaeology and Anthropology, 1994), fig. 14:2; N. P. Cohen and A. Mazar, eds., *Excavations at Tel*

*Beth-Shean 1989–1996*, vol. III: *The 13–11th Century B.C.E. Strata in Areas N and S* (Jerusalem: Israel Exploration Society, 2009), 231–42.

103. H. J. Franken, *Excavations at Tell Deir 'Alla: The Late Bronze Age Sanctuary* (Louvain: Peeters, 1992), fig. 5-16.

104. M. M. Ibrahim, "Sahab," *OEANE* 4:451.

105. M. M. Ibrahim, "The Collared-Rim Jar of the Early Iron Age," in *Archaeology in the Levant: Essays for Kathleen Kenyon* (Warminster: Aris & Philips, 1978), 116–26.

106. I. Finklestein, *The Archaeology of the Israelite Settlement* (Jerusalem: Israel Exploration Society, 1988), 283–84; A. Kempinski, "The Overlap of Cultures at the End of the Late Bronze Age and the Beginning of the Iron Age," in *Eretz-Israel* (Nahman Avigad Volume) 18 (1985): 399–407 (Hebrew). Derivation from a prior style would not preclude the vessel having been an Israelite innovation. At the time of his writing, Finkelstein thought the collared-rim jar was peculiar to the Israelites.

107. D. Wengrow, "Egyptian Taskmasters and Heavy Burdens: Highland Exploitation and the Collared-Rim Pithos of the Bronze/Iron Age Levant," *OJA* 15 (1996): 307–26.

108. A. Kempinski, "How Profoundly Canaanized were the Early Israelites?" *Zeitschrift des Deutschen Palästina-Vereins* 108 (1992): 6.

109. E. Yannai, "The Origin and Distribution of the Collared-Rim Pithos and Krater: A Case of Conservative Pottery Production in the Ancient Near East from the Fourth to the First Millennium BCE," in *"I Will Speak the Riddles of Ancient Times": Archaeological and Historical Studies in Honor of Amihai Mazar on the Occasion of His Sixtieth Birthday* (ed. A. M. Maeir and P. de Miroschedji; Winona Lake, Ind.: Eisenbrauns, 2006), 89–112.

110. A. Zertal, "The Water Factor during the Israelite Settlement Process in Canaan," in *Society and Economy in the Eastern Mediterranean (c. 1500–1000 B.C.): Proceedings of the International Symposium Held at the University of Haifa from the 28th of April to the 2nd of May 1985* (OLA 23; Leuven: Peeters, 1988), 341–52.

111. Ibrahim, "The Collared-Rim Jar of the Early Iron Age," 122.

112. L. G. Herr et al., "Madaba Plains Project: The 1989 Excavations at Tell el-'Umeiri and Vicinity," *ADAJ* 35 (1991): 159. In the four-room house at Tell el-'Umeiri, the broadroom contained the remains of twenty smashed collared-rim jars that lined the walls of the room, with tens of thousands of barley seeds scattered about, some from the base of a collared-rim jar. See L. Herr, "Excavation and Cumulative Results," in *The 1994 Season at Tall al-'Umayri and Subsequent Studies* (vol. 5 of Madaba Plains Project; ed. L. G. Herr et al.; Berrien Springs, Mich.: Andrews University Press, 2002), 11.

113. G. London, "Ethnicity and Material Culture," in *Near Eastern Archaeology: A Reader* (ed. S. Richard; Winona Lake, Ind.: Eisenbrauns, 2003), 148–49; cf. also idem., "A Comparison of Two Contemporaneous Lifestyles of the Late Second Millennium B.C.," *BASOR* 273 (1989): 37–55. Other archaeologists have concurred, e.g., W. G. Dever, "How to Tell a Canaanite from an Israelite," in *The Rise of Ancient Israel* (ed. H. Shanks; Washington, D.C.: Biblical Archaeology Society, 1992), 43–44.

114. E.g., E. Bloch-Smith, "Israelite Ethnicity in Iron I," 409; I. Finkelstein, "Ethnicity and the Origin of the Iron I Settlers in the Highlands of Canaan: Can the Real Israel Stand Up?" *BA* 59.4 (1996): 204; Dever, "How to Tell a Canaanite from an Israelite," 44; A. Mazar, "Jerusalem and Its Vicinity in Iron Age I," in *From Nomadism to Monarchy: Archaeological and Historical Aspects of Early Israel* (ed. I. Finkelstein and N. Na'aman; Jerusalem: Yad Ben-Zvi, 1994), 88.

115. E.g., R. B. Coote and K. W. Whitelam, *The Emergence of Early Israel in Historical Perspective* (2d ed.; Sheffield: Sheffield Phoenix Press, 2010), 124–25; D. Edelman, "Ethnicity and Early Israel," in *Ethnicity and the Bible* (ed. M. Brett; Leiden: Brill, 2002), 42–43;

N. P. Lemche, *The Israelites in History and Tradition*, 32; R. D. Nelson, *Joshua* (OTL; Louisville: Westminster John Knox, 1997), 4.

116. A. Faust, *Israel's Ethnogenesis: Settlement, Interaction, Expansion and Resistance* (London: Equinox, 2006), 194.

117. M. Dothan, "The Excavations at 'Afula," *'Atiqot* 1 (1955): 36.

118. Faust, *Israel's Ethnogenesis*, 195.

119. E.g., G. W. Ahlström, *The History of Ancient Palestine* (Minneapolis: Fortress, 1993), 338; E. Bloch-Smith, "Israelite Ethnicity in Iron I," 408; D. Edelman, "Ethnicity and Early Israel," 42.

120. Even the recent arguments of Yannai, "The Origin and Distribution of the Collared-Rim Pithos and Krater," 89–112, gloss over this issue. While he shows that various styles of collared-rim pithoi were in existence in Anatolia, Cyprus, western Syria, and Israel from the Chalcolithic period to the early Iron Age, his data also reinforce the fact that variations on body styles and decorative traditions also develop, come to predominate, and wane in various geographic areas as well. Most of Yannai's examples from the Late Bronze Age are from coastal Syria and Cyprus. The discussion about collared-rim jars in Cisjordan and Transjordan is the study of regional developments and stylistic emphases.

121. For references, see Killebrew, *Biblical Peoples and Ethnicity*, 177.

122. A. Mazar, *Excavations at Tell Qasile*, Part 2: *The Philistine Sanctuary: Various Finds, the Pottery, Conclusions, Appendixes* (Qedem 20; Jerusalem: Hebrew University of Jerusalem, 1985), 57–58.

123. A. Cohen-Weinberger and S. R. Wolff, "Production Centers of Collared-Rim Pithoi from Sites in the Carmel Coast and Ramat Menashe Regions," in *Studies in the Archaeology of Israel and Neighboring Lands* (SAOC 59; American Schools of Oriental Research Books 5; Chicago: Oriental Institute of the University of Chicago; Atlanta: American Schools of Oriental Research, 2001), 639–57.

124. A. E. Killebrew, "The Collared Pithos in Context: A Typological, Technological, and Functional Reassessment," in *Studies in the Archaeology of Israel and Neighboring Lands* (SAOC 59; American Schools of Oriental Research Books 5; Chicago: Oriental Institute of the University of Chicago; Atlanta: American Schools of Oriental Research, 2001), 377–98.

125. Killebrew, "The Collared Pithos in Context," 389–91.

126. L. G. Herr, "Tell el-'Umaryi and the Madaba Plains Region during the late Bronze-Iron Age I Transition," in *Mediterranean Peoples in Transition: Thirteenth to Early Tenth Centuries B.C.E.* (ed. S. Gitin, A. Mazar, and E. Stern; Jerusalem: Israel Exploration Society, 1998), 256.

127. L. G. Herr, "The History of the Collared Pithos at Tell el-'Umeiri, Jordan," in *Studies in the Archaeology of Israel and Neighboring Lands* (SAOC 59; American Schools of Oriental Research Books 5; Chicago: Oriental Institute of the University of Chicago; Atlanta: American Schools of Oriental Research, 2001), 237–50. The late Iron Age I was not represented at Tell el-'Umayri, but Herr suggests that the typological development of the collared-rim jar would have continued during this period. Based on the changes that had occurred by early Iron Age II, he suggests that in the late Iron Age I the vessel was probably characterized by a shortening of the neck and collar and reducing the significance of the rim.

128. L. G. Herr, "Tell el-'Umaryi and the Madaba Plains Region During the late Bronze-Iron Age I Transition," 256–57.

129. Killebrew, "The Collared Pithos in Context," 391.

130. J. A. Callaway, "A New Perspective on the Hill Country Settlement of Canaan in Iron Age I," in *Palestine in the Bronze and Iron Ages: Papers in Honour of Olga Tufnell* (ed. J. N. Tubb; London: Institute of Archaeology, University of London, 1985), 31–49.

131. Ibid., 31–49; cf. also idem., "Ai (et-Tell): Problem Site for Biblical Archaeologists," in *Archaeology and Biblical Interpretation: Essays in Memory of D. Glenn Rose* (ed. L. G. Perdue, L. E. Toombs, and G. L. Johnson; Atlanta: John Knox Press, 1987), 95–97.

132. W. G. Dever, "Ceramics, Ethnicity, and the Question of Israel's Origins," *BA* 58 (1995): 204–7; idem., "Is There Any Archaeological Evidence for the Exodus?" in *Exodus: The Egyptian Evidence* (ed. E. Frerichs and L. H. Lesko; Winona Lake, Ind: Eisenbrauns, 1997), 73–80; idem., *Who Were the Early Israelites and Where Did They Come From?* (Grand Rapids: Eerdmans, 2003); J. M. Miller, "The Israelite Occupation of Canaan," in *Israelite and Judaean History* (ed. J. H. Hayes and J. M. Miller; Philadelphia: Trinity Press International, 1977), 255.

133. D. Edelman, "Ethnicity and Early Israel," 44.

134. Cf. W. G. Dever, "Ceramics, Ethnicity, and the Question of Israel's Origins," 202–206; idem., *Who Were the Early Israelites and Where Did They Come From?* 122–23.

135. W. G. Dever, "Earliest Israel: God's Warriors, Revolting Peasants, or Nomadic Hordes?" in *Eretz-Israel* 30 (Jerusalem: Israel Exploration Society, 2011), 5.

136. E.g., R. E. Hendrix, P. R. Drey, and J. B. Storfjell, *Ancient Pottery of Transjordan: An Introduction Utilizing Published Whole Forms, Late Neolithic through Late Islamic* (Berrien Springs, Mich.: Institute of Archaeology/Horn Archaeological Museum, 1996).

137. D. R. Clark and G. A. London, "Investigating Ancient Ceramic Traditions on Both Sides of the Jordan," in *The Archaeology of Jordan and Beyond: Essays in Honor of James A. Sauer* (Studies in the Archaeology and History of the Levant 1; ed. L. E. Stager, J. A. Greene, and M. D. Coogan; Winona Lake, Ind.: Eisenbrauns, 2000), 100–10.

138. First published in A. F. Rainey and R. S. Notley, *The Sacred Bridge: Carta's Atlas of the Biblical World* (Jerusalem: Carta, 2006), 130. An updated version was published in A. F. Rainey, "Whence Came the Israelites and Their Language?" *IEJ* 57.1 (2007): 51.

139. Rainey, "Whence Came the Israelites and Their Language?" 50.

140. Dever, "Earliest Israel," 6.

141. Ibid.

142. E. J. van der Steen, "The Central East Jordan Valley in the Late Bronze and Early Iron Ages," *BASOR* 302 (1996): 51–74.

143. W. G. Dever, "Earliest Israel," 6.

144. H. J. Franken and J. Kalsbeek, *Excavations at Tell Deir 'Allā: A Stratigraphical and Analytical Study of the Early Iron Age Pottery* (Leiden: Brill, 1969), 119.

145. Herr, "Tell el-'Umayri and the Madaba Plains Region During the late Bronze-Iron Age I Transition," 256.

146. Ø. S. LaBianca, "Sociocultural Anthropology and Syro-Palestinian Archaeology," in *Benchmarks in Time and Culture: An Introduction to Palestinian Archaeology. Essays in Honor of Joseph A. Callaway* (ed. Joel F. Drinkard Jr., Gerald L. Mattingly, and J. Maxwell Miller; Atlanta: Scholars Press, 1988), 375–77.

147. LaBianca, "Sociocultural Anthropology and Syro-Palestinian Archaeology," 377.

148. LaBianca, *Sedentarization and Nomadization*, 244.

149. Gary A. Herion, "The Impact of Modern and Social Science Assumptions on the Reconstruction of Israelite History," in *Journal for the Study of the Old Testament* 34 (1986): 3–33.

150. LaBianca, *Sedentarization and Nomadization*, 245.

151. D. C. Hopkins, *The Highlands of Canaan: Agricultural Life in the Early Iron Age* (Decatur, Ga.: Almond Press, 1985), 137.

152. Hopkins, *The Highlands of Canaan*, 168.

153. O. Borowski, *Agriculture in Iron Age Israel* (Boston, Mass.: American Schools of Oriental Research, 2002), 6–7.

154. Finkelstein, *Archaeology of the Israelite Settlement*, 268–69.
155. E. Firmage, "Zoology (Animal Profiles)," *ABD* 4:1133.
156. LaBianca, *Sedentarization and Nomadization*, especially chs. 1–2.
157. Borowski, *Agriculture in Iron Age Israel*, 5.
158. Ibid., 6.
159. Ibid., 71–82.
160. See, however, E. Firmage, "Zoology (Animal Profiles)," 1134, who suggests that "it may be that the author(s) of the biblical dietary law took a pre-existing avoidance of pork and incorporated it into a systematic ideological superstructure."
161. I. Finkelstein, "Pots and People Revisited: Ethnic Boundaries in the Iron Age I," in *Ethnicity and the Bible* (ed. Mark G. Brett; Leiden: E. J. Brill, 1996), 227.
162. Ibid., 228.
163. Ibid., 230.
164. Ibid., 230.
165. Ibid. Finkelstein argues that most real "ethnic" features only came later, and were invented by the monarchy, "because the new state controlled vast areas with mixed elements. It was essential to unite them by creating a sense of nationalism and ethnic identity."
166. Faust, *Israel's Ethnogenesis*, 11–29.
167. F. Barth, "Ethnic Groups and Boundaries," in *Ethnic Groups and Boundaries: The Social Organization of Culture Difference* (Bergen: Universitets-Forlag and Boston: Little, Brown, 1969), 299.
168. Barth, "Ethnic Groups and Boundaries," 296.
169. Cf. J. Goldingay, "Covenant, OT and NT," *NIDB* 1:770–72. See also G. E. Mendenhall, *Law and Covenant in Israel and the Ancient Near East* (Pittsburgh, Pa.: Presbyterian Board of Colportage of Western Pennsylvania, 1955).
170. See G. E. Mendenhall, *Law and Covenant in Israel and the Ancient Near East* (Pittsburgh, Pa.: Presbyterian Board of Colportage of Western Pennsylvania, 1955).
171. G. E. Mendenhall, *Ancient Israel's Faith and History: An Introduction to the Bible in Context* (ed. G. A. Herion; Louisville: Westminster John Knox Press, 2001), 55–70.
172. F. A. Spina, "Reversal of Fortune: Rahab the Israelite and Achan the Canaanite," *BR* 17.4 (2001): 24–30, 53–54.
173. Numerous commentators have observed the importance of the stories of Rahab and Achan and include eloquent discussions of them. See, for example, the recent discussions of L. D. Hawk, *Joshua* (Berit Olam: Studies in Hebrew Narrative and Poetry; ed. D. W. Cotter; Collegeville, Minn.: Liturgical Press, 2000), 19–33; M. S. Ziese, *Joshua* (NIV Commentary; Joplin, Mo.: College Press, 2008), 79–98.
174. R. K. Hawkins, "From Disparate Tribes to 'All Israel,'" *NEASB* 50 (2005): 27–39.

# 8. 'Izbet Sartah: A Prototypical Israelite Settlement Site

1. A. Zertal, *The Israelite Settlement in the Hill Country of Manasseh* (Haifa, 1988), 24–26.
2. Map ref. 14675/16795.
3. See A. Eitan, "Aphek (in Sharon)," *NEAEHL* 1:62–64; P. Beck and M. Kochavi, "Excavations in the 1970s and 1980s," *NEAEHL* 1:64–72.
4. I. Finkelstein, *'Izbet Sartah: An Early Iron Age Site near Rosh Ha'ayin, Israel* (BAR International Series 299; Oxford: Oxford University Press, 1986).
5. For a discussion of the traits that suggest this, see ch. 7.

6. E. Netzer, "Domestic Architecture in the Iron Age," in *The Architecture of Ancient Israel: From the Prehistoric to the Persian Periods* (ed. A. Kempinski and R. Reich; Jerusalem: Israel Exploration Society, 1992), 193–201; Z. Herzog, "Settlement and Fortification Planning in the Iron Age," in *The Architecture of Ancient Israel: From the Prehistoric to the Persian Periods* (ed. A. Kempinski and R. Reich; Jerusalem: Israel Exploration Society, 1992), 231–74.

7. See M. D. Green, "Shephelah," *NIDB* 5:228.

8. The Late Mycenaean IIIB falls within Palestine's Late Bronze Age, and tend to be found specifically in Late Bronze IIB strata (1300–1200 B.C.E.). For further discussion of imported Mycenaean pottery, see R. Amiran, *Ancient Pottery of the Holy Land: From the Beginning of the Neolithic Period to the End of the Iron Age* (New Jersey: Rutgers University Press, 1970), 179–86.

9. I. Finkelstein, "Pottery and Stone Artifacts," in *'Izbet Sartah: An Early Iron Age Site near Rosh Ha'ayin, Israel* (ed. I Finkelstein; BAR International Series 299; Oxford: Oxford University Press, 1986), 45ff.

10. See the discussion on pottery in ch. 7.

11. A. Demsky, "The 'Izbet Sartah Ostracon Ten Years Later," in *'Izbet Sartah: An Early Iron Age Site near Rosh Ha'ayin, Israel* (ed. I. Finkelstein; BAR International Series 299; Oxford: Oxford University Press, 1986), 104–5.

12. A. Dotan reconstructed these lines as an exercise that consisted of three short sentences that dealt with the bringing of food, drink, and clothing to a certain individual. Cf. A. Dotan, "New Light on the 'Izbet Sartah Ostracon," *Tel Aviv* 8 (1981): 160–72.

13. A. Demsky, "A Proto-Canaanite Abecedary Dating from the Period of the Judges and Its Implications for the History of the Alphabet," *Tel Aviv* 4 (1977): 14–27; J. Naveh, "Some Considerations on the Ostracon from Izbet Sartah," *IEJ* 28 (1978): 31–35.

14. A. Millard, "An Assessment of the Evidence for Writing in Ancient Israel," in *Biblical Archaeology Today: Proceedings of the International Congress on Biblical Archaeology, Jerusalem, April 1984* (ed. J. Amitai; Jerusalem: Israel Exploration Society, 1985), 301–12. On abcedaries in general, see "Abecedaries," by A. Demsky (*COS* 1.107:362–65).

15. A mid-tenth-century B.C.E. abecedary was discovered at Tel Zayit in 2005. This, along with the Gezer Calender, remains the earliest writing in Canaan to diverge from Phoenician (Paleo-Hebrew), which makes them the earliest ancestors of Hebrew. For the Gezer Calender, cf. K. L. Sparks, *Ancient Texts for the Study of the Hebrew Bible: A Guide to the Background Literature* (Peabody, Mass.: Hendrickson, 2005), 450. For the Tel Zayit inscription, cf. R. E. Tappy et al., "An Abecedary of the Mid-Tenth Century from the Judaean Shephelah," *BASOR* 344 (2006): 5–46; R. E. Tappy and P. K. McCarter Jr., eds., *Literate Culture and Tenth-Century Canaan: The Tel Zayit Abecedary in Context* (Winona Lake, Ind.: Eisenbrauns, 2008).

16. R. Giveon, "An Egyptian Scarab of the 20th Dynasty," in *'Izbet Sartah: An Early Iron Age Site near Rosh Ha'ayin, Israel* (ed. I. Finkelstein; BAR International Series 299; Oxford: Oxford University Press, 1986), 104–5.

17. Finkelstein surveys a number of these. Cf. I. Finkelstein, "Architectural Analysis," in *'Izbet Sartah: An Early Iron Age Site near Rosh Ha'ayin, Israel* (ed. I. Finkelstein; BAR International Series 299; Oxford: Oxford University Press, 1986), 106–9.

18. As was the case at Ai, Tell en-Nasbeh, and Beer-sheba VII.

19. Finkelstein, "Architectural Analysis," 114.

20. The traditional 5-by-5-meter excavation square.

21. See Z. Herzog, "Settlement and Fortification Planning in the Iron Age," in *The Architecture of Ancient Israel: From the Prehistoric to the Persian Periods* (ed. A. Kempinski and R. Reich; Jerusalem: Israel Exploration Society, 1992), 233.

22. E.g., A. Faust, *Israel's Ethnogenesis: Settlement, Interaction, Expansion and Resistance* (London: Equinox, 2006), 182; I. Finkelstein, "The Iron Age 'Fortresses' of the Negev Highlands: Sedentarization of the Nomads," *Tel Aviv* 11 (1984): 189–209; idem., *Living on the Fringe: The Archaeology and History of the Negev, Sinai and Neighbouring Regions in the Bronze and Iron Ages* (Sheffield: Sheffield Academic Press, 1995), 46–49; T. E. Levy and A. F. C. Holl, "Migrations, Ethnogenesis, and Settlement Dynamics: Israelites in Iron Age Canaan and Shuwa-Arabs in the Chad Basin," *JAA* 21 (2002): 83–118; A. Shmueli, *Nomadism about to Cease* (Tel Aviv: Reshafim, 1980 [Hebrew]), 83, 154–55. Roger Cribb has discussed this same phenomenon in the context of the settlement sites of Iranian nomads. Cf. R. Cribb, *Nomads in Archaeology* (Cambridge: Cambridge University Press, 1991), 149–51.

23. J. D. Seger, "Halif, Tel," *NEAEHL*, 2553–59.

24. S. Bunimovitz and Z. Lederman, "Beth-Shemesh," *NEAEHL* 1:249–53.

25. I. Finkelstein, *The Archaeology of the Israelite Settlement* (Jerusalem: Israel Exploration Society, 1988), 264–69.

26. Ibid., 266.

27. D. H. K. Amiran and Y. Ben-Arieh, "Sedentarization of Bedouin in Israel," *IEJ* 13 (1963): 168.

28. Finkelstein, *The Archaeology of the Israelite Settlement*, 266.

29. B. Rosen, "Subsistence Economy of Stratum II," in *'Izbet Sartah: An Early Iron Age Site near Rosh Ha'ayin, Israel* (ed. I. Finkelstein; BAR International Series 299; Oxford: Oxford University Press, 1986), 171.

30. S. Hellwing and Y. Adjeman, "Animal Bones," in *'Izbet Sartah: An Early Iron Age Site near Rosh Ha'ayin, Israel* (ed. I. Finkelstein; BAR International Series 299; Oxford: Oxford University Press, 1986), 144.

31. Ibid., 145.

32. Exod 29:22; Lev 7:28-36. While critical scholars have traditionally regarded Exodus and Leviticus as being comprised of P and non-P materials, which are both generally seen as having a late date, both of these sources may have recorded more ancient traditions.

33. As per Lev 11:7; Deut 14:8. See the caveat in the preceding note. Similarly, D is conventionally assigned to a later period by critical scholars, but it may have recorded more ancient traditions.

34. Rosen, "Subsistence Economy of Stratum II," 174–80.

35. Most recently, see W. G. Dever, *Who Were the Early Israelites and Where Did They Come From?* (Grand Rapids: Eerdmans, 2003), 193.

36. W. G. Dever, "Archaeological Data on the Israelite Settlement: A Review of Two Recent Works," *BASOR* 284 (1991): 79.

37. A. Mazar, "The Iron Age Dwellings at Tell Qasile," in *Exploring the Longue Durée: Essays in Honor of Lawrence E. Stager* (ed. J. D. Schloen; Winona Lake, Ind.: Eisenbrauns, 2009), 334.

38. G. W. Ahlström, *Who Were the Israelites?* (Winona Lake, Ind.: Eisenbrauns, 1986), 31.

39. I. Finkelstein, "Historical Conclusions," in *'Izbet Sartah: An Early Iron Age Site near Rosh Ha'ayin, Israel* (ed. I. Finkelstein; BAR International Series 299; Oxford: Oxford University Press, 1986), 202.

40. The description of its allotment can be found in Josh 16:5-9; 17:7-10a.

41. Finkelstein, *The Archaeology of the Israelite Settlement*, 119–204.

42. Ibid., 264–69.

43. P. Beck and M. Kochavi, "Aphek, Excavations in the 1970s and 1980s," *NEAEHL* 1:64–72.

44. See R. E. Tappy, P. K. McCarter, M. J. Lundberg, B. Zuckerman, "An Abecedary of the Mid-Tenth Century B.C.E. from the Judaean Shephelah," *BASOR* 344 (2006): 5–46; R. E. Tappy and P. K. McCarter, *Literate Culture and Tenth-Century Canaan: The Tel Zayit Abecedary in Context* (Winona Lake, Ind.: Eisenbrauns, 2008).

45. C. F. Keil, *The Lamentations of Jeremiah*, vol. 8 (trans. J. Kennedy; Edinburgh: T&T Clark, 1865–1892), 466–67.

46. For bibliography on Kuntillit Ajrud, see K. L. Sparks, *Ancient Texts for the Study of the Hebrew Bible*, 450–52.

47. "Abecedaries," by A. Demsky (*COS* 1.107:363).

48. A. Demsky and M. Kochavi, "An Alphabet from the Days of the Judges," *BAR* 4.3 (1978): 24. The recently discovered Khirbet Qeiyafa ostracon provides another parallel. Like the 'Izbet Sartah abecedary, it too seems to run left to right. Cf. H. Misgav, Y. Garfinkel, and S. Ganor, "The Ostracon," in *Khirbet Qeiyafa, Vol. 1: Excavation Report, 2007–2008* (ed. Y. Garfinkel and S. Ganor; Jerusalem: Israel Exploration Society, 2009), 259–260.

49. M. Kochavi, "The History and Archaeology of Aphek-Antipatris: A Biblical City in the Sharon Plain," *BA* 44 (1981): 80–82.

50. Some have identified 'Izbet Sartah* with Ebenezer. Cf. F. M. Cross, "Newly Found Inscriptions in Old Canaanite and Early Phoenician Scripts," *BASOR* 238 (1980): 1–20; M. Kochavi, "An Ostracon of the Period of Judges from 'Izbet Sartah," *TA* 4 (1977): 1–13; M. Kochavi and A. Demsky, "An Israelite Village from the Days of the Judges," *BAR* 4/3 (1978): 19–21.

51. For a much more detailed discussion of the history of settlement at 'Izbet Sartah, see I. Finkelstein, "Historical Conclusions," in *'Izbet Sartah: An Early Iron Age Site near Rosh Ha'ayin, Israel* (ed. I. Finkelstein; BAR International Series 299; Oxford: Oxford University Press, 1986), 205–11.

52. Kochavi, "The History and Archaeology of Aphek-Antipatris," 82.

53. See chs. 5 and 6.

54. Finkelstein, "Historical Conclusions," 212.

55. Ibid.

56. 1 Sam 13:19-20.

57. Finkelstein, "Historical Conclusions," 212.

58. Ibid., 213.

59. V. H. Matthews, "Villages," *NIDB* 5:781–82; A. M. T. Moore, "Villages," *OEANE* 5:301–3.

60. V. H. Matthews, *Manners and Customs in the Bible: An Illustrated Guide to Daily Life in Bible Times* (3d ed.; Peabody, Mass.: Hendrickson, 2006), 49–50. The work involved in village life will be discussed further in ch. 10.

# 9. Early Israelite Sanctuaries and the Birth of a Nation

1. B. D. Bibb, "Amphictyony," *NIDB* 1:141.

2. F. S. Frick, *A Journey through the Hebrew Scriptures* (2d ed.; Belmont, Calif.: Thomson/Wadsworth, 2003), 271. See also A. D. H. Mayes, "The Period of the Judges and the Rise of the Monarchy," in *Israelite and Judaean History* (ed. J. H. Hayes and J. M. Miller; London and Philadelphia: SCM Press and Westminster, 1977), 306–7.

3. Since the Patristic period, Christian interpretation has regarded the scroll discovered in the Temple as that of Deuteronomy, while Jews have identified it as the Torah as a whole.

4. See the summaries of the interpretation of the "altar law" and the issue of centralization of the cult in G. J. Wenham, "Deuteronomy and the Central Sanctuary," in *TynBul* 22 (1971): 103–18; J. G. McConville, "The Altar-Law and Centralization of the Cult," in *Law and Theology in Deuteronomy* (Sheffield: Sheffield Academic Press, 1984), 21–38.

5. P. Pitkänen, *Central Sanctuary and Centralization of Worship in Ancient Israel: From the Settlement to the Building of Solomon's Temple* (Gorgias Dissertations 6, Near Eastern Studies 4; Piscataway, N.J.: Gorgias Press, 2003), 272.

6. E. S. Kalland, *Deuteronomy* (vol. 3 of *The Expositor's Bible Commentary*; ed. F. E. Gaebelein; Grand Rapids: Zondervan, 1992), 93.

7. P. T. Vogt, *Deuteronomic Theology and the Significance of Torah: A Reappraisal* (Winona Lake, Ind.: Eisenbrauns, 2006), 203.

8. C. F. Keil and F. Delitzsch, *The Fifth Book of Moses (Deuteronomy)* (vol. 1, Commentary on the Old Testament; trans. J. Martin; Edinburgh: T&T Clark, 1865–1892), 907.

9. Z. Zevit, "Seeing God in All the Right Places" (paper presented at the annual meeting of the SBL, Boston, Mass., 24 November 2008).

10. E.g., Exod 34:23–24; Deut 31:11; Isa 1:12.

11. J. Milgrom, "The Desecration of YHWH's Name: Its Parameters and Significance," in *Birkat Shalom: Studies in the Bible, Ancient Near Eastern Literature, and Postbiblical Judaism Presented to Shalom M. Paul on the Occasion of His Seventieth Birthday* (ed. C. Cohen et al.; 2 vols; Winona Lake, Ind.: Eisenbrauns, 2008), 69–81.

12. 1 Sam 9:12-14, 19, 25.

13. 1 Sam 10:5, 13.

14. 1 Kgs 3:4.

15. 1 Kgs 3:2-3.

16. 1 Chr 16:39; 21:29; 2 Chr 1:3, 13.

17. 2 Chr 33:17.

18. 2 Kgs 18:4, 22.

19. 2 Kgs 23:8-9, 13, 15, 19-20.

20. See D. L. Christensen, ed., *A Song of Power and the Power of Song: Essays on the Book of Deuteronomy* (Winona Lake, Ind.: Eisenbrauns, 1993); G. N. Knoppers and J. G. McConville, eds., *Reconsidering Israel and Judah: Recent Studies on the Deuteronomistic History* (Winona Lake, Ind.: Eisenbrauns, 2000); For recent reappraisals of the traditional view, see Pitkänen, *Central Sanctuary*; Vogt, *Deuteronomic Theology and the Significance of Torah*.

21. M. Noth, *Das System der zwölf Stämme Israels* (BWANT 4.1; Stuttgart: Kohlhammer, 1930). The discussion of an Israelite "amphictyony" had already been under way for some years by that time. Albrecht Alt, for example, had discussed it in the 1920s. Cf. A. Alt, "Israel, politische Geschichte," *RGG* 3: Cols. 437–42.

22. See the reviews in A. G. Auld, "Amphictyony, Question of," in *Dictionary of the Old Testament: Historical Books* (ed. B. T. Arnold and H. G. M. Williamson; Downers Grove, Ill.: InterVarsity, 2005), 26–32; B. D. Bibb, "Amphictyony," *NIDB* 1:141; T. C. Butler, *Joshua* (WBC 7; Waco, Tex.: Word, 1983), xxxiii–xxxv; A. D. H. Mayes, *ABD* 1:212–16; K. L. Sparks, *Ethnicity and Identity in Ancient Israel: Prolegomena to the Study of Ethnic Sentiments and Their Expression in the Hebrew Bible* (Winona Lake, Ind.: Eisenbrauns, 1998), 120–21.

23. Mayes, "Amphictyony," 212.

24. M. Noth, *The History of Israel* (2d ed.; trans. P. Ackroyd; New York: Harper, 1960), 88.

25. Mayes, "Amphictyony," 212.

26. Ibid.

27. Auld, "Amphictyony, Question of," 26.

28. Alt, "Israel, politische Geschichte," 438–39; M. Weber, *Ancient Judaism* (trans. and ed. H. H. Gertha and D. Martindale; Glencoe: Ill.: Free Press, 1952), 81ff, 90; Noth, *Das System der zwölf Stämme Israels*, 3–39; idem., *The History of Israel*, 92–106.

29. E.g., R. De Vaux, "Was There an Israelite Amphictyony?" *BAR* 3/2 (1977): 40–47; idem., *The Early History of Israel* (Philadelphia: Westminster Press, 1978): 695–715; C. H. J. de Geus, *The Tribes of Israel: An Investigation into Some of the Presuppositions of Martin Noth's Amphictyony Hypothesis* (Amsterdam: Van Gorcum, 1976); A. D. H. Mayes, *Israel in the Period of the Judges* (Studies in Biblical Theology, Second Series, no. 29; London: SCM, 1974); N. P. Lemche, "The Greek Amphictyony: Could It Be a Prototype for the Israelite Society in the Period of the Judges," *JSOT* 4 (1977): 48–59.

30. Mayes, "Amphictyony," 215.

31. B. Mazar, "Biblical Archaeology Today: The Historical Aspect," in *Biblical Archaeology Today: Proceedings of the International Congress on Biblical Archaeology, Jerusalem, April 1984* (ed. J. Amitai; Jerusalem: Israel Exploration Society, 1985), 17–18.

32. See the following discussion of the Gilgalim.

33. A. Zertal, *The Manasseh Hill Country Survey*, vol. 2: *The Eastern Valleys and the Fringes of the Desert* (Tel Aviv: University of Haifa and the Ministry of Defense, 1996), 394–97 (Hebrew); idem., *The Manasseh Hill Country Survey*, vol. 4: *From Nahal Bezek to the Sartaba* (Tel Aviv: University of Haifa and the Ministry of Defense, 2005), 238–42, 305–7, 333–37 (Hebrew).

34. A. Zertal, "Israel Enters Canaan: Following the Pottery Trail," *BAR* 17 (1991): 42–43; idem., *The Mannasseh Hill Country Survey, Vol. 2*, 394–97.

35. See A. Zertal, "To the Land of the Perizzites and the Giants: On the Israelite Settlement in the Hill Country of Manasseh," in *From Nomadism to Monarchy: Archaeological and Historical Aspects of Early Israel* (ed. I. Finkelstein and N. Na'aman; Washington, D.C.: Biblical Archaeology Society, 1994), 54–55; cf. also I. Finkelstein, *The Archaeology of the Israelite Settlement* (Jerusalem: Israel Exploration Society, 1988), 286–87.

36. A. Zertal, *From Nahal Bezek to the Sartaba*, 238–42, 724–70; D. Ben-Yosef, "The Jordan Valley During Iron Age I: Aspects of Its History and the Archaeological Evidence for Its Settlement" (Ph.D. diss., University of Haifa, 2007), 228–78; A. Zertal and D. Ben-Yosef, "Bedhat esh-Sha'ab: An Iron Age I Enclosure in the Jordan Valley," in *Exploring the Longue Durée: Essays in Honor of Lawrence E. Stager* (Winona Lake, Ind.: Eisenbrauns, 2009), 517–29.

37. See chs. 6–7.

38. D. Ben-Yosef, "The Jordan Valley During Iron Age I: Aspects of Its History and the Archaeological Evidence for Its Settlement" (Ph.D. diss., University of Haifa, 2007 [Hebrew]), 215–27.

39. A. Zertal, "Israel Enters Canaan," 42–43; idem., "The Iron I Culture in the Hill-Country of Canaan: A Manassite Perspective," in *Mediterranean Peoples in Transition: Thirteenth to Early Tenth Centuries B.C.E.* (ed. S. Gitin, A. Mazar, and E. Stern; Jerusalem: Israel Exploration Society, 1998), 247. On Gilgal, see W. R. Kotter, "Gilgal," *ABD* 2:1022–24; E. Levine, "Gilgal," *NIDB* 2:572–73.

40. B. Waltke, "Gilgal," *TWOT* 1:164.

41. Deut 11:30; Josh 8:30-35.

42. D. Merling Sr., *The Book of Joshua: Its Theme and Role in Archaeological Discussions* (AUSDDS 23; Berrien Springs, Mich.: Andrews University Press, 1997), 199–205; see also Joshua 15–19.

43. 1 Sam 7:16; 2 Sam 19:15.

44. Mic 6:5; Hos 4:15; 9:15; 12:11; Amos 4:4–5, 15.

45. As observed by Adam Zertal in "Archaeological Discovery In Jordan Valley: Enormous 'Foot-Shaped' Enclosures," *Science Daily* 6 (April 2009). Cited 9 July 2010. Online: http://www.sciencedaily.com/releases/2009/04/090406102600.htm.

46. *BDB*, 295.

47. *HALOT* 1:289.

48. On the historical development of the Hajj, see F. E. Peters, *The Hajj: The Muslim Pilgrimage to Mecca and the Holy Places* (Princeton, N.J.: Princeton University Press, 1994).

49. Zertal and Ben-Yosef, "Bedhat esh-Sha'ab," 527.

50. E.g., G. von Rad, *Old Testament Theology* (vol. 1 of *The Theology of Israel's Historical Traditions;* trans. D. M. G. Stalker; New York: Harper & Row, 1962), 15–35; Hans-Joachim Kraus, *Worship in Israel: A Cultic History of the Old Testament* (trans. G. Buswell; Oxford: Basil Blackwell, 1966), 152–65.

51. Exod 12:14; 23:16.

52. M. D. H., "Festivals," *EJ* 6:1238–43.

53. *HALOT*, 1184–86.

54. Cf. D. I. Block, *Judges, Ruth* (NAC 6; Nashville: Broadman & Holman, 1999), 717–18.

55. J. Monson, "The New 'Ain Dara Temple: Closest Solomonic Parallel," *BAR* 26/3 (2000): 26–27.

56. I use the feminine here because the 'Ain Dara temple is thought to have belonged to Ishtar. The interpretation of the footprints as those of the deity is uncertain, since the deities depicted in the reliefs inside the 'Ain Dara temple are wearing shoes with upturned toes.

57. See C. J. H. Wright, *God's People in God's Land: Family, Land and Property in the Old Testament* (Grand Rapids: Eerdmans, 1990).

58. For an overview of the discovery of the site and its excavation, see Adam Zertal, "Ebal, Mount," *NEAEHL* 1:375–77.

59. B. Brandl, "Two Scarabs and a Trapezoidal Seal from Mount Ebal," *Tel Aviv* 13–14 (1986/87): 166–72.

60. Sheep and goats.

61. A. Zertal, "Has Joshua's Altar Been Found on Mt. Ebal?" in *BAR* 1 (Jan/Feb: 1985): 26–43.

62. A. Kempinski, "Joshua's Altar or an Iron Age I Watchtower?" in *BAR* 1 (Jan/Feb, 1986): 42–49.

63. A. F. Rainey, "Zertal's Altar: A Blatant Phony: Queries and Comments," *BAR* 12 (1986): 66.

64. William G. Dever, "How to Tell an Israelite from a Canaanite," in *The Rise of Ancient Israel* (ed. Hershel Shanks; Washington, D.C.: The Biblical Archaeology Society, 1997), 34. For more information see: R. K. Hawkins, "The Iron Age I Structure on Mount Ebal: Excavation and Interpretation" (Ph.D. diss., Andrews University, 2007).

65. B. Wood and R. Young, "A Critical Analysis of the Evidence from Ralph Hawkins for a Late-Date Exodus-Conquest," *JETS* 51/2 (2008): 241.

66. W. C. Kaiser Jr. and D. A. Garrett, eds., *NIV Archaeological Study Bible: An Illustrated Walk Through Biblical History and Culture* (Grand Rapids: Zondervan, 2005), 288.

67. Pitkänen, *Central Sanctuary*, 182.

68. E.g., Josh 4; 22:9-34.

69. The preposition *b* (*beth*) has "in" as its primary meaning. Cf. F. Brown, S. R. Driver, and C. A. Briggs, *The New Brown-Driver-Briggs-Gesenius Hebrew and English Lexicon* (Peabody, Mass.: Hendrickson, 1979), 88.

70. A. Zertal, "Has Joshua's Altar Been Found on Mt. Ebal?" *BAR* 11 (1985): 43.

71. P. Pitkänen, *Central Sanctuary and Centralization of Worship in Ancient Israel: From the Settlement to the Building of Solomon's Temple*, 227.

72. Debate about the SP's presumed change from Ebal to Gerizim is quite ancient. See Josephus, *Ant.* 13.3.4, § 74–79.

73. Eusebius, *Onom*, 65.

74. I. Magen, "Gerizim, Mount," *NEAEHL* 2:484–92.

75. See A. Zertal, *A Nation is Born: The Altar on Mount Ebal and the Emergence of Israel* (Tel Aviv: Yedioth, 2000 [Hebrew]), 225–39.

76. B. Wood and R. Young, "A Critical Analysis of the Evidence from Ralph Hawkins for a Late-Date Exodus-Conquest," 242–43.

77. P. Heger, "Comparison and Contrast Between the Two Laws of the Altar: Exod 20:22 כי חרבך הנפת and Deut 27:5 לא תניף עליהם ברזל in Consideration of Their Historical Setting," in *Proceedings of the Twelfth World Congress of Jewish Studies, Jerusalem, July 29–August 5, 1997* (Jerusalem: World Union of Jewish Studies, 1999), 106.

78. Z. Zevit, *Religions of Ancient Israel: A Synthesis of Parallactic Approaches* (London: Continuum, 2001) 199.

79. Hawkins, "The Iron Age I Structure on Mount Ebal," 260.

80. Zevit, *Religions of Ancient Israel*, 199–200.

81. Wood dates it to Iron Age I. The dating of the sanctuary has been vigorously debated. For recent discussion, see Z. Herzog, "The Date of the Temple at Arad: Reassessment of the Stratigraphy and the Implications for the History of Religion in Judah," in *Studies in the Archaeology of the Iron Age in Israel and Jordan* (ed. A. Mazar, with the assistance of Ginny Mathias; JSOTSS 331; Sheffield: Sheffield Academic Press, 2001), 156–78; W. G. Dever, "Were There Temples in Ancient Israel? The Archaeological Evidence," in *Text, Artifact, and Image: Revealing Ancient Israelite Religion* (ed. G. Beckman and T. J. Lewis; Providence, R.I.: Brown University, 2006), 300–16; A. F. Rainey, "Hezekiah's Reform and the Altars at Beersheba and Arad," in *Scripture and Other Artifacts: Essays on the Bible and Archaeology in Honor of Philip J. King* (ed. M. D. Coogan, J. C. Exum, and L. E. Stager; Louisville: Westminster John Knox Press, 1994), 333–54.

82. For Ebal's special characteristics, see Hawkins, "The Iron Age I Structure on Mt. Ebal," 34–100.

83. See Hawkins, "The Iron Age Structure on Mt. Ebal," 181–216. "Manoah's altar," near Zorah, and the four-horned altar near Shiloh, may date to the Iron Age I.

84. See Hawkins, "The Iron Age I Structure on Mount Ebal," 224–67.

85. R. D. Haak, "Altar," *ABD* 1:162–67.

86. An example of the type Ib open altar is Altar 4017 at Megiddo, though it is fundamentally different from the Ebal structure in its shape and design. The Ebal structure also resembles the Iron Age I structure at Giloh, which may be a *bamah* or other cultic structure. For a brief discussion, see Ralph K. Hawkins, "Giloh," *NIDB* 2:574. I have carried out a detailed comparison of the Ebal structure with altars in the southern Levant from the Middle Bronze to Iron Ages. Cf. R. K. Hawkins, *The Iron Age I Structure on Mount Ebal* (Winona Lake, Ind.: Eisenbrauns, 2012).

87. Cf. M. Rowton, "Enclosed Nomadism," *JESHO* 17/1 (1974): 1–30.

88. A. Zertal, "A Cultic Center with a Burnt-Offering Altar from Early Iron Age I Period at Mt. Ebal," in *Wünschet Jerusalem Frieden: Collected Communications to the XIIth Congress of the International Organization for the Study of the Old Testament* (ed. M. A. Klaus and D. Schunk; Frankfurst am Main: Peter Lang, 1988), 144.

89. The Ebal tradition within Deuteronomy and Joshua has been given little attention in the scholarly literature. S. L. Richter suggests that the reason for this is that those traditions

were assumed to be "a somewhat peripheral addition" to a text whose very reason for existence was to function as an apologetic for the centralization of the cultus in Jerusalem. See S. L. Richter, "The Place of the Name in Deuteronomy," *VT* 57 (2007): 342–66.

90. Other possible cultic sites are discussed in R. K. Hawkins, "The Iron Age I Structure on Mount Ebal."

91. Haak, "Altar," 162–67.

92. S. L. Richter has recently argued that Mount Ebal is the "place of the name" in Deuteronomy. If Deut 12:5 indeed commands centralization, as has been traditionally understood, then Richter makes a convincing case that Mount Ebal was the site at which the author(s) intend to say that Yahweh had "placed his name." See Richter, "The Place of the Name in Deuteronomy," 342–66.

## 10. A CULTURE-SCALE MODEL OF THE EARLY ISRAELITE SETTLEMENT

1. M. Bunge, *Scientific Research* (2 vols.; New York: Springer-Verlag, 1967), 384.

2. G. Gibbon, *Anthropological Archaeology* (New York: Columbia University Press, 1984), 353.

3. Ibid.

4. E.g., H. M. Blalock, *Theory Construction* (Englewood Cliffs, N.J.: Prentice-Hall, 1969); idem., "The Formalization of Sociological Theory," in *Theoretical Sociology* (ed. J. McKinney and E. A. Tiryakian; New York: Appleton-Century-Crofts, 1970), 271–300.

5. J. Hage, *Techniques and Problems of Theory Construction in Sociology* (New York: Wiley, 1972).

6. Ibid., 173.

7. G. Gibbon, *Anthropological Archaeology* (New York: Columbia University Press, 1984), 370.

8. W. G. Dever, "Impact of the 'New Archaeology,'" in *Benchmarks in Time and Culture: Essays in Honor of Joseph A. Callaway* (ed. J. F. Drinkard, Jr., G. L. Mattingly, and J. M. Miller; Atlanta: Scholars Press, 1988), 344–45. Dever suggests that a consensus recognizes the following six major emphases within the New Archaeology: (1) The use of cultural-evolutionary paradigms; (2) a multidisciplinary orientation; (3) the necessity for a holistic approach; (4) the adoption of scientific methods for the formulation and testing of laws of cultural change; (5) the value of ethnography and modern material culture studies; and (6) the potential of archaeology for elucidating patterns of human thought and action.

9. E.g., R. L. Carneiro and S. L. Tobias, "The Application of Scale Analysis to Cultural Evolution," *Transactions of the New York Academy of Sciences* (Series II) 26 (1963): 196–207; V. G. Childe, *Piecing Together the Past* (London: Routledge and Kegan Paul, 1956); L. Freeman, "An Empirical Test of Folk-Urbanism" (Ann Arbor: University Microfilms No. 23, 502); M. Fried, *The Evolution of Political Society* (New York: Random House, 1967); A. W. Johnson and T. Earle, *On the Evolution of Human Societies: From Foraging Groups to Agrarian State* (Stanford: Stanford University Press, 1987); C. McNett Jr., "A Settlement Pattern Scale of Cultural Complexity," in *A Handbook of Method in Cultural Anthropology* (ed. R. Naroll and R. Cohen; Garden City, N.Y.: Natural History Press, 1973), 872–86; R. Marsh, *Comparative Sociology* (New York: Harcourt, Brace & World, 1967); R. Naroll, "A Preliminary Index of Social Development," *American Anthropologist* 58 (1956): 687–715; M. Sahlins, *Tribesmen* (Englewood Cliffs, N.J.: Prentice-Hall, 1968); E. Service, *Primitive Social Organization: An Evolutionary Perspective* (New York: Random House, 1962); J. Steward, *Theory of Culture Change* (Urbana: University of Illinois Press, 1955).

10. Gibbon, *Anthropological Archaeology*, 347–48.

11. J. H. Bodley, *Cultural Anthropology: Tribes, States, and the Global System* (3d ed.; Mountain View, Calif.: Mayfield, 2000), 18–29. Though Bodley's book is now in its fifth edition (Landham, Md.: Rowman & Littlefield, 2011), I intentionally use the third edition, because Bodley abandons his focus on scale in later editions in order to shift to a focus on imperia. See also J. H. Bodley, *The Power of Scale: A Global History Approach* (Armonk, N.Y.: M. E. Sharpe, 2003).

12. There have been a number of recent surveys of the current state of scholarship regarding the settlement that demonstrate this. W. G. Dever, "Archaeology and the Israelite 'Conquest,'" *ABD* 3:545–58; idem., *Who Were the Early Israelites and Where Did They Come From?* (Grand Rapids: Eerdmans, 2003); N. K. Gottwald, *The Hebrew Bible: A Brief Socio-Literary Introduction* (Minneapolis: Fortress, 2009), 150–64; P. J. Ray Jr., "Classical Models for the Appearance of Israel in Canaan," in *Critical Issues in Early Israelite History* (ed. R. S. Hess, G. A. Klingbeil, and P. J. Ray Jr.; Winona Lake, Ind.: Eisenbrauns, 2008), 79–93; K. L. Younger, "Early Israel in Recent Biblical Scholarship," in *The Face of Old Testament Studies: A Survey of Contemporary Approaches* (ed. D. W. Baker and B. T. Arnold; Grand Rapids: Baker, 1999), 176–206.

13. A. Alt, "Erwägungen über die Landnahme der Israeliten in Palästina," in *Kleine Schriften* 1 (4th ed.; Münich: 1968), 156; M. Noth, "Grundsätzliches zur geschichtlichen Deutung archäaologischer Befunde auf dem Boden Palästinas," *Palästina-Jahrbuch* 34 (1938): 7–22.

14. M. Weinfeld, "Historical Facts behind the Israelite Settlement Pattern," *VT* 38/3 (1988): 324–32.

15. A. Zertal, "To the Land of the Perizzites and the Giants: On the Israelite Settlement in the Hill Country of Manasseh," in *From Nomadism to Monarchy: Archaeological and Historical Aspects of Early Israel* (ed. I. Finkelstein and N. Na'aman; Washington: Biblical Archaeology Society, 1994), 58–59.

16. Cf. the discussion of the "Divine Warrior," in F. M. Cross, *Canaanite Myth and Hebrew Epic: Essays in the History of the Religion of Israel* (Cambridge, Mass: Harvard University Press, 1973), 91–111; Hans-Joachim Kraus, *Worship in Israel* (trans. G. Buswell; Richmond: John Knox, 1966), 152–65; J. Wilcoxen, "Narrative Structure and Cult Legend: A Study of Joshua 1–6," in *Transitions in Biblical Scholarship* (ed. J. C. Rylaarsdam; Chicago: University of Chicago Press, 1968), 43–70.

17. Since the nineteenth century, scholars have assumed that the book of Joshua painted a picture of a sweeping military conquest of Canaan, while the book of Judges presented a more accurate, "alternative" account. While the study of Joshua has moved from literary-critical approaches to tradition-historical approaches, this understanding of the relationship between Joshua and Judges continues to predominate in much of contemporary scholarly literature. In place of this focus on a supposed tension between the books of Joshua and Judges, however, some scholars have recently argued that the idea of a sweeping conquest is a modern scholarly construct imposed on the book of Joshua, and when it is read with greater nuance, it is seen to acknowledge a more complex and protracted settlement process. The text does not claim that the ancient Israelites occupied the land, but that they made sorties into the land and planned its apportionment.

18. As discussed in ch. 9, there was likely more than one Gilgal.

19. D. Merling, "The Book of Joshua: Its Structure and Meaning," in *To Understand the Scriptures: Essays in Honor of William H. Shea* (ed. D. Merling; Berrien Springs, Mich.: Institute of Archaeology, Siegfried H. Horn Archaeological Museum, Andrews University, 1997), 199–205.

20. Josh 4:19; 5:1-9, 10-12.
21. Josh 5:14; 9:6.
22. Josh 10:1-5, 15.
23. Merling, "The Book of Joshua: Its Structure and Meaning," 199–205.
24. R. K. Hawkins, "The Survey of Manasseh and the Origin of the Central Hill Country Settlers," in *Critical Issues in Early Israelite History* (ed. R. S. Hess, G. A. Klingbeil, and P. J. Ray, Jr.; Winona Lake, Ind.: Eisenbrauns, 2008), 177–79.
25. E.g., Josh 13:1-7; Judg 1:1–2:5. Cf. M. Weinfeld, *The Promise of the Land: The Inheritance of the Land of Canaan by the Israelites* (Berkeley: University of California Press, 1993), 388–400.
26. A. Zertal, "To the Land of the Perizzites and the Giants: On the Israelite Settlement in the Hill Country of Manasseh," in *From Nomadism to Monarchy: Archaeological and Historical Aspects of Early Israel* (ed. I. Finkelstein and N. Na'aman; Washington: Biblical Archaeology Society, 1994), 60.
27. Josh 14:12; 16:63; 17:11-12.
28. Josh 14–15 and Judg 1; Josh 16–17; 18–22.
29. Y. Aharoni, "The Settlement of Canaan," in *Judges* (ed. B. Mazar; *The World History of the Jewish People*, vol. 3; New Jersey: Rutgers University, 1971), 96.
30. A. Zertal, *The Manasseh Hill Country Survey*, vol. 2, *The Eastern Valleys and the Fringes of the Desert* (CHANE 21.2; Leiden: Brill, 2008), 19.
31. E.g., Deut 32:14; Judg 4:19; 5:16, 25; 6:25.
32. T. E. Levy and A. F. C. Holl suggest that the surfeit of terms related to pastoralism in the Hebrew Bible substantiates its attribution of a pastoral nomadic heritage to the early Israelites. Cf. T. E. Levy and A. F. C. Holl, "Migration, Ethnogenesis, and Settlement Dynamics: Israelites in Iron Age Canaan and Suwa-Arabs in the Chad Basin," *JAA* 21 (2002): 93–94.
33. For background studies of nomadism, see T. J. Luke, "Pastoralism and Politics at Mari in the Mari Period" (Ph.D. diss., University of Michigan, 1965); M. B. Rowton, "Enclosed Nomadism," *JESHO* 17 (1974): 1–30; idem., "Dimorphic Structure and the Parasocial Element," *JNES* 36 (1977): 181–98; V. H. Matthews, *Pastoral Nomadism in the Mari Kingdom, ca. 1830–1760 B.C.* (Cambridge, Mass.: American Schools of Oriental Research, 1978); idem., "Pastoralism and Patriarchs," *BA* 44 (1981): 215–18; idem., "The Wells of Gerar," *BA* 49 (1986): 118–26.
34. L. E. Stager, "The Archaeology of the Family in Ancient Israel," *BASOR* 260 (1985): 1–35.
35. For clearing of the forests, see Josh 17:14-18.
36. E.g., Deut 33:28.
37. E.g., Deut 32:14; Judg 6:11; 15:1; 1 Sam 6:13.
38. E.g., Judg 7:13; 13:7, 14.
39. O. Borowski, *Agriculture in Iron Age Israel* (Boston, Mass.: American Schools of Oriental Research, 2002); D. Hopkins, *The Highlands of Canaan: Agricultural Life in the Early Iron Age* (Sheffield: Almond Press, 1985).
40. V. H. Matthews, "Village," *NIDB* 5:781–82. Cf. B. A. Nakhai, "Contextualizing Village Life in the Iron Age I," in *Israel in Transition: From Late Bronze II to Iron IIa (c. 1250–850 B.C.E.)*, (ed. L. L. Grabbe; vol. 1 of *The Archaeology*; New York: T&T Clark, 2008), 121–37.
41. J. H. Bodley, "Socioeconomic Growth, Culture Scale, and Household Well-Being: A Test of the Power-Elite Hypothesis," in *Current Anthropology* 40/5 (1999): 597.
42. As, for example, at Tel Masos, though it is not clear whether this was an Israelite city. Cf. G. W. Ahlström, "The Early Iron Age Settlers at Hirbet el-Mšāš (Tel Masos)," *ZDPV* 100 (1984): 35–52; V. Fritz, "Überlegungen zur Identifikation von Hirbet el-Msas," in *Ergebnisse*

*Der Ausgrabungen auf der Hirbet el-Mšāš (Tēl Māśōś)* (ed. V. Fritz and A. Kempinski; Wiesbaden: Otto Harrassowitz, 1983), 238.

43. M. L. Chaney, "Ancient Palestinian Peasant Movements and the Formation of Premonarchic Israel," in *Palestine in Transition: The Emergence of Ancient Israel* (ed. D. N. Freedman and D. F. Graf; Sheffield: Almond Press, 1983), 51; G. Lenski and J. Lenski, *Human Societies: An Introduction to Macrosociology* (3d ed.; New York: McGraw-Hill, 1978), 229. The term *egalitarian* must be used with caution, however. Mendenhall called it an "absurdity" and stressed there is no word in biblical Hebrew that can thus be translated, but there is plenty of terminology that indicates the opposite. See G. E. Mendenhall, "Ancient Israel's Hyphenated History," in *Palestine in Transition: The Emergence of Ancient Israel* (ed. D. N. Freedman and D. F. Graf; Sheffield: Almond Press, 1983), 92–93. P. McNutt notes that ethnographic studies have shown that "even in societies with an egalitarian ideology, there is some differentiation in status, power, and wealth." Cf. P. M. McNutt, *Reconstructing the Society of Ancient Israel* (Louisville: Westminster John Knox, 1999), 74. If the term *egalitarian* is to be used, it must be with the caveats noted in the text. Domestic-scale cultures may not have had a king, but they typically still had a "chief" of some kind. Even the Book of the Covenant, generally recognized as the oldest law code in the Pentateuch, presupposed a *nasi'* or "chieftain." This text may be the product of this era, as suggested by E. M. Meyers, "Israel and Its Neighbors Then and Now: Revisionist History and the Quest for History Today," in *Confronting the Past: Archaeological and Historical Essays on Ancient Israel in Honor of William G. Dever* (ed. S. Gitin, J. E. Wright, and J. P. Dessel; Winona Lake, Ind.: Eisenbrauns, 2006), 258. C. Meyers has proposed that the pre-monarchic highland villages can be understood through the lens of the "complex chiefdom," and she suggests that the egalitarian social dynamics can be understood through a notion of "heterarchy," in which the whole community is involved in the management of village life. See C. L. Meyers, "'Tribes and Tribulations: Retheorizing Earliest 'Israel,'" in *Tracking the Tribes of Yahweh: On the Trail of a Classic* (ed. R. Boer; JSOTSup 351; Sheffield: Sheffield Academic Press, 2002), 42–45.

44. J. W. Burton, "Ghost Marriage and the Cattle Trade among the Atuot of the Southern Sudan," *Africa: Journal of the International African Institute* 48/4 (1978): 398–405; E. E. Evans-Pritchard, *Kinship and Marriage among the Nuer* (Oxford: Clarendon, 1951); R. S. Oboler, "Is the Female Husband a Man? Woman/Woman Marriage among the Nandi of Kenya," *Ethnology* 19/1 (1980): 69–88.

45. Cf. V. P. Hamilton, "Marriage (OT and ANE)," *ABD* 4:567–68; M. E. Shields, "Marriage, OT," *NIDB* 3:819.

46. Ø. S. LaBianca, *Sedentarization and Nomadization: Food System Cycles at Hesban and Vicinity In Transjordan* (Hesban 1; Berrien Springs, Mich.: Andrews University Press, 1990), 39; idem., "Tribe," *Eerdmans Dictionary of the Bible* (ed. D. N. Freedman; Grand Rapids, MI.: Eerdmans, 2000), 1333.

47. R. deVaux, *Ancient Israel: Its Life and Institutions* (London: Darton, Longman & Todd, 1961), 76–77.

48. J. W. Rogerson argues against this, concluding that the identification of early Israel as a segmentary society on the basis of African political systems is "hardly persuasive." Cf. J. W. Rogerson, "Was Early Israel A Segmentary Society?" *JSOT* 36 (1986): 17–26. D. Fiensy carefully reevaluated the "Nuer model," and while he observes that several features of the model have come under criticism, he suggests that the comparison warrants further study. Fiensy urges Old Testament scholars to carefully follow the anthropological literature to make sure that they do not base their own research on "discredited ethnological theories." Cf. D. Fiensy, "Using the Nuer Culture of Africa in Understanding the Old Testament: An Evaluation," *JSOT* 38 (1987): 73–83, esp. 80. Two decades of subsequent scholarly research seems

to have verified that there are indeed parallels between African political systems and ancient Israel's usage of lineages. Cf. the discussion and references in J. H. Walton, "Genealogies," in *Dictionary of the Old Testament: Historical Books* (ed. B. T. Arnold and H. G. M. Williamson; Downers Grove, Ill.: InterVarsity, 2005), 309–16.

49. P. M. McNutt, *Reconstructing the Society of Ancient Israel* (Lousiville.: Westminster John Knox, 1999), 77.

50. J. H. Bodley, *Cultural Anthropology*, 115–17; M. D. Sahlins, *Tribesmen* (Englewood Cliffs, N.J.: 1968), 10–11. See also E. E. Evans-Pritchard, *The Nuer: A Description of the Modes of Livelihood and Political Institutions of a Nilotic People* (New York: Oxford University Press, 1940), 181. A contemporary example of the age-class system can be found among the Hutterites. See G. E. Huntington and J. A. Hostetler, *The Hutterites in North America* (Mason, Ohio: Cenage Learning, 2002), 25–26.

51. I am hypothesizing these age sets on the basis of analogy with other domestic-scale cultures. It appears that age groups within agrarian communities, regardless of culture, share many basic functions. Cf. R. McC. Netting, *Smallholders, Householders: Farm Families and the Ecology of Intensive, Sustainable Agriculture* (Stanford, Calif.: Stanford University Press, 1993), 58–59.

52. Cf. Exod 20:12.

53. Prov 19:25, 29; 20:30; 22:15; 26:3; 29:15.

54. Prov 22:15.

55. Cf. Prov 13:24; 19:18; 23:13-14.

56. J. L. Crenshaw, "Education, OT," *NIDB* 2:195–205; J. M. Gundry-Volf, "Child, Children," *NIDB* 1:588–90.

57. Netting, *Smallholders, Householders*, 70.

58. C. Meyers, "The Family in Early Israel," in *Families in Early Israel* (ed. L. G. Perdue et al.; Louisville: Westminster John Knox, 1997), 30–32.

59. V. P. Hamilton, "Marriage (OT and ANE)," *ABD* 4:559–69.

60. Meyers, "The Family in Early Israel," 22–32.

61. While one might think of the women's work as less important or less strenuous than the work of the men, this is certainly not true. Carol Meyers has shown that the work of the ancient Israelite woman, in a premodern agrarian family, was virtually the same as that of a man and almost certainly consumed more total hours per day. Cf. C. Meyers, "Hierarchy or Heterarchy? Archaeology and the Theorizing of Israelite Society," in *Confronting the Past: Archaeological and Historical Essays on Ancient Israel in Honor of William G. Dever* (ed. S. Gitin, J. E. Wright, J. P. Dessel; Winona Lake, Ind.: Eisenbrauns, 2006), 245–54.

62. D. C. Hopkins, "'All Sorts of Field Work': Agricultural Labor in Ancient Palestine," in *To Break Every Yoke: Essays in Honor of Marvin L. Chaney* (ed. R. B. Coote and N. K. Gottwald; Sheffield: Sheffield Phoenix Press, 2007), 149–72.

63. E.g., Exod 20:12; 21:15, 17.

64. Meyers, "The Family in Early Israel," 31.

65. G. E. Mendenhall and G. A. Herion, "Covenant," *ADB* 1:1179–202; D. Patrick, "Covenant, Book of the," *NIDB* 1:767.

66. D. A. Knight, "Village Law and the Book of the Covenant," in *"A Wise and Discerning Mind": Essays in Honor of Burke O. Long* (ed. S. M. Olyan and R. C. Culley; Brown Judaic Studies 325; Providence, R.I.: Brown Judaic Studies, 2000), 174–78; idem., *Law, Power, and Justice in Ancient Israel* (Louisville: Westminster John Knox, 2011), 115–56.

67. See D. A. Knight's full discussion, in "Village Law and the Book of the Covenant," 163–74.

68. W. L. Holladay, *A Concise Hebrew and Aramaic Lexicon of the Old Testament* (Grand Rapids: Eerdmans, 1988), 91.

69. E.g., 1 Sam 16:4.

70. H. Reviv, *The Elders in Ancient Israel* (Jerusalem: Magnes, 1989), 11.

71. E.g., Prov 7:24; 8:32-36.

72. E.g., Ruth 4:1-2; 1 Sam 16:4; Jer 26.

73. See F. M. Cross, *From Epic to Canon: History and Literature in Ancient Israel* (Baltimore: Johns Hopkins University Press, 1998); D. N. Freedman, "Divine Names and Titles in Early Hebrew History," in *Magnalia Dei: Essays in Honor of G. Ernest Wright* (ed. F. M. Cross et al.; New York: Doubleday, 1976), 55–107; idem., "Early Israelite History in the Light of Early Israelite Poetry," in *Unity and Diversity: Essays in the History, Literature and Religion of the Ancient Near East* (Baltimore: Johns Hopkins University, 1975), 3–35; idem., "Early Israelite Poetry and Historical Reconstructions," in *Symposia Celebrating the Seventy-Fifth Anniversary of the Founding of the American Schools of Oriental Research (1900–1975)* (ed. F. M. Cross; Cambridge: American Schools of Oriental Research, 1979), 85–96; D. N. Freedman and D. Miano, "'His Seed Is Not': 13th-Century Israel," in *Confronting the Past: Archaeological and Historical Essays on Ancient Israel in Honor of William G. Dever* (ed. S. Gitin, J. E. Wright, and J. P. Dessel; Winona Lake, Ind.: Eisenbrauns, 2006), 295–301.

74. W. F. Albright, *Yahweh and the Gods of Canaan* (New York: Doubleday, 1969), 12–13.

75. Freedman, "Early Israelite Poetry and Historical Reconstructions," 85–96.

76. Ibid., 95.

77. Cf. the discussion of G. A. Herion, "The Impact of Modern and Social Science Assumptions on the Reconstruction of Israelite History," *JSOT* 34 (1986): 3–33.

78. F. S. Frick, "Religion and Socio-Political Structure in Early Israel: An Ethno-Archaeological Approach," in SBL Seminar Papers, 1979 (Missoula, Mont.: Scholars Press, 1979), 448–70, esp. 234.

79. Aboriginal law is derived from the Dreaming, and is the moral authority for behavior in Australian aboriginal society. When it is referred to as such, it is called the "Dreaming Law" or simply the "Law." It is inextricably linked to aboriginal religion. See the articles on the Dreaming, law, and mythology in D. Horton, ed., *The Encyclopedia of Aboriginal Australia: Aboriginal and Torres Strait Islander History, Society, and Culture* (Canberra: Aboriginal Studies Press, 1994); J. Jupp, ed., *The Australian People: An Encyclopedia of the Nation, Its People and Their Origins* (2d ed.; Cambridge: Cambridge University Press, 2002); S. Kleinert and M. Neale, *The Oxford Companion to Aboriginal Art and Culture* (Oxford: Oxford University Press, 2001); M. D. Prentis, *A Concise Companion to Aboriginal History* (Kenthurst: Rosenberg Publishing, 2008). See also the Australian Law Reform Commission, "Traditional Aboriginal Society and Its Law," in *Traditional Aboriginal Society* (2d ed.; ed. W. H. Edwards; Melbourne: MacMillan, 1998), 213–26.

80. The East African cattle peoples have not had a written law, and this has led many observers to conclude that they had no law. Evans-Pritchard, for example, concluded that "in a strict sense, the Nuer have no law" (*The Nuer: A Description of the Modes of Livelihood*, 162). There are, however, conventional compensations for a wide range of disputes, and one can speak of "law" among the Nuer in the sense of "a moral obligation to settle disputes by conventional methods, and not in the sense of legal procedure or legal institutions" (*The Nuer: A Description of the Modes of Livelihood*, 168). This traditional Nuer civil law addresses reparations or punishments with regard to damages, adultery, loss of limb, and so on, and it has, in recent times, been recognized by the Sudanese government, as explained in P. P. Howell, *A Manual of Nuer Law: Being an Account of Customary Law, Its Evolution and Development in the Courts Established by the Sudan Government* (London: Oxford University Press, 1954). See also

articles related to law and justice in H. L. Gates Jr., and K. A. Appia, eds., *Africana: The Encyclopedia of the African and African-American Experience* (5 vols.; New York: Oxford University Press, 2005); F. A. Irele and B. Jeyifo, eds., *The Oxford Encyclopedia of African Thought* (New York: Oxford University Press, 2010). For focused studies, see S. Eboh, *An African Concept of Law and Order: A Case Study of Igbo Traditional Society* (Oslo: IKO Press, 2004); M. A. Mohamed, T. Dietz, and A. G. Mohamed, eds., *African Pastoralism: Conflict, Institutions and Government* (London: Pluto Press, 2001).

81. D. M. Merling, *The Book of Joshua: Its Theme and Role in Archaeological Discussions* (Andrews University Seminary Doctoral Dissertation Series, vol. 23; Berrien Springs, Mich.: Andrews University, 1996), 229.

82. B. Mazar, "King David's Scribe and the High Officialdom of the United Monarchy of Israel," in *The Early Biblical Period: Historical Studies* (ed. S. Ahituv and B. Levine; Jerusalem: Israel Exploration Society, 1986), 135–36.

83. W. G. Dever, "Archaeology, Urbanism, and the Rise of the Israelite State," in *The Archaeology of Israel: Constructing the Past, Interpreting the Present* (ed. Neil Asher Silberman and David Small; England: Sheffield Academic Press, 1997), 172.

84. Bodley, *Cultural Anthropology*, 18.

85. Ibid., 166.

86. Ibid., 18.

87. Ibid., 167.

88. See, for example, Morton H. Fried, *The Evolution of Political Society: An Essay in Political Anthropology* (New York: Random House, 1967). For contemporary views, see Matthews and Benjamin, who essentially adopt this view in their reconstruction of the transition from tribal confederation to monarchy. Cf. Victor H. Matthews and Don C. Benjamin, *Social World of Ancient Israel: 1250–587 B.C.E.* (Peabody, Mass.: Hendrickson, 1993), 159–61.

89. W. G. Dever, "Archaeology, Urbanism, and the Rise of the Israelite State," 187.

90. Cf. the insightful article by D. M. Master, "State Formation Theory and the Kingdom of Ancient Israel," in *Journal of Near Eastern Studies* 60:2 (2001): esp. 123–27.

91. Ibid., 128.

92. M. Weber, *Economy and Society*, vol. 2 (ed. G. Roth and C. Wittick; Berkeley: University of California Press, 1978), 1007.

93. L. E. Stager, "The Patrimonial Kingdom of Solomon," in *Symbiosis, Symbolism, and the Power of the Past: Canaan, Ancient Israel, and Their Neighbors from the Late Bronze Age through Roman Palestine* (ed. William G. Dever and Seymour Gitin; Winona Lake, Ind.: Eisenbrauns, 2003), 70.

94. Ibid.

95. Certainly at the covenant-making ceremony of Josh 8:30-35 and the covenant renewal of Josh 24, the people were officially recognizing Yahweh as such.

96. Stager, "The Patrimonial Kingdom of Solomon," 71.

97. P. J. King and L. E. Stager, "Of Fathers, Kings, and the Deity: The Nested Households of Ancient Israel," in *Biblical Archaeology Review* 28, no. 2 (March/April 2002): 45.

98. Ibid., 62.

99. Master, "State Formation Theory and the Kingdom of Ancient Israel," 130.

100. R. S. Hess, "Early Israel in Canaan: A Survey of Recent Evidence and Interpretations," *PEQ* 125 (1993): 139.

101. For bibliography on each of these models, see Hess, "Early Israel in Canaan," 140.

102. 1 Kgs 3:2-5; 1 Chr 16:39; 21:29.

103. See F. A. Spina, "Israelites as *gērîm*, 'Sojourners,' in Social and Historical Context," in *The Word of the Lord Shall Go Forth: Essays in Honor of David Noel Freedman in Celebration*

*of His Sixtieth Birthday* (ed. C. L. Meyers and M. O'Connor; Winona Lake, Ind.: Eisenbrauns, 1983), 321–35.

104. Y. Aharoni, "The Settlement of Canaan," 127–28; see also K. L. Younger, "Early Israel in Recent Biblical Scholarship," in *The Face of Old Testament Studies: A Survey of Contemporary Approaches* (ed. D. W. Baker and B. T. Arnold; Grand Rapids: Baker, 1999), 200.

105. F. Braudel, *Capitalism and Material Life 1400–1800* (trans. M. Kochan; New York: Harper & Row, 1973), xii; idem., *The Structures of Everyday Life*, vol. 1 (trans. S. Reynolds; New York: Harper & Row, 1981), 23–26.

# AFTERWORD

1. In scholarly parlance, these stories are known as "foundation myths." Based primarily on his experiences with the Trobriand Islanders, the anthropologist Bronislaw Malinowski argued that the primary function of such myths was to provide a "sacred charter" to legitimize political identity, status, or power. A clan, for example, might legitimize its right to a particular geographical area by pointing to stories of the clan's ancestor who first inhabited the area under question. See B. Malinowski, *A Scientific Theory of Culture* (Chapel Hill: University of North Carolina Press, 1944).

2. J. H. Walton, *Ancient Near Eastern Thought and the Old Testament* (Grand Rapids: Baker), 235–36.

3. A task I hope to undertake in a commentary on the book of Joshua.

4. M. S. Smith, "God in Israel's Bible: Divinity between the World and Israel, between the Old and the New," *CBQ* 74/1 (2012): 10.

5. Ibid.

# INDEX

Abravanel, Don Isaac, 52, 54
Acts, historiographical purpose of writers, 20–21
'Adam sanctuary site, 179
Adams, R. B., 72–73
Adamthwaite, M. R., 88
adults in culture-scale model, 198
age sets in culture-scale model, 197–99
agrarian reform movements, 46–47
agriculture, 152–55, 173, 195–96
Aharoni, Yohanan, 38, 89, 96, 115, 121, 130, 147, 205
Ahlström, Gösta W., 13, 16, 18, 26, 71, 78, 143
Ai, 30–31, 105–111. *See also* et-Tell
'Ain Dara, 183
Albright, William Foxwell, 2–3, 30–32, 34–35, 93, 106, 147, 200
Aling, Charles, 72
Allen, J. P., 114
Alt, Albrecht, 36–40, 108–9, 132, 178, 192–93
Alt-Noth hypothesis, 37–38, 192–93
altars. *See* sanctuaries
Alter, Robert, 11
Amarna Correspondence, 67–70, 112, 114, 122
Ammonites, 144
amphictyony hypothesis, 177–78
'Amrah list, 71–72
animal husbandry, 169, 195–96
Annals of Amenophis II, 5
Annals of Thutmose III, 5–6, 89, 117
anthropology, 25–26, 190
'apiru people, 68–70, 122
Arad sanctuary site, 186–87
Arameans, 144
Archaeological Survey of Israel, 130, 159
Archaeological Survey Society, 130

archaeology
    biblical faith based on, 2–3, 32, 36
    biblical studies, impact on, 31–36, 96–105, 107–10
    excavations, 35. *See also specific sites*
    'Izbet Sartah remains, 161–65
    in reconstruction of Israeli settlement, 25–26
    Wadi Fidan Regional Archaeological Project, 72–73
architecture
    four-room house, 45–46, 141–46, 170–71
    of 'Izbet Sartah, 165–68
Ark of the Covenant, 178
Arndt, Karl J. R., 47
Arnold, B. T., 4
ascriptive approach to ethnicity, 155–57
assimilation of foreigners, 22, 154–56, 193, 201, 204
Assyrian Annals, 5, 13
Assyrian Chronicles, 12–13
Astour, Michael, 72
authorial intent and historical nature of writings, 15–18

Babylonian Chronicle Series, 5, 13
Barth, Frederick, 155
Bede, the Venerable, 55
behavioral evidence of ethnicity, 138, 146–47
Ben-Tor, Amnon, 112, 116
Ben-Yosef, Dror, 127–28, 182
Beth-Shean Valley, Israelite settlement at, 122–23
Bethel, 31, 34
bias and historical nature of writings, 11–12
Bibb, B. D., 175

## Index

bible as fact. *See* historical nature of writings
biblical evidence of date of exodus-conquest, 49–66
biblical faith, 2, 32, 39
biblical interpretation, 30–32, 38, 53–63, 96–100
biblical studies, archaeology's impact on, 31–36, 96–105, 108–10
Biblical Theology Movement, 2, 3, 25, 32
Bienkowski, Piotr, 95
Bietak, Manfred, 145
Billington, Clyde, 72
Biran, Avraham, 117–19
Block, D. I., 51
Bodley, John H., 191–92, 202
Boling, Robert G., 51, 54, 103
Borger, R., 69
Borowski, Oded, 153–54
boundaries of ethnicity, 154–56
Bowersock, G. W., 134
Braudel, Fernand, 24
Brettler, Mark Z., 4, 16
Briggs, Peter, 110–11
Bright, John, 2, 30, 31
Browning, Daniel, 50
Browning, R., 81–82
Brueggemann, Walter, 35, 59–60
Bryan, B. M., 89
Bunimovitz, S., 88, 145–46
Burke, Aaron, 94
Butler, T., 18

Callaway, J. A., 38–39, 107–9, 149
Canaanite texts, 67–70
central hill-country, 123–24
centralization ideal, 175–76, 187
ceramic traditions. *See* pottery
Chavalas, Mark, 14
children in culture-scale model, 197–98
Chilton, Bruce, 62
circle of stones, 179–84
Cisjordan, 132–134
cisterns at 'Izbet Sartah, 159, 168, 172–73
cities of conquest, 91–119
city, interpretation of, 102–3
classical models of settlement, 30–43
collared-rim jar. *See* pottery
Collingwood, R. G., 4
Collins, John J., 12, 15

column base fragment, 75–76
commercial-scale cultures, 191–92
Comte, Auguste, 35
conquest, 18–23, 91–19, 193–94. *See also* date of exodus-conquest
Conquest Model, 2–3, 30–36, 38
continuity of settlers, 141
Coote, R. B., 26, 98
coronation of King David, 19–20
covenant ceremony, 155–56
covenant renewal, 59–60
Creach, J. F. D., 100
Cross, F. M., 132
culture of settlers. *See* ethnicity and culture of settlers
culture scale, 190–92
culture-scale model, 189–205
  age sets, 197–99
  culture scale defined, 190–92
  egalitarian society, 196
  elders, 198–99, 200
  environment, 195
  family organization, 196–200
  flexible marriage, 196–97
  gender roles, 198
  law, 199
  lineage, 197
  marriage, 196–97
  overview, 189–90
  politicization, 201–3
  sedentarization, 194–201
  segmentary lineage, 197
  synthesis of, 204–5
  transhumance, 193–94
  Yahwism, 200–201, 205
cuneiform tablets, 10, 67–70
cycles of history, Jewish, 53–63

Dalman, Rodger, 64
Dan (Laish), 34, 117–19
date of exodus-conquest, evidence of, 49–66, 67–90
  Canaanite texts, 67–70
  Conquest model and, 30–36
  Egyptian texts, 49, 70–80
  Exodus, 63–65
  Greek and Phoenician texts, 80–82
  Jubilee years, 56–57, 60–63
  Judges, 51–52

# Index

date of exodus-conquest (*continued*)
   1 Kings, 480 years of, 51–55
   Palestine, conditions in, 82–90
   Sabbatical cycles, 57–63
date of 'Izbet Sartah settlement, 163, 172
David (King), coronation of, 19–20
Davies, Philip, 11, 78
de Vaux, Roland, 79
de Wette, W. M. L., 16, 175
Dearman, J. A., 102
deity invocation and historical nature of writings, 14–15
Delitzsch, F., 103, 176
Delphi league, 177–78
demographic change, 134, 137, 139, 205
destruction of cities. *See* conquest; Conquest model
Deuteronimist, 4–5
Deuteronomistic History (DtrH), 9, 16, 18, 96
Deuteronomy, 175–76
Dever, William G., 3, 13, 18, 25, 26, 32–34, 46, 129–30, 131, 145, 150–51, 190, 202
DeVries, L. F., 103
Dillard, R., 14
Dinur, U., 124
*Distanzangabe*, 480 years as, 63
domestic-scale cultures, 191–92, 193–201
Douglas, Mary, 146
*duwwar* camps, 140–41

Ebal sanctuary site, 184–187
economy of 'Izbet Sartah, 169–70, 172
Edelman, Diana, 138, 140, 143, 149–50
Edomites, 44, 71–72, 144
egalitarian society in culture-scale model, 196
Egyptian influence in Palestine, 88–89
Egyptian texts, 5–6, 36, 49, 70–80
Eichrodt, Walter, 56
Eissfeldt, Otto, 77–78
el-Amarna tablets, 67–70
el-Burnat (Mount Ebal), 184–86
elders in culture-scale model, 198–99, 200
Eleazar De Beaugency, 57
Engberg, R., 147
environment in culture-scale model, 195
Ephraim, 123

Esarhaddon's Apology, 15
et-Tell (Ai), 38, 106–8, 108–10
ethnic behavior, 138, 146–47
ethnicity, boundaries of, 154–56
ethnicity, defined, 137–38, 139
ethnicity and culture of settlers, 137–57. *See also* 'Izbet Sartah
   ascriptive approach to, 155–57
   foodways, 152–55
   four-room house, 45–46, 141–46, 170–71
   identity of, 36
   pottery, 138, 147–52
   racism and, 139
   settlement patterns, 139–40
   site layout, 140–41, 165–68, 170
ethos, 145–46, 169
etiological legend, conquest as, 96–98, 108
Eusebius of Caesarea, 91, 106
evidence of exodus-conquest. *See* date of exodus-conquest, evidence of
evolutionary development, 37, 40, 74–75, 201–3
excavations, 35. *See also specific sites*
Exodus, 63–65
exodus-conquest date. *See* date of exodus-conquest, evidence of
extrabiblical evidence
   of conquest of Hazor, 114
   of exodus date, 67–90
   of settlement, 36–40
Ezekiel, Jubilee years, 56–57

faith, 2, 32, 39, 41
family organization, 169–70, 196–200
farming. *See* agriculture
Faust, Avraham, 144–46, 148, 155
Feig, N., 124
Felix, Yehuda, 52
fictionalized history, 11
Finkelstein, Israel, 79, 115, 121, 123, 130, 138–39, 140–41, 154–55, 159, 161, 167, 172, 173
Firmage, E., 153
Fishbane, Michael, 57
Fleming, D., 69
flexible marriage in culture-scale model, 196–97
foodways and ethnic identity, 152–55, 173
footprints, symbolism of, 183

283

## Index

four-room house, 45–46, 141–46, 170–71
480 years of 1 Kings 6:1, 51–55
Frankel, R., 121
Franken, H. J., 151
Freedman, D. N., 200
Frendo, Anthony J., 80
Frick, F. S., 175
Fritz, Volkmar, 45–46, 115, 140–41

Gal, Z., 122, 130
Galilee, 38, 121–22
gapping in historiographical writings, 19–21
Garstang, John, 92–93, 95, 106–7, 112
Geldstein, F., 124
gender roles in culture-scale model, 198
genealogies, 197
geographic expansion, 128–29
Gibbon, Guy, 189
Gibeonites, assimilation of, 22, 193, 201, 204
Gilgal, 22–23, 182
gilgalim as sanctuaries, 179–84
Gluek, Nelson, 130
Gonen, R., 95
Görg, Manfred, 75–76
Gottwald, Norman K., 41–42, 48, 74, 153
Gray, J., 97–98
Grayson, A. Kirk, 5
Grdseloff, B., 71
Greek texts, 80–82
Green, M. D., 123

Habachi, Labib, 64
Habiru people, 68–70, 112
Hage, Jerald, 189–90
Hallo, W. W., 7
Halpern, Baruch, 15, 43–44, 101
Harmony Society, 47–48
Hasel, Michael, 77, 78–80
*hatser*-style site layout, 140
Hatti historiography texts, 6
Hazor, 30–31, 34, 89, 111–17
Hebrews in extrabiblical texts, 68–70, 70–75
Herion, G. A., 101
Herodotus, 6
Herr, L. G., 132, 149, 151

Hess, Richard S., 53, 102, 104–5, 204
Higginbotham, Carolyn, 89
historical nature of writings, 7–18
  authorial intent, 15–18
  invocation of deity, 14–15
  literary artistry, 10–11
  objectivity/bias, 11–12
  propaganda, 12–14
  proximity, 8–10
historiography, 3–8. *See also* historical nature of writings
  ethnicity as, 138
  Joshua as, 18–23, 96–100
  warfare, tool for, 98–99
history
  defined, 3–5
  fictionalized history, 11
  importance of, 208
  Jewish cycles of, 53–63
  pattern of, 41
  speeds of (Braudel), 24
  Synchronistic History, 13, 15
Hittite historiography texts, 6
Hjelm, Ingrid, 77, 79–80
Hoffmeier, J. K., 51, 52–53, 63, 64, 72, 76, 113
Holl, A. F. C., 45, 140
Holladay, J. S., 142
Hopkins, David C., 153
housechildren in culture-scale model, 197–98
houses of Israelites, 141–46, 170–71
Howard, D. M., Jr., 100
Huizinga, Johan, 4
Hyatt, J. P., 58
hymn to Merneptah, 76–80

Ibrahim, M. M., 142–43, 147
identity of Israelites, determining. *See* ethnicity and culture of settlers
immigration models of settlement, 30–40, 48, 108–9
indigenous models of settlement, 40–43, 45–46, 48
invasion. *See* conquest; Conquest model
invasions of Palestine, 85–86
Ionic Cities, 178
Isaiah, Sabbatical years in, 59–60
Israel in Merneptha Stele, 76–80

## Index

Israelite settlement, 121–35. *See also* culture-scale model; models of settlement
  central hill-country, 123–24
  extrabiblical evidence of, 36–40
  Galilee, 121–22
  Jezreel and Beth-Shean Valley, 122–23
  in Joshua, 21
  Manasseh, 125–30
  Negev desert, 124–25
  Transjordan, 131–34
Israelites, determining identity of. *See* ethnicity and culture of settlers
'Izbet Sartah, 159–73
  archaeological remains of, 161–65
  architecture of, 165–68
  cisterns at, 159, 168, 172–73
  date of settlement, 163, 172
  economy of, 169–70, 172
  ethnic identity of inhabitants, 170–71
  historical connections of, 171–72
  Israelite settlement and, 172–73
  location of, 159–61
  ostracon of 'Izbet Sartah, 45, 164–65, 171
  pottery, 162–63, 171, 173

Jack, James, 50, 64
Jephthah, 50
Jeremiah, Sabbatical years in, 57–59
Jericho, 30–31, 38, 91–105
Jerome, 91
Jewish cycles of history, 53–63
Jezreel, 77, 122–23
Josephus, 51
Joshua
  Ai, conquest of, 106, 111
  archaeological findings and, 96–105
  Conquest Model and, 3, 31, 32, 34
  historical value of, 9–10, 207
  historiographical purposes of writers, 18–23, 96–100
  interpretation of, 102–5
  Israel defined in, 154–56
  sanctuary of, 184–87
  Yahweh's promise in, 183
Josiah, 9, 57, 59–60, 99–100
Jubilee years as evidence of exodus, 56–57, 60–63
Judges, date of exodus and, 51–52

Kallai, Z., 124
Kalland, Earl, 176
Kalsbeek, J., 151
Kautz, J. R., 144
Keil, C. F., 57, 103, 176
Kempinski, A., 147
Kenyon, Kathleen, 93–97, 102, 104
Keown, Gerald L., 58
Kessler, Rainer, 24–25
Khazanov, A. M., 75
Killebrew, A. E., 149
king at Jericho, 104–5
1 Kings, 480 years in, 51–55
kinship systems, 197, 201–2
Kitchen, Kenneth A., 50, 77, 78, 80, 89–90, 114–15
Kjaer, Hans, 147
Knauf, E. A., 9, 13
Knight, D. A., 199
Kochavi, Moshe, 130, 159

LaBianca, Ø. S., 26, 74, 152–53
Lachish, 31, 34
Laish (Dan), 34, 117–19
law in culture-scale model, 199
leagues of cities, 177–78
Lemche, N. P., 12, 29, 78, 143
Lemche, Niels Peter, 138
Lenski, G., 139
Levy, T. E., 45, 72–73, 140
Licht, J., 8
lineage in culture-scale model, 197
list making in historiography, 6, 7–8, 11
literary artistry and historical nature of writings, 10–11
Liverani, M., 13–14
Livy, 17–18
London, Gloria, 137–38, 148
Long, Burke, 34
Long, V. Phillips, 11
Longman, T., 14

Madaba map, 132–33
Manasseh, Israelite settlement at, 125–30
Manetho, 6
Manor, Dale, 63
Marchetti, N., 96
Marquet-Krause, Judith, 106–7

*Index*

marriage in culture-scale model, 196–97
Marxism and Social Revolution Model, 41
Master, D. M., 201
material culture, 171, 173. *See also* ethnicity and culture of settlers
May, Herbert G., 56–57
Mayes, A. D. H., 177–78
Mazar, Amihai, 148, 170
Mazar, Benjamin, 179, 201
McCarter, P. K., 69
McKenzie, S. L., 103
McNutt, P. M., 197
Mendenhall, G. E., 40–43
Mendenhall-Gottwald hypothesis, 41–42, 192
Merling, David M., 22, 34, 101, 102, 104–5, 110–11, 200–201
Merneptah (son of Ramesses II), 49, 64, 72
Merneptah Stele, 44, 49, 76–80
Merrill, Eugene, 50
*mesharum* acts, 58, 60
metallurgy, 73
methodology for reconstruction of settlement, necessity for, 23–27
Meyer, F. B., 92
Meyers, Eric, 137
Milgrom, Jacob, 176
military activity. *See* conquest; violence
Miller, Clyde, 54
Miller, J. Maxwell, 32, 101
Miller, Robert, II, 141
Mitchell, G., 18
Moabite Stone, 53, 131
Moabites, 144
models of settlement, 30–48. *See also* culture-scale model
  Conquest Model, 30–36
  immigration models of settlement, 30–40, 48, 108–9
  indigenous models of settlement, 40–43, 45–46, 48
  Peaceful Infiltration Model, 36–40, 108–9
  recent models, 43–48
  Social Revolution Model, 40–43
mosaics, 132–34
Moses of Khoren, 81–82
Mount Ebal sanctuary site, 184–87
Mount Gerizim, 185–86
Muniz, A., 73

Musell, Mary Louise, 42
Musil, A., 141
myth in historical writings, 7, 9

name changes of nomadic peoples, 73–74
names, modernization of, 64–65
national consciousness of Israelites, 187
national history, 4–5
natural disasters in Palestine, 86
nature of Israel in Merneptah Stele, 77, 79–80
Negev desert, Israelite settlement in, 124–25
Nelson, Richard, 9, 98, 104
nested households, 202
New Archaeology, 25–26, 38, 190
Niditch, Susan, 15–16
Nigro, L., 96
Nolan, P., 139
Noll, K. L., 138
nomadic peoples. *See* pastoral nomadism
Noth, Martin, 9, 18, 37–38, 77, 79, 96, 107, 177–78

objectivity and historical nature of writings, 11–12
Old Testament as propaganda, 13–14
ostracon of 'Izbet Sartah, 45, 164–65, 171

Palermo Stone, 5
Palestine, conditions in, 82–90
pastoral nomadism. *See also* transhumance
  evolutionary development and, 37, 40
  Manasseh, people of, 127–29
  name discrepancy and, 73–74
  origin of Israelites and, 37–40, 43–46, 69
  Shasu people and, 44–45, 70–75
  site layout evidence of, 140
  warrior stereotype of, 74–75
patrimonial state, 202–3
Peaceful Infiltration Model, 36–40
Peasant's Revolt Theory, 40–43
Petrie, Sir William Flinders, 30, 49, 76
Phoenician texts, 80–82
Pi-Ramesses (Qantir), 64
pig bones, 154, 169

pilgrimage, 182–83
Pitkänen, Pekka, 175, 185
poetry of ancient Israel, 200
political-scale cultures, 191–92, 201–3
politicization in culture-scale model, 201–3
Polybius, 16–18
Polzin, R., 18–19
population size, 196. *See also* demographic change
positivism, 35–36, 100–101, 200
postmodern skepticism, 11–12
postmodernism in biblical scholarship, 35
pottery
  el-Burnat, 184
  et-Tell, 106
  ethnic identity and, 138, 147–52
  Hazor, 116
  'Izbet Sartah, 162–63, 171, 173
  Manasseh, 128–30
  Tel Dan, 118
  Tell es-Sultan (Jericho), 92, 94, 95, 100
  Transjordan, 132
Pressler, C., 99
procession road, 182
Procopius, 80–81
propaganda and historical nature of writings, 5, 12–14
prose fiction, bible as, 11
proximity and historical nature of writings, 8–10

Qadesh, battle of, 84, 85
Qantir (Pi-Ramesses), 64

racism and ethnicity, 139
Rahab, assimilation of, 156, 201, 204
Rainey, A. F., 42, 69, 150
Rameses (city), 63–65
Ramesses II (pharaoh), 49–50
Ramsey, G. W., 105
Rapp, George, 47–48
Ray, Paul J., Jr., 52, 132
recent models of settlement, 43–48
Redford, Donald, 43–44, 71
religion, reform based on, 46–48
religion, role of in domestic-scale culture, 200–201
Robinson, E., 92, 106, 109, 117

Rogerson, John, 26
Rosen, S. A., 26, 101

Sabbatical years as evidence of exodus, 57–63
Salzman, Philip Carl, 75
Samuel, propagandistic nature of, 14
sanctuaries, 175–88
  amphictyony hypothesis, 177–78
  gilgalim, 179–84
  Mount Ebal, 184–87
  multiple sites of, 179
sandal, symbolism of, 183
sandal-shaped enclosures, 127–28, 179–86
sapienization process, 191, 195, 197, 201, 205
Sarna, Nahum, 54
Sarrie, I., 96
Scalise, Pamela J., 58
Schmitz, P. C., 81–82
Schröder, Paul, 82
scientific theory, 189–90
sedentarization in culture-scale model, 194–201
*Seder 'Olam Rabbah,* 60–62
Seeher, Jürgen, 84
segmentary lineage in culture-scale model, 197
Sellin, Ernst, 92, 109
settlement. *See* Israelite settlement; models of settlement
settlement patterns for ethnic identity, 139–40
Shasu people, 44–45, 70–75
Shechem, 37
Shiloh, Yigal, 142–43, 145
shrines, 175
silos, significance of, 168–69, 171
site layout and ethnic identity, 140–41, 165–68, 170
Smelik, K.A.D., 13
Smith, E., 92
Smith, Mark, 208–9
Smothers, Thomas G., 58
Social Revolution Model, 40–43
social tension in Palestine, 86
Soggin, J. A., 97
Spanier, Y., 124
Sparks, Kenton, 6, 8–9

## Index

Spina, Frank, 156
Stager, Lawrence E., 119, 129, 142, 202
Steinmann, Andrew, 52
Sternberg, Meir, 11, 19
surveys. *See* excavations
Symbiosis Hypothesis (Fritz), 45
symbolic numbers, 53–63
Synchronistic History, 13, 15

tabernacle altar, 186–87
Talmud, Jubilee years in, 56–57
Tel Dan, 117–19
Tell Beit-Mirsim, 30
Tell el-Qedah (Hazor), 112–13
Tell es-Sultan (Jericho), 92–96, 100–102, 103
Ten Ionic Cities, 178
"termination rituals" at Hazor, 115
Tetrateuch, pre-priestly, 98
theory of Israelite emergence in Canaan. *See* culture-scale model
Thompson, Thomas L., 12, 26, 77, 79–80, 138
Thucydides, 6–7
Torah, 54–55, 56
traits of political-scale society, 202
transhumance, 73, 193–94
Transjordan, Israelite settlement in, 131–34

Van De Mieroop, Marc, 10–11, 73–74, 84–88
van der Steen, E. J., 150
Van Seters, John, 4–5
Victory Stela of King Piye, 6
Vincent, R. P. L.-H., 93
violence, 41, 75. *See also* warfare
Vogt, Peter, 176
von Rad, Gerhard, 13, 23
von Ranke, Leopold, 4, 11

Wadi Fidan Regional Archaeological Project, 72–73
walls of Hazor, 112–13
walls of Jericho, 104. *See also* Tell es-Sultan
Waltke, B. K., 182
Walton, John H., 8, 15, 208

warfare
 Conquest Model and, 3, 30
 at Hazor, 115–17
 in Palestine, 82–84, 85
 in pastoralist societies, 75
 Peaceful Infiltration Model and, 37, 39
 as tool in historiography, 98–99
Warren, Charles, 92
Watzinger, Carl, 92
Weber, Max, 178, 201–2
Weidner Chronicle, 5, 8, 12, 15
Weinfeld, Moshe, 146, 192
Weippert, Manfred, 40
Wellhausen, Julius, 53–54, 75
Wheeler, Mortimer, 93
White, Hayden, 11
Whitelam, K. W., 26
"width stratigraphy," 130
Wildberger, Hans, 59
Willis, T. M., 102
Wilson, Charles, 106
Wood, Bryant G., 51–52, 68, 76, 100, 109, 113, 185–87
Worcestor, Samuel, 47
worship. *See* sanctuaries
Woudstra, M. H., 100
Wright, G. Ernest, 2–3, 31–32, 35–36, 52, 103
Wright, J. E., 34
writings. *See also* historical nature of writings
 history of development of, 5–7

Yadin, Yigal, 31, 112, 114, 115
Yahwism, 15, 44, 71–72, 200–201, 205
Yamauchi, E., 10
Young, Rodger, 51–52, 54, 55–62, 65, 186–87
Younger, K. L., 13, 34, 52
Younker, R. W., 44–45, 132
youth in culture-scale model, 198

Zertal, Adam, 125–26, 128, 182, 185–86, 194
Zevit, Ziony, 2, 176, 186
Zuckerman, Sharon, 115–16

www.ingramcontent.com/pod-product-compliance
Lightning Source LLC
Chambersburg PA
CBHW010719300426
44115CB00020B/2959